and endlessly fought for again … Her superb narrative brings that history vividly into the present, weaving individual lives into the sweeping changes of the century.' —*Wall Street Journal*

'In pursuit of Wonder Woman, Jill Lepore has tackled archives, interviewed contemporaries and dug through court transcripts, college records, the literature of the early 20th-century suffragism and the annals of Wonder Woman and her rivals. The result is a tour de force.' —Helen DeWitt, *Literary Review*

'A meticulously researched account on the life and influences of the female superhero's eccentric male creator.' —*Financial Times*

'*The Secret History of Wonder Woman* is the fullest and most fascinating portrait ever created about the complicated, unconventional family that inspired one of the most enduring feminist icons in pop culture … In [Lepore's] hands, *The Secret History of Wonder Woman* is its own magic lasso, one that compels history to finally tell the truth about Wonder Woman – and compels the rest of us to behold it.' —*Los Angeles Times*

'Few historians handle weirdness as deftly or thoughtfully as Lepore … [Her] brilliance lies in knowing what to do with the material she has. In her hands, the Wonder Woman story unpacks not only a new cultural history of feminism, but a theory of history as well.' —*New York Times Book Review*

'Wonderfully vivid … Intertwining biography, history and fiction, this is about much more than a comic book character.' —*Prospect*

'Jill Lepore's generously illustrated *The Secret History of Wonder Woman* impressively links the iconic superhero's 1941 creation by William Moulton Marston (also the inventor of the lie detector) both to the aims of mid-twentieth-century feminism and to the influential Marston family's deep domestic intrigues.' —*Elle*

'*The Secret History of Wonder Woman* relates a tale so improbable, so juicy, it'll have you saying, "Merciful Minerva!" ... An astonishingly thorough investigation of the man behind the world's most popular female superhero.' —NPR

'If it makes your head spin to imagine a skimpily clad pop culture icon as (spoiler alert!) a close relation of feminist birth control advocate Margaret Sanger, then prepare to be dazzled by the truths revealed in historian Jill Lepore's *The Secret History of Wonder Woman*. The story behind Wonder Woman is sensational, spellbinding and utterly improbable. Her origins lie in the feminism of the early 1900s, and the intertwined dramas that surrounded her creation are the stuff of pulp fiction and tabloid scandal ... It took a super-sleuth to uncover the mysteries of this intricate history, hidden from view for more than half a century. With acrobatic research prowess, muscular narrative chops and disarming flashes of humor, Lepore rises to the challenge, bringing to light previously unknown details and deliberately obfuscated connections.' —*San Francisco Chronicle*

'Enthralling ... It is hard to do justice to the many layers of this wonderful book. Meticulously detailed and lovingly constructed, it is part biography, part social history, part detective story. Above all, it is a portrait of an extraordinary family – and the women who made the man who made Wonder Woman.' —*Daily Mail*

'On the one hand, the story [*The Secret History of Wonder Woman*] relates has more uplift than Wonder Woman's invisible airplane or her eagle-encrusted red bustier. It's a yea-saying tale about how this comic book character, created in 1941, remade American feminism and had her roots in the ideas and activism of Margaret Sanger, the founder of Planned Parenthood. On the other hand, *The Secret History of Wonder Woman* is fundamentally a biography of Wonder Woman's larger-than-life and vaguely creepy male creator, William Moulton Marston ... [Lepore] fully tells Marston's history for the first time, as well as the complete history of how so many crisp feminist ideas made

's

WONDER WOMAN

'*The Secret History of Wonder Woman* is as racy, as improbable, as awesomely righteous, and as filled with curious devices as an episode of the comic book itself. In the nexus of feminism and popular culture, Jill Lepore has found a revelatory chapter of American history. I will never look at Wonder Woman's bracelets the same way again.' —Alison Bechdel, author of *Fun Home*

'Jill Lepore's obsessively researched book on Wonder Woman, the four-color embodiment of the women's rights movement, reveals that the life of the character's creator, Dr. William Marston – inventor of the lie detector, charming crank, ardent feminist and secret polygamist – was waaay more colorful than any comic book superhero. Suffering Sappho!' —Art Spiegelman, author of *Maus*

'An absolutely unputdownable book. The life history of polymath charlatan and/or genius (I couldn't ever decide) William Moulton Marston, who worked his way through law, movie scenarios, lie detection, ménages a trois, free love, BDSM and polygamy before creating the first feminist super-person had me saying "wow" practically every other page. And that's not even mentioning the tough-as-nails women he exalted, lifted from and, uh, shared who make up the molten core of this newly-revealed story. Rocketing from the suffragism of the 1910s to the ERA of the 1970s on a wave of home-spun pop culture righteousness, this story's head-spinning weirdness ultimately makes you question your own accomplishments, aims, and – almost like a great modern novel – your real motives.' —Chris Ware, author of *Building Stories*

'All superheroes have strange myths of origin, but the politically and erotically charged back-story of Wonder Woman outstrips any comic book. Jill Lepore unmasks the comic-strip heroine as the strange daughter of early 20th-century women's suffrage and the bondage-fixated imagination of William Moulton Marston, a hucksterish psychologist who invented the lie-detector test and lived in a covert threesome with his wife and girlfriend ... A startling and intelligent double biography.' —*Sunday Times*

'Hugely entertaining ... Lepore calls Wonder Woman the missing link between the first and second waves of feminism, as they're known – that is, between the suffragist era that so inspired Marston and the 1970s women's-liberation movement.' —*The Atlantic*

'All credit to Jill Lepore for simultaneously rescuing Wonder Woman from indifference, establishing her as an expression of first-wave feminism and introducing her creator, who must be one of the more repellent individuals ever to call himself a feminist ... Terrific reading.' —*The Observer*

'The book I read most eagerly and discussed most avidly in 2014 was *The Secret History of Wonder Woman* ... Lepore is among the most productive, intellectually invigorating and surprising cultural critics in the US.' —Elaine Showalter, *Times Literary Supplement*

'This book is several things at once: a history of Wonder Woman's creator, Marston; a reflection on the themes underpinning the comic; and an exploration of how it was influenced by the early women's suffrage and reproductive rights movements ... Where [*The Secret History of Wonder Woman*] shines is in laying bare how explicitly political the comic book was always intended to be.' —*New Statesman*

'Ms. Lepore's lively, surprising and occasionally salacious history is far more than the story of a comic strip. The author, a professor of history at Harvard, places Wonder Woman squarely in the story of women's rights in America – a cycle of rights won, lost

their way into Wonder Woman comics. It's complicated material that she capably explores.' —*New York Times*

'Seamlessly combining rigorous scholarship and riveting readability, this richly rewarding book illuminates the histories of a problematic comics icon. A must-read.' —*SFX Magazine*

'To my generation, Wonder Woman is most famous for being played by the former Miss World USA Lynda Carter in the 1970s television series, wearing the bare minimum of pre-watershed clothing; a patriotic pin-up girl ... But she was conceived by Marston as a feminist symbol, an Amazon from a man-free land who "came to the United States to fight for peace, justice and women's rights". It's a bit like finding out that Barbie was a post-dated Pankhurst plant to get women into the workplace ... Lepore's voice is fresh, clear and often cheeky ... [*The Secret History of Wonder Woman*] is brilliantly written and splendidly researched.' —Julie Burchill, *Spectator*

'With a defiantly unhurried ease, Lepore reconstructs the prevailing cultural mood that birthed the idea of Wonder Woman, carefully delineating the conceptual debt the character owes to early-20th-century feminism in general and the birth control movement in particular ... Again and again, she distills the figures she writes about into clean, simple, muscular prose, making unequivocal assertions that carry a faint electric charge ... [and] attain a transgressive, downright badass swagger.' —*Slate*

'Cultural history doesn't get more enthralling.' —*Times Higher Education*

'In the spirited, thoroughly reported *The Secret History of Wonder Woman*, Jill Lepore recounts the fascinating details behind the Amazonian princess' origin story ... Fascinating.' —*Newsday*

'Deftly combines biography and cultural history to trace the entwined stories of Marston, Wonder Woman, and 20th-century feminism ... Lepore – a professor of American history at Harvard, a *New Yorker* writer, and the author of *Book of Ages* – is an endlessly energetic and knowledgeable guide to the fascinating backstory of Wonder Woman. She's particularly skilful at showing the subtle process by which personal details migrate from life into art.' —*Christian Science Monitor*

'Not just for serious comics historians, *The Secret History of Wonder Woman* is also a must-read for anyone interested in feminist or utopian literature.' —*A.V. Club*

'The secret identity and ironic origin of Wonder Woman, gleefully revealed here, lie less in comic book fantasy than in the racy life of her creator and the history of women's liberation.' —*The Times*

'The Marston family's story is ripe for psychoanalysis. And so is *The Secret History*, since it raises interesting questions about what motivates writers to choose the subjects of their books. Having devoted her last work to Jane Franklin Mecom, Benjamin Franklin's sister, Lepore clearly has a passion for intelligent, opinionated women whose legacies have been overshadowed by the men they love. In her own small way, she's helping women get the justice they deserve, not unlike her tiara'd counterpart ... It has nearly everything you might want in a page-turner: tales of S&M, skeletons in the closet, a believe-it-or-not weirdness in its biographical details, and something else that secretly powers even the most "serious" feminist history – fun.' —*Entertainment Weekly*

'What Lepore seeks to do here is tell the story of women's experience in the 20th century through this pop-culture icon ... A cracking narrative.' —*Independent*

'Lepore's discipline is worthy of a first-class detective ... [*The Secret History of Wonder Woman*] convinces us that we should know more about early feminists whose work Wonder Woman drew on and carried forward ... A key spotter of connections,

Lepore retrieves a remarkably recognizable feminist through-line, showing us 1920s debates about work-life balance, for example, that sound like something from *The Atlantic* in the past decade.' —*New York Review of Books*

'Immensely readable ... More than a treat for comic fans, Lepore's superb book is for anyone interested in the social history of America.' —Martin Gray, *Scotland on Sunday*

'This wham-bang-thank-you-superma'am book is thrilling, amazing, unexpectedly weird and right-on righteous!' —*Saga*

'Lepore, a Harvard historian, is the first scholar to have full access to the Marston family papers and she mines these to marvellous effect. She also situates Wonder Woman's story in multiple historical contexts, especially that of twentieth-century women's history. Wonder Woman, she finds, was the bridge between the originary feminism of the 1900s and the modern women's movements beginning in the 1960s. Where others have seen only kinky chains, she perceives direct connections to earlier feminist images of fettered women overcoming social and political restraints ... For Lepore the real superhero, here, is that of her own field, History ... Lepore notes that "history raises questions about the nature of truth", and that the historian's diligent sifting through evidence is more effective in distinguishing fact from fiction than Marston's lie detector and Wonder Woman's lasso ... *The Secret History of Wonder Woman* is an exemplary case by a model practitioner.' —*Times Literary Supplement*

'A fascinating and eclectic study ... Lepore has added to our understanding of an iconic literary character ensconced deep within the mythology of our modern society; but more importantly she has used this character to shape a new understanding of that society's own history ... Her research is surprising not only because it reveals what we did not know about Wonder Woman, but because it underscores what we did not know about our own history.' —*Pop Matters*

JILL LEPORE

Jill Lepore is the David Woods Kemper '41 Professor of American History at Harvard University and a staff writer at *The New Yorker*. *Book of Ages,* her most recent book, was a finalist for the National Book Award. She lives in Cambridge, Massachusetts.

THE SECRET HISTORY OF
WONDER
WOMAN

JILL LEPORE

SCRIBE

Melbourne • London

Scribe Publications
18–20 Edward St, Brunswick, Victoria 3056, Australia
2 John St, Clerkenwell, London, WC1N 2ES, United Kingdom

This edition first published in the United States by Vintage Books, 2015
Published in Australia and the United Kingdom by Scribe 2015

Front-of-jacket image: WONDER WOMAN is ™ and © DC Comics.
Print: Courtesy of the Smithsonian Institution Libraries, Washington, D.C.
Author photograph © Dari Michele
Book design by Maggie Hinders

Printed and bound in the UK by CPI Group (UK) Ltd, Croydon CR0 4YY

National Library of Australia Cataloguing-in-Publication data

Lepore, Jill, 1966- author.

The Secret History of Wonder Woman / Jill Lepore.

9781925106985 (AU edition)
9781925228113 (UK edition)
9781925113822 (e-book)

1. Marston, William Moulton, 1893-1947. 2. Feminism in literature.
3. Literature and society–United States. 4. Wonder Woman (Fictitious character).
5. Women superheroes–United States. 6. Comic books, strips, etc.–Social aspects.
7. Women's rights–United States–History. 8. Feminism–United States–History.

741.5973

A CIP record for this title is available from the British Libary

scribepublications.com.au
scribepublications.co.uk

To Nancy F. Cott,
for making history

As lovely as Aphrodite—as wise as Athena—with the speed of Mercury and the strength of Hercules—she is known only as Wonder Woman, but who she is, or whence she came, nobody knows!

—*All-Star Comics*, December 1941

With the announcement yesterday that the popular comics heroine "Wonder Woman" will now rate a whole magazine to herself beginning July 22, M. C. Gaines, publisher of All-American Comics at 480 Lexington Avenue, also revealed officially for the first time that the author of "Wonder Woman" is Dr. William Moulton Marston, internationally famous psychologist.

—Press release, *All-American Comics,* Spring 1942

"What's the idea of calling me *Wonder Woman?"*

—Olive Byrne, *Family Circle,* August 1942

Wonder Woman was from the start a character founded in scholarship.

—The *ΦBK Key Recorder,* Autumn 1942

Frankly, Wonder Woman is psychological propaganda for the new type of woman who should, I believe, rule the world.

—William Moulton Marston, March 1945

CONTENTS

From *Wonder Woman #1* (Summer 1942)

THE SPLASH PAGE

WONDER WOMAN is the most popular female comic-book superhero of all time. Aside from Superman and Batman, no other comic-book character has lasted as long. Like every other superhero, Wonder Woman has a secret identity. Unlike every other superhero, she also has a secret history.

Superman first bounded over tall buildings in 1938. Batman began lurking in the shadows in 1939. Wonder Woman landed in her invisible plane in 1941. She was an Amazon from an island of women who had lived apart from men since the time of ancient Greece. She came to the United States to fight for peace, justice, and women's rights. She had golden bracelets; she could stop bullets. She had a magic lasso; anyone she roped had to tell the truth. To hide her identity, she disguised herself as a secretary named Diana Prince; she worked for U.S. military intelligence. Her gods were female, and so were her curses. "Great Hera!" she cried. "Suffering Sappho!" she swore. She was meant to be the strongest, smartest, bravest woman the world had ever seen. She looked like a pin-up girl. In 1942, she was recruited to the Justice Society of America, joining Superman, Batman, the Flash, and Green Lantern; she was the only woman. She wore a golden tiara, a red bustier, blue underpants, and knee-high, red leather boots. She was a little slinky; she was very kinky.

Over seven decades, across continents and oceans, Wonder Woman has never been out of print. Her fans number in the millions. Gen-

Wonder Woman, newspaper strip, May 12–13, 1944

erations of girls have carried their sandwiches to school in Wonder Woman lunch boxes. But not even Wonder Woman's most ardent followers know the true story of her origins. She's as secret as a heart.

In an episode from 1944, a newspaper editor named Brown, desperate to discover Wonder Woman's secret past, assigns a team of reporters to chase her down. She easily escapes them, outrunning their car in her high-heeled boots, leaping like an antelope. Brown, gone half mad, suffers a breakdown and is committed to a hospital. Wonder Woman, taking pity on him, puts on a nurse's uniform and brings him a scroll. "This parchment seems to be the history of that girl you call 'Wonder Woman'!" she tells him. "A strange, veiled woman left it with me." Brown leaps out of bed and, not stopping to change out of his hospital johnny, races back to the city desk, where he cries out, parchment in hand, "Stop the presses! I've got the history of Wonder Woman!"

Brown's nuts; he hasn't really got the history of Wonder Woman. All he's got is her Amazonian legend.

This book has got something else. *The Secret History of Wonder Woman* is the result of years of research in dozens of libraries, archives, and collections, including the private papers of Wonder Woman's creator, William Moulton Marston—papers that have never been seen by anyone outside of Marston's family. I read the published material first: newspapers and magazines, trade journals and scientific papers, comic strips and comic books. Then I went to the archives. I didn't find anything written on parchment; I found something better: thousands of pages of documents, manuscripts and typescripts, photographs and drawings, letters and postcards, criminal court records, notes scribbled in the margins of books, legal briefs, medical records, unpublished memoirs, story drafts, sketches, student transcripts, birth certificates, adoption papers, military records, family albums, scrapbooks, lecture notes, FBI files, movie scripts, the carefully typed meeting minutes of a sex cult, and tiny diaries written in secret code. Stop the presses. I've got the history of Wonder Woman.

Wonder Woman isn't only an Amazonian princess with badass boots. She's the missing link in a chain of events that begins with the woman suffrage campaigns of the 1910s and ends with the troubled place of feminism fully a century later. Feminism made Wonder Woman. And then Wonder Woman remade feminism, which hasn't been altogether good for feminism. Superheroes, who are supposed to be better than everyone else, are excellent at clobbering people; they're lousy at fighting for equality.

But Wonder Woman is no ordinary comic-book superhero. The secrets this book reveals and the story it tells place Wonder Woman not only within the history of comic books and superheroes but also at the very center of the histories of science, law, and politics. Superman owes a debt to science fiction, Batman to the hard-boiled detective. Wonder Woman's debt is to the fictional feminist utopia and to the struggle for women's rights. Her origins lie in William Moulton Marston's past, and in the lives of the women he loved; they created Wonder Woman, too. Wonder Woman is no ordinary comic-book character because Marston was no ordinary man and his family was no ordinary family. Marston was a polymath. He was an expert in deception: he invented the lie detector test. He led a secret life: he had four children by two women; they lived together under one roof. They were masters of the art of concealment.

Their favorite hiding place was the comics they produced. Marston was a scholar, a professor, and a scientist; Wonder Woman began on a college campus, in a lecture hall, and in a laboratory. Marston was

Wonder Woman, disguised as a man, trying to hide an injured Steve Trevor from reporters. From "Racketeer's Bait," an unpublished *Sensation Comics* story

a lawyer and a filmmaker; Wonder Woman began in a courthouse and a movie theater. The women Marston loved were suffragists, feminists, and birth control advocates. Wonder Woman began in a protest march, a bedroom, and a birth control clinic. The red bustier isn't the half of it. Unknown to the world, Margaret Sanger, one of the most influential feminists of the twentieth century, was part of Marston's family.

Wonder Woman has been fighting for women's rights for a very long time, battles hard fought but never won. This is the story of her origins—the stuff of wonders, and of lies.

★ **PART ONE** ★

VERITAS

From "In the Clutches of Nero," *Sensation Comics #39*
(March 1945)

IS HARVARD AFRAID OF MRS. PANKHURST?

WILLIAM MOULTON MARSTON, who believed women should rule the world, decided at the unnaturally early and altogether impetuous age of eighteen that the time had come for him to die. In everything, he was precocious.

Moulton Castle, Newburyport, Massachusetts

He had arrived, however, remarkably late, or at least his mother thought so; for years, she had been under considerable pressure to produce him. She was one of five sisters; her only brother had died in 1861, after which her grieving father had built a turreted medieval manor north of Boston, where he'd closeted himself in a Gothic library in the tallest of its crenellated towers to write a treatise titled *Moulton Annals,* in which he traced his family back to the Battle

The Moulton sisters inside the castle, 1885. Left to right: Susan, Claribel, Molly, Alice, and Annie

of Hastings, in 1066. One Moulton had signed the Magna Carta; another—"thin-flanked, broad-chested, long-armed, deep-breathed, and strong-limbed"—had tramped through the pages of Sir Walter Scott's *Tales of the Crusaders.* Measured against the valiance of such men, the annalist, a fainthearted veteran of the American Civil War, could hardly fail to find his own derring and doing a disappointment. ("Capt. Moulton's enterprise was made evident by his attempt to establish a large carriage manufacturing business," he wrote about himself, feebly.) The further his researches progressed, the more he despaired of his descendants: girls who glided idly over the parquet floors of Moulton Castle in lacy, wasp-waisted gowns, their hair twisted on the tops of their heads in tottering piles. Susan and Alice never married; Claribel and Molly bided their time. That left Annie, a spinster schoolteacher. In 1887, she married Frederick William Marston, a merchant of quality woolens for gentlemen's suits; he was, it was whispered, beneath her. And so it came to pass that, upon this unpromising match, Captain Moulton staked the succession of a lineage that dated back to the Norman Conquest. At last, in 1893, at the late age of thirty-four, Annie Moulton Marston gave birth to a baby, a boy. They named him William. The conqueror.[1]

It might be said, then, that it was at once a betrayal and rather in the spirit of these romantic beginnings that in the winter of 1911, eighteen-year-old William Moulton Marston, a student at Harvard College, procured from a chemist in Cambridge a vial of hydrocyanic acid, with which he prepared to end his life.

He had been born in a three-story Victorian house on Avon Street, in Cliftondale, Massachusetts. He was cherished; he was adored. His mother and alike his aunts, having no need to divide their attentions, lavished them upon him, tucking him into their laps. He ate Sunday dinner at

William Moulton Marston in 1894

Moulton Castle. He liked to gauge the distance between the genuine and the fake; he collected stuffed birds. He won his first school prize when he was seven years old. He held literary ambitions: he wrote poems and stories and plays.[2] His mother detected signs of genius.

His boyhood philosophy of suicide is what happens when pragmatism, fed by observation, finds a nest in the home of a very clever child, unquestioned by his parents. On Avon Street, a neighbor of the Marstons' one day looked in the bathroom mirror, said, "What the hell," and slit his throat.[3] Boy Marston turned this over in his mind. "From the age of twelve to my late twenties," he later explained, "I believed firmly in suicide." If success could be achieved with ease, he reasoned, life was worth living; if not, "the only sensible thing to do was to sign off."[4]

He was not, early on, tempted to sign off: he triumphed at everything he attempted. He grew tall and devilishly handsome, even if his ears poked out. His hair was dark and curly, his chin broad and dimpled. He grew from cub to lion. In eighth grade, at Felton Grammar School, he fell in love with a sharp, spindly girl named Sadie Elizabeth Holloway. She was whip-smart. She'd come to New England from the Isle of Man; she was a Manx. The next year, he was elected class president and she class secretary; no other outcome had been, to either

Marston in 1911, as a Harvard freshman

of them, imaginable.[5] Maybe it was then that he told her that they would name their first son Moulton.

At Malden High School, Marston was elected class historian, president of the Literary Society, and editor in chief of the student literary magazine the *Oracle*. He wrote a class history in the form of a conversation with Clio, the goddess of history, "she, first of all the nymphs who sprung from Zeus." He presided over a debate about woman suffrage. He played football: a six-foot, 184-pound left guard. During his senior year, his team won the state championship. When Charles W. Eliot, the emeritus president of Harvard, came to speak to the senior class, Marston decided where his destiny lay. "The effect of Harvard upon the after life of a man cannot be estimated," he wrote in the *Oracle*.[6] On his college application, in the blank marked "Intended Occupation," he wrote one word: "Law."[7] His mind was unclouded by any doubt of his admission.

He moved to Cambridge in September 1911, lugging a trunk stuffed with suits and books into a cramped room in a boardinghouse on the corner of Hancock Street and Broadway, east of Harvard Yard. And then he met, for the first time, an obstacle.

"I had to take a lot of courses that I hated," he explained. English A: Rhetoric and Composition was a required course for freshmen. "I wanted to write and English A, at Harvard, wouldn't let you write," he complained. "It made you spell and punctuate. If you wrote anything you felt like writing, enjoyed writing, your paper was marked flunk in red pencil."[8]

"During my Freshman year," he wrote, "I decided that the time had come to die."[9] English A had crushed him. But the course that convinced him to kill himself was History 1: Medieval History, taught by Charles Homer Haskins.[10] Haskins, who wore a waxed, handlebar mustache, was dean of the graduate school. His interest was medieval scholasticism, the subject of his monograph *The Rise of Universities*.

Later, he founded the American Council of Learned Societies. Professor Haskins's Middle Ages weren't half as swashbuckling as Captain Moulton's *Annals:* Haskins loved scholars better than knights.

History raises questions about the nature of truth. In a lecture Haskins delivered to freshmen, he distinguished the study of the past from the investigation of nature. "The biologist observes plants and animals; the chemist or physicist conducts experiments in his laboratory under conditions which he can control," Haskins said. "The historian, on the contrary, cannot experiment and can rarely observe." Instead, the historian has got to collect his own evidence, knowing, all the while, that some of it is useless and much of it is unreliable.[11] Haskins loved pawing through the cluttered junk drawer of the past and finding the gemstones among the shards of broken glass. To Marston, everything in that drawer looked like rubbish.

"I didn't care who had married Charlemagne's great-grandmother's sister, nor where Philip had breakfast the day he wrote a letter to the Pope," Marston explained. "I'm not saying such facts are unimportant, only that they didn't interest me and that I had to learn them. So I made arrangements to procure some hydro-cyanic acid from a chemist friend."[12]

Hydrocyanic acid kills in less than a minute. It smells of almonds. It is also the poison that Henry Jekyll uses to kill himself in *Dr. Jekyll and Mr. Hyde,* a story published in 1886, which Marston had read as a boy in his bedroom on Avon Street, a story about a man who becomes a monster.[13]

What checked Marston's hand as he held the vial was the study of existence itself. There was one course he loved: Philosophy A: Ancient Philosophy. It was taught by George Herbert Palmer, the frail, weak-eyed, sixty-nine-year-old Alford Professor of Philosophy and chairman of Harvard's Philosophy Department. Palmer had thin, long white hair, bushy black eyebrows, blue eyes, and a walrus mustache. He lived at 11 Quincy Street, where he pined for his wife, Alice Freeman Palmer, who had been president of Wellesley College, an advocate for female education, and a suffragist. She'd died in 1902. He refused to stop mourning her. "To leave the dead wholly dead is rude," he pointed out, quite reasonably.[14]

Early in his career, Palmer had made a luminous translation of the *Odyssey*—its aim, he said, was to reveal "that the story, unlike a bare record of fact, is throughout, like poetry, illuminated with an underglow of joy"—but his chief contribution to the advancement of philosophy was having convinced William James, Josiah Royce, and George Santayana to join what became known as "the Great Department": Harvard's faculty of philosophy.[15]

The key to teaching, Palmer believed, is moral imagination, "the ability to put myself in another's place, think his thoughts, and state strongly his convictions even when they are not my own." He "lectured in blank verse and made Greek hedonism a vital, living thing," Marston said.[16]

In the fall of 1911, Philosophy A began with a history of philosophy itself. "According to Aristotle," Palmer told his class, as Marston sat, rapt, "the rise of philosophy has three influential causes: freedom, leisure, and wonder." For weeks, he raved about the Greeks: they, to Palmer, were geniuses of dialectics and rhetoric. After Thanksgiving, he lectured on Plato's *Republic;* by December, he was expounding on how man was "a rational being in a sensuous physical body," underscoring, as he often did, that by "man," he meant men and women both. He eyed his class of Harvard men sternly. "Girls are also human beings," he told them, "a point often overlooked!!"[17]

The equality of women was chief among Palmer's intellectual and political commitments, and it was a way, too, that he remembered his wife. George Herbert Palmer, who saved Marston's life, was faculty sponsor of the Harvard Men's League for Woman Suffrage.

The American suffrage movement dates to 1848, when the first women's rights convention was held in Seneca Falls, New York (a story later told in *Wonder Woman*), where delegates adopted a "Declaration of Sentiments," written by Elizabeth Cady Stanton and modeled on the Declaration of Independence: "We hold these truths to be self-evident: that all men and women are created equal; that they are endowed by their Creator with certain inalienable rights; that among these are life, liberty, and the pursuit of happiness." Its demands included women's "immediate admission to all the rights and privileges which belong to them as citizens of these United States."[18]

From "Wonder Women of History: Susan B. Anthony," *Wonder Woman #5* (June–July 1943)

At the beginning of the twentieth century, American suffragists grew militant. They'd been inspired by the British suffragist Emmeline Pankhurst. In 1903, Pankhurst founded the Women's Social and Political Union. Its motto was "Deeds, not words." Pankhurst went to prison for trying to deliver a petition to the House of Commons. Suffragists shackled themselves to the iron fence outside 10 Downing Street. "The condition of our sex is so deplorable that it is our duty to break the law in order to call attention to the reasons why we do what we do," Pankhurst insisted.[19] "The incident of the Suffragettes who chained themselves with iron chains to the railings of Downing Street is a good ironical allegory of most modern martyrdom," G. K. Chesterton observed, predicting that the tactic would fail.[20] He was wrong.

The Harvard Men's League for Woman Suffrage was formed in

British suffragists chained to the railings outside 10 Downing Street. From the *Illustrated London News*, 1908

Emmeline Pankhurst being arrested outside Buckingham Palace

the spring of 1910 by John Reed, then a senior, and by a Harvard Law School student who'd been converted to the cause by Max Eastman, a philosophy graduate student at Columbia University who'd helped found a Men's League for Woman Suffrage in New York. In the fall of 1911, the Harvard Men's League for Woman Suffrage announced a lecture series. The first lecture, to be held on October 31, was to be given by Florence Kelley, who'd fought for a minimum wage, an eight-hour workday, and an end to child labor. The announcement caused a ruckus: women were not allowed to speak at Harvard. Abbott Lawrence Lowell, the university's president, said he feared "a mob of women trooping around the Yard." The league submitted a petition to the Harvard Corporation, which ruled that Kelley could speak, but only if the lecture was closed to anyone outside the university.[21] The league obliged. In her lecture, Kelley insisted that the conditions of the working poor could not be addressed without granting women the right to vote.[22] The corporation, anxious that the university not be seen to be endorsing women's rights, demanded that the league bring, as its next guest, a speaker opposed to woman suffrage.[23] Instead, the league announced that its next guest would be, of all people, Emmeline Pankhurst.

She was slated to speak in Sanders Theatre, the largest and most prestigious hall on campus (it seats one thousand people). Terrified, the corporation issued a ruling barring Pankhurst from speaking anywhere on campus, noting that, its earlier exception for Kelley notwithstanding, "the college halls should not be open to lectures by women."[24]

"Is Harvard Afraid of Mrs. Pankhurst?" asked the editors of the *Detroit Free Press*. (The answer was yes.) The news made headlines all over the United States. Most papers took the side of the suffrage league. "The question of universal suffrage is now in the public eye as never before in our history," the *Atlanta Constitution* observed. "It is a subject for legitimate debate, one upon which the young and formative mind demands, and is entitled to, information." The *New York Times'* editorial board was all but alone in endorsing the corporation's decision, on the grounds that "the curriculum of Harvard does not include woman suffrage."[25]

In Cambridge, suffrage was all anyone talked about. "The undergraduate body is split into two camps, the 'sufs' and the 'antis,'" the *New York Times* reported. "In class room, lecture hall, college yard, and Harvard Union, suffrage, and the action of the corporation, is the principal topic of conversation."[26]

The corporation had ruled that Pankhurst couldn't speak on campus; it couldn't stop her from speaking in Cambridge. The league announced that it had arranged for Pankhurst to speak in Brattle Hall, a dance hall at 40 Brattle Street, just a block from Harvard Yard. The editor of the *New York Evening Post,* a prominent alumnus, urged as many students as possible to attend "for the double purpose of thus making amends for the University's lamentable blunder and of hearing one of the ablest orators of the day." Pankhurst's lecture, held on the afternoon of December 6, was open only to Harvard and Radcliffe students; admission required a ticket. It was mobbed: fifteen hundred students showed up in a hall designed to hold not more than five hundred. They scrambled up the walls and tried to climb in through the windows.[27]

Pankhurst proved as severe as ever. "The most ignorant young man, who knows nothing of the needs of women, thinks himself a competent legislator, because he is a man," Pankhurst told the crowd, eyeing the Harvard men. "This aristocratic attitude is a mistake."[28]

Marston was fascinated; he was thrilled; he was distracted. With a revolution taking place on his very doorstep, he could not bring himself to care about Professor Haskins's Middle Ages. "It was mid-year examination time when I reached my final decision to stop existing," he explained. Then he thought that maybe he ought to take his exams, "to see how badly I was doing."[29]

Dr. Poison. From "Dr. Poison," *Sensation Comics #2* (February 1942)

On the day of the exam in Philosophy A, George Herbert Palmer handed out the questions to his class, along with a word of advice: "A scholar approaches a task for the sake of himself, not for that of someone else, as the schoolboy does."[30]

Marston took that to heart. He aced the exam. Palmer, who almost never gave A's, gave one to Marston.[31]

Eighteen-year-old William Moulton Marston did not, then, swallow that vial of cyanide. But he never forgot it. And he never forgot Emmeline Pankhurst and her shackles, either. Three decades later, when Marston created a female comic-book superhero who fights for women's rights ("Wonder Woman, Wonder Woman! She's turning this man's world topsy-turvy!"), her only weakness is that she loses all her strength if a man binds her in chains. And the first villain she faces is a chemist rumored to be developing a cyanide bomb. His name is Dr. Poison.[32]

THE AMAZONIAN
DECLARATION OF INDEPENDENCE

SADIE ELIZABETH HOLLOWAY, who liked to pretend she was a boy, was the first girl in four generations of Holloways. She was named after her grandmothers. She was born on the Isle of Man in 1893, the same year that William Moulton Marston was born, an ocean away. Her grandfather, an Englishman named Joseph Goss, was the captain of Queen Victoria's yacht; one day, when the king of Spain fell overboard, Goss saved him, for which he was knighted; ever after, he was known as Don José de Gaunza. Her mother, Daisy, married an American bank clerk named William George Washington Holloway. When Sadie was five, the Holloways moved to America. Summers, she went home. She never lost her Manx accent. She was fierce and she was picky. Mostly, she was fearless.

She had a little brother; she liked to boss him around. In Massachusetts, the Holloways lived at first in a boardinghouse on Beacon Hill and then in a seaside cottage in Revere before settling in Cliftondale, in a house on Morton Avenue, where they installed indoor plumbing and replaced all the windows with stained glass. Sadie had an orange tabby cat named Sandy Alexander MacTabish. She and her best friend, Pearl, put on plays together. Sadie always played all the parts for boys because she had clothes that could pass for pants: "I was the only one who had pajamas."

From "Introducing Wonder Woman," *All-Star Comics #8* (December 1941–January 1942)

On Morton Avenue, the Holloways lived across the street from a flower shop. It smelled of jasmine. An Irish family lived two doors away. "Once the two boys in the family got my brother down and were pummeling him," Sadie said, in a story she liked to tell. "I jumped on their backs and banged their heads on the pavement." But what she remembered most about growing up on Morton Avenue was the day those boys' mother accidentally killed herself after piercing a wire through her cervix, hoping to lose a baby she could not afford to keep.[1]

Wonder Woman came not from the Isle of Man but from the isle of woman. "In the days of ancient Greece, many centuries ago, we Amazons were the foremost nation in the world," Hippolyte explains to her daughter, Princess Diana, in the first Wonder Woman story Marston ever wrote. "In Amazonia, women ruled and all was well." Alas, that didn't last. After Hippolyte defeated Hercules, the strongest man in the world, he stole her magic girdle, which had been given to her by Aphrodite, the goddess of love. Without it, Hippolyte lost all her power and the Amazons became the slaves of men, bound in chains. They escaped only after pledging to live apart from men forever. They sailed across the ocean until they found an uncharted place they named Paradise Island. There they lived, blessed with eternal

Wonder Woman, newspaper strip, August 16, 1944

life, for centuries—until, one day, Captain Steve Trevor, a U.S. Army officer, crashed his plane onto the island.

"A man!" Princess Diana cries when she finds him. "A man on Paradise Island!"

She carries him in her arms like a baby. She falls in love with him. Hippolyte consults the gods.

"You must deliver him back to America, to help fight the forces of hate and oppression," Aphrodite advises.

"You must send with him your strongest and wisest Amazon," says Athena, the goddess of war, to "America, the last citadel of democracy, and of equal rights for women!"

The strongest and wisest of the Amazons turns out, of course, to be Hippolyte's daughter, who then flies Trevor, in her invisible plane, to the United States, "to help him wage the battle for freedom, democracy, and womankind!"[2] She brings him to an army hospital. After he recovers, she joins him at the headquarters of U.S. military intelligence, where Princess Diana disguises herself as Diana Prince, a prim, bespectacled secretary. She takes dictation in Greek, which, more than once, nearly gives her away. "That's not shorthand!" another secretary cries. "It's not Gregg, nor Pitman, nor any other system." Diana: "It's—er—Amazonian!"[3]

Sadie Elizabeth Holloway met William Moulton Marston when they were both in the eighth grade, at a grammar school in Cliftondale. Later, the Holloways moved to Dorchester, south of Boston. At Dorchester High School, Sadie studied Greek. For her sixteenth birthday, her mother gave her a copy of John Ruskin's *Sesame and Lilies*. "A girl's education should be nearly, in its course and material of study, the same as a boy's," Ruskin advised.[4] When Sadie graduated from high school, she went to Mount Holyoke College, in South Hadley, Massachusetts, the first women's college in the United States.

Female education was, as yet, a novelty. Until the end of the eighteenth century, girls had not typically been taught even how to write. In the new nation, ideas about educating girls began to change; in a republic, women had to know enough of the world to raise sons who could be virtuous citizens. Mount Holyoke was founded in 1837. Plenty of critics were on hand to warn its students not to get carried away with any fancy ideas about equality. On July 4, 1851, during a celebration marking the seventy-fifth anniversary of the Declaration of Independence, C. Hartwell, from a nearby boys' theological seminary, read to the assembled Mount Holyoke girls a parody he'd written of Elizabeth Cady Stanton's 1848 "Declaration of Sentiments." He called it an "Amazonian Declaration of Independence."

"We hold these truths to be intuitive and indisputable, that all men and women are created free and equal," Hartwell read aloud, finding that very funny.[5]

Suffragists, though, didn't think Amazons were preposterous; they thought they were amazing. From the time of Homer, an Amazon had meant a member of a mythic ancient Greek race of women warriors who lived apart from men. By the end of the nineteenth century, some suffragists, following the work of male anthropologists, had come to believe that a land of Amazons—an ancient matriarchy that predated the rise of patriarchy—had, in fact, once existed.[6] "The period of woman's supremacy lasted through many centuries—undisputed, accepted as natural and proper wherever it existed, and was called the matriarchate, or mother-age," Elizabeth Cady Stanton explained in 1891.[7]

American girls started going to college in significant numbers only at the end of the nineteenth century. Many, like Sadie Holloway, went

From "The Adventure of the Life Vitamin," *Wonder Woman #7* (Winter 1943)

to women's colleges, one of the "Seven Sisters" founded before 1889: Mount Holyoke, Barnard, Bryn Mawr, Radcliffe, Smith, Vassar, and Wellesley. (Wonder Woman founds an all-girls school, too: Wonder Woman College.) Others went to coeducational schools. In 1910, 4 percent of Americans between the ages of eighteen and twenty-one went to college; by 1920, that number had risen to 8 percent, 40 percent of which were women.[8]

By the time Sadie Holloway packed her bags for Mount Holyoke, in 1911, an "Amazon" meant any woman rebel—which, to a lot of people, meant any girl who left home and went to college. "New Women," they were called, and they meant to be as free as men: Amazons, all.

Sadie Holloway had wide-set blue eyes and stood five feet flat. She was stern and stoic and tight-lipped. At Mount Holyoke, she tied her long, dark, wavy hair on top of her head,

Sadie Elizabeth Holloway as a student at Mount Holyoke in 1915

like a Gibson girl. She wore lacy white dresses that fell to her ankles; she rolled the sleeves up past her elbows. She joined the debating society, the Philosophy Club, the Baked Bean Club, the choir. She worked for the student magazine, the *Mount Holyoke*. She was bold; she was unflinching: she played field hockey.[9]

The right to an education was as hard fought a battle as the right to vote; the first had to be achieved before the second could be won. "The time will come when some of us will look back upon the arguments against the granting of the suffrage to women with as much incredulity as that with which we now read those against their education," said Mary Woolley, the president of Mount Holyoke, in a speech she gave at the National American Woman Suffrage convention in Baltimore in 1906.[10]

Woolley was a tireless supporter of women's rights. Inez Haynes Gillmore, a Radcliffe graduate, had founded the College Equal Suffrage League in 1900, the first college suffrage league. In 1908, Woolley had a hand in making that campaign a nationwide effort, helping to found the National College Equal Suffrage League.[11] A Mount Holyoke chapter of the Equal Suffrage League began meeting in the spring of 1911, the semester before Holloway arrived on campus. Not every woman's college was a hotbed of suffragism, but Mount Holyoke was. The faculty was nothing but "rank women suffragists," one student said. By 1914, when a Mount Holyoke student submitted a paper for English 1 called "Reasons for Opposition to the Further Extension of the Suffrage," her professor applauded her effort—"a clear presentation of one side of the question"—and then argued with her in the margins. In the spring of Holloway's junior year, the *Mount Holyoke* reported that the Equal Suffrage League had wanted to sponsor a debate on the subject of suffrage and that an archaeology professor had agreed to argue in favor of granting women the vote but "no one was willing to speak for the opposition." By the time Holloway graduated, in 1915, nearly half the student body belonged to the Equal Suffrage League.[12]

Mary Woolley wasn't only a suffragist; she was also a feminist. "Feminism is not a prejudice," she said. "It is a principle."[13]

The word "feminism," hardly ever used before 1910, was everywhere by 1913. It meant advocacy of women's rights and freedoms and a vision of equality markedly different from that embraced by

Holloway (first row, left), on the staff of the *Mount Holyoke*, 1915

the "woman movement" of the nineteenth century, which, nostalgic for a prehistoric, matriarchal "mother-age," had been founded less on a principle of equality than on a set of ideas about women's moral superiority. "All feminists are suffragists, but not all suffragists are feminists," as one feminist explained. Feminists rejected the idea of women as reformers whose moral authority came from their different-ness from men—women were supposedly, by nature, more tender and loving and chaste and pure—and advocated instead women's full and equal participation in politics, work, and the arts, on the grounds that women were in every way equal to men.

Suffrage was a single political goal. Feminism's demand for equality was broader, both more radical and more difficult. "I hang in a void midway between two spheres—the man's sphere and the woman's sphere," Inez Haynes Gillmore wrote in "Confessions of an Alien" in *Harper's Bazaar* in 1912. "The duties and pleasures of the aver-age woman bore and irritate. The duties and pleasures of the average man interest and allure."[14] Could a life be lived in between? Women involved in the nineteenth-century woman's movement had often subscribed to the belief that women had no interest in sex—no lust, no hunger, no passion. Feminists disagreed. They wanted to separate sex from reproduction, so that sex, for women, could be, as it was

THE
WOMAN
REBEL

NO GODS NO MASTERS

VOL I.   MARCH 1914   NO. 1.

THE AIM

This paper will not be the champion of any "ism."

All rebel women are invited to contribute to its columns.

The majority of papers usually adjust themselves to the ideas of their readers but the WOMAN REBEL will obstinately refuse to be adjusted.

The aim of this paper will be to stimulate working women to think for themselves and to build up a conscious fighting character.

An early feature will be a series of articles written by the editor for girls from fourteen to eighteen years of age. In this present chaos of sex atmosphere it is difficult for the girl of this uncertain age to know just what to do or really what constitutes clean living without prudishness. All this slushy talk about white slavery, the man painted and described as a hideous vulture pouncing down upon the young, pure and innocent girl, drugging her through the medium of grape juice and lemonade and then dragging her off to his foul den for other men equally as vicious to feed and fatten on her enforced slavery — surely this picture is enough to sicken and disgust every thinking woman and man, who has lived even a few years past the adolescent age. Could any more repulsive and foul conception of sex be given to adolescent girls as a preparation for life than this picture that is being perpetuated by the stupidly ignorant in the name of "sex education"?

If it were possible to get the truth from girls who work in prostitution to-day, I believe most of them would tell you that the **first** sex experience was with a sweetheart or through the desire for a sweetheart or something impelling within themeselves, the nature of which they knew not, neither could they control. Society does not forgive this act when it is based upon the natural impulses and feelings of a young girl. It prefers the other story of the grape juice procurer which makes it easy to shift the blame from its own shoulders, to cast the stone and to evade the unpleasant facts that it alone is responsible for. It sheds sympathetic tears over white slavery, holds the often mythical procurer up as a target, while in reality it is supported by the misery it engenders.

If, as reported, there are approximately 35,000 women working as prostitutes in New York City alone, is it not sane to conclude that some force, some living, powerful, social force is at play to compel these women to work at a trade which involves police persecution, social ostracism and the constant danger of exposure to venereal diseases. From my own knowledge of adolescent girls and from sincere expressions of women working as prostitutes inspired by mutual understanding and confidence I claim that the **first** sexual act of these so-called wayward girls is partly given, partly desired yet reluctantly so because of the fear of the consequences together with the dread of lost respect of the man. These fears interfere with mutuality of expression —the man becomes conscious of the responsibility of the act and often refuses to see her again, sometimes leaving the town and usually denouncing her as having been with "other fel-

lows." His sole aim is to throw off responsibility. The same uncertainty in these emotions is experienced by girls in marriage in as great a proportion as in the unmarried. After the first experience the life of a girl varies. All these girls do not necessarily go into prostitution. They have had an experience which has not "ruined" them, but rather given them a larger vision of life, stronger feelings and a broader understanding of human nature. The adolescent girl does not understand herself. She is full of contradictions, whims, emotions. For her emotional nature longs for caresses, to touch, to kiss. She is often as well satisfied to hold hands or to go arm in arm with a girl as in the companionship of a boy.

It is these and kindred facts upon which the WOMAN REBEL will dwell from time to time and from which it is hoped the young girl will derive some knowledge of her nature, and conduct her life upon such knowledge.

It will also be the aim of the WOMAN REBEL to advocate the prevention of conception and to impart such knowledge in the columns of this paper.

Other subjects, including the slavery through motherhood; through things, the home, public opinion and so forth, will be dealt with.

It is also the aim of this paper to circulate among those women who work in prostitution; to voice their wrongs; to expose the police persecution which hovers over them and to give free expression to their thoughts, hopes and opinions.

And at all times the WOMAN REBEL will strenuously advocate economic emancipation.

THE NEW FEMINISTS

That apologetic tone of the new American feminists which plainly says "Really, Madam Public Opinion, we are all quite harmless and perfectly respectable" was the keynote of the first and second mass meetings held at Cooper Union on the 17th and 20th of February last.

The ideas advanced were very old and time-worn even to the ordinary church-going woman who reads the magazines and comes in contact with current thought. The "right to work," the "right to ignore fashions," the "right to keep her own name," the "right to organize," the "right of the mother to work"; all these so-called rights fail to arouse enthusiasm because to-day they are all recognized by society and there exist neither laws nor strong opposition to any of them.

It is evident they represent a middle class woman's movement; an echo, but a very weak echo, of the English constitutional suffragists. Consideration of the working woman's freedom was ignored. The problems which affect the

for men, about pleasure, not sacrifice. In 1914, Greenwich Village feminist Margaret Sanger founded a magazine called the *Woman Rebel*. The "basis of Feminism," Sanger said, had to be a woman's control over her own body, "the right to be a mother regardless of church or state."[15]

New Women like Sadie Holloway held every expectation of political equality with men. They expected to control their fertility, to forge relationships of equality with the men they married, if they chose to marry, and to rise to the top of their profes-

Marston and Holloway in 1914

sions, whether or not they also chose to have children. Quite how all this could be accomplished was less clear; apparently, equality with men required servants; much of early feminism was a fantasy of the wealthy, equality for the few. M. Carey Thomas, president of Bryn Mawr, said, "No woman can amount to anything who does her own dusting." To that, Holloway said, "Oh yes she can, if she gets up early enough in the morning."[16] Holloway always wanted everything.

Holloway loved Marston, but at Mount Holyoke, she didn't much mind being apart from him. "We did our biggest fighting at around 14 so that by the time we hit college we were going pretty well as a team," she said.[17] To visit her, Marston took a train from Cambridge. Holloway liked to meet him at the station—a streetcar ran from South Hadley to campus—but Mount Holyoke girls weren't allowed to ride with a man without a chaperone. "A stupid rule," Holloway called it. She complained to the dean. Then she rode with Marston anyway.[18]

During Holloway's sophomore year, Woodrow Wilson, a professor of history who'd once taught at Bryn Mawr, ran for president. Wilson ran as a Democrat against William Howard Taft, the Republican incumbent; Theodore Roosevelt, who ran on a third-party ticket; and Eugene Debs, the Socialist. College girls all over the country followed the election avidly. The Mount Holyoke Equal Suffrage League sponsored a mock presidential debate, a torchlight parade, stump speeches, a mass political meeting, and a mock election. "The question of suffrage for women was, of course, well to the front in almost all the speeches," the *New York Evening Post* reported, in a story titled "The College Girl and Politics."[19] The Amazons were declaring independence.

At Mount Holyoke, Holloway studied English, history, math, and physics, but she loved Greek best.[20] She loved the language and the stories, and she loved, especially, the women. Her favorite book was *Sappho: Memoir, Text, Selected Renderings and a Literal Translation,* edited and translated by Henry Thornton Wharton and first published in 1885. Sappho had lived on the Greek island of Lesbos in the Aegean Sea, around 600 B.C. Wharton's was the first complete English translation of her poetry, which survives only in fragments. Wharton's *Sappho* was part of a Victorian Sappho revival, a Sapphic obsession that found especially ardent expression at women's colleges. The use of the word "lesbian"—literally a resident of Sappho's island of Lesbos—to mean a woman attracted to other women dates to this era, though it wasn't yet part of the vernacular. Sappho of Lesbos had become the symbol of female love.[21]

Sappho held a special place at Mount Holyoke. When Mary Woolley accepted the presidency of the college, she arranged for Jeannette Marks, a literary scholar who was also a suffragist, to be offered a position in the English Department. They had met when Woolley was teaching at Wellesley and Marks was a freshman; they lived together for fifty-five years.[22] In 1912, when Holloway was a sophomore, Mount Holyoke celebrated its seventy-fifth anniversary. Students staged an original play called *The Thirteenth Amendment,* a musical comedy about a world without men: a feminist utopia.[23] In a parade led by Woolley, students from the Department of Greek marched dressed as Helen of Troy, Penelope, Electra, Antigone, Sophocles, and Sappho.[24]

Holloway read Sappho in the original Greek. "The prose I really didn't give a hoot about," she said, "but the poetry was something else again."[25] From fragment 31:

> *no: tongue breaks, and thin*
> *fire is racing under skin*
> *and in eyes no sight and drumming*
> *fills ears*
> *and cold sweat holds me and shaking*
> *grips me all, greener than grass.*[26]

It set her shuddering.

Later, much later, Sadie Holloway, a whip-smart tomboy from the Isle of Man, wrote a memo to DC Comics explaining what exclamations Wonder Woman, an Amazon from an island of women, ought and ought not to use. Avoid: "Vulcan's Hammer!" Preferred: "Suffering Sappho!"[27]

"I still have a Wharton's *Sappho* and still read it," Holloway wrote when she was in her eighties.[28] She once inscribed a book, "Χρυδοφάη Φεράπαlναv Αφροδίraς": "Aphrodite's handmaid, bright as gold." She signed it, simply, "Sappho."[29]

DR. PSYCHO

AT HARVARD, William Moulton Marston wore owl's-eye spectacles, a tweed suit, and a coonskin coat. The coat had pockets specially sized to hide a fifth of whiskey. He liked rye best. He drank and he smoked; he swooned and he staggered. He wrote a parody of Poe's "The Raven": "Desperately, I wished the morrow; foolishly I sought to borrow / From the beer, relief from sorrow." In it, an undergraduate is visited by the ghost of the philosopher Josiah Royce—"Flowing hair but slightly matted"—who, "Wandering round in endless circles," cries out that skepticism endures "Evermore!"[1]

The last of the Moultons of Moulton Castle fell for philosophy just when philosophy was falling for psychology. In an essay called "The Hidden Self," published in 1890, four years after *Dr. Jekyll and Mr. Hyde,* William James explained that a man has both a public self, the sum of his performances, and a private self, the sum of his passions.[2] Every Jekyll has his Hyde. James was writing decades before either comic books or superheroes were invented, but his line of argument is no small part of why

Wonder Woman changing into Diana Prince. From "The Purloined Pressure Coordinator," *Comic Cavalcade #4* (Fall 1943)

Passing through the gates of Holliday College. *Wonder Woman*, newspaper strip, September 9, 1944

comic-book superheroes have secret identities: Superman his Clark Kent, Batman his Bruce Wayne, and Wonder Woman her Diana Prince. The distance between philosophy and pop is, really, remarkably small.

Psychology began as a branch of philosophy. James, a philosopher who had trained as a physician, taught the first course in experimental psychology ever offered in the United States. He believed that the science of the mind lies within the study of philosophy because, as he argued in *The Principles of Psychology*, the passions that constitute the hidden self are manifestations of physical sensations: "Whatever moods, affections, and passions I have, are in very truth constituted by, and made up of, those bodily changes we ordinarily call their expression or consequence."[3] The study of psychology, therefore, required experimentation, which is why James became convinced that Harvard had to have a "psychological laboratory," a place where Mr. Hyde could be found by Dr. Seek.

Wonder Woman disguises herself to attend a lecture at Holliday College. *Wonder Woman*, newspaper strip, September 14, 1944

Marston had a hidden self, too. He kept

Dr. Psycho in his psychological laboratory. From "Battle for Womanhood," *Wonder Woman #5* (June–July 1943)

it as well stowed as the flask of rye he tucked into the pocket of his coonskin coat—until, later in his life, he spilled his secrets all over the pages of his comic books.

Harvard not only didn't allow women to speak on campus, it also didn't admit women as students. But Wonder Woman can't keep away. She's like Emmeline Pankhurst, swooping in and stirring everyone up. Much of the action in Wonder Woman comics takes place at "Holliday College": the name's a mash-up of "Holloway" and "Holyoke." Once, disguised in a varsity sweater with an *H* on it—an unmissable allusion to a Harvard varsity sweater—Wonder Woman attends a lecture at Holliday College given by Dr. Hypno. Holliday College is full of sinister professors with names like "Professor Manly" whose chief villainy is their opposition to feminism. Wonder Woman's arch-nemesis is Dr. Psycho, an evil professor of psychology whose plan is "to change the independent status of modern American women back to the days of the sultans and slave markets, clanking chains and abject captivity." He is shriveled and lecherous. He is brilliant and dastardly. Plotting to himself, he snickers, "Women shall suffer while I laugh—Ha! Ho! Ha!" When Wonder Woman first meets Dr. Psycho, in an episode

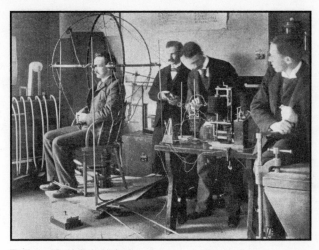

The Harvard Psychological Laboratory

called "Battle for Womanhood," he locks her in an iron cage in the basement of his "psycho laboratory."[4]

William James didn't much like experimental work. But he wanted Harvard to have a state-of-the-art psychological laboratory. To build it, he invited to the department a German psychologist named Hugo Münsterberg.[5] "The situation is this," James wrote to Münsterberg in 1892. "We are the best university in America, and we must lead in psychology. I, at the age of 50, disliking laboratory work naturally, and accustomed to teach philosophy at large, altho I could, *tant bien que mal,* make the laboratory run, yet am certainly not the kind of stuff to make a first-rate director thereof."[6]

In 1897, after several visits, Münsterberg accepted a permanent appointment at Harvard; James, with no small relief, changed his own title from "professor of psychology" to "professor of philosophy." The next year, Münsterberg was elected president of the American Psychological Association.[7] Soon, he began planning the construction of a psychological laboratory in the Philosophy Department's new home, a four-story brick building on Harvard Yard, to be called Emerson Hall.[8]

Hugo Münsterberg

It opened in 1905. Birds and monkeys were kept in iron cages six feet by four, rabbits and guinea pigs in pens twice as small, and mice in tiny hutches.[9]

Münsterberg earned extra money by teaching at the "Harvard Annex," a makeshift campus for women students that opened in 1879. The annex didn't have its own faculty; annex students took all their courses with Harvard professors, although they were banned from earning Harvard degrees.[10] George Herbert Palmer, who championed female education as ardently as he championed woman suffrage, taught at the annex from the start. He also insisted, to no avail, that annex students ought to be allowed to attend his Harvard lectures, alongside Harvard men. Palmer's wife, Alice Freeman Palmer, had tried to convince Harvard president Charles Eliot to admit women to Harvard. Eliot had said no but promised her that the annex could become part of Harvard—and that annex students could be awarded Harvard degrees—if she could raise $250,000 for an endowment. She raised that money, only to be told by Eliot that he had changed his mind. In 1894, the annex, instead of becoming part of Harvard, was incorporated as Radcliffe College.[11]

Münsterberg's research concerned perception, emotion, reaction, and sensation. He liked to experiment on his students, especially on his female students. "One is indeed all things to all men in a laboratory," Gertrude Stein wrote after, as a Radcliffe student, she found herself in Münsterberg's laboratory in 1894, "with a complicated apparatus strapped across her heart to register her breathing, her finger imprisoned in a steel machine and her arm thrust immovably in a big glass tube."[12] He was trying to find Stein's mind.

Despite teaching at Radcliffe, Münsterberg was notorious for his opposition to both female education and woman suffrage. He believed in neither the intellectual nor the political equality of women. "To be sure, there are several American women whose scientific work is admirable," he allowed, "but they are still rare exceptions. The tendency to learn rather than to produce pervades all the great masses of women." The only reason to educate women, he thought, was to make them more interesting wives: "The woman should not strive for intellectual cultivation to do away with marriage but to ennoble it."[13] Women, in his view, had little capacity for reason. There was no question, for instance, of women serving on juries. As the *San Francisco Chronicle* reported, "Professor Hugo Munsterberg says that women are not fit for jury duty because they are unwilling to listen to argument and cannot be brought to change their opinion on any subject."[14] Münsterberg also believed that, if ever women were to succeed in gaining the right to vote, their enfranchisement would be a "dead letter for the overwhelming majority of women," since "the average woman does not wish to go into politics." Decent, moral women had too much to do at home to cast a ballot, he thought, and any women who *would* show up at the polls would be easily corrupted, with the result that "the political machines would win new and disgusting strength from the feebleness of these women to resist political pressure." Not to mention the danger that "politics might bring about differences between husband and wife." In short, "the self-assertion of women in political matters is hardly a practical question."[15]

William James died in 1910, the year before Marston arrived at Harvard. George Santayana retired during Marston's freshman year. After acing Philosophy A, Marston enrolled in Ethics with Palmer, Metaphysics with Royce, and Experimental Psychology with a lean young lecturer named Herbert Langfeld.[16] He earned one A after another, at a time when A's were altogether rare.[17] In 1912, when Marston was a sophomore, Harvard's Department of Philosophy was renamed the Department of Philosophy and Psychology.[18] That year, Marston began studying with Münsterberg, who found Marston so impressive that he hired him to assist him in teaching at Radcliffe, strapping girls to machines.

It was an age of experiment, and of philosophy, applied. The historian Charles Homer Haskins insisted that knowledge is always partial. Royce, the philosopher, had a different notion. "The idea of truth is essentially a social idea," Royce told his students. "When you assert that a proposition is true, you are actually making an appeal to somebody."[19] From Münsterberg, Marston learned another path to truth. The experimental psychologist needn't dive for his evidence in a dustbin; he could create his own evidence, in a laboratory.

The experiments Münsterberg and Marston conducted together in the Psychological Laboratory in Emerson Hall and on their students at Radcliffe were designed to detect deception. They wanted to tell truth from lies. Marston began conducting a series of "reaction-time" experiments: he wanted to know whether people who are lying hesitate when they speak.[20] Haskins defined the historical method as the discrimination between the trustworthy and untrustworthy; Münsterberg wanted to predict trustworthiness. To understand how the mind works—to discover the physical manifestation of truth and deceit—would be to know whose evidence was to be trusted, not by making a subjective judgment, the way the historian applied to a mass of evidence the intellectual skills of criticism and interpretation, but through observations made and tests developed. Truthfulness—truth itself—was to be established not through discrimination but through observation.

Münsterberg had begun this research before Marston moved to Cambridge. Following work being done in Europe, he had devised a series of tests to measure what he believed to be indicators of deceit: the heat of the skin, the rate of the heartbeat, the speed of speech. In 1907, he'd tried to put his theory into practice when he accepted an assignment from *McClure's Magazine* to go to Idaho to report on the trial of Harry Orchard.[21]

Orchard had been charged with the assassination of the state's former governor, an assassination allegedly ordered by Big Bill Haywood, head of the Industrial Workers of the World. He'd confessed to that crime, and to eighteen other murders, too; he said he was a hit man for the union. On the strength of Orchard's confession, Haywood had been charged with murder. Haywood pled not guilty. He was defended by Clarence Darrow, the most celebrated trial lawyer in the country.

Münsterberg visited Orchard in the state penitentiary in Boise. "I had come to examine his mind and to find out what was really at the bottom of his heart," he said. For seven hours, over two days, he subjected Orchard to nearly one hundred deception tests. The press watched the professor's every trip to the prison. "The entire reading

world had its attention attracted by the visit of Professor Hugo Munsterberg of Harvard University to Boise, Idaho," as one newspaper
reported. All around the country, the devices Münsterberg brought
with him to that jail in Idaho to hook up to Orchard's arms and legs
and chest and head captured headlines: "Machines That Tell When
Witnesses Lie," read one. Before Münsterberg began his tests, he was
sure Orchard was lying. By the time he was done, he'd become convinced that Orchard was telling the truth.[22]

Münsterberg left Boise before the trial ended, having promised the
defense that he would keep the results of his tests secret until after
the verdict, but on a train ride to his summer home in Massachusetts,
he broke his promise: he told a reporter that "every word in Orchard's
confession is true."[23] Darrow accused Münsterberg of having been
bribed by the prosecution. In his closing statement to the jury, Darrow
called Orchard "monstrous" and "a liar." It was preposterous, Darrow
said, that anyone could be asked to take Orchard's word for anything.

"Gentlemen," Darrow said to the jury, "I don't believe that anywhere where the English language is spoken or where common law
prevails any intelligent lawyer would ever have dreamed of convict-
ing defendants upon evidence like this." And a Harvard psychologist,
Darrow hinted, had nothing to teach a juror. "You can't take Harry
Orchard's face or his form and make it over again in a second, and
you can't take his crooked brain and his crooked, dwarfed soul, and
make it new in a minute, and if you, gentlemen, are going to bank on
that in this case, then you are taking a serious responsibility with Bill
Haywood's life."[24]

Haywood was acquitted. Münsterberg, afraid that he might be sued,
decided not to publish "Experiments with Harry Orchard," the article
he had written for *McClure's*. Instead, he published an essay about
the importance of psychological testimony in criminal court cases.[25]
He predicted that a science of testimony, hard and exact, would one
day replace standards of judicial proof, as sloppy and unreliable as the
evidence and methods used by the historian—or a defense lawyer. He
called into question the very idea of a jury: Why leave a finding of
guilt or innocence to fallible jurors?[26]

In 1908, Münsterberg published a book called *On the Witness
Stand*, an anthology of his essays. The collection was reviewed by

John Henry Wigmore, who was both the dean of Northwestern Law School and the author of the definitive four-volume *Treatise on the Law of Evidence* (1904–5).[27] Wigmore set about reading everything written, in every language, on the *Psychologie der Aussage*—the psychology of testimony—an investigation centered in Germany whose objective was to evaluate the reliability of testimony by staging scenes in front of unsuspecting bystanders to be called as witnesses.[28] Wigmore's review took the form of a farcical trial in which a plaintiff—the legal profession—charges Münsterberg with libel for having declared "that there existed certain exact and precise experimental and psychological methods of ascertaining and measuring the testimonial certitude of witnesses and the guilty consciousness of accused persons." Münsterberg's defense is handled by two worthless attorneys named R. E. Search and X Perry Ment. The jury, unsurprisingly, finds for the plaintiff.[29]

Even before Wigmore's review, though, Münsterberg's reputation had been devastated, partly because of his fidelity to Germany, despite its growing militarism, and partly because of his criticism of the United States as a nation suffering from an excess of equality. Münsterberg believed in hierarchy, order, and Germany. To him, there was no better illustration of American decay and German purity than the ridiculous aspirations of American women: "the aim of the German woman is to further the interests of the household," he maintained, but "that of the American woman is to escape."[30] By 1905, William James had become so exasperated with Münsterberg that he threatened to resign. "I want a world of anarchy," James said. "Münsterberg wants a world of bureaucracy." Calls for Münsterberg's deportation began in 1907. He spent 1910–11 in Berlin, where he founded the Amerika Institut: he wanted to explain Germans to Americans and Americans to Germans. When he returned to the United States, a Harvard alumnus, convinced that Münsterberg was a spy, attempted to have him removed from the faculty.[31]

By 1912, when William Moulton Marston walked into Harvard's Psychological Laboratory in Emerson Hall, Hugo Münsterberg was nearly ruined. The last of the Moultons of Moulton Castle would be Dr. Psycho's last student.

JACK KENNARD, COWARD

MARSTON WORE HIS COONSKIN COAT; Holloway wore her hair pinned up, ringlets dangling. Arm in arm, they'd stride from Harvard Yard, down Massachusetts Avenue to Central Square, to the Scenic Temple, "The Home of High Class Entertainment in Cambridge." Tickets cost ten cents. The price to get into a nickelodeon was almost never a nickel.[1]

They had to watch where they stepped. Cambridge was a jungle of pits and cranes. In 1909, the Boston Elevated Railway Company had begun building a subway line meant to begin at Park Street station, tunnel under Boston Common, rise over the Charles River Bridge, burrow again at Kendall Square, bore beneath a corner of Harvard Yard, and end at a station beneath Harvard Square, where the pillars on the platform were painted with crimson *H*'s, like the letters on varsity sweaters.[2] The digging alone took two years. On March 10, 1912, the mauled and decapitated body of James B. Dennehey, twenty-three, was found on the subway tracks under Harvard Yard. He'd been inspecting the tracks when he was killed during a practice run.[3] Still, the subway opened as scheduled on March 23, 1912, at 5:24 a.m. By horse, the ride between Harvard Square and Boston's Park Street station, a distance of 3.2 miles, had taken twenty-five minutes; by subway, it took eight.[4]

The opening of the subway meant more trips to the movies. That spring, Holloway, when she visited, could have ridden with Marston from Harvard Square to Park Street to go to the Tremont Theatre, on the Common, to see an adaptation of Homer's *Odyssey*. Holloway would have liked that; she adored anything Greek.[5] Marston had other reasons to go. His father's business in quality woolens for gentlemen's suits was failing, and Marston had decided to work his way through college by writing for the movies.

In the Psychological Laboratory in Emerson Hall, Marston had been experimenting with machines that might tell truth from lies. To write movies, he had to turn lies into truths: he had to learn how to tell a story that wasn't true but that, on film, would seem to be.

Motion pictures—pictures that moved, or "movies," as they were called starting in 1902—were so new that what to call a script hadn't yet been settled. ("Screenplay" wasn't used before 1916.) The word "photoplay," meaning a dramatic film, was coined in 1909. Using "scenario" to mean a movie script dates to 1911.

"I took up scenario writing during my second year at Harvard—the year 1912–1913," Marston explained in an interview he gave in 1915 to a trade magazine called *Moving Picture World*. "I purchased a book on the subject and spent considerable time at the picture shows studying the plots, style of pictures produced by different companies, and the visual effects possible with moving pictures."[6]

The book he bought during his sophomore year was *How to Write a Photoplay,* by Herbert Case Hoagland, who worked for Pathé Frères.[7] "To write a photoplay requires no skill as a writer," Hoagland reassured his readers. There was no need to write dialogue, for instance, since movies had no sound. The work mostly involved thinking of a good story and picturing how it could be told by piecing together scenes shot on reels of film that could be threaded through a projector. This was all so unfamiliar that much of Hoagland's book is an explanation of the fundamentals: "After the actual taking of the pictures the undeveloped film is sent to the factory where it is developed, dried, and wound in a roll. . . . Each scene is developed and printed separately and the positives are all joined afterwards in their proper order with title and subtitles in proper place." But the book was also bursting with practical tips for aspiring writers: "Life—everyday life—as you see it about you is full of good ideas for films," he suggested. Girls are important: "Remember that very few stories are of great interest without the rustle of a skirt."

The going rate for a scenario was about twenty-five dollars, Hoagland reported, and "the market for photoplays is large and growing." *How to Write a Photoplay* included a list of motion picture companies, along with their addresses and an account of the kinds of films they preferred, from the American Film Manufacturing Company of Chicago ("They are strong on the American cowboy") to the Victor Film Manufacturing Company of New York ("This company has been formed to present photoplays in which Miss Florence Lawrence will be the star").[8]

"I sold several scenarios to various companies," Marston boasted, but at the end of his sophomore year, he said, he "became too busy to pursue the work further."[9] Marston liked to say he stopped writing for the movies because he was drawn into his scientific research. In truth, he was broke. In the spring of his sophomore year, citing his father's debts, he applied for a scholarship.[10]

In his junior year, Marston returned to his research. He designed an experiment to determine whether systolic blood pressure could be used to detect deception.[11] He wrote to Holloway, told her about his idea for an experiment, and asked for her help.[12] He intended to conduct an experiment on ten psychology graduate students. (One of them was Leonard Troland, a friend from Malden High School who had studied physics and psychology at MIT before joining Münsterberg's laboratory.) For each of the ten subjects, Marston needed a different story, and for the experiment to work, Marston wasn't supposed to know what was in the stories, so Holloway wrote them.[13] Each story involved a friend of the subject who'd been accused of a crime. Marston tucked each story into an envelope, gave it to the subject to read, told the subject to say something that could save his friend, and asked him to choose whether to do that by lying or by telling the truth. He then attached the subject to a blood pressure cuff, or sphygmomanometer, affixed to a machine that recorded the readings on a graph paper. So that he couldn't see his subjects' faces, Marston hid behind a screen. (To establish a baseline, Marston also took his subjects' blood pressure while they were reading William James's *Pragmatism*, during which, it turned out, their blood pressure remained entirely stable and regular.) Next, he questioned each subject about the fictional crime in the presence of a "jury" consisting of between two and ten

Marston, with glasses, giving a lie detector test to Leonard Troland at the Harvard Psychological Laboratory in 1914

students from Münsterberg's elementary psychology course. At the end of the questioning, Marston attempted to determine whether each subject was lying or telling the truth, using only the blood pressure readings, while the jury made the same determination from having watched the subjects and listened to them speaking. Out of 107 cases, Marston was right in 103 instances, or 96 percent of the time, while the jurors, on average, were right only about half the time.[14]

If he had never created Wonder Woman, William Moulton Marston would be remembered for this experiment. He invented the lie detector test. A century on, it's still in use. It's also all over Wonder Woman.

"Come, Elva, you'll have to take a lie detector test," Diana Prince tells Elva Dove, a secretary she suspects of spying, as she drags her down a hallway.

"I'll ask you questions," Diana says, strapping Elva to the machine while Trevor looks on. "Answer truthfully or your blood pressure curve will go up.

"Did you take that rubber report from the secret files?" Diana asks.

"No, no!" Elva insists.

"Well, I'll be jiggered," Trevor exclaims, reading the graph. "She *is* lying."[15]

In the spring of 1914, when Marston was conducting his early blood pressure experiments, Hugo Münsterberg went to the movies for the very first time. He went to see *Neptune's Daughter,* released by Universal Pictures on April 25. After that, he went to every motion picture he could. "Reel after reel moved along before my eyes— all styles, all makes," Münsterberg wrote in *Cosmopolitan.* "I went with the crowd to Anita Stewart and Mary Pickford and Charles Chaplin; I saw Pathé and Vitagraph, Lubin and Essanay, Paramount and Majestic, Universal and Knickerbocker. I read the books on how to write scenarios; I visited the manufacturing companies, and, finally, I began to experiment myself."[16]

Diana Prince administering a lie detector test. From "A Spy in the Office," *Sensation Comics #3* (March 1942)

Motion pictures were an entirely new art form—as comic books would be later—one that psychologists could observe from its infancy and use to conduct experiments into how the workings of the mind are written on the body. In a 1916 book called *The Photoplay: A Psychological Study,* Münsterberg offered a theory of cinema at a time when cinema had hardly begun. He interviewed directors; he spoke to actresses. He explained the close-up. He explained crosscutting. He wanted to know: "What psychological factors are involved when we watch happenings on the screen?"[17] What, to the mind, are movies?

Münsterberg came to believe that there is no better psychological laboratory than a nickelodeon, in much the same way that Marston later came to believe that there is no better form of psychological propaganda than a comic book. Watching people watch movies, Münsterberg thought, might one day allow him to answer every question he had spent his life's work asking—questions about perception, emotion, sensation, reaction, and deception. "To picture emotions," Münsterberg insisted, "must be the central aim of the photoplay." Consider the sequence of scenes in a motion picture that tells the story of a man brought to trial for murder: "The man who shot his best friend has not offered an explanation in the court trial which we witness. It remains a perfect secret to the town and a mystery to the spectator; and now as the jail door closes behind him the walls of the prison fuse and melt away and we witness the scene in the little cottage where his friend secretly met his wife and how he broke in and how it all came about and how he rejected every excuse which would dishonor his home."[18] Couldn't this new kind of storytelling reveal this character's hidden self—Mr. Hyde—and reveal, too, how the mind works, how a man sees and knows, remembers and forgets, feels and deceives?

Marston took all this in with the air he breathed. Maybe he even went to the movies with Münsterberg. And then, at the end of his junior year, just as he was completing his first set of deception experiments, he read an advertisement in the *Harvard Crimson*: "$100 Offered for 'Movies' Scenario."[19] The Edison Company was holding a nationwide talent search among American college students, promising a cash prize to the author of the best scenario submitted by a student at one of ten colleges: Harvard, Yale, Columbia, Cornell, Princeton, and the Universities of California, Chicago, Michigan, Pennsylvania, and Wisconsin.

"I began to attend the picture theatres again," Marston said, "looking especially for Edison films."[20] He made a study of story, reel by reel.

By the time of the contest deadline, 337 scenarios had been submitted. The winner was announced in February 1915. "Ten colleges—the brainiest men of the country—were invited to this contest and 'Jack Kennard, Coward,' is the result," the Edison Company reported. It was written by William Moulton Marston.[21]

A reporter from a Boston newspaper interviewed Marston, now a senior, in his room at 8 Hollis Hall: "Lying on the couch in his study, the author, famous overnight, told how he worked his way through college by selling scenarios, how he introduced the college atmosphere, and real deeds into the prize-winner and what he thinks will happen when the photo-play bursts like a bombshell into the quaint and sedate yard."[22]

"For the past three years I have led a rather stupid life," Marston said. "I have done nothing but study and write these scenarios. I am taking an A.B. course and intend to enter the Law School next fall when I get my degree."

Marston had been elected to Phi Beta Kappa, voted the chapter president, and admitted to Harvard Law School. (Till the end of his days, he kept his Phi Beta Kappa key on his watch chain. He once had Harry G. Peter, the artist who drew Wonder Woman, sketch her

From the Phi Beta Kappa *Key Recorder,* 1944

wearing an academic cap and gown and lassoing a professor with a Phi Beta Kappa key.)[23] "This study of psycho-physics of deception is going to prove a great help to me when I begin to practice law," Marston announced from his couch. He was awesomely cocky. He explained his research. "I have tried 100 experiments and every one has come out right. You can see what a valuable thing it will be to me when I cross-examine a witness. A blood pressure machine can be attached to the witness' arm and by my knowledge of this course I can tell whether I am getting the truth or not."[24]

The reporter asked about the prizewinning scenario.

"My inspiration for the plot of 'Jack Kennard, Coward' arose, in the first place, from a systematic search for a 'big' situation as a climax which would contain plenty of action," Marston said. "I then built the plot with the purpose of constantly leading up to the climax. The ideas in the plot itself were drawn from various incidents of personal experience here at college."[25]

Jack Kennard, Coward tells the story of a high school football star from a small town who comes to Harvard, joins the football team, and then quits, leading everyone, including his girlfriend, to think he's too scared to play. At the time, Harvard's varsity football squad was led by two all-Americans from Marston's class, H. R. "Tack" Hardwick and Stan Pennock.[26] (It was a famously good squad. Even two decades later, the *Harvard Crimson* was still insisting, "This team was the greatest team in Harvard history.")[27] The names Tack Hardwick and Stan Pennock sound plenty like Jack Kennard. Still, if Kennard was based on a real person, that person was Bill Marston: a high school football star whose high school won the state championships but who never appeared on any football roster at Harvard.[28]

"You see," Marston said, leaping up from his couch, "here is where I bring my own experiences into the scenario and introduce the Harvard characters. The real reason why Kennard stopped playing football was because he got into trouble with the college office with his gambling debts. That really happened to one of the players on the Harvard team."

Later in life, Marston always said he chose not to play football at Harvard because he was so committed to his research. "Considerable pressure was put on me my first year to come for the freshman team," he maintained, but "I resisted it." This was a lie. Marston didn't conduct any experiments his freshman year. More likely, he'd tried out and hadn't made it, or had been too intimidated to try out, or maybe he'd tried out and then quit. Marston fell into a depression in the fall of his freshman year and very nearly killed himself; part of what pushed him there might have had to do with football. Three of his teammates from Malden High School had gone on to spectacular college football careers; one was the captain of the team at Dartmouth. Not Marston. "I went to Harvard and decided to quit athletics," he said. He claimed to have been asked, again and again, even as an upperclassman, to try out. He declined: "It would have forced me to break off my psychological laboratory course."[29] Maybe. Meanwhile, his father had fallen into debt—or at least that's what Marston told his dean, in his scholarship application, though maybe it was Marston who'd fallen into debt, gambling. Maybe Holloway thought he was a coward.

Jack Kennard, Coward was cast, shot, and edited in less than two months. In its climactic final scene (the "'big' situation" upon which Marston had based the plot), Kennard proves his bravery when, in the brand-new Harvard Square subway station, he leaps onto the tracks to rescue his girlfriend, who is about to be run over by a train. For all his study of storytelling, Marston only ever patched together his fictions from his facts: the accident in the Harvard Square subway station,

A scene from *Jack Kennard, Coward*, 1915

the high school football player who can't play college ball, the student plagued by debts. Even his lies told the truth.

Jack Kennard, Coward was released on May 5, 1915.[30] It played at scattered theaters across the country. In Gettysburg, it shared billing with Charlie Chaplin's Keystone comedy *Getting Acquainted*. In Cambridge, where it played at the Durrell Hall theater, across the street from city hall, it was advertised as "a college play to stir the young and make the older patrons dream of younger days."[31] One reviewer said, "William Marston has written a fairly convincing tale of a young collegian in this one-reel drama. Charles M. Seay has brought its good points to the front, and Thomas MacEvoy looks and acts the title role capitally."[32]

It wasn't a good week for the movies. Two days after the film opened, a German U-boat sank the *Lusitania* off the coast of Ireland. More than eleven hundred people drowned, including more than a hundred Americans; four were recent Harvard graduates. Outside Harvard's Germanic Museum, undergraduates draped a statue of a lion, a gift from the kaiser, in black.[33]

"To my German friends and colleagues," Josiah Royce announced in his metaphysics class, all but addressing Hugo Münsterberg directly, "if they chance to want to know what I think, I can and do henceforth only say this: 'You may triumph in the visible world, but at the banquet where you celebrate your triumph there will be present the ghosts of my dead slain on the *Lusitania*.'"[34]

Holloway and Marston at Marston's Harvard
graduation, 1915

A month of mourning passed. And then, on Thursday, June 24,
1915, an unseasonably cold day, Marston graduated from Harvard. In
exercises held at Sanders Theatre, E. E. Cummings, a member of Marston's class, delivered a speech about modernism called "The New Art."
He quoted a poem by Amy Lowell: "Little cramped words scrawling
all over the paper / Like draggled fly's legs"; he quoted a stream of
prose by Gertrude Stein: "Please pale hot, please cover rose, please
acre in the red stranger, please butter all the beef-steak with regular
feel faces." Then President Lowell conferred 124 degrees, handing out
diplomas written in Latin on parchment.

After four years in Cambridge, Gvilielmvs Movlton Marston carried
home a scroll of sheepskin marked *magna cvm lavde* and engraved
with the university's motto: VERITAS.[35] Truth.

MR. AND MRS. MARSTON

SADIE HOLLOWAY graduated from Mount Holyoke on June 16, 1915.[1] She'd gotten her hair cut. Beneath her tasseled graduation cap, she wore her hair in a bob, her curls cut above the nape of her neck. Feminists in Greenwich Village had begun bobbing their hair in 1912. In 1915, it was still radical. "The idea, it seems, came from Russia," the *New York Times* reported. "The intellectual women of that country were revolutionaries. For convenience in disguising themselves when the police trailed them, they cropped their hair."[2] Holloway was something of a revolutionary, too.

When Holloway turned twenty-two, Marston gave her a book of poems written by the American poet Vachel Lindsay. (Holloway always wanted poems for presents.) He'd underlined a poem called "The Mysterious Cat." She liked to be mysterious; she loved cats; she thought of herself as a Manx, a cat without a tail; Marston thought of himself as her slave. Marston liked these lines: "I saw a cat—'twas but a dream / Who scorned the slave that brought her cream." It sounds a little filthy. In the margin, Marston wrote, "Ha! Ha!"[3]

He proposed; she accepted; he gave her

Holloway at Mount Holyoke commencement, 1915

Holloway and Marston in 1916

an engagement ring he bought with the prize money he'd gotten for *Jack Kennard, Coward*.[4]

Marston was going to go to law school; Holloway decided she'd go, too. "It never occurred to me not to go if that's what I wanted to do," she said. She'd once gotten in trouble, at Mount Holyoke, in an ethics class, when the professor asked, "Now in the case of a lawyer who is hired to defend a guilty man, what should he do?"

Holloway said: "Change his profession."[5]

She liked the idea of studying law. She liked arguing about rules. Her father objected.

"As long as I am able to keep you in gingham aprons," he told her, "you should be content to stay home with your Mother." Holloway ignored him. To earn her tuition, she spent the summer selling cookbooks, door to door.[6]

In September, Holloway and Marston married. Holloway was the first in her class to become a wife, at a time when only one in two Mount Holyoke graduates ever married.[7] To the wedding, in the parlor of her parents' house, she wore a white satin gown and a veil caught with lilies of the valley.[8] Marston wanted her to take his name. She did, but she resented it. "As for names, we are stuck with either our father's name or our husband's, so choose the one you like the best," she once advised a friend. "There's no such thing in this civilization as 'your own name.'"[9]

Marston didn't like the name Sadie, even though Holloway liked it rather a lot, especially, she said, "if you use its oriental spelling, Zaidee, the Earth Mother." Marston didn't like the name Elizabeth, either, so Sadie Elizabeth Holloway became Betty Marston. (I'll keep calling her "Holloway.") She was bitter about it, but she gave in. "I was stuck," she said later.[10]

They honeymooned in Maine. Then they moved to a two-bedroom apartment in Cambridge, on Remington Street.[11] Marston began studying at Harvard Law School.

"Those dumb bunnies at Harvard wouldn't take women," Holloway said, "so I went to Boston University."[12]

"Studying at Boston University Law School and keeping house" is what Holloway listed as her occupation in the first report she sent to the Mount Holyoke alumni office in 1916. She tried to teach herself to cook, using a Fannie Farmer cookbook given to her by her mother-in-law.[13] She never loved cooking but she did love law school.

Boston University, founded in 1869, had admitted women from the start; it was the first coeducational college in Massachusetts. But in 1915, Holloway, with her bobbed hair, was one of only three women in her law school class. During a course in criminal law, when the topic was something like rape, the female students were asked to leave.[14]

Holloway was an excellent law student, Marston an indifferent one. "I plugged along doggedly, doing every bit of the drudgery prescribed and getting exceptionally poor results," he admitted.[15] (He never earned higher than a C.) He'd gone to law school to learn the law of evidence. In the fall of 1916, his second year, he enrolled in Evidence with Arthur Dehon Hill. For a textbook, Hill used the second edition of James Bradley Thayer's *Select Cases on Evidence*. Thayer, who taught at Harvard until his death in 1902, had taught John Henry Wigmore, Hugo Münsterberg's nemesis. (When Wigmore wrote his *Treatise on the Law of Evidence*, he dedicated it to Thayer.) As Thayer saw it, there weren't any rules of evidence; or, to be exact, there were two, and only two: "(1) that nothing is to be received which is not logically probative of some matter requiring to be proved; and (2) that everything which is thus probative should come in, unless a clear ground of policy of law excludes it."[16] What Marston wanted to figure out was how to introduce his lie detector test into court.

The presidential election of 1916 turned on two questions: the war in Europe and woman suffrage. Wilson, who was running for a second term, advocated neutrality and remained opposed to a constitutional amendment guaranteeing women the right to vote. He was challenged by Charles Evans Hughes, a former New York governor and U.S. Supreme Court justice. Hughes urged American entry into the war.[17] "A vote for Hughes is a vote for war," explained a senator from Oklahoma. "A vote for Wilson is a vote for peace." At the Republican National Convention in Chicago, five thousand women staged a

Women as U.S. states, those in chains representing states where women could not vote, 1916

protest. Hughes began supporting woman suffrage. Some women supported Hughes, because of his position on suffrage; others supported Wilson, because of his position on peace. In the end, it was women voters who, by rallying behind the peace movement, gained Wilson a narrow victory: he won ten of the twelve states where women had already been enfranchised. Without them, he would have lost.[18]

All fall, Lowell, Harvard's president, had been pressured to fire Münsterberg, for his support for Germany. In a letter written on November 2, Lowell refused, staunchly stating his decision as a matter of principle: "It has fallen to the lot of this University to be among the foremost in maintaining the principle of academic freedom, which has been severely strained by the present war. That principle, we believe to be of the greatest importance, and not to be put in jeopardy without tangible proof of personal misconduct, apart from the unpopularity of the views expressed."[19]

Münsterberg did not survive the controversy. On the morning of December 16, 1916, he woke up feeling uneasy and unsteady and walked more slowly than usual from his home at 7 Ware Street to Radcliffe Yard. He entered the lecture hall. Marston may well have been there, acting as his assistant. Münsterberg began to speak; he began to sway. In the middle of a sentence, he slumped to the floor. He had had a cerebral hemorrhage. He died within the hour. He was fifty-three.[20]

There is a page in a Wonder Woman comic book that features a tombstone. It reads, "Rest in Peace Prof. Psycho."[21]

THE EXPERIMENTAL LIFE

IN DECEMBER 1916, while Wilson delivered his State of the Union address, suffragists flooded the galleries in the Capitol and unfurled a banner that read, "MR. PRESIDENT, WHAT WILL YOU DO FOR WOMAN SUFFRAGE?" They were members of what became the National Woman's Party, founded by Alice Paul and Lucy Burns after they split from the National American Woman Suffrage Association, whose strategy was to change voting laws, state by state. Paul and Burns fought, instead, for a federal constitutional amendment.

New Women wanted to change the world. Burns had graduated from

Suffragists from the National Woman's Party outside the White House, 1917

Vassar in 1902 and gone on to study at Yale, Columbia, and Oxford, but mainly, in England, she'd studied the methods of militant suffragism. So had Paul; she'd been in England between 1908 and 1910, where she'd been arrested during protests organized by Emmeline Pankhurst's Women's Social and Political Union. Back in the United States, Paul earned a PhD from the University of Pennsylvania, writing a dissertation on women's legal rights. In January 1917, suffragists began a silent vigil outside the White House, carrying banners reading, "HOW LONG MUST WOMEN WAIT FOR LIBERTY?" and pledging not to cease their vigil until the amendment passed. On March 4, 1917, on the eve of Wilson's inauguration, more than a thousand women marched around the White House in an icy rain.[1]

Days after Wilson's inauguration, German U-boats sank three American ships. On April 2, a constitutional amendment to grant women the right to vote was introduced in Congress. That same day, Wilson asked Congress to declare war. Then he went back to the White House and wept.[2] When the picketers around the White House refused to stop their protest, they were arrested. At trial, the judge said, "We are at war and you should not bother the president."[3]

On April 6, the day Congress declared war, experimental psychologists from across the country gathered at Harvard, in Emerson Hall. They were led by Herbert Langfeld, Marston's undergraduate adviser, and Robert Yerkes, president of the American Psychological Association.[4] Yerkes, who had earned his PhD at Harvard in 1902 and had studied in Münsterberg's laboratory, was a specialist in both primate behavior and intelligence testing; he was a prominent eugenicist. Out of that meeting came the Psychology Committee of the National Research Council, headed by Yerkes. Its first task was "the psychological examining of recruits to eliminate the mentally unfit."[5]

The war that Wilson hoped would end all wars all but silenced the campaign for woman suffrage, a campaign that had been closely aligned with the peace movement. Congress passed the Espionage Act in 1917 and the Sedition Act in 1918; both were aimed chiefly at socialists, anarchists, and pacifists (Wilson had called for authority to censor the press as well; Congress struck that down by a single vote). Winning the war seemed to the federal government to require the suppression of dissent and to require, too, the nation's psychologists;

Steve Trevor administers test. From "The Milk Swindle," *Sensation Comics #7* (July 1942)

war itself had become a psychological laboratory.

Marston described his life during these years as a series of experiments:

> First experiment, teaching psychology at Radcliffe while still a Harvard undergraduate; result, unfortunate for the girls, who may have learned psychology, but not love. Second experiment, studying law; result, unfortunate for the law, which gained a poor advocate. Third experiment, 1917–1918, War and Army.[6]

Marston's research had obvious wartime applications: the interrogation of prisoners of war and suspected spies. He filled out a draft card on June 5, 1917, ten days before Congress passed the Espionage Act, and two weeks before the end of his second year of law school.[7] By fall, he'd begun a correspondence with Yerkes.[8] He wanted to continue his deception studies, asking Yerkes, "Why not set me at researching upon them in the Harvard Psych. Lab.?"[9] Yerkes consulted with Columbia psychologist Edward L. Thorndike, who met with Marston and reported to Yerkes, "I have spent most of the afternoon with Marston and like him very much and have confidence in him. I am still a little shaky about his findings, but I think they deserve a real try-out with real cases."[10] Langfeld told Yerkes he would be glad to give Marston the use of the facilities in Emerson Hall. "He has much energy and push and is very resourceful," he wrote. "He is very intelligent." Still, Langfeld was not without worry about what he by now perceived to be Marston's Achilles' heel: "I have a mere suspicion that he may be slightly overzealous in grasping opportunities, which causes him to take the corners a little too sharply."[11]

Marston sent Yerkes a research proposal.[12] In response, Yerkes established a special Committee on Tests for Deception, "to make inquiry concerning the reliability and practicability of certain procedures proposed by William M. Marston for the detection of deception."[13] Marston began a study in Emerson Hall, aided by Leonard Troland and another scientist named Harold Burtt. They conducted deception tests—using "iron clad precautions"—on ten men: five Harvard undergraduates and five second-year law school students. The results, Marston reported to Yerkes, were remarkable.[14] Yerkes ordered Marston "to make application of his methods to a number of cases of actual crime."[15]

Marston undertook this next investigation in the fall of 1917, conducting deception tests on twenty criminal defendants who had been recommended by the Municipal Criminal Court of Boston for medical and psychological evaluation. His case reports read like this:

CASE NO. 2. WOMAN (COLORED). AGE, 31 YEARS.

Record of Case Given to Examiner Previous to Deception Test.
Colored woman, 31 years of age. Arrested six months ago for larceny of a ring and placed on probation on the strength of the testimony of a colored man from whom a ring was alleged to have been stolen. Defendant during the six months had not made restitution, as she had been ordered to do, and was suspected by the probation officer of having avoided her calls. Examination was to determine whether or not she stole the ring in the first place.

B.P. Judgment.
Innocent. Woman telling the truth as to the ring, having been given to her.

Verification
The judge dismissed the case, although probation officer advised six months further probation. New evidence had turned up indicating that the colored man who first alleged that defendant stole ring was a disreputable character, etc.

In each of the twenty cases, the judgment of the blood pressure machine, as read by Marston, was subsequently verified by other evidence.[16] Yerkes began to wonder whether Marston had cut his corners too sharply.

During Harvard Law School's winter break, Marston went to Washington. The National Woman's Party vigil around the White House had ended, only to be followed by pickets protesting the treatment of the women who'd been arrested. Many, including Alice Paul, had gone on hunger strikes and were being forcibly fed. Burns had been beaten and hanged from chains. In November, a delegation of suffragists, including a feminist cartoonist named Lou Rogers, had gone to Washington to plead with Wilson to let the picketers out of jail. Paul and Burns, they said, were being tortured. At the end of the month, Burns, Paul, and twenty other women were released. In January 1918, while Marston was in Washington, Wilson announced that he had decided to support a federal woman suffrage amendment.[17]

In Washington, Yerkes arranged for Marston to discuss his research with John Henry Wigmore, who was serving in the army in the Judge Advocate General's office. Yerkes also tried to secure Marston a position that would allow him to apply his work in the field. At the Department of Justice, Marston met with the chief of the Bureau of Investigation (later called the FBI) and with a young J. Edgar Hoover. Asked to hire Marston, the bureau demurred. Yerkes then sent Marston to New York to meet with the chief of the Office of Military Intelligence, who turned him down, and handed him over to the New York chief of police, who wasn't interested, either. For all of Marston's charm, his near-perfect laboratory results generally failed to impress men involved in actual criminal investigation. Marston was exasperated. "I don't care whether they call me Mr. or Mud," he wrote Yerkes. "But I firmly believe that unless Headquarters orders that these tests be instituted in a certain definite place and that I be given certain definite powers to get at cases, we'll go on and on piling up interesting thesis data and getting nowhere practically."[18]

Supervised by Wigmore, Marston conducted an investigation into a series of petty thefts, of scientific instruments, that had taken place in the building where Yerkes worked: "I was asked to examine all the negro messengers in the Mills Building who could have had access to the room from which the instruments were taken," Marston explained. He subjected eighteen messengers to his deception test and reported that Subject #4, a man named Horace Dreear, was guilty. But he'd got the wrong man: it turned out, beyond any doubt, that someone else had committed the crime. Desperate to vindicate himself, Marston went to New York, where, he told Yerkes, he found out that Dreear came from a " 'bad lot' of the New York negroes." (Even if Dreear hadn't stolen the instruments, he was still a guilty man, Marston was trying to argue; it's just that he was just guilty of something else.) Marston told Yerkes that he had begun to think that the problem with his experiment might have been that he had failed to account for what he now suspected might be a racial difference: "The factor of voluntary control which, with white men, seems to make a deception rise regular and almost an absolute one, apparently is almost altogether lacking in negroes."[19]

Yerkes's support weakened. Marston had been turned down by the Office of Military Intelligence, the Bureau of Investigation, the New York Police Department, the Department of War, and the Department of Justice. He'd also accused an innocent man. Yerkes decided Marston's best use might be in the classroom. He began making arrangements for Marston to teach a course in military psychology to soldiers. This required Marston to leave his third year of law school without finishing his coursework, to which the dean reluctantly agreed.[20]

Marston and Holloway graduated from law school in June 1918. In August, they took the bar exam together. Holloway got through it faster. "I finished the exam in nothing flat," she said, "and had to go out and sit on the stairs waiting for Bill."[21]

In October 1918, Marston was commissioned as a second lieutenant and sent to Camp Greenleaf, Georgia, where he was appointed a professor at the U.S. Army School of Military Psychology.[22] Holloway stayed in Cambridge. "During the war," she said, "women left at home were bored stiff."[23]

There's a Wonder Woman episode in which Dr. Psycho disguises himself as the ghost of George Washington in order to shout down the idea that women ought to be allowed to contribute to the war effort.

Marston, second from left, at Camp Greenleaf in 1918

"Women will lose the war for America! Women should not be permitted to have the responsibilities they now have!" he warns. "They must not be trusted with war secrets or serve in the armed forces. Women will betray their country through weakness if not through treachery!"

"Why that loose-tongued double-talking phony!" Wonder Woman cries out, leaping to the stage. "I'll stop him."[24]

Holloway, though, wasn't able to stop anything. Mr. Marston went to war. Mrs. Marston stayed home.

At Camp Greenleaf, Marston taught a course called Military Problems of Testimony. He designed an *Aussage* experiment: he took ten nickels and "about 50 articles, each of some intrinsic value to a soldier," and hid them in a room on the second floor of the camp's Psychology Building. He instructed thirty-five soldiers to go into the room, one at a time, and either steal nothing or steal something and hide it in a nearby barracks. Fourteen officers, some of them lawyers, were to watch the soldiers as they entered and exited the room, follow them, and, eventually, hook them up to a blood-pressure cuff and question them.[25]

Nineteen soldiers had stolen something; sixteen had stolen nothing. (Before being interrogated, they wrote confessions, which were then sealed until the completion of the experiment.) The officers, using Marston's deception test, were able to determine a soldier's guilt or innocence in twenty-six out of thirty-five cases, or 74.3 percent. Marston, who did not conduct the interrogations but merely read graphs documenting the soldiers' blood-pressure changes, was

From "Victory at Sea," *Sensation Comics #15* (March 1943)

right thirty-four out of thirty-five times, achieving the astonishing success rate of 97.1 percent. His test, he concluded, was nearly perfect; the only problem with it was that some people weren't as good at applying it as he was.[26] It looked very fishy. As Yerkes delicately put it, Marston's results "did not command the confidence of all members of the Psychology Committee."[27]

But Wigmore was impressed. He urged Marston to write up the research he'd conducted at Camp Greenleaf and submit it to the *Journal of Criminal Law and Criminology,* a publication Wigmore had founded. Marston's article was accepted.[28]

"Say," Steve Trevor is forever saying to Diana Prince, "you're quite the little psychologist!"[29]

MACHINE DETECTS LIARS, TRAPS CROOKS

MARJORIE WILKES, who believed in both suffrage and bondage, was born in Atlanta, Georgia, in 1889. She was an only child. Her father worked for the Georgia railroad.[1] She smoked from the age of thirteen. She was tough as nails and thin as a twig. She had eyes like a doe's and hair as brown as a mouse's. In 1912, when she was twenty-two, she worked on a suffrage campaign in Chicago. She married a man named Huntley because she wanted a new name: she didn't want to share a name with the man who assassinated Abraham Lincoln. In 1914, having left her husband, she started working as a librarian. In 1916, she marched in a suffrage parade at the Republican National Convention in Chicago; one Chicago newspaper cartoonist depicted suffragists marching with their wrists in shackles, dragging balls chained to their feet, slaves to the men who ruled them.[2]

"No one knows more about the production of Wonder Woman than Marjorie W. Huntley," Holloway liked to say.[3] In the 1940s, Huntley helped out with the inking and lettering of Wonder Woman, including panel after panel depicting women shackled, hands and feet. "How can she run with that ball and chains?" one of Wonder Woman's captors cries out.[4] Huntley was schooled in suffrage, but she believed, too, in what she called "love binding": the importance of being tied and chained. She also believed in extra-body consciousness, vibrations, reincarnation, and the psychic nature of orgasm.[5]

She met Marston in 1918, after Armistice was declared, on Novem-

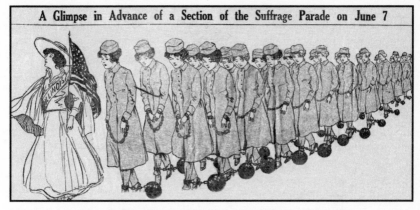

Suffragists as slaves in a parade during the Republican National Convention in Chicago in 1916

Wonder Woman and her friends as slaves in "Mole Men of the Underworld," *Wonder Woman #4* (April–May 1943)

ber 11, and he was sent to Camp Upton, New York, to treat shell shock victims. Huntley was the camp's librarian. Marston was twenty-five and far from his wife; Huntley was twenty-nine and divorced. They were together for six months. Marston was discharged from the army on May 9, 1919, the day he turned twenty-six.

The National Woman's Party, which had staged demonstrations throughout the war—burning Wilson's speeches, picketing the Capitol, and delivering addresses while wearing prison uniforms—finally achieved victory during the peace. On May 21, 1919, the House of Representatives passed the Nineteenth Amendment: "The right of citizens of the United States to vote shall not be denied or abridged by the United States or by any State on account of sex." It passed in the Senate on June 4 and went to the states for ratification.

Marston went home to Cambridge. Soon, Holloway was pregnant. They moved into a house on Lowell Street, off Brattle Street; Holloway's parents bought it for them.[6] They rented out rooms to law school friends, and in one room they kept a patient of Marston's, a boy who could not stop masturbating; he had to be watched night and day.[7] Huntley came to visit. Marston had left her with an understanding that she ought to come whenever she liked. She talked, later, about how she and Marston and Holloway became a "threesome"; that may have started in 1919.[8]

In September 1919, Marston enrolled in Harvard's PhD program in philosophy and Holloway, five months pregnant, enrolled in an MA program at Radcliffe. All of the courses taken by Radcliffe graduate students were taught at Harvard's graduate school, by Harvard professors. Mr. and Mrs. Marston enrolled together for two semesters of Psychological Laboratory with Herbert Langfeld.[9]

On January 7, 1920, Holloway gave birth to a stillborn baby. They named her Fredericka, after Marston's father. All Holloway's life, whenever she had to fill out a form that required her to list the names of her children, she included that baby born dead.[10]

That summer, the Marstons went on vacation in Bermuda; sailing back to the United States, they reached shore on August 9.[11] Nine days later, the Nineteenth Amendment became law. On Election Day that fall, Marjorie Wilkes Huntley escorted women to the polls. With suffrage won, the National Woman's Party began lobbying for the passage of equal rights bills in the states and for the ratification of an Equal Rights Amendment, drafted by Alice Paul.[12]

Holloway and Marston struggled to find their own kind of equality. "Can it be in the divine order of things that one Ph.D. should wash the dishes a whole lifetime for another Ph.D. just because one is a woman and the other a man?" asked the writer of a 1921 essay called "Reflections of a Professor's Wife."[13] Holloway might have asked the same question.

In the 1920–21 academic year, Holloway and Marston enrolled, once again, in the same courses, with the same professors.[14] As Holloway liked to tell it, much of Marston's research was really her research, and she earned a PhD from Harvard as surely as he had, even if she was never awarded the degree. "I suggested the original Lie Detector experiment," she always claimed.[15] The only reason Harvard didn't grant her a PhD, she said, was that she had balked at a requirement for proficiency in German. "I refused to accept the idea that it was necessary to read the German scientists if you were to keep up in your field, regardless of having completed the other requirements," she explained. "I went to Radcliffe, signed some forms, criticized them from a legal point of view, wrote a thesis on Studies in Testimony, and was granted an M.A."[16]

Holloway was either lying or misremembering. Harvard didn't admit women to doctoral programs; there was no question of a woman taking a qualifying examination, German or no German.[17] Nor did an MA from Radcliffe require a thesis. And "Studies in Testimony" isn't the title of a master's thesis written by Holloway—she didn't write one—but of a journal article later published by Marston.

Despite her MA and her JD, Holloway had a hard time finding work. At the time, less than 2 percent of all lawyers in the United States were women.[18] No one took a woman lawyer seriously, Holloway complained. "I have never met a woman who, in those days, actually tried a case before a jury," she said. She told this story about when she was clerking: "One day I was in Court filing papers when His Honor leaned over the bench and intoned, 'Young lady, please tell your employer not to send his secretary to court to file papers.'" She bided her time. She liked to say, about men who treated her that way, "I didn't spit in his eye but I would have liked to."[19]

During the war, Holloway sold Lifebuoy soap outside a nickelodeon in Central Square. Anyone who bought fourteen dollars' worth of soap got a free movie ticket.

"Would you like to try some Lifebuoy Soap, Madame?" she would ask.

"No, I wouldn't; it smells like a hospital."

"You mean a hospital smells like Lifebuoy," Holloway would say.

She traveled from town to town. She got to know the other traveling saleswomen; they always stuck together. She had a friend everyone called "Blackie," because she dyed her hair with shoe polish. Blackie's favorite saying got to be one of Holloway's favorite sayings, too. Blackie would say, "God, Missus, there ain't a man on Earth worth a foot in Hell."[20]

Except Marston.

The experimental life of William Moulton Marston involved a great many schemes. In his last year of graduate school, Marston opened the Tait-Marston Engineering Company, with a machine shop and foundry in Boston and offices at 60 State Street.[21] He became treasurer of a fabrics firm called United Dress Goods.[22] And, with two friends from law school—Felix Forte, who had helped Marston with his work on deception tests, and Edward Fischer, a founder of the Boston Legal Aid Society—he opened up a law firm: Marston, Forte & Fischer. Its offices, too, were at 60 State Street.[23] Tait-Marston Engineering, United Dress Goods, and Marston, Forte & Fischer all failed. But Marston only ever admitted to the failure of the law firm, the fourth in the series of experiments that made up his life: "Fourth investigation, 1918–21, practicing law while continuing psychological work at Harvard; result, general dissatisfaction of all subjects concerned, especially clients."[24]

He thought, though, that there might still be money to be made in the detection of deception. He had a series of photographs taken on the porch of his house on Lowell Street, where he'd constructed a makeshift stage: a wooden table covered with laboratory equipment, including wheels, cords, clocks, and a sphygmomanometer. In the photographs, Marston wears a three-piece tweed suit and his owl's-eye spectacles and is in the company of a very pretty young woman—the secretary at Marston, Forte & Fischer. Her long, dark hair is pinned back, her wide eyes impassive; she wears a pale dress. In one shot, she is seated in a chair, next to Marston, who leans over her. A blood pressure cuff is wrapped around her arm, and a strap is winched against

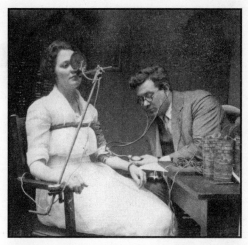

Marston administering a lie detector test to the secretary of his
law firm, 1921

her chest, just above her breasts. A black disk propped over one of her
eyes blocks half of her vision.

In May 1921, Marston distributed the photographs to newspa-
pers, along with a press release headed "Machine Detects Liars, Traps
Crooks." The story was picked up by papers all over the country:
"Successful lying will soon be a lost art."[25]

The next month, Marston graduated with a PhD. He had spent
nearly ten years at Harvard. He had studied history, philosophy, psychology, and law. He had earned three degrees. He liked to ponder
the nature of evidence. He believed he knew how to find out who was
telling the truth and who was not. He had become an excellent liar.
The time had come for his next experiment: "Fifth research, founding
the great (potentially) subject of legal psychology at American University."[26] For this experiment, Dr. Marston went to Washington.

STUDIES IN TESTIMONY

THE LECTURE had only just begun when there came a rap at the door. The professor walked across the room and opened the door. A young man entered. He wore gloves. In his right hand, he carried an envelope. Tucked under his left arm he held three books: one red, one green, and one blue. He said he had a message to deliver. He spoke with a Texas twang. He handed the professor the envelope. While the professor opened the envelope, pulled out a yellow paper, and read

A disguised Wonder Woman attends a lecture. *Wonder Woman*, newspaper strip, September 14, 1944

its contents, the messenger, using only his right hand, drew from his pocket a long, green-handled pocketknife. Deftly, he opened the knife and began scraping his gloved left thumb with the edge of the blade.[1]

The class was a graduate course called Legal Psychology, held at American University, in Washington, D.C. It met twice a week, in the evening, beginning in March 1922. There were eighteen students; all of them were lawyers. They had come to the lecture hall, a building at 1901 F Street, after either a day at the office or a day in court; many of them worked for the government. In the course catalog, the professor, William Moulton Marston, had listed a prerequisite: "Students must have a working knowledge of the principles of Common Law to qualify for this course, which is especially designed for practicing attorneys and lawyers having a genuine and active interest in raising the standards of justice in the actual administration of the law."[2] He remained possessed of a certain ambivalent idealism.

Marston finished reading whatever was written on that sheet of yellow paper, said something to the Texan, and sent him on his way. Then, turning to his class, he informed his students that the man who had just left the room was not, in fact, a messenger at all; he was, instead, an actor, following a script written by Marston, as part of an elaborate experiment.

Imagine, Marston went on, that the man who was here a moment ago has since been arrested and charged with murder. Imagine, too, that you have all been summoned as witnesses. Please write down everything you saw.

Eighteen lawyers picked up their pencils.

In preparing this experiment, Marston had identified 147 details the students could have noticed—the number and color of the books the messenger held, for instance, and that he held them under one arm, his left. After the students had written down all they had observed, Marston examined them, one by one; then he cross-examined them. After class, he scored their answers, grading them for completeness, accuracy, and "caution" (you'd get a point for caution if, upon either direct or cross-examination, you said, "I don't know"). Out of 147 possible observable details, the students, on average, noticed only 34.

Everyone flunked. And no one, not a single student, had noticed the knife.[3]

Marston based this experiment on one he'd read about in John Henry Wigmore's twelve-hundred-page book, *The Principles of Judicial Proof as Given by Logic, Psychology, and General Experience,* published in 1913.[4] Despite his feud with Münsterberg, Wigmore believed that no science was more important to the law than psychology and that no aspect of psychology was more important to judicial proof than the study of testimony.[5] Wigmore described an experiment conducted by Arno Gunther in 1905. Gunther had arranged for a messenger to enter a lecture hall, after which he had asked his students to report the details of the scene. Gunther's scene included thirty details, starting with these:

1. The time was 3:45 P.M.
2. The man was medium height, medium large.
3. His hair was brown.
4. He had a small brown mustache, no beard.
5. He wore glasses, *i.e.* spectacles.
6. He had on an overcoat, of black cloth, and buttoned.
7. He had on a dark suit.
8. A soft hat, dark brown.
9. No gloves.
10. In his hands he carried cane, hat, and a letter.
11. The cane was brown, with a black handle.
12. The man was 21¾ years old.
13. On entering he did not knock.
14. After entering, he said: "Excuse me, Mr. G, may I speak with you a moment?"
15. Mr. G replied, "Certainly. Come in."
16. The visitor stepped forward and handed a letter,
17. saying, "I have here a letter to be handed to you."[6]

Marston followed Gunther's design closely. But to Gunther's incident he added a knife. Marston was less interested in the reliability of testimony than in the reliability of juries, so, unlike Gunther, he didn't end his experiment after pointing out to his students that they'd flunked. Instead, he collected their evidence and submitted it to juries.[7] "I have arranged here for the entire testimony of my 18 witnesses to be submitted separately to two juries," Marston reported to Wigmore, "one of 12 men and one of 12 women."[8] Marston's study of the reliability of testimony was really a study about women's political participation.

Gaining the right to vote had by no means led automatically to female jury service. In 1921, after much lobbying by women, six states changed their laws to allow women jurors. But by 1922, women still did not serve on juries in thirty-one states, or in the territories of Alaska and Hawaii.[9] Marston wanted to see if he could get results that would cast light on the debate over whether women could be relied on to weigh evidence as well as men.

In this research, Holloway helped. She'd taken a job in Washington with an information service founded by Frederic Haskin in 1915. Haskin wrote a syndicated newspaper column, fielding readers' questions. Holloway researched his answers. She worked so fast, she said, that she could dictate forty letters before lunch. At the university, when Marston didn't feel like delivering his lectures, he had Holloway deliver them for him. She'd grown bitter; she resented his students. "There was a group of four men up front who obviously were brainier than I was and who talked to each other while I was lecturing," Holloway said. "So one day I called one of them up and said to him, 'You know, So and So, nobody is going to give a good G[od].D[amn]. when you flunk this course.'"[10]

For Marston's study of testimony, he asked Wigmore to serve as judge. Wigmore agreed. Marston enlisted two other judges, too: Dr. Charles C. Tansill, an American historian at the Library of Congress, and Emily Davis, a young "newspaper woman and correspondent." (Davis had interviewed Marston about the deception test.) One thing Marston was trying to determine was whether Wigmore, the nation's foremost authority on the law of evidence, would be any better at weighing testimony than Tansill, a historian, or Davis, a journalist and a woman. But what Marston was most keen to discover was whether women were competent as jurors.[11]

Working with Holloway, Marston found that, in measurements of accuracy and completeness in their evaluation of testimony, the women jurors scored better than the men jurors: "They were more careful, more conscientious, and gave much more impartial consideration to all the testimony than did the male juries." Women were also better judges. Davis scored better than both Tansill and Wigmore: "Her findings were more complete and more accurate than those submitted by any male judge."[12]

It was an interesting finding. Holloway, later in life, came to believe that this research had been her Radcliffe master's thesis. But nothing much came of it. Marston lost interest in the subject—nothing held his interest for long. Also, by the time he wound up his study of testimony, he'd got wrapped up in a murder trial.

On March 10, 1922, ten days before American University's spring semester began, James Alphonso Frye, twenty-two, was indicted on charges of first-degree murder, accused of killing a Washington physician named Robert Wade Brown. Brown had been shot to death in the front hall of his house. A $1,000 reward had been offered for information leading to the killer.[13] In the summer of 1921, Frye was arrested for robbery, and, in the course of the investigation of that crime, John R. Francis, a dentist, told the police that Frye had killed Brown.[14] Frye, Brown, and Francis were all black. During a police interrogation, Frye confessed to the murder. He said he had gone to Brown's house to get medicine for gonorrhea and had accidentally shot him during a struggle that began when Frye said he didn't have any money and Brown refused to give him the medicine. Frye said, "I tried to run to the door and he grabbed me again and knocked me down and I told him to put his hands up and he kept on hitting me, hitting me on the head, and in the struggle I think that my gun was fired."[15] The announcement that Brown's killer had been found, like the murder itself, made national news.[16]

In November 1921, Frye was tried for robbery in a criminal court headed by Chief Justice Walter McCoy; Lester Wood served as attorney for one of Frye's codefendants, a man named William N. Bowie.[17] Wood, twenty-five, was an auditor for the U.S. Shipping Board.[18] He was also a student at American University's law school, where he was studying with Marston. Wood was defending Bowie to gain court-

Frye, center, being tested by Marston, wearing glasses

room experience. Frye and Bowie were found guilty and sentenced to four years in prison. Frye's attorney, James O'Shea, filed a motion for a new trial. Wood, acting as Bowie's attorney, filed an appeal.[19] In December 1921, McCoy granted the motion for a new robbery trial for both Frye and Bowie, agreeing that the jury had not been sufficiently instructed regarding the presumption of innocence. The new trial, also in McCoy's court, produced the same verdict, and the same sentence.[20]

Frye told Lester Wood that his confession to the murder had been a lie. On March 11, 1922, Frye pled not guilty to the charge of murder.[21] He also switched lawyers, placing himself in the hands of Wood and another of Marston's students, Richard V. Mattingly. Mattingly, twenty-two, had graduated from Georgetown Law School but had been unable to find legal work. He was taking classes at night, toward a graduate degree in diplomacy and jurisprudence; during the day, he worked as a salesman.[22] Court documents from the Frye case refer to the firm of "Mattingly & Wood," with offices at 918 F Street; it seems to have been formed simply for the sake of this one case. Mattingly and Wood's handling of Frye's case was likely at Marston's instigation: he seems to have decided that James Frye could be, to him, what

Frye and Marston in the *Washington Daily News*, July 20, 1922

Harry Orchard had been to Hugo Münsterberg—a chance to change the history of jurisprudence. Neither he nor Wood and Mattingly ever disclosed to the court that Wood and Mattingly were enrolled in Marston's Legal Psychology class.[23]

On June 3, Marston sent Wigmore the statements he had taken from his eighteen students, as part of his study in testimony.[24] One week later, Mattingly and Wood brought Marston to the D.C. Jail, to meet Frye. Marston asked Frye if he would submit to the use of the lie detector; Frye agreed.[25] Frye himself later described what happened next: "He asked me several questions, none pertaining to the case, then suddenly he launched upon several questions going into every detail of the case."[26] The story was reported in the *Washington Daily News;* Marston sent Wigmore a clipping. Only when Frye saw that same story in the paper did he learn that Marston believed him innocent.[27] No one had ever bothered to tell him.

Frye's murder trial was scheduled to begin on July 17, in McCoy's court.[28] The prosecutor, assistant district attorney Joseph H. Bilbrey, brought to the stand the physicians who had examined the body, the police detectives who had witnessed Frye's confession, and two witnesses who testified that they had seen Frye at Brown's house on the night of the murder.[29] Mattingly and Wood opened their defense by calling a police detective who suggested that Frye had been bullied into confessing.[30] A crucial defense would have been an alibi. But Mattingly and Wood made only a halfhearted attempt to establish Frye's whereabouts on the night of the murder. Frye said he had been at the home of a woman named Essie Watson, in the company of a woman named Marion Cox. Essie Watson was too ill to appear in court; Mattingly and Wood requested a continuance; McCoy denied their request.[31] Cox never testified. (Frye later said that she refused.)[32] Instead, Mattingly and Wood tried to establish that Frye's confession was a lie and that, in disavowing it, Frye was telling the truth.[33] This line of defense required introducing the expert testimony of Professor William Moulton Marston. To that end, Mattingly and Wood submitted Marston's publications, including his Harvard dissertation, to the judge.[34]

Wonder Woman attempting to testify in court, *Wonder Woman*, newspaper strip, March 1945

In court the next day, the courtroom was full to overflowing, in anticipation of Marston's testimony.[35] Mattingly approached the bench.

> MR. MATTINGLY: If your honor please, at this time I intend to offer in evidence the testimony of Dr. William M. Marston as an expert in deception.
> THE COURT: His testimony on what?
> MR. MATTINGLY: Testimony as to the truth or falsity of certain statements of the defendant which were made at a particular time.

McCoy was skeptical; Marston, waiting with his blood pressure apparatus, restless. The prosecutor began to speak.

> MR. BILBREY: If your honor please—
> THE COURT: You do not need to argue it. If you object to it, I will sustain the objection.
> MR. BILBREY: I do not want to object, but I think that properly to make the offer the witness ought to be put on the stand and sworn and asked questions.

The prosecution didn't object to Marston's evidence; the judge did. The real experts at deciding whether or not a witness was telling the truth, McCoy told Mattingly, was a jury: "That is what the jury is for."

Mattingly suggested that an expert in deception was just like any other kind of expert witness. McCoy would have none of it: "We do not bring experimental matters into the court," he said. Mattingly made one request after another, trying to find a way to persuade McCoy to qualify Marston as a witness; McCoy denied each request. Mattingly asked whether a witness for the prosecution, a police officer named Jackson, might be subjected to a lie detector test. Again, McCoy denied his request.

"Mind you, I do not know anything about the test at all," McCoy said. "I had certain pamphlets submitted to me yesterday to look at, of some Dr. Marston—I believe his thesis when he got his Ph.D. degree. I am going to read them when I come back from my vacation. I see enough in them to know that so far the science has not sufficiently developed detection of deception by blood pressure to make it a useable instrument in a court of law."

Mattingly pressed him: "Your honor, of course, in looking over those papers, did not assume that Dr. Marston was the only authority on the subject?"

"Oh, no, indeed," said McCoy. "I take him as an authority." As to the lie detector test: "When it is developed to the perfection of the telephone and the telegraph and wireless and a few other things we will consider it. I shall be dead by that time, probably, and it will bother some other judge, not me."[36]

And with that, Marston's attempt to have lie detection introduced into the courts came to an end.[37] Nothing was left but the closing arguments. The jury, after deliberating for less than an hour, found Frye guilty of the lesser charge of second-degree murder. Mattingly announced that he would appeal, on the grounds that Marston's testimony ought not to have been excluded.[38] On July 28, McCoy sentenced Frye to life.[39]

Two days later, Marston wrote to Wigmore: "I'm enclosing some clippings in re our first attempt at the introduction of Deception Tests into court procedure, which may interest you. Of course, we did not expect any lower Court would take the responsibility of admitting the tests, but believed the time was ripe to carry the point up for a Supreme Court precedent."[40]

Marston decided to offer a new course, in the summer session. A notice appeared in the *Washington Post:* "Prof. William M. Marston, Ph.D., L.L.B., will give a course in the philosophy of law at the summer school of American University, starting this week."[41] Both Mattingly and Wood enrolled. Marston gave them both C's.[42] The dean granted Marston tenure and named him chairman of the Psychology Department, and American University opened, on his behalf, "the only psycho-legal research laboratory in the United States."[43] And James Alphonso Frye, twenty-two, went by train to Leavenworth, Kansas.

FRYE'D

IN THE EXPERIMENTAL LIFE of William Moulton Marston, James A. Frye was experiment number six. Marston had staked his academic reputation on the Frye case. He expected the appeal to reach the U.S. Supreme Court and make him famous the world over.

The brief for the appellant, very likely written by Marston himself, consisted almost entirely of an argument on behalf of Marston's work: "The question whether a witness is testifying or has testified truthfully or falsely is a scientific question which requires the aid of the study and experience of the scientific man to accurately determine."[1] The prosecution, in its brief, argued that the matter came down to Marston's credibility, which, in the prosecution's view, didn't amount to much. Bilbrey and U.S. Attorney Peyton Gordon cited a 1922 law review article written by Harvard Law School professor Zechariah Chafee in which Chafee (not mentioning that Marston had been a student of his) asserted that Marston's work was entirely inconclusive and that deception tests "cannot, of course, be substituted in courts generally for present methods of examination until their usefulness is thoroughly demonstrated."[2] As for Marston, the prosecution told the court, "Whether he can or can not detect deception is something that does not appear to be known to anyone except Dr. Marston."[3]

On December 3, 1923, the D.C. Circuit Court of Appeals denied the appeal. "Just when a scientific principle or discovery crosses the line between the experimental and demonstrable stages is difficult to define," the opinion read. "Somewhere in this twilight zone the evidential force of the principle must be recognized, and while courts will go a long way in admitting expert testimony deduced from a well-recognized scientific principle or discovery, the thing from which the deduction is made must be sufficiently established to have gained general acceptance in the particular field in which it belongs. We think the systolic blood pressure deception test has not yet gained such standing and scientific recognition among physiological and psychological authorities as would justify the courts in admitting expert testimony deduced from the discovery, development, and experiments thus far made."[4]

Frye v. United States is a landmark in the law of evidence and one of the most cited cases in the history of American law. It established what's known as the Frye test, under which, to be admitted as evidence, a new kind of scientific principle has to have gained general acceptance. "Frye," like "Miranda," has the rare distinction of having become a verb. To be "Frye'd" is to have your expert's testimony deemed inadmissible.[5]

Frye v. United States is also one of the bigger mysteries in American legal history. The appeals court's opinion, only 641 words long, contains not a single reference to case law or precedent, nor any references to any scientific literature.[6] But the ruling seems cryptic only because the details of the case itself have been long since forgotten. That's how case law works. People who cite *Frye* don't know or care who Frye was or whom he is supposed to have killed, and they haven't bothered to find out much about Marston, either. Case law obliterates context, and experimental science repudiates tradition; their rise marked a shift away from the idea that truth can be found in the study of the past. But there's a reason the court's ruling was brief, and it has to do with a set of facts that can be found only in the archives, in the junk drawer of history.

Among the many facts about the Frye case that have never been discovered by anyone who has ever cited or studied it are three that concern the man who would one day create Wonder Woman: first, Frye's lawyers were Marston's students; second, at the time Frye's lawyers were working on Frye's defense, they were also involved in an experiment in the reliability of testimony, undertaken in consultation with the twentieth century's most important scholar of the law of evidence, John Henry Wigmore; and third, on March 6, 1923, five days after Mattingly and Wood filed their appeal, their professor was arrested for fraud.[7]

Marston's legal troubles began with a suit filed in January 1922 by Edward G. Fischer, his former partner at Marston, Forte & Fischer. Alleging a breach of contract, Fischer sued Marston for $5,000. The case dragged on through spring.[8] The Tait-Marston Engineering Company was failing, too, not least because Marston had abandoned the company when he'd moved to Washington. But it was the bankruptcy of the third business he had launched in 1920, a fabrics company called United Dress Goods, that got him arrested.

Marston was indicted by a federal grand jury in Massachusetts on December 1, 1922. A warrant was issued for his arrest. On February 19, 1923, a U.S. marshal reported that he had been unable to find Marston in Boston.[9] A secret indictment was then forwarded to Washington, where Marston was arrested by federal agents on March 6. His arrest was reported in both the *Boston Globe*—"Arrest Inventor of Lie Detector"—and the *Washington Post*. "Marston, Lie Meter Inventor, Arrested," read the headline in D.C., in a story that made a point of remarking on Marston's role in the Frye case.[10] The irony—expert at deception arrested for lying—wasn't lost on anyone.

Marston was charged with two crimes: using the mails in a scheme to defraud, and aiding and abetting in the concealment of assets from the trustee in the United Dress Goods bankruptcy. The grand jury charged that Marston had placed orders with businesses in New York for large quantities of fabric and, in that correspondence, had made "false and fraudulent pretenses" regarding the firm's financial condition.[11] United Dress Goods filed for bankruptcy in January 1922; Marston was charged with having knowingly and fraudulently concealed from the firm's trustee $2,400 (an amount roughly equal to his annual salary as a professor).[12]

After his arrest, Marston was brought to Boston. He was held on $2,600 bail, which he paid. He was arraigned on March 16, 1923.[13] He pled not guilty, insisting that he had no knowledge of the transactions of which he was accused.[14] On March 17, an account of his arraignment appeared in newspapers in Boston, Washington, and New York (" 'Lie Detector' Inventor Arraigned"). According to one reporter, Marston claimed that "the publicity was ruining him."[15] To defend himself against the charges, Marston retained a friend from law school, Richard Hale, founder of the Boston firm of Hale and Dorr, whose offices were in the same building where Marston, Forte & Fischer had been, at 60 State Street.[16]

At the time of his arrest, in March 1923, Marston was teaching a slate of courses—including Psycho-Physiology, Advanced Theoretical Psychology, and an applied course called Psycho-Legal Laboratory.[17] It's not clear whether he finished the term, but, in any case, he was fired.

His arrest and arraignment were reported in Washington newspapers the month Mattingly and Wood filed their appeal. The publicity could hardly have helped their cause. In the summer and fall of 1923, Mattingly and Wood applied for extra time while they prepared an additional brief, "Memorandum of Scientific History and Authority of Systolic Blood Pressure Test for Deception." (Marston wrote to Wigmore, asking for help in preparing the Frye appeal, but Wigmore proved unreachable.)[18] The chief purpose of this second brief, the science brief, was to diminish Marston's role in establishing the detection of deception, placing him as only one among a larger number of scientists working in the field.[19] It reads as Frye's attorneys' attempt to separate the credibility of deception tests from the credibility of their expert witness. It didn't work. The D.C. Circuit Court of Appeals issued its ruling in *Frye v. United States* on December 3, 1923: "While courts will go a long way in admitting expert testimony deduced from a well-recognized scientific principle or discovery, the thing from which the deduction is made must be sufficiently established to have gained general acceptance in the particular field in which it belongs." The opinion was brief and cryptic because so little else needed to be said: the appellant's chief witness—the expert upon whose testimony the case turned—was under a federal grand jury indictment for fraud.

On December 31, 1923, Marston sent Wigmore "Studies in Testimony," his report on the testimony experiment he had conducted in his Legal Psychology class, not mentioning his own legal troubles.

Wonder Woman, newspaper strip, March 1945

Wigmore applauded the article as "marked by great scientific care and caution" and recommended its publication. About the Frye verdict, Marston affected detachment. "I think it was confirmed in the District Court of Appeals, tho I have not seen the decision," he wrote, vaguely, to Wigmore. "Counsel, of course, expected that result, but wanted to get it before the U.S. Supreme Court in proper form."[20]

Richard Hale was successful in defending Marston against the charges of a federal grand jury. "I persuaded the United States authorities here that they had no case whatever against Marston," Hale wrote to the president of American University after Marston was fired. As to the charges, "I investigated those things fully and was convinced they had no taint of criminality in them."[21]

Even though the case never went to trial, the scandal cost Marston the chairmanship of the Psychology Department at American University, the directorship of the only psycho-legal research laboratory in the United States, and his professorship. The charges against him were dropped on January 4, 1924.[22] "Studies in Testimony" appeared in the *Journal of Criminal Law and Criminology* in May.[23]

In June, Mattingly and Wood were admitted to the Supreme Court bar. It doesn't seem as though they pursued the appeal to the Supreme Court; or, if they did, the Court refused to hear the case.[24] After *Frye,*

Marston gave up on the study of law, which is what made it possible for him, one day, to create Wonder Woman.[25] For Marston, the end of one experiment always marked the beginning of another.

It wasn't until 1945, in a Wonder Woman comic strip, that Marston finally extracted his vengeance on Judge Walter McCoy of the D.C. Circuit Court of Appeals. A bumbling, balding Judge Friendly calls Wonder Woman to the witness stand, in a case in which Priscilla Rich is being tried for crimes committed by a villain known as the Cheetah (who is the other half of Priscilla's split personality). Instead of dismissing Wonder Woman's testimony—and her lie detector—as inadmissible, Judge Friendly welcomes her.

"I understand you—er—examined this defendant with your—ah—remarkable Amazonian lasso," the judge says to her.

"Yes, I asked Priscilla if she was the Cheetah."

"Ahem! While it's highly irregular—hm—I'd like to hear your—ah—findings!"

"I will *show* you, judge," offers Wonder Woman, who then lassoes Priscilla and drags her to the witness stand.

"I object!" cries the prosecuting attorney.

"Objection sus—" the judge begins, only to be cut off by Wonder Woman, who, ignoring the objection, interrogates her witness. Priscilla, within the lasso, is compelled to speak nothing but the truth. At the trial's end, the judge shakes Wonder Woman's hand.

"Your advice was—humpf—invaluable, Wonder Woman! I—ah—wish you'd give me—er—further help—"

"Call on me anytime!" Wonder Woman says. And she smiles her sly smile.[26]

PART TWO

FAMILY CIRCLE

From "Grown-Down Land," *Sensation Comics #31* (July 1944)

10

HERLAND

OLIVE BYRNE, who was thrown away, was born in February 1904 in the back of a four-room house in Corning, New York, a city of glass. She was delivered by her mother's older sister, a twenty-four-year-old nurse named Margaret Sanger.[1]

The baby squirmed and screamed. Her mother, Ethel, could not get her to stop crying. Her father, Jack, was at Jimmy Webb's saloon, down the street. He came home drunk and hollering, stomping the snow off his boots. He opened the back door and threw the baby into a snowbank. Sanger ran outside, pulled Olive from the snow, and brought her inside. Jack Byrne went back to Jimmy Webb's. He stayed there for two days.[2]

Ethel Byrne and Margaret Sanger were the youngest daughters of Michael Hennessey Higgins, who was born in Ireland and who, in Corning, carved tombstones, although he spent most of his time drinking, and making speeches, and fuming. He had a temper as hot as the fires at the Corning Glass Works. He and his wife, Anne, had eleven children. Margaret, when she was only eight years old, deliv-

Margaret (left) and Ethel Higgins in the 1880s

ered the youngest of them. Anne Higgins died at the age of forty-nine of tuberculosis, but Margaret and Ethel knew that she had died, really, of motherhood: she had been pregnant eighteen times in twenty-two years.

The Higgins sons went to work in the glassworks. Mary, the oldest daughter, went to work as a servant for a family named Abbott, taking care of a little girl named Olive, which is how Mary Olive Abbott Byrne got saddled with a very long name. (She hated it. "I would have liked to have been a Dorothy," she said.)[3] Anna, the next oldest Higgins daughter, went to work in New York City, so she could earn money to send Margaret to boarding school, because Margaret was clever and wanted to be a doctor. Ethel, who had brown eyes and auburn hair and all the fury of her father, was even cleverer than Margaret. ("She was the intellectual," one of Margaret Sanger's granddaughters liked to say, later.)[4] But there wasn't enough money for Ethel to follow Margaret to boarding school, so she went to the Corning Free Academy, where she met Jack Byrne, and got pregnant. In 1901, when he was nineteen and she was eighteen, they eloped.[5]

Margaret Higgins never became a doctor. Instead, she went to nursing school and married an architect named William Sanger. She delivered Ethel's first baby, Jack, in 1902. (Ethel delivered Margaret's children, and Margaret delivered Ethel's.) By February 1904, when Olive Byrne was born, Margaret Sanger had a baby of her own, and she had tuberculosis.[6]

The only thing that seemed to quiet Olive when she was a baby was a patent medicine called Mrs. Winslow's Soothing Syrup; it knocked her out. (It contained morphine.) Once, Ethel gave Olive so much syrup that she slept for two days straight; it took a doctor to wake her up. After a while, Ethel Byrne decided there was nothing to do but leave. When Olive's brother was three and Olive was two, Ethel walked them down the street to her husband's parents' house, at 310 East Tioga Avenue, left them there, and disappeared.

"That was the last time anyone in Corning saw her for four years," Olive said. Olive's grandparents put her in a crib in an upstairs bedroom. She said, "I think I spent a lot of time in that crib."

Ethel Byrne carried a suitcase to the train station and bought a one-way ticket to New York. She studied nursing at Mount Sinai Hospital.

Married women were not allowed to train as nurses; she said she was single. She was lying.

Olive's grandparents adopted Olive and her brother. Olive's grandmother told Olive that her mother was dead.[7] She was lying. Later, Ethel told Olive that she'd tried to get her and her brother back.[8] She was lying. "Deceit comes easy to the Irish," Olive Byrne liked to say.[9]

"Oh Lord I am not worthy that thou shoudst come to me," Olive Byrne sang in church when she was five years old, and she meant it. She had straight, jet-black hair, blue eyes, pale skin, and freckles. She bit her fingernails until they bled. She played with paper dolls; she loved to make paper families, a tissue of fictions. When she was six, her mother came to visit—she had risen, it seemed to Olive, from the very grave—and hugged her so close that the brooch on her dress left a scratch on Olive's cheek. All she could ever remember of her mother, after that, was the scratch.[10]

Olive Byrne in 1906

Olive Byrne's father died in 1913; both of her grandparents died the next year. Olive and her brother, twelve and ten, were bundled off to two different Catholic orphanages: one for boys and one for girls.

By then, Ethel Byrne was living in Greenwich Village with Robert Allerton Parker, a drama critic, in a second-floor apartment in a brownstone at 246 West 14th Street. Margaret Sanger sometimes lived there, too. Sanger had three children, and her marriage was falling apart.[11]

Ethel Byrne and Margaret Sanger believed in free love, socialism, and feminism.[12] They worked for the Socialist Party Women's Committee, the IWW, and the *Masses,* a socialist monthly. They joined the Liberal Club, "A Meeting Place for Those Interested in New Ideas," and went to meetings of Heterodoxy, a women-only club that held meetings on subjects like "What Feminism Means to Me."[13] (Both clubs were founded in 1912.) They knew Upton Sinclair, Emma Goldman, John Reed, and Crystal Eastman and her brother Max. They lived in a

The feminist cartoonist Lou Rogers, c. 1910

world of free love, of heterodoxy, and of Amazons, breaking chains.

Max Eastman edited the *Masses;* John Reed was a staff writer. Max Eastman was also secretary of the New York Men's League for Woman Suffrage, and it was Reed who, as a senior at Harvard in 1910, the year before Marston enrolled as a freshman, had helped start the Harvard Men's League for Woman Suffrage, sponsored by George Herbert Palmer. Crystal Eastman helped start the Congressional Union for Woman Suffrage in 1913 and the Woman's Peace Party in 1914. She was also a member of the Heterodoxy Club. She wanted to know "how to arrange the world so that women can be human beings, with a chance to exercise their infinitely varied gifts in infinitely varied ways, instead of being destined by the accident of their sex to one field of activity—housework and child-raising."[14]

Annie Lucasta Rogers, another member of the Heterodoxy Club, was a feminist cartoonist whose way of depicting the struggle for women's rights greatly shaped Wonder Woman. Born in Maine in 1879, she'd come to New York to draw editorial cartoons. She got her first cartoon published after bringing it to the *New York Call,* a socialist daily. She'd gone to see a Hearst editor who told her that newspapers had "no use for women in this particular line of work and not much use for them in any other." After that, she sent in her work by mail, signing it "Lou Rogers."[15]

Rogers's cartoons appeared in everything from the *Call* to the *New York Tribune* and the *Ladies' Home Journal.* She specialized in suffragist publications like the *Woman Citizen* and the *Suffragist.* The *Woman's Journal* called her "the only woman artist to devote all her time to feminism." "In attempting to interpret the woman's movement," she told *Cartoons Magazine* in 1913, "I think that the cartoon should aim to arouse men and women to the realization that the ideals of the movement are part of human progress." When the *New York Evening Post* published a special issue devoted to suffrage, Rogers pro-

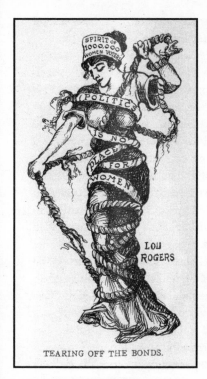

TEARING OFF THE BONDS.

Lou Rogers, *Tearing Off the Bonds*, pen and ink drawing for *Judge*, October 19, 1912

Harry G. Peter, pen and ink drawing. From Marston's "Why 100,000 Americans Read Comics," *American Scholar* 13 (1943–44)

vided the cartoons (the *Post* called her "the only woman cartoonist"). In 1914, when the New York Woman Suffrage Association offered a $50 prize for the best scenario about the suffrage movement, in a contest much like that which Marston won the next year, for *Jack Kennard, Coward,* Rogers served on the prize jury with Charlotte Perkins Gilman, another member of Heterodoxy. That same year, Rogers started "a suffrage cartoon service," charging $5 for a four-column cartoon to a syndicate that included *Harper's Weekly* and *Judge,* a humor magazine that Rogers had been drawing for since 1908. When Heterodoxy organized a mass debate with topics like "The Right to Work," "The Right of the Mother to Her Profession," "The Right to Her Convictions," and "The Right to Her Name," the title for the meeting came from a Rogers cartoon in which a woman using nothing but her fists smashes holes labeled "Education" and "Suffrage" in a brick wall: it was called "Breaking into the Human Race."[16]

Rogers was also a staff artist at the swank humor magazine *Judge,* where she illustrated a page called "The Modern Woman," which ran from 1912 to 1917. Rogers's cartoons often featured an allegorical woman, chained or roped, breaking her bonds. Another staff artist at *Judge* sometimes filled in for her. His name was Harry G. Peter, and he was the artist who, one day, would draw Wonder Woman.

Wonder Woman was born in bohemia. In the 1910s, when Ethel Byrne and Margaret Sanger were living in Greenwich Village, Amazons were everywhere. In 1913, Max Eastman published a book of verse called *Child of the Amazons and Other Poems.* In the title poem, an Amazonian girl tells the Amazonian queen that she has fallen in love with a man. To marry him and bear his children, though, would violate an Amazonian law: "No Amazon shall enter motherhood / Until she hath performed such deeds, and wrought / Such impact on the energetic world / That thou canst it behold and name her thine." So she decides, in the end, that she cannot follow love until "the far age when men shall cease / Their tyranny" and "Amazons their revolt."[17] The next year, Inez Haynes Gillmore, who had helped Maud Wood Park found the National College Equal Suffrage League and who was also a member of Heterodoxy, published a novel called *Angel Island.* Its plot involves five American men who are shipwrecked on a desert island that turns out to be inhabited by "super-humanly beautiful" women with wings, "their bodies just short of heroic size, deep-bosomed, broad-waisted, long-limbed; their arms round like a woman's and strong like a man's." The men, overcome with desire, capture the women, tie them up, and cut off their wings, leaving them utterly helpless because, although the women have feet, they have never used them before and cannot walk. Eventually, the strongest of them leads the other women in waging a revolution: she learns to walk "with the splendid, swinging gait of an Amazon."[18]

Wonder Woman's origin story, in which Captain Steve Trevor crashes his plane on Paradise Island and Diana, princess of the Amazons, falls in love with him—an attachment that is both in violation

The Amazons in Inez Haynes Gillmore's 1914 novel, *Angel Island*

of Amazon law and a threat to her independence—comes straight out of Eastman's poem and Gillmore's novel. But it wasn't only "Child of the Amazons" and *Angel Island:* in the 1910s, this story line was a stock feminist plot. In 1915, Heterodoxy's Charlotte Perkins Gilman published *Herland,* a utopian novel in which women live entirely free from men, bearing only daughters, by parthenogenesis. (On Paradise Island, Queen Hippolyte carves her daughter out of clay.) In prewar, early-twentieth-century feminist fiction, women rule the world in peace and equality, until men come, threatening to bring war and inequality. In *Angel Island* and *Herland,* men have to be taught that if they want to live with women—if they want to marry them and have children with them—they will be allowed to do so only on terms of equality. And for that to happen, there has got to be a way for the men and women to have sex, but without the women getting pregnant all the time. The women in Gilman's utopia practice what at the time was called "voluntary motherhood," a subject Gilman approaches with a certain primness. "You see they were Mothers, not in our sense of helpless, involuntary fecundity, forced to fill and overfill the land, every land, and then see their children suffer, sin, and die, fighting horribly with one another," Gilman wrote, "but in the sense of Conscious Makers of People."[19]

Margaret Sanger, who dug Olive Byrne out of a snowbank, thought women ought to be conscious makers of people, too. But she had a different word for that kind of thing.[20] She called it birth control.

THE WOMAN REBEL

IN 1912, when Olive Byrne was eight years old, Margaret Sanger wrote a twelve-part series in the *New York Call*, the socialist daily that published Lou Rogers's cartoons. The series was called "What Every Girl Should Know." It covered, matter-of-factly, the subjects of sexual attraction, masturbation, intercourse, venereal disease, pregnancy, and childbirth. The U.S. Post Office banned Part 12, "Some Consequences of Ignorance and Silence," on grounds of obscenity. In its place, the *Call* ran an announcement: " 'What Every Girl Should Know': NOTHING!"[1]

Sanger was not easily silenced. In 1914, with help from Ethel Byrne, she began publishing *Woman Rebel*, an eight-page feminist monthly, in which she coined the term "birth control." (To fund it, she tried to enlist the support of the Heterodoxy Club but was turned down; instead, she raised money through advance subscriptions.)[2] Its first issue included a manifesto called "Why the Woman Rebel?"

> Because I believe that deep down in woman's nature lies
>   slumbering the spirit of revolt.
> Because I believe that woman is enslaved by the world
>   machine, by sex conventions, by motherhood and its present
>   necessary child rearing, by wage-slavery, by middle-class
>   morality, by customs, laws and superstitions.
> Because I believe that woman's freedom depends upon

awakening that spirit of revolt within her against these
things which enslave her.
Because I believe that these things which enslave woman must
be fought openly, fearlessly, consciously.[3]

In *Woman Rebel*, Sanger promised to expose the bondage of motherhood and to explain birth control, asking, "Is there any reason why women should not receive clean, harmless, scientific knowledge on how to prevent conception?" Six of the magazine's seven issues were declared obscene and seized.[4] Sanger was indicted. John Reed raised money for her defense, but Sanger fled the country; she left her children, two boys and a girl, with Ethel Byrne.[5]

In England, Sanger collected information about contraception. She also met Havelock Ellis, a doctor, psychologist, and theorist of sex. Ellis celebrated sexual candor, sexual expression, and sexual diversity. His 1897 book, *Sexual Inversion,* which had been banned, treated homosexuality with sympathy, as did his six-volume *Studies in the Psychology of the Sex.* To discredit the idea that women were without passion, Ellis argued that the evolution of marriage as an institution had resulted in the prohibition on female sexual pleasure, which was derided as wanton and abnormal. Ellis insisted on what he called "the erotic rights of women" and criticized heterosexual men who, "failing to find in women exactly the same kind of sexual emotions that they find in themselves . . . have concluded that there are none at all." Erotic equality, Ellis insisted, was no less important than political equality, if more difficult to achieve: "The right to joy cannot be claimed in the same way as one claims the right to put a voting paper in a ballot box," he wrote. "That is why the erotic rights of woman have been the last of all to be attained."[6]

The day Sanger met Ellis, she wrote in her diary, "I count this as a glorious day to have conversed with the one man who has done more than anyone in this Century toward giving women & men a clear & sane understanding of their sex lives & of all life." Sanger and Ellis became friends, then lovers.[7]

Sanger next wrote a fifteen-page pamphlet called *Family Limitation,* in which she gave frank instructions on how to use the best methods she'd been able to discover in Europe. "It seems inartistic and sordid to insert a pessary or a tablet in anticipation of the sexual act," she told her readers. "But it is far more sordid to find yourself, several years later, burdened down with half-a-dozen unwanted children, helpless, starved, shoddily clothed, dragging at your skirt, yourself a dragged-out shadow of the woman you once were." *Family Limitation* was marked "for private circulation" and was handed out on the streets.[8] That was illegal, too.

In September 1915, the month William Moulton Marston married Sadie Elizabeth Holloway in Massachusetts, Margaret Sanger's husband, William Sanger, was tried and convicted in New York for distributing *Family Limitation*. "Your crime is not only a violation of the laws of man, but of the law of God as well," the judge told him. "If some persons would go around and urge Christian women to bear children, instead of wasting their time on woman suffrage, this city and society would be better off."[9]

The month after her husband's trial, Margaret Sanger returned to the United States to be with her daughter, Peggy, who had contracted pneumonia and was being cared for by Ethel Byrne at Mount Sinai Hospital.

"I want Aunt Ethel to hold me; not you," Peggy said when she first saw her mother.[10] Peggy died. Sanger was devastated.

Olive Byrne was eleven, and living in a convent school in Rochester in January 1916, when Margaret Sanger appeared in federal court in New York to face the charges against her for *Woman Rebel*. Appeals on her behalf had been sent to President Wilson, pleading the cause: "While men stand proudly and face the sun, boasting that they have quenched the wickedness of slavery, what chains of slavery are, have been or ever could be so intimate a horror as the shackles on every limb—on every thought—on the very soul of an unwilling pregnant woman?"[11] Sanger refused a lawyer and insisted on representing herself. In February, the charges against her were dropped, the court believing that prosecuting a mother grieving the death of a five-year-old daughter would only aid her cause.[12] Sanger, disappointed not to have her day in court, was determined to provoke another arrest.

In October 1916, Margaret Sanger and Ethel Byrne rented a storefront in Brooklyn and posted handbills in English, Italian, and Yiddish:

MOTHERS!
Can you afford to have a large family?
Do you want any more children?
If not, why do you have them?
DO NOT KILL, DO NOT TAKE LIFE, BUT PREVENT
Safe, Harmless Information can be obtained of trained nurses at
46 AMBOY STREET.

Mothers pushing baby carriages and holding toddlers' tiny hands lined up around the corner. They paid ten cents to register. Sanger or Byrne met with seven or eight at once to show them how to use pessaries and condoms. Nine days after the clinic opened, an undercover policewoman posing as a mother of two came and met with Ethel Byrne, who discussed contraception with her. The next day, Byrne and Sanger were arrested. They were charged with violating a section of the New York State Penal Code, under which it was illegal to

Margaret Sanger (in fur-trimmed coat) and Ethel Byrne (to the right of the woman holding the baby) leaving the Brooklyn birth control clinic in 1916

Margaret Sanger (left) and Ethel Byrne in court in 1917

distribute "any recipe, drug, or medicine for the prevention of conception."[13]

Byrne was tried first, beginning on January 4, 1917. Her lawyer argued that the penal code was unconstitutional, insisting that it infringed on a woman's right to the "pursuit of happiness." That proved unconvincing. Byrne was found guilty on January 8.[14]

In the national news, Byrne's trial and imprisonment dwarfed the attention given to the suffrage movement. On January 10, Alice Paul and the National Woman's Party began their suffrage vigil outside the White House, carrying signs reading, "MR. PRESIDENT HOW LONG MUST WOMEN WAIT FOR LIBERTY?"[15] That was dramatic, but not quite as dramatic as what was happening to Ethel Byrne in New York.

On January 22, Byrne took two hours off from her hospital work to attend a hearing. She was sentenced to thirty days at Blackwell's Island. "The children Mrs. Ethel Byrne was nursing through the measles will have to get another nurse," the *New York Tribune* reported. Nothing was said, in any of the coverage of Byrne's trial, about her own two children; reporters seem not to have known about them.

"I shall go on a hunger strike at once," Ethel Byrne announced in court. "They can take me to the Workhouse, but they cannot make me eat or drink or work while I am there."[16]

Byrne's inspiration was Emmeline Pankhurst.[17] Byrne's grandson believes that Byrne, like Alice Paul and Lucy Burns, spent time in England sometime before 1916, working for Pankhurst's Women's Social and Political Union, whose members, when jailed, went on hunger strikes. Photographs of these women being force-fed—steel devices bracing open their mouths—had only advanced their cause, which is why, in the fall of 1911, the Harvard Corporation had refused to allow Pankhurst to speak on campus, and which is also why, in the winter of 1917, Byrne's decision to follow Pankhurst's lead riveted the nation's attention, even while suffragists were picketing outside the White House day and night. The *New York Times* ran the Byrne story on its front page for four days in a row.[18]

In the police van, on her way to Blackwell's Island, Byrne told other women prisoners how to use contraception. On the second day of her hunger strike, she was brought back to federal court. Her lawyer attempted to secure her release through a writ of habeas corpus but failed. Byrne collapsed during the hearing, after which she spent the night at a prison called the Tombs. Brought back to Blackwell's Island, she issued a statement through her lawyer, from cell 139.

"I will eat nothing until I am released," she said. "It does not make much difference whether I starve or not, so long as my plight calls attention to the archaic laws which would prevent our telling the truth about the facts of life. The fight is to go on." (The worst part, she later said, was going without water: "At night the woman whose duty it was to go up and down the corridors to give the prisoners a drink if they wanted it stopped right by my cell and cried, 'Water! Water' till it seemed as if I could not stand it.")[19]

Failing fast, Byrne was moved to the prison hospital. She compared her fate to the fate of women who die during abortions. "With the Health Department reporting 8,000 deaths a year in the State from illegal operations on women, one more death won't make much difference, anyway," Byrne said. Her supporters compared her struggle to the battle for suffrage, finding the fight for the right to contraception more urgent: "No amount of votes women ever get will do as much as the solution of this age-old problem."[20]

At Carnegie Hall, speaking at a rally in Byrne's honor—attended by more than three thousand supporters—Sanger said, "I come not from the stake of Salem where women were tried for blasphemy, but from the shadow of Blackwell's Island where women are tortured for obscenity." After five days without eating or drinking, Byrne was unable to get out of bed. Newspapers reported her vital signs daily. Byrne's attorney said she was in imminent danger of falling into a coma. Sanger, who was not allowed to visit, said her sister was on the verge of death. "I didn't advise her to undertake this hunger strike, but I certainly would not tell her to end it now," Sanger told reporters. An editorial in the *New York Tribune* begged the governor to issue a pardon, threatening him with the judgment of history: "It will be hard to make the youth of 1967 believe that in 1917 a woman was imprisoned for doing what Mrs. Byrne did."[21]

On the sixth day of Byrne's hunger strike, Sanger went to Rochester, ostensibly to speak at the local Birth Control League. (While Sanger was in Rochester, the Birth Control League sent a petition to the governor, in Albany, asking him to stop "the further persecution of the noble women who are leading the birth control movement.") But really, she'd gone to Rochester to see Olive Byrne, who was twelve years old, and living in a convent school called the Nazareth Academy. In Rochester, Sanger, hoping to help the cause, revealed to the press, for the first time, that her sister had two children. Sanger told reporters that Byrne had been preparing to bring her children to New York to live with her, and had finally gotten an apartment ready for them, but that this plan had been derailed by her arrest. (None of this was true.) Then she said she had come to Rochester to tell Olive what had happened to her mother. "Mrs. Byrne's sister explained that she feels the children should know about their mother and understand her motives," one paper reported.[22] That part, anyway, was true.

"There is a woman here who says she is your aunt and she wants to see you," the mother superior of the Nazareth Academy said to Olive Byrne when she sent for her. "You don't have to see her, you know."

"Oh, I don't mind," Olive said, stifling her excitement. No one had ever visited her before.

At first the nuns had refused to let Sanger past the gates. It had taken Sanger three days and a lawyer to get in. "But Margaret was not a pioneer of women's rights for nothing," Olive later wrote. "She threatened to call the police and charge abduction. At last the matter was referred to the Bishop who reluctantly agreed that she could see me in the presence of the Mother Superior."

Olive was escorted to a room filled with nuns, two priests, a bishop, and Margaret Sanger, who was tiny and glamorous. Olive thought she looked like a movie star. (Later that year, Sanger starred in a silent film called *Birth Control;* it was suppressed.)[23]

Olive was astonished. "I was a dumpy kind of child with a freckled face and wearing a most unbecoming school uniform, but that beautiful woman came to me, swept me into her arms and said, 'Oh, you lovely darling.' As no one had ever made such an extravagant gesture of love to me before, I was overcome with shyness and could not speak. But a wonderful glow filled me so I thought I would cry, and I was afraid they might send her away if I did."

Sanger hugged Olive and told her that her mother loved her very much. She did not, as the bishop feared, tell this little girl about birth control.[24]

By then, Ethel Byrne had been refusing to eat or drink for a week. Prison doctors began forcibly feeding her milk and eggs through a rubber tube. Sanger said that Byrne had been unable to resist the start of the feedings because she was unconscious at the time. Byrne was the first woman prisoner in the United States submitted to forced feeding.[25]

On January 31, Sanger and a delegation of birth control advocates met with the governor in Albany; he offered to pardon Byrne if she would agree to never again participate in the birth control movement.[26] The next day, Sanger was allowed to visit Byrne in prison. Byrne was too weak to speak. Sanger sent the governor a telegram, begging him to pardon her sister. The governor, en route from Albany to New York, missed the telegram, but later that day, Sanger and her delegation met with him in New York.

"My sister is dying," she told him.

"You know, Mrs. Sanger," he said, "that if she will only promise not to break the law henceforth I will free her at once."

"She is in no mental condition to promise anything," Sanger said. "She will perish if you do not set her free. I will take the responsibility of guaranteeing that she will not violate the law if you will release her."

The governor signed the pardon that night.

Byrne was released from prison. "Eyes closed, her face twitching with pain, Mrs. Byrne was carried from her hospital cell," the *New York Tribune* reported. She went by stretcher from the warden's office

to a boat to Manhattan, and then by ambulance to the apartment at
246 West Fourteenth Street. She had served ten days of a thirty-day
sentence.[27]

She had also gained the spotlight. Sanger, meanwhile, had started a
new journal, the *Birth Control Review;* its first issue appeared in February 1917. For an art editor, Sanger hired Lou Rogers.[28]

During Sanger's trial, the district attorney called to the witness
stand a parade of women who had gone to the Brooklyn clinic.

> "Have you ever seen Mrs. Sanger before?"
> "Yess. Yess, I know Mrs. Sanger."
> "Where did you see her?"
> "At the cleenic."
> "Why did you go there?"
> "To have her stop the babies."

Sanger's attorney cross-examined the same witnesses:

> "How many children have you?"
> "Eight and three that didn't live."[29]

In the end, the judge ruled that no woman has "the right to copulate
with a feeling of security that there will be no resulting conception":
if a woman isn't willing to die in childbirth, she shouldn't have sex.
Sanger was found guilty on Friday, February 2, the day after Byrne
was pardoned. Sentencing was scheduled for the following Monday.

"Will you go on a hunger strike if you are sent to the workhouse?"
a reporter asked. Sanger said she hadn't decided.[30]

On February 5, Sanger was sentenced to thirty days. She refused
to pay a fine instead of going to prison. But she didn't go on a hunger strike; she served her time. From the Queens County Penitentiary,
on Long Island, Sanger wrote to Byrne, telling her sister that she
had "made the finest fight ever made by any woman in the U.S.A."
("Women from the workhouse keep coming here & ask for you," she
told her.)[31]

"What would you think of speaking now & then?" Sanger asked

Byrne. "Think it over."[32] But speaking, even now and then, would have violated the terms of Byrne's pardon.

The day Margaret Sanger was released from prison, Ethel Byrne met her and brought her home.[33] But Ethel Byrne never forgave her sister for making that promise, on her behalf, to the governor of New York. She thought her sister had wanted, all along, to nudge her out of the movement.[34] For the movement Margaret Sanger wanted to lead, Ethel Byrne was too radical.

12

WOMAN AND THE NEW RACE

WHEN OLIVE BYRNE WAS A GIRL, she spent the summer far from orphanages and convents, on the vaudeville circuit. Her uncles Billie and Charlie Byrne were female impersonators known as the Giddy Girls. "The BYRNE & BYRNE MUSICAL COMEDY COMPANY Announce Their Giddy Girls," the billing read. In 1917 and 1918, they went from Pennsylvania to Ohio to Kansas and back again, three shows a day. Olive sang in the chorus.[1]

In 1918, when Olive Byrne was fourteen, she left Nazareth Academy for the Mount St. Joseph Academy in Buffalo. She started studying to be a nurse. At St. Joseph's, the nuns had crushes on the girls and the girls had crushes on the nuns, but Olive managed to keep out of trouble by becoming an excellent liar.[2]

When she was sixteen, she visited her mother in New York; it was the first time she'd seen her in ten years. She stayed with Ethel Byrne and Rob Parker in the apartment in Greenwich Village, at 246 West Fourteenth Street. Margaret Sanger had gone to California, where she was writing a book she was calling "Voluntary Motherhood." "Got off a chapter," Sanger wrote in her diary one day. But Olive always insisted that it was Parker who wrote Sanger's books.[3]

Olive knew that her mother and Parker were sleeping together. At the time, she said, "I looked for sexual overtones in a handshake." And she knew, too, that they weren't married, even though "Aunt Margaret Sanger told me that Bob and Ethel had been married in Nantucket." At that, Ethel Byrne had only laughed and said, "Margaret was known to invent 'nice covers' for circumstances that she thought might become a matter of scandal, embarrassing to herself."[4]

There was more than scandal at stake. The Espionage and Sedition Acts, passed in 1917 and 1918, had exposed many of Sanger's and Byrne's Greenwich Village friends to persecution. For their opposition to the war, Max Eastman, John Reed, and other editors and writers for the *Masses* were indicted for conspiracy. Emma Goldman spent two years in prison for opposing the draft. For making an antiwar speech in Ohio, Eugene Debs was sentenced to ten years in prison. Sanger decided to cut all of her ties with anyone whose stance on the war threatened the success of the birth control movement. That meant leaving Ethel Byrne out of it. "I think what Margaret was doing was not so much dropping my mother per se as it was getting the movement away from the fringes of socialism, out of Greenwich Village and into uptown New York because the money for anything is where the people are who have money and not in your ragtag, bobtail people," Olive Byrne later said. "My mother was not a good 'uptown' person: she was a rebel, far more a rebel than Margaret ever was and she never was anything else. You have to comply a little bit, you know, to get anywhere, and my mother wouldn't comply with anybody for anything."[5]

Sanger forged new alliances. At her trial in 1917, the judge had ruled that Sanger had no right to distribute contraception but that physicians did, so Sanger decided to ally the birth control movement with doctors, and with an emerging medical literature on the importance of female sexual pleasure. In 1918, in the *Birth Control Review*, Sanger published an essay by Havelock Ellis called "The Love Rights of Women"; Lou Rogers contributed the drawings.[6] The next year, Sanger, who had divorced her husband, began a decades-long affair with H. G. Wells. (A barely fictionalized Sanger is the hero's lover in Wells's autobiographical 1922 novel, *The Secret Places of the Heart*.)[7] Meanwhile, Sanger courted alliances with conservatives and eugenicists, who were interested in using contraception to control the population of "mental defectives"—by force, if necessary. In 1921, Sanger founded the American Birth Control League; six years later, a survey conducted of nearly a thousand of its members found them to be dis-

Women chained by unwanted pregnancies. From Sanger's *Birth Control Review*, 1923

proportionately Republican, from small towns or suburbs, and Rotarians. Faced with a membership who objected to her feminism, Sanger was forced to resign as the league's president.[8]

Sanger's feminism was of a very particular sort. Olive Byrne, living with Parker and Ethel Byrne in the winter of 1920, heard a lot about the book Sanger was working on, "Voluntary Motherhood," whose title changed, first to "The Modern Woman Movement." It was published in October 1920, two months after the passage of the Nineteenth Amendment, with a new title: *Woman and the New Race.* Between 1920 and 1926, *Woman and the New Race* and Sanger's next book, *The Pivot of Civilization,* sold more than half a million copies.[9]

Woman and the New Race placed the birth control movement on the stage of history as a struggle of even greater importance than suffrage. "The most far-reaching social development of modern times is the revolt of woman against sex servitude," Sanger wrote, promising that contraception would "remake the world." No freedom was more important: "No woman can call herself free who does not own and control her own body." And to that revolt against slavery, no one had been more important than her sister: "No single act of self-sacrifice in the history of the birth-control movement has done more to awaken

Wonder Woman chained by men. From "The Count of Conquest," *Wonder Woman #2* (Fall 1942)

the conscience of the public or to arouse the courage of women, than did Ethel Byrne's deed of uncompromising resentment at the outrage of jailing women who were attempting to disseminate knowledge which would emancipate the motherhood of America," Sanger wrote. (Or maybe it was Parker who wrote that.) Woman, Sanger argued, "had chained herself to her place in society and the family through the maternal functions of her nature, and only chains thus strong could have bound her to her lot as a brood animal."[10] The time had come to break those chains.

Picturing and talking about women as chained and enslaved was ubiquitous in feminist literature, a carryover from the nineteenth-century alliance between the suffrage and abolitionist movements. Charlotte Perkins Gilman described a feminist this way: "Here she comes, running out of prison and off pedestal; chains off, crown off, halo off, just a live woman."[11] Chained women inspired the title of another of Sanger's books, *Motherhood in Bondage,* a compilation of some of the thousands of letters she had received from women begging her for information about birth control; she described the letters as "the confessions of enslaved mothers."[12] An illustration commissioned by Lou Rogers for the cover of Sanger's *Birth Control Review* pictured a weakened and desperate woman, fallen to her knees and chained at the ankle to a ball that reads, "UNWANTED BABIES."[13]

Birth control could unlock those chains. Voluntary motherhood, Sanger argued in *Woman and the New Race,* "is for woman the key to the temple of liberty." The emancipation of women, Sanger argued, wasn't a matter of ballots; it was part of a struggle that went all the way back to ancient Greece. It was a matter of liberating the "feminine spirit"—a spirit well represented in the poems of Sappho of Lesbos, who, Sanger explained, "sought to arouse the Greek wives to the expression of their individual selves," their sexual selves. The feminine spirit, Sanger wrote, "manifests itself most frequently in motherhood, but it is greater than maternity." It had been suppressed by force: the laws, religions, and customs that had denied women recourse to contraception. Women's struggles had led, the world over, to woman seeking out "violent means of freeing herself from the chains of her own reproductivity." Overpopulation is the cause behind all human misery, including poverty and war, Sanger argued. But "force and fear have failed from the beginning of time." Birth control is "the real cure for war" and "love is the greatest force of the universe." When love defeats force, "the moral force of woman's nature will be unchained," Sanger predicted, and the world will be made anew.[14]

"Let this book be read by every man and woman who can read," Havelock Ellis said about *Woman and the New Race.*[15] Among the people who read it were Mr. and Mrs. William M. Marston, who in 1920 were studying for graduate degrees in psychology, at Harvard and Radcliffe. The philosophy of Margaret Sanger's *Woman and the New Race* would turn out to be the philosophy of Wonder Woman, precisely.

> With the beauty of Aphrodite, the wisdom of Athena, the strength of Hercules, and the speed of Mercury, she brings to America woman's eternal gifts—love and wisdom! Defying the vicious intrigues of evil enemies and laughing gaily at all danger, Wonder Woman leads the invincible youth of America against the threatening forces of treachery, death, and destruction.[16]

Women should rule the world, Sanger and Marston and Holloway thought, because love is stronger than force.

Years later, when Marston hired a young woman named Joye Hummel to help him write Wonder Woman, Olive Byrne gave Hummel a copy of *Woman and the New Race*. Read this, she told her, and you'll know everything you need to know about Wonder Woman.[17]

THE BOYETTE

IN 1922, when Olive Byrne was eighteen, she left Byrne & Byrne and the Giddy Girls and spent the summer with her mother in Truro, on Cape Cod. Margaret Sanger had bought a house in Truro from John Reed, who sold it to her in 1917, just before he left the United States for Russia to report on the Bolshevik Revolution. (Reed was arrested in 1918, on his way home.) Ethel Byrne bought a house nearby, a sea captain's house on Mill Pond Road, a short walk from the railway depot. Byrne's house had no electricity and nothing but a cast-iron stove in the kitchen. She put up a sign: EAT, DRINK, AND BE MERRY. She drank at all hours. She made a colored glass path out back, out of empty liquor bottles, planted neck side down. It's still there, glinting, like sea glass, in the sand.

Ethel Byrne liked to go to Provincetown, one town over, to visit friends. Truro and Provincetown were refuges for Greenwich Village radicals and a haven for homosexuals. Ethel Byrne and Margaret Sanger believed in free love, which meant they believed in sex outside of marriage, and considered marriage itself a form of oppression. People who believed in free love didn't necessarily regard homosexuality as simply another form of sexual expression. But Ethel Byrne did.[1]

In the summer of 1922, Ethel and Olive Byrne rode the narrow, winding road from Truro to Provincetown in a beat-up Ford touring car. One night, they went to a party where eight men were sitting with their arms around one another, kissing. "Though I'd heard of homosexuals," Olive later wrote, "I'd never met any."[2]

Margaret Sanger didn't spend the summer of 1922 in Truro with Ethel and Olive Byrne. She spent it on a world tour, raising money and contemplating an offer of marriage from a millionaire. She knew that accepting it would look like a betrayal of her principles; she also knew that the movement she was leading needed money. On September 14, 1922, Sanger's forty-third birthday, she married J. Noah Slee, a sixty-one-year-old oil magnate, at a city clerk's office in London. They kept the marriage secret for over a year. But Sanger must have telegrammed her sister and told her the news because days later and out of the blue, Ethel took Olive Byrne to New York, to a college directory office on Forty-second Street, and insisted that Olive apply to college, straight-away. Ethel Byrne might have been shut out of the birth control movement, but she was determined that her sister's millionaire husband would pay for her daughter to become not a nurse but a doctor.

At the college directory office, Olive and her mother pored over admissions applications and cabled admissions offices. The semester had already begun; most freshmen classes were already filled. In the end, Ethel Byrne decided to send her daughter to Jackson, the women's college of Tufts University. Olive Byrne packed her bags, went to Grand Central Station, got on a train to Boston, and arrived at Tufts, alone and two weeks into the semester. Her tuition was paid by J. Noah Slee.[3]

She threw herself into college life. She joined the glee club and the staff of the *Tufts Weekly*. She was chairman of the Social Committee. She was tall and lean; she played basketball. She won a leading role in the class operetta, *The Wisdom of Neptune*. She had her hair bobbed and got the nickname Bobbie. (She makes an appearance in Wonder Woman as a Holliday College student named Bobbie Strong.) Olive Byrne was a freethinker and a radical; she believed, too, in free love. "We thought we were very daring," she said. She founded the Tufts Liberal Club, modeled on the Liberal Club her mother and aunt had belonged to in Greenwich Village, inviting anyone who was "a chivalrous free-thinker, ie, free of all bias" to join. She was elected vice president (the highest-ranking office open to a woman; the president was always a man).[4]

In her studies, though, Olive Byrne was behind even before she arrived. "The important subjects for medical school, chemistry and

Olive Byrne (front row, with headband) with Alpha Omicron Pi at Tufts in 1923, at the end of her freshman year. Mary Sears, the inspiration for Etta Candy, is to her right, wearing a tie.

biology, were not difficult for me," she explained, but she found the math hard. At the end of the first semester of her freshman year, she was put on academic probation. She was saved, she liked to say, by a friend: "Deliverance came in the rotund shape of a junior named Mary Sears." With Sears's tutoring, Byrne scraped by with C's.[5]

Mary Sears was the inspiration for Wonder Woman's best friend, a Holliday College student named Etta Candy. At Tufts, Sears belonged to a sorority, Alpha Omicron Pi. At Holliday College, Etta Candy belongs to Beeta Lambda. Like Mary Sears, Etta Candy is "rotund." She is addicted to sweets and is forever offering up exclamations like "Bursting brandy drops!" and "Great chocolates!" (Etta's father's name is Sugar Candy; her brother's name is Mint. Her boyfriend goes to Starvard College.)[6]

"You know, Etta, you ought to cut down on the candy. It will ruin your constitution," Diana Prince tells her.

"My constitution has room for lots of amendments."[7]

In an Alpha Omicron Pi photograph taken in the spring of Olive Byrne's freshman year, she's in the front row, wearing a short-sleeved,

Wonder Woman is rescued by Etta Candy and the Holliday College girls. From "America's Guardian Angel," *Sensation Comics #12* (December 1942)

boat-necked polka-dotted dress and a flapper's thick band in her short hair, smiling. Mary Sears is sitting next to her.[8]

"I wasn't a very gung-ho type of sorority sister," Byrne explained, but, in February of her freshman year, she was initiated. "I felt good about that," she wrote. "At last I belonged to a family."[9]

During her sophomore year, Byrne helped manage the basketball team and performed in the class play. Her grades improved.[10] She invited her aunt to campus to speak, as a guest of the Liberal Club. The Tufts administration refused to allow Sanger on campus, just as, years before, Harvard had banned Emmeline Pankhurst. Sanger was used to that. In 1929, when Sanger visited Boston to lecture at Ford Hall, city authorities banned her lecture, so she appeared on stage with a gag over her mouth, while Harvard historian Arthur Schlesinger Sr. read a

Margaret Sanger gagged, in protest of censorship

Wonder Woman and her mother gagged. From "The Four Dooms," *Wonder Woman #33* (February 1949)

statement on her behalf. "I see immense advantages in being gagged," it read. "It silences me, but it makes millions of others talk."[11] When the Tufts administration banned Margaret Sanger from campus, Olive Byrne arranged for her to speak instead at a church in Somerville, nearby.[12] Wonder Woman is gagged by villains all the time, too. But in the end, she always has her say.

Feminism and the birth control movement were not without effect on the sex lives of college girls. In the 1920s, college women were far more likely to engage in premarital sex, and to achieve orgasm, than their counterparts just ten years earlier. In his pioneering sex surveys in the 1930s, Alfred Kinsey found that of women born before 1900 (like Sadie Holloway, born in 1893), only 14 percent had sex before marriage, compared to 36 percent of women born between 1900 and 1910 (like Olive Byrne, born in 1904). Women of Olive Byrne's generation, who came of age right after women gained the right to vote, were also more likely than women of Holloway's generation to embrace sex as a source of pleasure. But they were less likely than women of Holloway's generation to tie sex-as-pleasure to feminism.[13]

During Christmas vacation, Olive Byrne worked in New York, at

Margaret Sanger's Clinical Research Bureau, on Sixteenth Street. Sanger had opened the clinic, with Slee's money, in 1923. At Tufts, Olive Byrne became the undergraduates' source for contraception. Everyone knew she was Sanger's niece. "Always there were people when I was in college coming around asking me if I knew birth control methods," she said. "The only thing was you had to go to New York to get the material." It helped if you could say you were a friend of Olive Byrne's. "If any of the people you know at school are down in

Olive Byrne during her senior year at Tufts

New York and want to come in and get some information you tell them to ask for me," Sanger told her. "Tell them to say you sent them and we will take care of them."[14]

One way Olive Byrne got by at Tufts was by trading on her radicalism and her sophistication: she was voted the wittiest, cleverest, and most distinctive student in the class of 1926.[15] And one way in which she was distinctive was her androgyny. During her senior year, she got her hair cut in what was known—for its boyishness—as an "Eton crop." She dressed like a boy, too, a fashion far more common in England than in the United States. "The 'Boyette' not only crops her hair close like a boy but she dresses in every way as a boy," the London *Daily Mail* reported in 1927. "Her ambition is to look as much like a boy as possible."[16]

In the fall of 1925, Olive Byrne, boyette, took a class with a wildly charismatic young professor who'd come from Washington, D.C., where he'd been involved in a sensational murder trial.[17] She found him irresistible.

THE BABY PARTY

WILLIAM MOULTON MARSTON, professor of psychology, arrived at Tufts University in the autumn of 1925. He was thirty-two years old, and hulking. He weighed more than two hundred pounds. Since being arrested for fraud and fired from American University, he'd worked for the National Committee for Mental Hygiene, administering psychological tests to students in a school on Staten Island and to inmates in a Texas penitentiary. He'd also published an article in which he attempted to salvage his academic career by venturing into a new field: the study of sex.

In the 1920s, psychologists were fascinated by sex, sexual difference, and sexual adjustment, not only because of Freud's influence, but also because of the rise of behavioralism. Lewis Terman, who helped develop the IQ test, invented a test to measure "masculinity" and "femininity"; its purpose was to identify deviance. According to the behavioralist John B. Watson, feminism itself was a form of deviance: a feminist was a woman unable to accept that she wasn't a man. "Most of the terrible women one must meet, women with the blatant views and voices, women who have to be noticed, who shoulder one about, who can't take life quietly," Watson wrote in the *Nation*, "belong to this large percentage of women who have never made a sex adjustment."[1]

Marston first revealed his fascination with sex and sexual difference in an article he published in the *Journal of Experimental Psy-*

chology at the end of 1923. In "Sex Characteristics in Blood Pressure," he reported on the results of an investigation he had conducted at Harvard between 1919 and 1921, aided by "Mrs. E. H. Marston" and "supplemented by subsequent work by the writer." He'd wanted to discover in what ways women's brains work differently than men's. He and Holloway had conducted blood pressure tests on ten men and ten women. They'd tried to get them upset, and then they'd tried to arouse them.

"With female subjects, the most effective sex-stimulus was found to be, not the presence or conversation of a strange man," Marston reported, "but sex topics of conversation with a person well known." He believed his study demonstrated that women are more emotionally volatile than men ("Emotions capable of producing major b.p. changes fluctuate within the female consciousness with great facility and rapidity, while any emotional influences that find their way into expression in the male organism tend to persist") and that most of women's emotions were founded in their sexuality ("there being a far greater number of adequate stimuli to sex-emotion in the female organism"). The emotion women were most likely to experience was anger, Marston reported; the emotion men were most likely to experience was fear. The kinds of statements that got women agitated were things like "I was so mad I could have killed her!" What got men riled were statements like "I may not get that teaching job."[2] But what this kind of research had most clearly proved to Marston was how much he liked doing this kind of research, especially the part about getting women excited.

In the fall of 1925, a Tufts newspaper announced his arrival: "Dr. William M. Marston will be Assistant Professor of Philosophy, centering his attention particularly on psychology."[3] At American University, Marston had been a full professor and chairman of the Psychology Department. Tufts appointed him an untenured assistant professor. He was climbing down the academic ladder, not up. With every step down, his teaching load got heavier. At Tufts, he taught eight courses in two semesters: Experimental Psychology, Abnormal Psychology, Comparative Psychology, the History of Psychology, the Psychology of Human Behavior, a research seminar, and two sections of Applied Psychology.[4]

From "The Fun Foundation," *Sensation Comics #27* (March 1944)

Holloway didn't come with him to Massachusetts. Instead, she took a job in New York, as managing editor of a psychology journal, *Child Study: A Journal of Parent Education,* where she worked with Josette Frank, an expert on children's literature who was one of the journal's editors.[5] *Child Study,* started in 1924, was published by the Child Study Association of America; its purpose was to teach parents how to raise children. Using birth control, wealthier women were having fewer children; they were expected to devote more attention to them; they needed to be taught the science of motherhood. It was in this same spirit that *Parents' Magazine* was founded, in 1926.[6]

In his Experimental Psychology class at Tufts in the fall of 1925, Marston had as a student a girl whose hair was cut like a boy's. She was Margaret Sanger's niece. She was chic and sophisticated and radical and desperately unhappy; she had had an unbearably lonely childhood. Possibly, she was suicidal. He suggested that she come to a clinic he had just opened to treat students with adjustment problems.

Marston later wrote a story in which Wonder Woman leaps into Niagara Falls to rescue a pretty girl named Gay, who is attempting to drown herself. (Women who loved other women began referring to themselves as "gay" in the 1920s; Gertrude Stein used the word that way in 1922.)[7] "Poor child! You've lived a terrible life," Wonder Woman says to Gay, after rescuing her. "You're *fun-starved!*" She brings her to Holliday College and introduces her to Etta Candy at Beeta Lambda: "I want you to take charge of this girl and *make* her have *fun!*" Etta teaches Gay how to play. "Having fun has made a new girl of me," Gay says. "It'll do the same for others. I'm going to start a Fun Clinic and teach despondent people how to enjoy life!"[8] Inspired by Gay's newfound happiness, Wonder Woman raises $1 billion for a Fun Foundation and opens Fun Clinics across the country, "giving healthy recreations to millions of fun-starved Americans."[9]

Before meeting Professor Marston, Olive Byrne had taken three courses in the Psychology Department; she'd earned three C's. Her coursework was stronger in her major, English, where she'd earned B's. In Experimental Psychology, Marston gave her an A. Before that, the only A she'd gotten was in a gym class. In the spring of her senior year, she took three more classes with Marston: Applied Psychology, Abnormal Psychology, and a research seminar that was usually restricted to graduate students. Marston gave her three more A's.[10]

She began working as his research assistant. They decided—or maybe he decided and she agreed—to conduct a study together. He wanted to know how women felt when they were tied up and how other women felt when they beat them.

At the time, Marston was developing a theory of emotions derived from what he called the "basic psycho-neural mechanisms of emotion." He had begun this work while conducting psychological tests on more than three thousand men held in prisons in Texas; he was especially interested in "the homo-sexual relationships inevitable in prison life." The results of these tests had suggested to Marston that there exist four primary emotions: dominance, compliance, inducement, and submission. At Tufts, he focused on what he called captivation, which he described as "an essential constituent of sadistic teasing or torturing of weaker human beings or animals."[11]

Understanding his interest in captivation, Olive Byrne took her professor to Alpha Omicron Pi, where freshmen pledges were required

From "School for Spies," *Sensation Comics #4* (April 1942)

to dress up like babies and attend a "Baby Party." Marston later described it: "the freshmen girls were led into a dark corridor where their eyes were blindfolded, and their arms were bound behind them." Then the freshmen were taken into a room where juniors and seniors compelled them to do various tasks, while sophomores hit them with long sticks.[12] Each of these scenes appears in Wonder Woman comics, where initiates to Beeta Lambda are hit with sticks and, during "Baby Week," wear diapers.

At Tufts, Marston observed the party, and then he and Olive Byrne began conducting interviews together. "Nearly all the sophomores reported excited pleasantness of captivation emotion throughout the party," he reported. "The pleasantness of their captivation responses appeared to increase when they were obliged to overcome rebellious freshmen physically, or induce them by repeated commands and added punishments to perform the actions from which the captive girls strove to escape."[13] Marston was fascinated.

When Marston published his findings, he made sure to credit his assistant: "Studies of emotions reported by sophomores and upper class girls during their annual punishment of the freshmen girls were

From "Three Pretty Girls," *Sensation Comics #43* (July 1945)

made by Miss Olive Byrne and myself, during the academic year 1925–1926."[14] What more the psychologist and his assistant did together that year is hard to say.

Olive Byrne graduated from Tufts with a bachelor's degree in English on June 14, 1926, at a ceremony during which Jane Addams was awarded an honorary degree.[15] Ethel Byrne took the train from Truro to watch her graduate, celebrating an education that she hoped would allow her daughter an escape from the slavery of involuntary motherhood. Holloway came, too. "I'd like you to meet somebody special," Marston told his wife.[16]

In a photograph taken on that day, Olive Byrne, one eye hidden by a lock of dark hair, wears her cap and gown and smiles, shyly, her head tilted down. On her right is Holloway, a good six inches shorter, wearing an elegant suit and a cloche, and carrying Olive's diploma. On Olive's left, and with his arm around her, stands Marston, tall and wide and grinning, in his academic regalia—cap and gown and Harvard hood. Set apart, on Marston's other side, is Ethel Byrne, in a pale

Left to right: Elizabeth Holloway Marston, Olive Byrne, William Moulton Marston, and Ethel Byrne, at Tufts commencement in 1926

coat and a brimmed hat. It's a family photograph but a bewildering one: Marston and Holloway look as if they must be Olive Byrne's parents, except that they're too young. (They were only eleven years older than she was.) Ethel Byrne looks as though she might be an aunt.

One day, Olive Byrne, pasting the photograph into a family album, took out a pen. "EHM," she wrote on Holloway's jacket. Over Ethel Byrne's coat, she wrote, in blue ink, a single word: "MOTHER."

HAPPINESS IN MARRIAGE

OLIVE BYRNE, the wittiest, cleverest, and most distinctive graduate of the Tufts class of 1926, never made it to medical school.[1] "I find that my plans for the coming year have not come to pass as I anticipated," she wrote to Margaret Sanger's husband, J. Noah Slee, on September 5, 1926, three months after she graduated from Tufts. Slee had offered to pay for Olive to go to medical school, but she decided instead to go to graduate school in psychology at Columbia, and to work for—and live with—Marston.

"I can make enough money this year to pay for my room, board and clothes working with Dr. Marston on his book and lecture work," she told Slee. "But in order to do graduate work at Columbia, I will have to ask for your assistance." She asked him to pay her tuition. "I do so want to be independent but I also want to do something worth while when I am independent."

Ethel Byrne did not approve.

"Mother only laughs when I tell her what I want to do," Olive told Slee.[2]

Marston left Tufts when Olive Byrne graduated. He'd been there less than a year. He was probably fired. If his relationship with Byrne and the business with the Baby Party had been discovered, the dean of the college would likely have told him to leave. That kind of thing happens all the time in Wonder Woman comics.

"What are you doing here?" Dean Sourpuss of Holliday College

Carolyn Marston Keatley, Marston's aunt

asks Professor Toxino. "You know you're not welcome at this college!"[3]

Byrne spent the summer after she graduated living with Marston and Holloway in Darien, Connecticut. "The Marstons have been awfully good, helping me with their almost unlimited knowledge of the subject I want to take up," she wrote Slee. Once classes started, she planned to move to the city, where Holloway kept an apartment. "I'm going to live up near Columbia with Mrs. Marston."[4]

According to one version of the family story, Marston had given Holloway a choice. Either Olive Byrne could live with them or he would leave her. This was something altogether different from whatever arrangement they had with Marjorie Wilkes Huntley.

"He had a rather strange appreciation of women," Sheldon Mayer, Marston's editor at DC Comics, once said. "One was never enough."[5]

Holloway was devastated. She walked out the door and walked, without stopping, for six hours, thinking.[6]

Decades later, Holloway explained that she, Marston, and Byrne had devised a "non-conformist" way to live. "All the basic principles" of their life together, she said, were arrived at "in the years 1925, 26, and 27 when a group of about ten people used to meet in Boston at Aunt Carolyn's apartment once a week."[7]

Aunt Carolyn was Carolyn Marston Keatley, a sister of Marston's father. She was a nursing supervisor at the Deaconess Hospital in Boston.[8] She was an Aquarian: she believed in the teachings in a book published in 1908 called *The Aquarian Gospel of Jesus the Christ*, by an American preacher named Levi H. Dowling. Dowling claimed to have found historical documents proving that Jesus, as a young man, had traveled to India and Tibet, where he learned a religion of peace. Keatley believed that she was living in the dawn of the Age of Aquarius, the beginning of a new astrological age, an age of love: the New Age.[9]

The ten or so people who met at Keatley's apartment during Olive Byrne's senior year at Tufts included Keatley, Holloway, Marston, Marjorie Wilkes Huntley, and Byrne. Theirs was a remarkably kinky New Age—kinkier, even, than the Baby Party. A ninety-five-page, single-spaced typescript of notes taken during the meetings at Keatley's apartment chronicle a cult of female sexual power—specifically, a "clinic"—involving "Love Leaders," "Mistresses" (or "Mothers"), and "Love Girls." It sounds something like a sexual training camp. Love Girls "do not believe in or practice escape from or concealment of the love organs"; at the meetings, presumably, Love Girls wore no clothes. There are astrological overtones: a Love Leader and a Mistress and their Love Girl form a "Love Unit," a perfect constellation. Much in the meeting notes refers to Marston's theory of dominance and submission; females "in their relation to males, expose their bodies and use various legitimate methods of the Love sphere to create in males submission to them, the women mistresses or Love leaders, in order that they, the Mistresses, may submit in passion to the males." Much in the notes concerns sex itself: "During the act of intercourse between the male and his Mistress, the male's love organ stimulates the inner love organs of the Mistress, and not the external love organs," but "if anyone wishes to develop the consciousness of submission, he or she must keep the sexual orgasm in check, and thus permit the nervous energy to flow freely and uninterruptedly into the external genital organs." (The submissive partner was supposed to hold back orgasm.)

Very few names are supplied in the meeting notes, although there are references to "the Messenger Betty," "the messenger R," and "the girl Zara."[10] Messenger Betty must have been Holloway: Marston called her Betty. Messenger R must have been Marston himself. In Olive Byrne's diaries, "R" is code for Marston (her secret name for him was Richard). And "the girl Zara" must have been Huntley. "Zara or Zaz is the name given me by Doctor and Ms. Marston when we became a threesome," Huntley once explained.[11]

How seriously anyone but Keatley and Huntley took this is difficult

The High Priestess Zara. From
"Mystery of the Crimson Flame,"
Comic Calvacade #5 (Winter 1943)

to know. In a Wonder Woman story called "Mystery of the Crimson Flame," a senator's daughter helps Diana Prince investigate a cult run by the "High Priestess Zara"; Wonder Woman exposes Zara as a fraud.[12] Marston's interests included what he called captivation and Huntley called "love binding": bondage. Imagining what happened in those meetings at Keatley's apartment, Holloway once told her children, would require "great flexibility in your thinking and the wide extension of your mental horizons in your exploration of what is against what is not."[13] Olive Byrne seems to have thought the whole thing was a little ridiculous. She also thought Huntley was nuts. "That woman's a lunatic," she used to say.[14]

But Byrne brought something crucial to those meetings: birth control, and her aunt's books, including *Woman and the New Race,* which everyone in the group read. They also likely read a book Sanger published in 1926, called *Happiness in Marriage.* Sanger didn't talk about love girls and love leaders, but she did stress a man's obligation to help a woman achieve orgasm by delaying his own: "The successful husband-lover will, during every act of the love drama, seek to redirect all egotistical impulses, and, like a skillful driver, at every moment hold himself under intelligent control." In a chapter titled "The Organs of Sex and Their Functions," she explained the importance of the clitoris, the "special seat of sex sensitiveness," and advised men regarding its stimulation: "Avoid hurry."[15]

The way Marston, Holloway, and Byrne decided to live—as a threesome and, when Huntley was around, as a foursome—began, Holloway later said, as an idea: "A new way of living has to exist in the minds of men before it can be realized in actual form."[16] It had something to do with Marston's theory of emotions, with Keatley and Huntley's ideas about a "Love Unit," and with Margaret Sanger's and Havelock Ellis's ideas about "Love Rights." Holloway tried to explain what she had taken away from reading *Woman and the New Race:* "The new

"A great movement [is] now under way—the growth in the power of women," William Moulton Marston wrote to his editor, Sheldon Mayer, in February 1941, submitting his first script. "Let that theme alone or drop the project." For an artist, Marston chose Harry G. Peter, who, like Marston, had ties to the Progressive Era suffrage and feminist movements. In 1911, Marston was a freshman at Harvard when the university banned the militant British suffragist Emmeline Pankhurst from speaking on campus. Elizabeth Holloway, whom Marston married in 1915, had been a suffragist at Mount Holyoke College, and Marjorie Wilkes Huntley, a librarian who began living with the Marstons, on and off, around 1918, had taken women to the polls. Olive Byrne, who met Marston in 1925, was the daughter of Ethel Byrne, who, in 1917, was the first woman in the United States to go on a hunger strike, after she and her sister, Margaret Sanger, were arrested for having opened the nation's first birth control clinic. In the 1910s, Harry G. Peter had contributed illustrations to "The Modern Woman," the pro-suffrage editorial page of the magazine *Judge,* where he was a staff artist, along with the feminist cartoonist Lou Rogers, whose work would greatly influence how Peter came to draw Wonder Woman. In 1941, Peter made some sketches and sent them to Marston; Marston liked everything but the shoes.

Wonder Woman made a spectacular debut on American newsstands just as the United States entered the Second World War, appearing in *All-Star Comics #8* (December 1941–January 1942), and then on the cover of *Sensation Comics #1* (January 1942). Both comic books were published by Maxwell Charles Gaines. The stories were credited to "Charles Moulton," a pseudonym made up of Gaines's and Marston's middle names. Wonder Woman appeared in every issue of *Sensation Comics* as the lead story, and on every cover. In March 1942, the National Organization for Decent Literature put *Sensation Comics* on its list of "Publications Disapproved for Youth." Gaines wrote to the bishop in charge of the list and asked why. The bishop wrote back, "Wonder Woman is not sufficiently dressed."

"Noted Psychologist Revealed as Author of Best-Selling 'Wonder Woman,'" Marston wrote in a press release in the summer of 1942, announcing the debut of *Wonder Woman*. "The only hope for civilization is the greater freedom, development and equality of women in all fields of human activity," Marston wrote, explaining that he intended Wonder Woman "to set up a standard among children and young people of strong, free, courageous womanhood; and to combat the idea that women are inferior to men, and to inspire girls to self-confidence and achievement in athletics, occupations and professions monopolized by men." Wonder Woman was the first female superhero to have her own magazine.

In most comics women's role was limited to answering the mail and taking the meeting minutes, Marston, in the stories he wrote, railed against what he called "domestic slavery," as in this story, "The Return of Diana Prince," *Sensation Comics #9* (September 1942). The theme, as well as the iconography, is taken directly from the suffrage and feminist writers and illustrators of the 1910s who had so powerfully influenced both Marston and Peter.

Marston also used Wonder Woman to feature his long-standing work, dating to his junior year of college, on the detection of deception, the subject of his 1921 doctoral dissertation in Harvard's Psychology Department. As early as 1923, newspapers referred to Marston as the "Lie Meter Inventor." In 1938, Marston published a book called *The Lie Detector Test,* staking his claim in the invention of what became the polygraph. In "The Duke of Deception," *Wonder Woman #2* (Fall 1942), Wonder Woman uses her magic lasso to compel a villain to tell the truth. Like her bracelets, the magic lasso was given to Wonder Woman on Paradise Island, before she left the land of the Amazons to journey to "America, the last citadel of democracy, and of equal rights for women!"

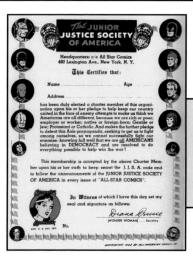

The Justice Society of America held its first meeting in the winter of 1940. "Each of them is a hero in his own right, but when the Justice Society calls, they are only members, sworn to uphold honor and justice!" Fans who joined a special Junior Justice Society were mailed membership certificates, signed by Wonder Woman. From *All-Star Comics #14* (December 1942–January 1943).

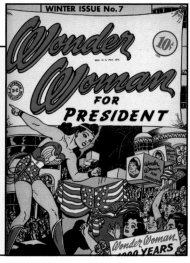

"Frankly, Wonder Woman is psychological propaganda for the new type of woman who, I believe, should rule the world," Marston wrote. He got that message across in a story from *Wonder Woman #7* (Winter 1943), in which Diana Prince becomes president of the United States. A League for a Woman President had been founded in 1935, in hopes of getting the first woman to the White House by 1940. In 1937, Marston held a press conference at which he announced that women would one day rule the world. "Women have twice the emotional development, the ability for love, than man has," he explained. "And as they develop as much ability for worldly success as they already have ability for love, they will clearly come to rule business and the Nation and the world." Marston thought the reign of women would usher in an age of peace, an argument that suffragists had used in attempting to secure for women the right to vote.

Wonder Woman is bound in almost every one of her adventures, usually in chains. The bondage in Wonder Woman comics raised hackles with Gaines's editorial advisory board, but Marston insisted that Wonder Woman had to be

chained or tied so that she could free herself—and, symbolically, emancipate herself. "My woman's power returns again!" she cries, here, in "The Rubber Barons," *Wonder Woman #4* (April–May 1943).

In 1943, Gaines asked one of his editors, Dorothy Roubicek, to propose a solution that might answer the members of the editorial advisory board who were troubled by the bondage in Wonder Woman comics, while also accommodating Marston, who insisted on the importance of this theme to his feminist argument. After meeting with Roubicek, Gaines sent Marston Roubicek's proposed "list of methods which can be used to keep women confined or enclosed without the use of chains." Marston was unmoved. "Please thank Miss Roubicek for the list of menaces," he wrote Gaines, drily. Nevertheless, in "Victory at Sea," *Sensation Comics #15* (March 1943), Wonder Woman is wrapped in a straitjacket and locked in a jail—the kind of menace Roubicek preferred.

Secret identities lie at the heart of all superhero comics, but for Marston, who had worked for U.S. military intelligence during the First World War, Wonder Woman's secret identity as Diana Prince, a secretary to U.S. military intelligence, takes on a special cast. Marston kept a lie detector in his house, and he liked to administer tests to his guests. Here, in "Victory at Sea," *Sensation Comics #15* (March 1943), Steve Trevor proposes administering a lie detector test to Diana Prince.

TOP In May 1942, Franklin Delano Roosevelt created the Women's Army Auxiliary Corps. One hundred fifty thousand women joined the army, filling jobs that freed more men for combat. "The Women's Army Auxiliary Corps appears to be the final realization of woman's dream of complete equality of men," Margaret Sanger wrote in the *New York Herald Tribune*. In "Battle for Womanhood," in 1943, just when American women's participation in the war effort, both at home and abroad, was most crucial, Dr. Psycho, disguised as the ghost of George Washington, attempts to convince Americans that "women will betray their country through weakness."

MIDDLE Meanwhile, also in "Battle for Womanhood," Dr. Psycho ties up his wife, Marva, in his psychological laboratory, much as Hugo Münsterberg had strapped Radcliffe students to machines in Harvard's Psychological Laboratory. Dr. Psycho insists, "No woman can be trusted with freedom!"

BOTTOM As women's involvement in the war increased, so did Wonder Woman's. In "The Invisible Invader," *Comic Cavalcade #3* (Summer 1943), she bests the German military. Later, she's promoted to "General Wonder Woman." "Women are gaining power in the man's world!" Wonder Woman reported to her mother, Hippolyte, at the end of 1943.

Marston met Olive Byrne at Tufts in 1925, when he was her psychology professor, and also the director of a student mental health clinic. Byrne's Tufts sorority, Alpha Omicron Pi, appears in Wonder Woman as Etta Candy's sorority, Beeta Lamba, and the mental health clinic appears as a "Fun Clinic." Gay, who was rescued by Wonder Woman after trying to drown herself in Niagara Falls, gets a new lease on life when she joins Etta's sorority, just as Olive Byrne did. At left, from "The Fun Foundation," *Sensation Comics #27* (March 1944). Olive Byrne moved in with Marston and his wife in the summer of 1926. (Marston gave his wife a choice: either he would leave her or Byrne could live with them.) Eventually, each woman had two children by Marston. Byrne and Marston marked their anniversary as November 21, 1928, which is when Byrne began wearing thick bracelets on her wrists—the same bracelets worn by Wonder Woman.

LEFT In 1944, *Wonder Woman* became a newspaper strip, syndicated by King Features. Out of the hundreds of comic books in circulation at the time, no other comic-book superhero, aside from Superman and Batman, had ever made the gigantic jump from comic books to newspaper syndication, with its vast daily circulation. Marston had so much work to do that he hired an assistant, a nineteen-year-old student of his named Joye Hummel. To celebrate the newspaper syndication, Gaines had his artists draw a panel in which Superman and Batman, rising out of the front page of a daily newspaper, call to Wonder Woman, who's leaping onto the page, "Welcome Wonder Woman!" Another advertisement promoting the newspaper strip appeared in *Sensation Comics #32* (August 1944).

TOP, RIGHT In "The Amazon Bride," *Comic Cavalcade #8* (Fall 1944), Wonder Woman agrees to marry Steve—until she wakes up and realizes, to her relief, that it was only a nightmare. The psychiatrist Frederic Wertham found the feminism in *Wonder Woman* repulsive: "As to the 'advanced femininity,' what are the activities in comic books which women 'indulge in on an equal footing with men'? They do not work. They are not homemakers. They do not bring up a family. Mother-love is entirely absent. Even when Wonder Woman adopts a girl there are Lesbian overtones." Wertham's rival, the psychiatrist Lauretta Bender, an expert on childhood aggression, disagreed. *Wonder Woman* comic books display "a strikingly advanced concept of femininity and masculinity," Bender wrote, admiring how the "women in these stories are placed on an equal footing with men and indulge in the same type of activities." Wertham wanted comic books banned. Bender thought comic books helped children grow.

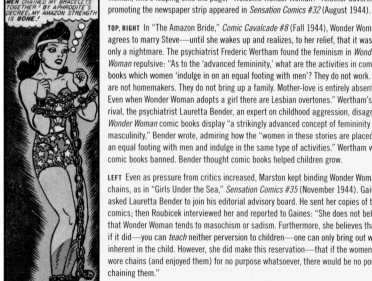

LEFT Even as pressure from critics increased, Marston kept binding Wonder Woman in chains, as in "Girls Under the Sea," *Sensation Comics #35* (November 1944). Gaines asked Lauretta Bender to join his editorial advisory board. He sent her copies of the comics; then Roubicek interviewed her and reported to Gaines: "She does not believe that Wonder Woman tends to masochism or sadism. Furthermore, she believes that even if it did—you can *teach* neither perversion to children—one can only bring out what is inherent in the child. However, she did make this reservation—that if the women slaves wore chains (and enjoyed them) for no purpose whatsoever, there would be no point in chaining them."

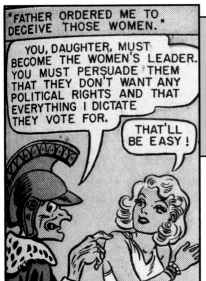

In 1948, Marston's widow, Elizabeth Holloway Marston, urged DC Comics to hire her as Wonder Woman's new editor. Instead, DC Comics appointed Robert Kanigher. Kanigher hated Marston's creation and, in his treatment of Marston's character the Duke of Deception, made clear his belief that women's political equality was a mistake— one that could be easily undone. In Kanigher's story "Deception's Daughter," *Comic Cavalcade #26* (April–May 1948), the Duke and his daughter, Lya, conspire to reverse women's political gains.

An unusually evocative cover from the Kanigher era depicts Wonder Woman bringing a woman trapped in Victorian clothing, and Victorian mores, into the modern world. Cover, *Wonder Woman #38* (November–December 1949).

After the war, Wonder Woman followed the hundreds of thousands of American women who had worked during the war, only to be told, when peace came, not just that their labor was no longer needed but also that it threatened the stability of the nation, by undermining men. She was also no longer drawn by Harry G. Peter, who died in 1958. Typical of the Kanigher era is this cover from *Sensation Comics #94* (November–December 1949). Wonder Woman grew weaker every year. In the 1950s, she became a babysitter, a fashion model, and a movie star. She wanted, desperately, to marry Steve. Kanigher also abandoned the "Wonder Women of History" pull-out; he replaced it with a series about weddings, called "Marriage a la Mode."

Wonder Woman #178 (September–October 1968) marks the beginning of what's known as the "Diana Prince Era," during which, as Joanne Edgar explained in *Ms.* magazine in 1972, "she relinquished her superhuman Amazon powers along with her bracelets, her golden magic lasso, and her invisible plane. She became a human being. Diana Prince, clad now in boutique pant suits and tunics, acquired conventional emotions, vulnerability to men, the wisdom of an adviser (a man, of course, named I Ching), and the skills of karate, kung fu, and jiujitsu. In other words, she became a female James Bond, but without his sexual exploits."

In December 1972, DC Comics published a "Special! Women's Lib Issue," *Wonder Woman #203*, written by a science-fiction writer named Samuel R. Delany and meant to be the first installment of a six-part storyline. In the first story, Diana Prince defeats a department store owner who is underpaying women workers. In each of the remaining five stories, she was to face another anti-feminist. "Another villain was a college advisor who really felt a woman's place was in the home," Delany later said. "It worked up to a gang of male thugs trying to squash an abortion clinic staffed by women surgeons. And Wonder Woman was going to do battle with each of these and triumph." Only the first story was ever published.

In 1972, the founding editors of *Ms.* put Wonder Woman on the cover of the magazine's first regular issue. They hoped to bridge the distance between the feminism of the 1910s and the feminism of the 1970s with the Wonder Woman of the 1940s, the feminism of their childhood. "Looking back now at these Wonder Woman stories from the '40s," Gloria Steinem said, "I am amazed by the strength of their feminist message." For all her controversy and ambiguity, Wonder Woman is best understood as the missing link in the history of the struggle for women's equality, a chain of events that begins with the woman suffrage campaigns of the 1910s and ends with the troubled place of feminism a full century later.

race will have a far greater love capacity than the current one and I mean physical love as well as other forms." As to the people who would bring about this new race, "Ethel and Mimi were willing to buck the crowd," Holloway allowed (Sanger's family called her Mimi), but "they both went into free love which won't work."[17]

What Marston wanted went well past free love. Olive Byrne wanted, desperately, to be part of a family. Holloway wanted something else.

When Marston told Holloway he wanted Byrne to move in with them—and told her she had to choose between that and living without him—she was thinking about more than the sexual arrangements. She was also wondering whether this way of living might offer a solution to the bind she was in as a woman who wanted to have both a career and children.

Hardly a magazine was sold, in 1925 and 1926, that didn't feature an article that asked, "Can a Woman Run a Home and a Job, Too?"[18] Freda Kirchwey, a Barnard graduate who was managing editor of the *Nation,* decided to tackle the question with a series of autobiographical essays she published under the title "These Modern Women." It spotlighted professional women; its aim was "to discover the origin of their modern point of view toward men, marriage, children, and jobs." One of the women Kirchwey featured was Lou Rogers, the feminist cartoonist who had been on the staff of *Judge* with Harry G. Peter and worked as the art director of Margaret Sanger's *Birth Control Review.* Most of the women Kirchwey invited to write for the *Nation* in 1926 shared more or less the same view about the crux of the matter. The modern woman, Crystal Eastman explained, is "not altogether satisfied with love, marriage, and a purely domestic career. She wants money of her own. She wants work of her own. She wants some means of self-expression, perhaps, some way of satisfying her personal ambitions. But she wants a husband, home and children, too. How to reconcile these two desires in real life, that is the question."[19] That was Holloway's question, too.

In "The Professional Woman's Baby," in an April 1926 issue of the *New Republic,* Helen Glynn Tyson, who had earlier written for Sanger's *Birth Control Review,* looked at the census data and the state of the conversation and despaired. The Equal Rights Amendment—"Men and women shall have equal rights throughout the United States"—had been introduced into Congress in 1923, but Tyson found it woefully naïve; it failed to offer any remedy for, or even any illumination of, the structural challenges of combining motherhood and work. "In college, when we discussed our 'careers' we had the whole thing neatly worked out," Tyson wrote ruefully. "The day-time care of the child, I remember, was to be delegated to 'experts,' skilled in that particular task. Alas! Where are those 'experts'? The devoted female relative is of course extinct; even if she were not, the modern mother would no longer be satisfied with the care Aunt Minnie could render." Group day care was deficient; there was hardly any. And who could find a nanny sufficiently trained in the psychological science of child study, promoted by *Child Study*, the magazine Holloway worked for? "This, then, is the dilemma of the modern mother," Tyson wrote, "stated so often, in one way or another, and as often left unsolved: on the one hand, a keen interest in her professional work, a real need of income, the fear of mental stagnation, and the restlessness that comes from filling all her day with petty things; on the other hand, new demands in child care that were unknown even a decade ago; a supply of domestic helpers that is fast diminishing both in quality and quantity; and, like a cloud over all her activities, her own emotional conflict that is rooted deep in her maternity."[20]

Nineteen twenty-six also saw the publication of a number of landmark books on this same subject. In *Woman's Dilemma*, Alice Beal Parsons asked "whether the physical and mental differences between the sexes are such to warrant different social functions, and whether the home will necessarily be endangered if the mother has an outside job." Parsons thought not. She argued that the solution to the "woman's dilemma" was for men to do more housework and child care. "When she does as much work outside the home as her husband," Parsons thought, "there would seem to be no reason why she should in the future be responsible for all the domestic chores."[21] Suzanne La Follete, in *Concerning Women*, took a dark view of whether this was likely, but she did believe that "women have equality almost within their grasp": since they'd achieved political equality and were on the way toward achieving legal equality, there remained only the pursuit of economic justice.[22] In *Marriage and Careers: A Study of One Hundred Women Who Are Wives, Mothers, Homemakers and Professional Workers,* Virginia MacMakin Collier reported the results of a study of professional married women with children, conducted for the Bureau of Vocational Information; she presented the problem this way: "Scores of eager girls just stepping out of college, scores even of already happily married women, are asking themselves the question: How shall they have the heritage of happiness implied in a husband and children and still retain the mental activity and stimulus of interesting work?" Between 1910 and 1920, the percentage of married women who worked had nearly doubled, and the number of married women in the professions had risen by 40 percent, Collier noted. "The question, therefore, is no longer, should women combine marriage with careers, but how?"[23]

Elizabeth Holloway Marston, a New Woman living in a New Age, made a deal with her husband. Marston could have his mistress. Holloway could have her career. And young Olive Byrne, trained in the science of psychology, would raise the children.[24] They'd find a way to explain it, to hide it. The arrangement would be their secret. No one else need ever know.

16

THE EMOTIONS OF NORMAL PEOPLE

"I WAS GOING ON FOR A PH.D. but I got sidetracked by marriage and motherhood," Olive Byrne later said, explaining why she never finished her dissertation. She didn't mention that she wasn't the one who got pregnant.[1]

Olive Byrne entered a doctoral program in psychology at Columbia in the fall of 1926. The Psychology Department at Columbia offered a PhD and a one-year master's degree. Before Byrne began, she told Noah Slee that she had done so much research for Marston during the summer after graduating from Tufts that she thought she might even be able to complete a doctoral degree in two years.[2] She finished the coursework required for a master's degree, thirty credits' worth, in one year. She received the degree on June 1, 1927, having submitted a master's thesis titled "The Evolution of the Theory and Research on Emotions," a review of the scholarship on the psychology of emotions, in which she featured Marston's work prominently.[3] One month later, the Columbia Psychology Department appointed Marston as a lecturer.[4]

Marston was still sliding down the academic ladder, rung by rung, from chairman of the department at American University, to assistant professor at Tufts, to lecturer at Columbia, where he was hired only because the department was in dire need of teachers. Psychology had become its own department at Columbia in 1920 and had grown so fast that it was suffering from both a shortage of faculty and an overabundance of graduate students. "In 1923–24 there were 67 candidates for the Ph.D. on our list, and with Master's Essays included there were 85 separate research problems under supervision," according to a department report. Hiring lecturers like Marston was one solution to the problem. Another solution, urged by the report, "was to keep the number of Ph.D. candidates down." Robert Woodworth, the department chair, made a study of recent alumni and found that although a significant number of women had received doctorates, only a few of them were working in the field.[5] The solution to the too-big graduate program seemed to be to encourage women to drop out.

By no means was Woodworth the only chairman or psychology the only department to arrive at this solution. Between 1900 and 1930, the percentage of PhDs awarded to women doubled, and then, for three decades, it fell.[6] The gains made by women in the beginning of the twentieth century were lost, everywhere, as women who had fought their way into colleges and graduate programs found that they were barred from the top ranks of the academy. No structural changes had been made that would have allowed women to pursue a life of the mind while raising children: many quit; many were kicked out; most gave up. In a 1929 study called *Women and the Ph.D.*, Barnard economist Emilie Hutchinson quoted an associate professor who said that when, across the country, "every president and head of department insists on having only men in higher positions, it seems to me idiotic to encourage women to take the higher degrees with the thought of getting anything like a fair deal."[7]

During Olive Byrne's second year of coursework, in 1927–28, she nearly completed the number of credits required for a doctorate, but she never submitted a dissertation.[8] She'd have been discouraged from finishing, because she was a woman. But she also had to quit, to take care of a baby. It wasn't hers.

"In 1927 we decided that if we were going to have children we'd better get started," Holloway explained.[9] She was thirty-four years old. Holloway wanted to get pregnant, but she had not the least intention of quitting her job. She had left *Child Study* to take a position as an editor in the New York offices of the *Encyclopaedia Britannica*.

The *Encyclopaedia Britannica,* begun in 1768, had had no complete revision since the eleventh edition, in 1910–11. Work on the fourteenth edition had begun in 1926; it was the first edition to have two staffs, one British and one American.[10] The plan was for this new edition to be not only more American than earlier editions but also more journalistic. The work took two and a half years and cost $2.5 million. The resulting encyclopedia consists of twenty-four volumes, and more than 37,000,000 words, written by more than 3,500 contributors. Nearly half of those contributors were American (the 1,500 contributors to the eleventh edition, by contrast, included only 123 Americans). "Here is no mere revision," a critic for the *New York Times* wrote, upon the encyclopedia's completion. "From A to Z, the book has been almost wholly rewritten."[11] Holloway was a senior editor, with responsibility for acquiring and editing articles in seven areas: psychology, law, home economics, medicine, biology, anthropology, and personnel relations. She edited more than six hundred articles.[12]

Holloway got pregnant in December 1927. Olive Byrne dropped out of Columbia in the spring of 1928 to prepare for the baby, just as the book she'd been helping Marston write, *Emotions of Normal People,* finally appeared, published under his name alone.

Emotions of Normal People is, among other things, a defense of homosexuality, transvestitism, fetishism, and sadomasochism. The book argues that forms of sexual expression commonly derided as "abnormal" are, in fact, entirely normal. Marston dedicated the book to five women: his mother, his aunt Claribel, Elizabeth Holloway Marston, Marjorie Wilkes Huntley, and Olive Byrne. *Emotions of Normal People* appeared in both London and New York, as part of a series called the International Library of Psychology, Philosophy and Scientific Method, edited by the British psychologist C. K. Ogden. It was in some ways a triumph. Authors who contributed to this series include Wittgenstein, Piaget, and Adler.[13]

The book outlines Marston's theory of the four primary emotions. Its chief argument is that much in emotional life that is generally regarded as abnormal (for example, a sexual appetite for dominance or submission) and is therefore commonly hidden and kept secret is actually not only normal but *neuronal:* it inheres within the very structure of the nervous system. The work of the clinical psychologist, Marston argued, is to provide patients with an "emotional re-education" (of the sort that he provided in a student clinic at Tufts). He wrote, "The only practical emotional re-education consists in teaching people that there is a norm of psycho-neural behaviour, not dependent in any way upon what their neighbours are doing, or upon what they think their neighbours want them to do. *People must be taught that the love parts of themselves, which they have come to regard as abnormal, are completely normal.*"[14]

But *Emotions of Normal People* failed to earn Marston the regard of his profession. For the most part, the book was ignored. One of the only reviews to appear in the United States ran in the *Journal of Abnormal and Social Psychology*. It was ecstatic. "This book presents the first logical and sensible treatise on emotions that psychology has ever offered," it read. "Dr. Marston says that his work is the result of 15 years of experimental and clinical study, and the reader can readily believe that those fifteen years have proven to be worth while." The review was written by Olive Byrne.[15]

Reviewing a book written by someone you're living with and sleeping with is, needless to say, wrong. At a time when male scientists and scholars routinely published their wives' and girlfriends' research and writing under their own names, Marston was remarkably forthright in publicly acknowledging the contributions of women to his scholarship as often as he did: he dedicated his books to them; he cited their assistance in the text and in footnotes; and, in a textbook he published called *Integrative Psychology,* he listed Holloway as coauthor.[16] Olive Byrne's work for Marston was, at times, merely secretarial; she marked letters and manuscripts she typed for him with the standard secretarial postscript "wmm/ob."[17] But there is an extraordinary slipperiness, too, in how Marston, Holloway, and Byrne credited authorship; their work is so closely tied together and their roles so overlapping that it is often difficult to determine who wrote what. This seemed not to trouble any of them one bit. Byrne's willingness to write a review of *Emotions of Normal People*—a book to which, in addition to the other ways in which she was involved with the author, she had contributed both significant original research (while at Tufts, studying the Baby

Party) and a review of the scholarly literature (her Columbia master's thesis)—suggests that the family rule regarding authorship amounted to: Anything goes.

But anything does not go in academia. Early in 1928, just after Holloway got pregnant, Marston learned that his lectureship at Columbia would not be renewed. He had now lost appointments at three different universities. He scrambled to find another. He must have known that his chances were slim. He turned to his alma mater.

"Do you know of any job for me next year?" Marston wrote to Edwin G. Boring, at Harvard, on March 18, 1928, enclosing his curriculum vitae.[18]

Boring had joined Harvard's Psychology Department in 1922, just after Marston left, but Marston knew him because they had both worked with Robert Yerkes during the war. Boring also knew Holloway. She'd begun corresponding with him at the end of 1927, just before Boring was elected president of the American Psychological Association. Boring was Holloway's chief source for articles on the subject of psychology in the *Encyclopaedia Britannica*. Not only did Boring contribute a number of articles himself, including the entry on experimental psychology, he also recruited his colleagues to write for Holloway.[19]

Holloway was a feisty and decisive editor. But she never passed up a chance to promote her husband's work. She wrote to Boring about an article on emotions that had come from the British office, describing it as "a nice misty, mossy, philosophical article full of timely Wundtian witticism." What she wanted, though, was "a good, live, up-to-date American article." What she wanted was thirty-five hundred words and, she wrote Boring, "I want Bill to write it, he having just completed a survey of the most important work now being done in this field."[20] (It wasn't her husband who had just completed a survey of the most important work now being done in the field of emotions; it was Byrne. That survey was her master's thesis.)

Holloway included Marston's entry for "Emotions, Analysis of," in the fourteenth edition of the *Encyclopaedia Britannica;* she published it under Marston's name alone. Its brief bibliography lists five sources, including a journal article by Marston and Byrne's master's thesis. But the entry's entire purpose seems to have been to promote Marston's theory of emotions, citing his work as demonstrating "a definite neurological basis for love and appetite as the two basic compound emotions."[21]

Marston had plenty of love and plenty of appetite. What he didn't have was a job. When he wrote to Boring looking for work, Boring suggested that he write to the Harvard Appointments Bureau.[22]

"I should like to register my name as desirous of a position teaching psychology next year at a salary of thirty five hundred dollars," Marston wrote to the bureau. "I am especially interested in personality work, and clinical work in emotions." He described himself as a "university and consulting psychologist." One kind of work he had done, and would be happy to continue doing, was running "personality clinics for emotional readjustment of students," like the clinic he'd run at Tufts, helping students learn to love their "love parts."[23]

"Dr. Marston has been serving as lecturer in our department during the present year and part of last year," Columbia's A. T. Poffenberger reported, in a letter of recommendation that he submitted to the Harvard Appointments Bureau. "He has made an excellent impression both in his teaching and in his immediate contact with students. He has directed a number of minor researches, although his work was primarily in our undergraduate department. We all like him as an associate and would seriously consider trying to retain him if a position suitable for him were available. Dr. Marston's qualities warrant an unusually good position in my opinion."[24] Still, if Marston's colleagues at Columbia had admired him, they'd have renewed his appointment, if only because the department had too many students and not enough teachers.

Marston's only unqualified letter of recommendation came from Leonard Troland, an expert in optics who was well versed in both physics and psychology. Troland had known Marston and Holloway since high school. He was also among the men in Emerson Hall whom Boring had roped into writing for the *Encyclopaedia Britannica* (Troland contributed the entry on the color black).[25]

"Dr. Marston is a personal friend of mine," Troland wrote in his letter of recommendation. "I have known him for about 20 years. He is a Harvard Ph.D. in psychology and took up some of his work under my instruction. I regard him as a man of high ability and initiative, particularly in the field of research and teaching. He has had training and practice in the legal profession, as well as in psychology. He is well known throughout the country for his investigations and writing concerning the physiology of the emotions. Perhaps his most striking work has to do with methods for detecting intentional falsehood. I recommend him very highly."[26]

Boring offered a much more limited endorsement. "Dr. Marston is a very dynamic and effective psychologist, who is an expert in physiological research on the emotions and on certain phases of the problems of personality. He can teach and interest students. He will always be productive. Some people think that he is a little too much of a specialist." Then he amplified this last point: "I may add that this matter of specialization is perhaps a little extreme, and that whatever he teaches it is likely to be colored by his own views. It is also true that his enthusiasm goes to the extent of a mild eccentricity. He might fit very well in some places, but in the average, normal, general department of psychology he would probably remain separated in his work, and even at times open to the charge of sensationalism."[27] This was candid and fair and, all things considered, generous.

A more critical report came from Edward Thorndike, a colleague of Marston's at Columbia. During the war, Thorndike had supported Marston's work for Yerkes's Psychology Committee. His opinion of Marston had since soured. Thorndike's typewritten letter included a remarkable correction: "Dr. W. M. Marston is a competent ~~psychologist~~ lecturer in psychology." The rest of the letter was not hopeful: "His success in past work is a measure of his future promise. It has been only moderate."[28]

But the most damning letter in Marston's file came from Marston's former adviser Herbert Langfeld, who had taught both Marston and Holloway and knew them both well. He had since left Harvard for Princeton. "As the Harvard records will undoubtedly show, Dr. Marston was an excellent student and always received very good grades as an undergraduate," Langfeld began. "He got his Ph.D. degree without any difficulty." Then Langfeld listed his reservations: "He has had several positions, which he has not been able to hold. Rumors have come to me from these various places, which I have not been able to substantiate. It therefore makes it very difficult for me to say anything further than that when he took his degree at Harvard he gave every promise of doing excellent work." On the bottom of this Langfeld typed, "Confidential: for office only."[29] With a letter like that in his file, no one would hire Marston, ever. It was blacklist language. It was the kind of thing said about homosexuals. Marston never again secured a regular academic appointment.

Olive Byrne, wearing bracelets, holding Moulton Marston in the fall of 1928

Holloway worked throughout her pregnancy. "If you don't quit that job, that child will never be born," Marston said to her. She left work on a Tuesday and took the train home to Darien, Connecticut. (Holloway never learned how to drive.) She nearly had the baby in the house, but when the contractions started, Marjorie Wilkes Huntley was there; she put Holloway in Marston's car and raced her to Lenox Hill Hospital in Manhattan. "Zaz got me to New York on time," Holloway said.[30] The baby was born on August 26, 1928. They named him Moulton.

"You are quite a sport to keep on with your job as you did," Boring wrote to Mrs. Marston, sending congratulations.[31] But Mrs. Marston very much intended to keep on with her job. Her husband was out of work. They had made other arrangements for the baby.[32] Once, asked on a questionnaire about how soon she had returned to work after a pregnancy, she refused all the answers offered, checked off "Other," and wrote in, "as soon as physically able."[33]

Holloway went back to work in New York, leaving her newborn in the country with Marston and Byrne.

"The city air didn't agree with the baby," Olive Byrne wrote to J. Noah Slee that November, from Connecticut.

"Them's the facts of my seeming flitting about," she told her uncle.[34] More she did not say.

17

THE CHARLATAN

ON JULY 21, 1928, Carl Laemmle, the head of Universal Studios in Hollywood, took out an advertisement in the pages of the *Saturday Evening Post:*

Wanted—A Psychologist

Somewhere in this country there is a practical psychologist—accomplished in the science of the mind—who will fit into the Universal organization. He can be of real help in analyzing certain plot situations and forecasting how the public will react to them. As moving pictures are reaching out more and more for refinements, such a *mental showman* will have great influence on the screens of the world. I will pay well for such a person.[1]

Laemmle, who was sixty-one and barely five feet tall, had opened his first nickelodeon in Chicago in 1906, when he was thirty-nine: he put 120 folding chairs in a converted clothing store on Milwaukee Avenue that he rented from an undertaker. Three years later, he founded the Independent Moving Pictures company, in New York, and began producing films in a makeshift studio on Eleventh Avenue. In 1912, he made the first "feature film," a five-reeler. After earning millions of dollars making silent films starring Mary Pickford ("Uncle Carl," as he was called, established the star system), he founded Universal

Marston and Byrne (together, in the back) conducting experiments at Columbia in 1928

Pictures in 1915 (the year Marston's film, *Jack Kennard, Coward,* won the Edison prize), moved his operation to Los Angeles, and built Universal City Studios on four hundred acres. Laemmle wanted a mental showman in 1928 because the era of the silent film was coming to an end and he had no idea what to do. He was tired and ready to retire. He didn't much like talkies. And he was worried about the growing threat of censorship, against which a psychologist, he thought, might prove the best defense.[2]

And so he took out an ad in the *Saturday Evening Post.* "While a lot of people may have taken the ad for a gag," *Variety* reported, hundreds of letters poured in, some from "the greatest minds, psychologically speaking, in the country."[3] When Marston read Laemmle's ad, he'd been blacklisted from academia and was about to become a father. He needed work.

Marston's interest in the movies had lately resurfaced. In January 1928, right after Holloway got pregnant, Marston and Byrne had conducted an experiment at the Embassy Theatre in New York. Marston invited reporters and photographers to watch as he seated an audience of six chorus girls—three blondes and three brunettes—in the front row of the theater. (When Boring said, in his letter of recommendation, that Marston had a penchant for sensationalism, he was alluding to the Embassy Theatre experiment.) Then he hooked the girls up to blood pressure cuffs—he called the device a "Love Meter"—and recorded their level of excitement as they watched the romantic climax of MGM's 1926 silent film *Flesh and the Devil,* starring Greta Garbo. He claimed his findings proved that brunettes are more easily aroused than blondes.[4]

"The experiment was made by Dr. William Marston, a lecturer on psychology at Columbia University; his laboratory was a Broadway theatre, and his audience was mostly press agents," a newspaper in Wisconsin reported.[5] Marston had founded an advertising agency; the MGM study was a publicity stunt. It worked. The story, picked up by the Associated Press and sometimes accompanied by a publicity photo featuring Marston, Byrne, and beautiful chorus girls hooked up to a tangle of machinery, appeared in papers all over the country. It was even featured in a newsreel, and shown in theaters: "Dr. William Marston tests his latest invention: The Love Meter!"[6]

Marston was by no means the only psychologist in America interested in the movies. He wasn't even alone among psychologists at Columbia interested in the movies. There was Walter Pitkin, for one. Pitkin, the American editor of the *Encyclopaedia Britannica,* was Holloway's boss. He was also a psychologist. In 1905, Pitkin, who held no college degrees, had been hired as a lecturer in psychology at Columbia on the strength of a recommendation from William James. He also worked as an editor for the *New York Tribune* and the *New York Evening Post.* He was one of the most influential editors of the first half of the twentieth century. He was appointed professor of journalism at Columbia's School of Journalism in 1912, its founding year. He taught there until his retirement in 1943. One of his best-known books was *How to Write Stories,* published in 1923.[7] Marston met Pitkin through Holloway. He became one of Pitkin's closest friends.[8] They shared an interest in film, and in the intersection of storytelling and psychology. They went to a great many movies together.

"He and I used to study the talking pictures from a psychological point of view," Pitkin later wrote, "and we quickly agreed that Charlie Chaplin & Cohorts were either fools or liars (maybe both) in asserting that the talkie had a weaker appeal than the silent. You didn't have to be terribly learned in matters of perception and general esthetics to know that, if the integration of sight and sound could be perfected, the esthetic effect would enormously surpass that of sight alone. So Bill and I became noisy rooters for the talkies. We were, I think, the first among academes."[9]

Other psychologists were interested in film, too, following Münsterberg's pioneering work of the 1910s. An MA student in Byrne's graduate program at Columbia had conducted a study about how much people remembered after watching a movie.[10] In 1929, Will Hays, president of the Motion Picture Producers and Distributors of America, wrote to the president of Columbia, offering money to fund research. (Hays was interested in gathering evidence in support of a censorship code.)[11] Marston's friend Leonard Troland had worked for the Technicolor Motion Picture Corporation of California; in 1925, while still teaching at Harvard, he had been named Technicolor's director of research. Later, he moved to California. (Troland, who killed himself in 1932, has been credited with developing both two-color photography and the technology behind color motion pictures.)[12]

Not many psychologists, though, had as much experience as Marston in thinking about films and feelings. Universal Studios called him in for an interview.

"Carl Laemmle Digs the Doc," *Variety* reported on December 26, 1928, announcing that Marston, "Who Went Through Harvard Three Times Without Quitting, Will Tell 'Em How and What at Universal City." Said Laemmle, "I have at last found the man."[13]

The next day, Marston was interviewed by a reporter for the *New York Evening Post* in Universal's offices in New York. "Dr. Marston, who won't write B.A., PhD, and LLB after his name in another week because Hollywood is touchy about such things, is going to be the psychological authority behind all forthcoming motion pictures from one big concern," the *Post* reported. "He has just signed a contract as director of the new public service bureau of that corporation. His job will be to test out the emotional value of stories and treatment, to run the film through the chemical path of scientific scrutiny. That spells revolution for the good old blood and thunder, slush and sentiment school of the cinema."

"A motion picture must be true to life," Marston said. "If a picture portrays a false emotion it trains people seeing it to react abnormally. It is a false emotion which shows man as the leader and dictator in a love affair. Woman should be shown as the leader every time. She controls and directs the love affair. Maybe she uses her supposed submission to a cave man to get more of a grip on him ultimately. But the picture should show cave man appeal operates only as a challenge to that woman to captivate that pretty tough bird!"

He trotted out his theory of emotions and explained how he'd apply it to Universal films.

"We expect to show the actual mechanics of the emotion of love, with the interesting aspects of submission and domination and captivation," he said. "People always accept the truth once it is applied to their own experience. What they want is a successful love affair, and they will take anything that will help them to achieve this."

He explained that Hollywood offered him a bigger psychological laboratory than Harvard had.

"The movies are the only known type of emotional stimulus wherein the experimenter can control the emotions of those who watch," Marston said. "It can't be done with any other vehicle at all. I hope to present these emotional problems to the audiences themselves by a series of educational aims showing the mechanics of emotion and also by letting spectators write their own endings to a picture."

The reporter concluded: "No regret tinges this optimistic scientist's desertion of the laboratory and lecture platform for the motion picture studio. He is dedicating himself to a greater work."[14]

Marston had just finished a stint of teaching at NYU, where he'd offered a course during the fall semester, as an adjunct instructor.[15] The first week of January, he went to Washington Square to clean out his office, and there, and then at Grand Central Station while waiting for the train back to Darien, he was interviewed by a student writing for the school newspaper—a piece of publicity Marston had no doubt arranged himself. Marston explained that his new job would involve approving every story before shooting. "In this manner," he said, "a scenario will be made psychologically sound before it is turned over to the moving picture technicians for actual production." He'd approve every film after production and before distribution, too. "No other

Left to right: Carl Laemmle Jr., Elizabeth Holloway Marston, Moulton ("Pete") Marston, William Moulton Marston, and Carl Laemmle in 1929, when the Marstons and Olive Byrne (not pictured) arrived in Hollywood

organization," Marston said, "not even the church, is so powerfully equipped to serve the public psychologically as is the motion picture company."[16]

In January 1929, Marston, Holloway, Byrne, and five-month-old Moulton took a train across the country. (Everyone called the baby Pete.) They left Huntley behind. They stopped in Chicago, where they stayed with Marston's aunt Claribel, who, according to Holloway,

Marston, right, on the set of *The Charlatan*, at Universal
Studios, in 1929

"was so intent on having her friends meet the 'GRREAT Doctor Marston' that the baby, my companion, and I were completely neglected." (By "my companion" Holloway meant Byrne.)[17]

In California, they rented a house in the hills overlooking Los Angeles. Marston drove a Model T to Universal City. Holloway returned to her work for *Encyclopaedia Britannica;* she worked by post. And Byrne took care of baby Pete.[18]

Marston's title at Universal was director of the Public Service Bureau. The plan was for him to work on a trial basis for a few months, with the possibility of signing a five-year contract. But first, *Variety* said, "he's got to prove to the boys out west that a story shouldn't have a happy ending simply because it is sobby in the preceding five and a half reels." He was supposed to help with casting, story editing, and setting up camera shots and, in general, to "apply psychology wherever psychology is needed."[19]

Marston's first idea was to run a contest for moviegoers. He persuaded Laemmle to offer $2,000 in cash prizes for the best answers to the question "Why do alluring women love homely men?" It wasn't an experiment; it was a gimmick, designed to promote Laemmle's latest film, *The Man Who Laughs,* one of the producer's first attempts to use sound. The film, based on a Victor Hugo novel, tells the story of a blind girl who falls in love with a man whose face has been disfigured; his features are contorted into a hideous, permanent grin. Working in Hollywood, Marston said, would allow him to "read the riddle of the public taste." Audience reaction to the love story in *The Man Who Laughs*, he said, "opens up an interesting discussion on an elemental psychological phenomenon": Why do beautiful women love ugly men? He pointed, by way of example, to Arab sheiks and their harems. The sheiks, he said, are "middle-aged, swarthy, leathery skinned, hawk-nosed, thin-lipped men with bristly dirty beards, but who are the objects of adoration on the part of the captivating women whom they have cruelly treated."[20]

Marston conducted some of his work for Laemmle in a laboratory of his own making, at the University of California, Los Angeles. In one experiment, he showed Universal's 1929 film *The Love Trap* to one thousand students, except without the final scene, or "tag," that was later appended to it, in which our heroine, a chorus girl who has been spurned by her husband's well-heeled family, enjoys the satisfaction of humbling them. He wanted to know how audiences handle movies that end badly.[21]

Marston had views on sound in films, too. "Sound and talking undoubtedly increase the entertainment value of a picture," he told a Hollywood reporter. "There is a distinct conflict, however, between pictorial and sound elements, which cannot be entirely avoided until third dimensional pictures are made."[22]

Marston urged Laemmle to hire Walter Pitkin as a story editor. "So to Bill, bless him, I owe an everlasting debt for having taken five years off my age," Pitkin later wrote, "and to Uncle Carl an equal debt for clipping off another five years. I was fifty-one when I went to Hollywood. I couldn't have been more than forty-one when I left, some six months later."[23]

Marston liked to tell a story about a producer calling him into his office and asking for his help in raising $10 million for a new film. Marston said he'd need a few months to set up some meetings with wealthy New Yorkers. An hour and fifteen minutes later, the producer called back.

"Never mind, Marston, about that plan we discussed," he said. "I have the money and we don't need you in the picture." Pitkin had gotten the money by sending a two-foot-long telegram to a friend on Wall Street.[24]

Marston and Pitkin decided to write a book together. *The Art of Sound Pictures* was published in November 1929.[25] "The talkies are the only art that would attract Leonardo da Vinci were he alive to-day," Pitkin and Marston wrote. This art, they explained, "is a baby giant, as clumsy as all babies are. . . . We don't know what the baby will be doing and saying when it grows up. But we are sure it will make its mark in the world."[26]

Much of the book is advice for would-be screenwriters. "Probably nine out of ten stories which fail to sell in Hollywood contain some serious defect in emotional handling," Marston explained. And, because "no successful screen story can contain a universal emotional appeal unless it is highly flavored with erotic passion," would-be screenwriters needed to understand the psychology of sex, and to know that every story ought to demonstrate what he described as psychological laws: the facts that "woman possesses the superior love power," that love always vanquishes force, that "passion is predominantly a male emotion, and that submission in love belongs to the man and not to the woman."[27]

Much of *The Art of Sound Pictures* is a guide to eluding censorship. Marston and Pitkin dedicated a great deal of their attention to explaining, point by point and state by state, what could pass the censors and what couldn't. Branding—"Scene showing branding iron in fire, if application of it is not shown"—okay in New York, Ohio, and Virginia, not allowed in Pennsylvania, Maryland, or Kansas. Sex—"Man and woman (married or unmarried) walking toward bedroom, indicating contemplated intimacy, if they are not shown after the door closes on them"—depends on action. Homosexuality—"Action of characters, indicating they are perverted, as scene showing women kissing each other, if shown in long shot"—generally, not allowed.[28]

Although the book was advertised as "the first complete, practical book on how to write for the talkies," the *New York Times* dismissed it: "What there is in sound pictures to attract the attention of two eminent psychologists is one of those things that nobody can ever understand."[29]

At Universal Studios, Marston had a hand in films like *Show Boat,* in 1929. He also helped get films past the censors, including *All Quiet on the Western Front,* in 1930. When Carl Laemmle's son, Junior Laemmle, took over Universal, he turned it into a specialty shop for horror films: Marston's theory of emotions lies behind the particular brand of psychological terror in Laemmle's *Frankenstein* (1931), *Dracula* (1931), and *The Invisible Man* (1933). Before Marston left Hollywood, he also worked for Paramount. For *Dr. Jekyll and Mr. Hyde* (1931), he tested audience reaction by strapping viewers to blood pressure cuffs while they watched the rushes.[30]

Marston ran his contests, offered his advice, strapped up audiences to his Love Meter, and pottered around from one studio lot to another, drinking with Pitkin, criticizing directors, and giving actors psychological advice. A lot of people thought he was selling hokum.[31] One film Marston worked on, before he was fired from Universal, was a silent film about a fortune-teller. It was called *The Charlatan.*[32]

Marston never got that five-year contract. In 1930, the Motion Picture Producers and Distributors of America adopted what came to be called the Hays Code. It prohibited films from depicting anything that would "lower the moral standards of those who see it," including nudity, childbirth, and homosexuality. The code wasn't much enforced until 1934, but, by then, Carl Laemmle's son and successor had found a better "mental showman" than Marston to vet Universal's films.

When Universal began screening the rushes of Junior Laemmle's *Frankenstein,* starring Boris Karloff, it brought in a rival lie detector developer, Leonarde Keeler, of Keeler, Inc., to test audience reactions. During the war, Marston's colleagues on the Psychology Committee of the National Research Council had found the detection of deception lacking in scientific credibility. In *Frye v. United States,* the courts had roundly rejected its admissibility as evidence in criminal cases. But in 1921, John Larson, a police detective who had earned a PhD in physiology from the University of California, read one of Marston's scholarly papers—"Physiological Possibilities of the Deception Test"—and decided to figure out how to apply the technique to police interrogation. He hired Keeler, a Berkeley high school student, as his assistant. In 1925, Keeler tried to patent what he sometimes called the Emotograph or the Respondograph but eventually settled on calling the Keeler Polygraph ("poly" because it recorded different kinds of things—blood pressure, heart rate, and so on). After Larson moved to Chicago, to work with the Chicago police, Keeler followed him there, to work at the Scientific Criminal Detection Laboratory, the United States' first forensic laboratory—founded by John Henry Wigmore. In 1931, with adjustments to his original design, Keeler was awarded a patent for his polygraph.[33]

Marston, Holloway, Byrne, and baby Pete, along with Walter Pitkin, went back to New York. Marston and Pitkin decided to start their own motion picture company: Equitable Pictures Corporation. Marston, named vice president, owned 15 percent of the stock. Pitkin always had a thousand projects going on, all at once. ("When you walk into a man's house expecting to discuss the financial details of a business deal and find him sitting at the piano with a pencil and musical score composing a symphony it is likely to prove disconcerting," Marston once wrote about him.)[34] He had a lot of story ideas. Once, on *Encyclopaedia Britannica* letterhead, Pitkin scratched out an idea for a film whose plot was to revolve "Around Bill Marston's thesis: How can a woman love & yet make a living? How be *economically* independent & also *erotically* independent?" Its point would be to "Show that free love isn't the solution."[35]

Marston wanted to make that film, a film about the dilemma of the New Woman. He wanted to call it either "Brave Woman" or "Giddy Girl," after his ladies: Holloway and Byrne. He couldn't choose which.

Equitable Pictures was incorporated in October 1929, with ten thousand shares of common stock. Days later, the stock market collapsed.[36] So did Equitable Pictures. A woman, one woman, who could be both economically and erotically independent, would have to wait out the Depression. She'd have to have been a superhero, anyway. And superheroes hadn't been invented yet.

VENUS WITH US

OLIVE BYRNE married William K. Richard of Los Angeles on November 21, 1928, when she was twenty-four years old.[1] She took his name and became Olive Richard. Their first son, Byrne Holloway Richard, was born on January 12, 1931. Another boy, Donn Richard, was born on September 20, 1932. Shortly after that, she told her sons, their father died. William K. Richard had been a very ill man: he had been gassed in the war and suffered from lung problems, from which he'd never recovered. Oddly, she didn't have a single photograph of him.[2]

She had no photograph because there was no William K. Richard. "Olive Richard" was a fiction. (From here on out, I'll call her "Olive," to avoid confusing her with her son Byrne.) Byrne and Donn's father was William Moulton Marston. The wedding date, though, wasn't a lie. In November 1928 Olive Byrne began wearing a pair of close-fitted, wide-banded bracelets. She never took them off. Wonder Woman wears the very same bracelets.

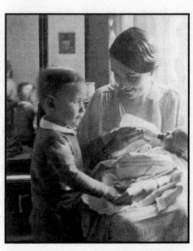

Olive, with bracelets, with Pete and baby Byrne in 1931

Marston and Olive Byrne celebrated November 21, 1928, as their anniversary. As in many families, it often slipped their minds. She wrote in her diary for November 21, 1936: "Anniversary. Which we forgot entirely." And again, on November 21, 1937, bitterly: "Again forgot anniversary which is just as well."[3]

On December 6, 1928, two weeks after the wedding, Marston sent an extraordinary letter to the alumni office at Mount Holyoke College, trumpeting Holloway's accomplishments.

"Do you know," he asked, that "Betty (you used to call her Sadie)"

1. Was Managing Editor of Child Study Magazine, for year 1925–6.
2. Wrote many interesting and successful trade articles, "broadsides", etc. etc. for the Policy Holders Service Bureau, Metropolitan Life Ins. Col., 1926–7, and was offered many inducements to stay with them when, in 1927 she left to become a member of the Editorial Dept. of the Encyclopaedia Britannica, handling psychology, anthropology, medicine, physiology, law, and some biology?
3. Worked as editor and wrote article on "Conditioned Reflex" (to appear as signed article in forthcoming Britannica) until Aug. 21, 1928, when she left to have a large sized infant son, Moulton Marston, weighing 8 lbs. [torn] oz., on August 26?
4. That said son now weighs 11 lbs. 10 oz.? (That's most important!)
5. That she moved her family to the country, to wit, Darien, Conn., for benefit of His Nibs? where we all now reside with varying degrees of resignation, commuters at last.
6. That Betty has been doing graduate work at Columbia, in psychology, for her Ph.D. degree?
7. That she collaborated very largely with her somewhat soft-witted husband in writing EMOTIONS OF NORMAL PEOPLE, published recently in New York and London, Kegan Paul and Harcourt Brace?

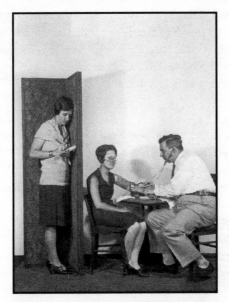

Marston, right, conducting experiments with Olive Byrne,
behind the screen, with bracelets

8. That she is now working as joint author, with same afore-
   said person, on a General Psychology, to appear next Fall,
   published by Prentice-Hall?
9. That Betty, Esq., has been an Instructor in Psychology at
   Washington Square College, New York University for a
   couple of years—and still is such?
10. That she's the best wife and mother who ever lived?[4]

The family arrangement, in which Marston had two wives, one to
work and one to raise the children, involved the promotion of Holloway's career. Olive Byrne had the best possible modern-day psychological training necessary for the modern, scientific management of
children. Her staying home with Holloway's baby allowed Holloway
to lead the life of a professional woman, unencumbered by the duties
of motherhood. And Holloway's income supported Olive's children,
when they came. Marston had never been able to hold a job for more
than a year. He needed Holloway's income, too.

Left to right: Marston, Huntley, Pete, Holloway, and baby Byrne, in 1931

"Many classmates can testify with me that it is very hard to earn a living; the only thing to do is to have a wife, like mine, who will go to work to support you," Marston reported to Harvard in 1930, on the occasion of his fifteenth reunion, when Holloway was working as an assistant editor at *McCall's* magazine. "With the idea of helping her out, I have taught psychology at Columbia and New York universities, and practiced as a 'consulting psychologist'—you know, one of those bennies who tells reluctant business men what the public really thinks of the stuff they're trying to sell, and listens to the confessions of disappointed brides." For a time, Marston occupied offices at 723 Seventh Avenue.[5] But, mostly, in the 1930s, he was out of work.

The census for 1930 records Marston and Holloway, both thirty-six, living at 460 Riverside Drive with Pete, age one, and Marjorie Wilkes Huntley, age forty; Huntley is listed as a "roomer."[6] Huntley was a member of the family, but she came and went; she was restless. She lived, in the course of her life, in thirty-five cities. For a long time, she was a librarian at the Metropolitan Hospital, New York.[7] Neither Olive Byrne nor "Olive Richard" is listed as part of the Marston household in the 1930 census. When she got pregnant, she must have moved out to hide her pregnancy.

Olive's first baby was a towheaded boy. She kept a journal in which she chronicled his childhood. On the cover she wrote, "Byrne Holloway Richard, Jan. 12, 1931 at 7:57 PM." She gave him her name and Holloway's, too, stitching the family together. She was a doting, loving mother. Her book about Byrne is part baby book, part laboratory notebook, a record kept by a woman who wanted to be a doctor and who had trained as a nurse and a psychologist. It is an epitome of scientific motherhood. During baby Byrne's second year: "About Jan. 25. Began handing objects back to adult or putting object back in place. . . . Feb. 7. Paid marked attention to French words spoken to him by W.M.M.—laughed at them, and tried to say 'adieu.' "[8]

Olive also kept diaries, in which she used secret codes. "The only practical emotional re-education consists in teaching people that there is a norm of psycho-neural behaviour, not dependent in any way upon what their neighbours are doing, or upon what they think their neighbours want them to do," Marston had written in *Emotions of Normal People*. But the problem with the way the Marstons lived was that their neighbors would have considered it abnormal. Olive believed the truth was best kept secret: in particular, she didn't want her children to know about it, ever. But keeping up the story required layers of deception. So she invented William K. Richard, a fictional husband. In her diary, when she wrote about Marston, as Holloway's husband, she referred to him "W.M.M." When she wrote about him as her sons' father, she referred to him as "R" or "Ri," for "Richard."[9]

As Olive Byrne's life became more hidden, Margaret Sanger's became more visible. While the Marstons were keeping their family arrangements as secret as possible, Sanger was reaching new levels of fame as the international leader of the birth control movement. In 1931 she testified in Congress on behalf of what she called a "Mothers' Bill of Rights." Awarded the medal of the American Women's Association, Sanger was celebrated in the *New York Herald Tribune:* "Mrs. Sanger deserves this honor; she deserves more honors than a world against whose darkness of mind she has fought bravely and consistently for twenty years is ever likely to give her. Mrs. Sanger has carved, almost single-handed and in the face of every variety of persecution, a trail through the densest jungles of human ignorance and helplessness. She has been many times arrested, assailed and covered with mud—which remains perhaps the most substantial tribute to her pio-

Olive, with bracelets, is holding Donn, with Holloway, pregnant, behind her. Byrne and Pete are at right. Christmas 1932, the year Marston published *Venus with Us*

neering genius." She published an autobiography called *My Fight for Birth Control*. One reviewer wrote, "Margaret Sanger is one of our generation's world-changers."[10]

Marston patched together odd jobs. He taught courses in psychology here and there: at Long Island University, the New School, the Rand School, and, finally, at Katharine Gibbs. In 1931, he talked to a reporter about coeds. "He believes the sexes have changed their professional status," the reporter said, "that the hunted has become the huntress, that men students have more ideas about women than about themselves and that a majority of men prefer to be 'unhappy masters' rather than 'happy slaves.'"[11] Maybe it was Marston who was, in those years, an unhappy master.

He founded a firm called Hampton, Weeks, and Marston. It failed. He explained that failure this way: "I started an advertising agency at the wrong time, lost my last dollar, and was laid low by appendicitis and complications following and took to writing while recovering."[12] He decided to try his hand at fiction.

In June 1932, Marston published a novel, *Venus with Us: A Tale of the Caesar*, set in ancient Rome. The plot concerns Florentia, a sixteen-year-old vestal virgin. "Youth surged within her slender body like a velvet flame." She'd grown up in ancient Rome's version of the convent schools where Olive Byrne was raised: "When she was a little girl, just before her eighth birthday, her mother had brought her to Vesta's Shrine." Before meeting the beautiful Gaius Caesar, who, in the course of the novel, spurns that name to become Julius Caesar, Florentia had known much of women but nothing of men: "Accustomed as she was, from childhood, to the soft beauties of the feminine forms about her, Florentia beheld in Gaius a delicacy of face and figure equal to that of any of her companions." Meeting him, she is overcome by passion. "Her mouth became suddenly dry, her legs trembled beneath her. A creeping fire swept under her skin from her ear tips to toes." Their love is thwarted by Metala, a woman from the island of Lesbos, who keeps Florentia bound in chains. As the story unfolds, various women are abducted and taken to Lesbos. But Caesar and Florentia are helpless before the power of their forbidden love: "They had found each other; and whatever the world might say about it, each felt that their relationship was quite as sacred as the Altar of Vesta." When Florentia has a baby by Caesar, she names her Dorothea. Dorothy was Olive Byrne's favorite name.

The story involves a great deal of dominance and submission. "Oh, my adored Master!" characters cry. Marston devotes lavish attention to describing slaves' chains. "The ceremonial chains used in Roman spectacles were heavy and elaborate. They were intended to symbolize utter subjection of the conquered ruler or other captive of distinction; yet also to ornament and emphasize the beauty or importance of the prisoner thus exhibited," he writes. "Besides leg and arm bands, with connecting chains, Florentia wore a heavy golden collar and belt of gold, with graceful, looping chains of hand-carved links falling from neck and waist to wrists and ankles." The story is an autobiographical erotic fantasy—Marston, hiding stories about his life in fiction— with Olive as Florentia, the cloistered "young girl who quivered with ecstasy at his every touch," and Caesar as a mouthpiece for Marston's psychological theories. When a former slave complains of her slavery, he replies, "The slavery part of it didn't hurt you, in my opinion. I have a notion it's really rather good for people to be compelled to submit to others."[13]

Venus with Us sold for $2.50, had a lurid cover, and was hardly noticed.[14] Marston had tried science. He'd tried law. He'd tried Hollywood. He'd tried advertising. He'd tried fiction. And yet: he still hadn't quite found the medium for his message: love binds.

FICTION HOUSE

ON MARCH 1, 1932, twenty-month-old Charles Augustus Lindbergh Jr., Little Lindy, the son of the aviator, was stolen from his crib. H. L. Mencken called it "the biggest story since the Resurrection." Everyone had a theory. Marston suspected the kidnapper was a woman desperate for a child. "The normal woman needs and desires children," he told the press. Keen to aid the search, he offered his services: "I wrote to Col. Lindbergh, placing the Lie Detector and my experience with it at his disposal." Lindbergh did not reply. In May, the baby was found dead.

Leonarde Keeler, who'd replaced Marston at Universal Studios in 1930 and had been granted a patent in 1931, was selling polygraphs to police departments all over the country. When Marston wrote to Lindbergh offering to help and presenting himself as the inventor of the lie detector, he was staking a claim. He was also trying to burnish his credentials as "the world's first consulting psychologist," which, with a nod to Sherlock Holmes, the world's first consulting detective, was what Marston liked to call himself. There was every reason to believe that Little Lindy's kidnapper was a woman, he explained to reporters, because every woman longs for a baby: "Her arms ache for babies in the same way that a born sculptor's fingers itch for clay and a naturally gifted artist's hands become restless for pencil or brush."[1]

Marston felt he knew a good deal about that ache. In 1932, both Olive Byrne and Elizabeth Holloway were pregnant. Olive gave birth

Left to right: Olive Byrne (in bracelets) holding Donn; Elizabeth Holloway Marston, holding Olive Ann; and Marjorie Wilkes Huntley, holding a doll, in 1933

to a boy, Donn, on September 20, 1932. Five months later, on February 22, 1933, Holloway, forty years old, gave birth to a girl named Olive Ann; everyone called her O.A. Marston took a photograph of his ladies. The three women, wearing pale dresses, sit on a wicker garden bench. In her lap, Olive holds Donn; in hers, Holloway holds O.A.; and in her lap, Huntley holds a baby doll. Huntley had had a hysterectomy.

Marston had nicknames for the women in his house. He called Holloway "Cutie," Olive "Docile," and Huntley "Yasmini." Even the nicknames had nicknames: Keetsie, for Holloway; Dotsie, for Olive; and Zaz or Yaya or Zara, for Huntley.[2]

Holloway went back to work right after O.A. was born. She'd taken a job at Metropolitan Life Insurance as assistant to the vice president in charge of farm mortgages.[3] Olive Byrne now had four children to care for; the youngest two were only five months apart. It must have been very much like raising twins.

Marston dabbled in all sorts of work. He was willing to give psychological advice to anyone who'd pay for it. "My real job, however," he said, "is trying to bring up four youngsters in the four different ways they should grow."[4] The apartment in the city was crowded, but Holloway couldn't leave New York; her paycheck was supporting the

Left to right: Olive Byrne; Marston holding O.A. and Donn, with Byrne in front; Holloway; and Pete, in Cliftondale, 1934

whole family. So Marston, Olive, and the four children went to Massachusetts and moved into the house Marston had grown up in, on Avon Street in Cliftondale, where Marston's mother was living alone. (His father had died in 1923.) Marston told his mother that Olive was the family's widowed housekeeper.[5]

They spent summers on Cape Cod, in a barn next to Ethel Byrne's house. They didn't stay at Ethel's house because, as Olive's son Byrne later explained, his father and his grandmother "didn't always see eye to eye." Ethel had never liked Marston. Olive's brother, Jack, and his wife, Helen, spent summers in Truro, too. Jack Byrne adored his sister, but, like his mother, he didn't trust Marston. "Your Dad is a great ladies man," he once told his nephew Byrne, "Watch him."[6]

Jack Byrne was a writer and editor of pulp fiction. (A "pulp" is a magazine printed on cheap, rough paper, as opposed to a "slick," a magazine printed with a glossy finish.) In the 1930s, Jack Byrne was the editor of Fiction House, a New York–based publisher of pulps—westerns and detective stories, especially. He published *Action Stories, Fight Stories,* and *Detective Book Magazine.* "We want fast-moving yarns," he told writers. "Woman interest is permissible, but must not overshadow action-adventure elements."[7] Marston gave that some thought.

The family at Truro in 1935. Olive Byrne is wearing the bandanna.

.   .   .

In February 1935, when Olive Byrne's sons Byrne and Donn were four and two, Holloway and Marston adopted them. The boys took Marston's name. Byrne Holloway Richard became Byrne Holloway Marston, bearing all three of his parents' names.[8] Becoming Marstons didn't weaken the boys' ties to their mother's side of the family, but it's possible that neither Margaret Sanger nor Ethel Byrne knew that Olive had given up her rights as a parent. The year of the adoption, Olive's family felt that she was hiding herself away.[9]

She relinquished her legal rights as a parent out of concern for her children's security. The Marstons' adopting the boys—giving the family legitimacy—may also have played a role in Holloway's parents' decision to help them out financially. In the summer of 1935, the whole family moved to Rye, New York, to a large wooden house on a lot covered with old cherry trees and surrounded by forty-eight acres of farmland. It was big enough for a family of seven or, when Huntley was there, eight, and close enough to the city that Holloway could live there and take the train to work every day. They named the place Cherry Orchard.[10]

The house had two full stories and an attic. There were three bedrooms in the attic: one for O.A., one for Huntley, and one that Donn and

Cherry Orchard, the Marstons' house in Rye, New York

Byrne shared. Huntley's room was under the eaves; she hung beads in the doorway, filled the room with crystals, and burned incense inside. Pete's bedroom was on the second floor, along with Marston's study, where Marston kept a daybed: he liked to write lying down. There were three other rooms on the second floor: Holloway's bedroom, a bathroom, and Olive's bedroom; these three rooms were adjoining. Marston could get from one bedroom to the other by walking through the bathroom. He slept in both.[11]

Margaret Sanger visited Cherry Orchard whenever she came to New York.[12] And Olive took the children—hers and Holloway's—to visit Sanger at Sanger's house in Fishkill. (The kids all called Sanger "Aunt Margaret.") In August 1935, Olive wrote to Sanger to postpone a visit. "Just at present I'm trying to land a writing job—interviews—for a magazine."[13]

She did land that job, as a staff writer for *Family Circle*, a weekly women's magazine that began appearing in grocery stores in 1932.[14] It was a giveaway; its publisher made money by selling advertising space to the grocery stores that stocked it at checkout counters. It soon became the sixth of what would eventually become known as the Seven Sisters of women's magazines, a group that included *Ladies' Home Journal*, *Good Housekeeping*, and *McCall's*. *Family Circle*'s audience was American mothers, who, in hard times, were shopping thriftily. Its circulation soon reached well over two million readers, nearly all of them women, nearly all of them mothers—homemakers—looking for advice about how to take care of their children and their husbands and their houses.[15]

Olive Byrne's first article for *Family Circle,* a cover story written by "Olive Richard," appeared on November 1, 1935. It was a profile of William Moulton Marston.

Everything about her life Olive Byrne at once hid and, like Marston, almost compulsively exposed. She titled her article about him "Lie Detector." She pretended she had never met him before. "Olive Richard" was a widowed mother of two. Eager to help a friend whose young son is an inveterate liar, she's curious about a device she's heard of, called a lie detector: "So I made up my mind to meet the man who invented it—Dr. William Moulton Marston, psychologist and lawyer." She writes him a letter. "A week later I boarded a train, keeping safe in my bag the gracious letter which I'd received from this famous man inviting me to come and see him. I arrived at his large rambling house set high on a hill." She didn't mention that she lived there. Approaching the house, she describes the scene:

> On the spacious side lawn four children and two cats were jumping hurdles. The hurdle was held by an enormous man with a shock of gray hair standing up on his head. He was shouting directions and helping the game along by suiting the height of the hurdle to the length of each contestant's legs. The children spied me first and drew back as children do in the presence of a stranger.

She didn't mention that she was the children's mother.

> Then the big man saw me and smiled a welcome.
> "Hello," he said. "I've been waiting for you."

She didn't mention that she'd known him for ten years and lived with him for nine.

"You know, you aren't at all the sort of man I expected to meet! I've seen a good many psychologists, but—"

"I know," laughed the doctor. "Lean, long-faced fellows, with high I.Q.'s and lots of academic dignity. I'm sorry to disappoint you, but it's hard for a fat man to be dignified."

And here—here, of all places, in the pages of a women's magazine—her love for him comes through. Maybe that's how she'd first seen him, the first day she walked into a classroom at Tufts and saw him standing at his desk, or the day she walked into a clinic for desperately unhappy students. He was tubby and undignified and funny and warm. She found him wonderful.

This noted scientist is the most genuine human being I've met. He isn't fat—that is, in the ordinary way. He's just enormous all over. We walked through the garden and about the grounds. The doctor asked me about my work and myself, and I told him more in 15 minutes than I'd tell my most intimate friend in a week. He's the kind of person to whom you confide things about yourself you scarcely realize.

She must have felt, from the moment she first met him, that he knew her, that he understood her, that he cared about her.

In the story, he takes her to his study, on the second floor of the house, with windows overlooking the garden.

"May I see the lie detector?" I asked.

"You're looking right at it," laughed the doctor, "or at *him*."

He explains the science of lie detection to her, insisting that telling a lie changes a person's heart rate and raises the blood pressure.

"That doesn't seem possible," I protested. "I couldn't *feel* the slightest change in my heart-beat if I were to tell you that my mother's name is Grace instead of Ethel."

"Want to try it?" asked Dr. Marston.

Marston then attaches a blood pressure cuff to her arm—the machine that, in the experiments they conducted together, Olive Byrne usually took charge of.

> "Tell me what you did last evening—truth or lie, just as you like."
>
> I thought for a minute. Then I decided to be clever. I'd mix truth and falsehood and see if he could tell which was which.[16]

Nearly every story Olive Byrne wrote for *Family Circle* follows this formula. A problem presents itself. Our intrepid reporter decides to visit the world's most famous consulting psychologist. She takes a train to his house. She spends an hour or two with him, Watson to his Holmes. Then she peppers her account of her time with him with true facts—Marston had four children; Olive's mother's name was Ethel—but these are only so many islands of truth in an ocean of lies. *I'd mix truth and falsehood and see if he could tell which was which.*

Maybe the problem she brings is her own shyness. "Olive Richard" tracks down Dr. Marston, summering on Cape Cod.

> The Doctor, who had taken off thirty pounds and put on a deep tan, greeted me with his usual heartiness. "So you're worried about shyness," he said when I had told him what was bothering me. "How lucky you are! Shyness is a great personality asset if you use it right."

She mentioned her own timidity—"Talking to anybody I didn't know was a horror"—but she didn't mention that his pet name for her was "Docile." She only mentioned how he made her feel.

> No one can feel shy in Dr. Marston's presence. He is the sort who brushes away social artificialities and makes you feel completely at ease. I said, "You're the most baffling person."[17]

Maybe the problem she brings him concerns a girl who doesn't know how far she should go with a man before marriage.

Dr. Marston dug a pipe out of a cluttered drawer, stuffed it, and burned three matches to get it going. "How far should a girl go?" he repeated. "I don't know. I'm neither a vice-squad detective nor a glamour girl. But I can give you a rough idea of how far I'd like to have my daughter go when she gets to the man-capturing age."

"That will do nicely," I agreed, amused at the thought of how the Doctor's daughter will handle Pop when she gets a few years older.

(O.A. was only three.)

"Well, first the girl should understand how far there is to go, and the consequences of each step. Then she must decide how far she has to go with a particular man to make him feel her challenge, and at what point she must stop to keep him from thinking she's submitting to him."[18]

Maybe the problem was a woman who was having "husband trouble." To discuss this dilemma, our reporter meets Dr. Marston for lunch at the Algonquin Club.[19] Or maybe the problem is love itself. No matter what the dilemma "Olive Richard" brings him, Dr. Marston charms her, endlessly and utterly.

Much of what Olive Byrne wrote for *Family Circle* is puff ("Puff Richard," her brother Jack called her).[20]

So many of you have made inquiries about Dr. William Moulton Marston's books that I thought I'd better read his "Emotions of Normal People" again to freshen my memory. Dr. Marston, the FAMILY CIRCLE psychologist, is, as you may know, probably the greatest authority in this country on the analysis of emotions, having written the article on that subject for the Encyclopaedia Britannica.[21]

Some of it, though, is penetrating, in its wily way. There were many ways Olive Byrne could have taught herself how to write for a magazine. She'd written for the college newspaper at Tufts. She was a quick study. She'd probably read Walter B. Pitkin's *How to Write Stories*. She'd typed Marston's magazine articles. She'd also talked to her brother. She even wrote a profile of him, for *Family Circle*. "Olive Richard," keen to write pulp fiction, goes to visit Jack Byrne, editor of Fiction House, to ask him for writing advice.

"Well now," drawled Mr. Byrne, a surprisingly young and good-looking New Yorker with an Irish twinkle in his blue eyes, "can you take it young lady? The pulp world is inhabited strictly by he-men and gals have to know their place."

He then explains to her that two hundred pulps are published a month, of which forty-three are detective-story magazines, forty-one are westerns, and five are love-story magazines, though even that many romances, he thought, were too many.

"The pulp world is going sissy," Mr. Byrne lamented. "Even I now have to admit that during the past five years the love interest in stories has become an integral part of our formula. It's a terrible change. Nevertheless, the chief appeal of our magazines is to he-men, who like their drama strong, fast, and straight from the shoulder; their heroes brawny and bold; and their heroines winsome, worried, and weak."

The piece includes a boxed-out feature, listing his rules for writing: "SO YOU'D LIKE TO WRITE FOR THE PULPS! Okay—then take the advice of Jack Byrne, chief Editor of Fiction House." Our reporter never mentions that her subject is her brother. But she does allow, in a wink to him, that he's full of malarkey.

When I asked Mr. Byrne to tell me something about himself, he looked positively disappointed in me.
"Haven't I been telling you all about myself? I'm a 100% pulp product."[22]

So was she. In *Family Circle*, Olive Byrne wrote her own kind of pulp: women's pulp, mother's pulp, homemaker's pulp. Her *Family*

Circle stories are amazingly playful—full of fictions, and full of ambition. Marston wrote a novel, but in the 1930s, it was Olive Byrne, not Marston, who was studying the rules of pulp fiction. She was a 100 percent pulp product: an avid reader of fiction, a student of pulp, and, in her own relentlessly self-effacing way, a daring writer.

"Struggling to write F.C. piece," she noted in her diary early in 1936. "I ain't no author." If only she could tell the truth, she often thought, the truth of her own life. "Idea family history story on my mind," she confided to her diary a few weeks later. "Wish I *could* write." Her confidence failing, she turned to Marston, asking him to write on her behalf. "Got up a new idea for a column—Ri did in my name—for F.C." This was always the temptation, with Marston: to hide behind him. But the great bulk of what she published under her name in *Family Circle* was her own writing. Sometimes the writing came slowly: "Started to work on F.C. story, didn't get far." Sometimes it was boring: "Will probably work on F.C. piece—Ho hum." Sometimes she procrastinated: "Fooled around with F.C. piece." But she knew, too, that some of what she wrote was good.

"Finished F.C. story," she reported. "Not bad."[23]

THE DUKE OF DECEPTION

"**LIE DETECTOR**," Olive Byrne's profile of William Moulton Marston in *Family Circle,* appeared in grocery stores on November 1, 1935. On November 21, Marston told the press that an attorney named Lloyd Fisher had asked him to administer a lie detector test on his client, Bruno Richard Hauptmann. Hauptmann had been arrested in 1934 for the murder of the Lindbergh baby. Early in 1935, in a trial that had gripped the nation, he'd been found guilty and sentenced to death. Fisher had filed an appeal and, on October 15, Hauptmann had been granted a stay of execution while the U.S. Supreme Court entertained a motion to review his case. On October 16, Harold G. Hoffman, governor of New Jersey, visited Hauptmann in jail; he'd begun to suspect that Hauptmann might be innocent. "By using the lie detector," Marston told the *Washington Post*, "we may learn new facts about the kidnapping and killing."[1]

Leonarde Keeler wanted to test Hauptmann, too. Because of the *Frye* ruling, the results from such a test weren't admissible in court, but they did carry weight in criminal detection; Keeler's patented polygraph had become routine in police interrogation. (It had become popular with businessmen, too: they used it to test their employees' fidelity.)[2] Contrary to what Marston told the press, though, Hauptmann's attorney had not asked him to administer a lie detector test. "Mr. Lloyd Fisher, questioned about the report, replied that he had never heard of Dr. Marston," one newspaper reported.[3] In January

1936, Marston brought his lie detector to the governor's office; Hoffman was considering Hauptmann's request for clemency. "Personally," the governor told the *New York Times,* "I would like to have a blood-pressure test made." Marston said the testing would take at least two weeks and that, for his services, he'd charge about $100 a day.[4] Marston never conducted the test, and the governor never granted Hauptmann clemency. Hauptmann died in an electric chair on April 3, 1936.

But, in a few short weeks, Marston, an out-of-work detector of lies, had gotten more publicity than he'd had in years. He decided to dedicate himself to writing a book about the detection of deception while the interest in the Lindbergh baby story was still high. "I hope, even yet, to find a living human being whose mind contains information about the Lindbergh kidnaping," he said. "If such a person exists, his secret knowledge can be read like print by the Lie Detector."[5]

The Lie Detector Test appeared on March 10, 1938. Marston inscribed a copy for his seven-year-old son: "For Byrne Marston—To help him always tell the truth. With love from Daddy."[6] His publisher sent a copy to J. Edgar Hoover, director of the Federal Bureau of Investigation, seeking an endorsement.[7] Hoover was not averse to providing blurbs—"Herbert A. Philbrick has performed an outstanding patriotic duty in his fearless presentation of facts in his book, *I Led 3 Lives,*" Hoover wrote on the back of a double agent's exposé—but, on this occasion, he demurred.[8] Instead, he opened a file on Marston.

Much of *The Lie Detector Test* is devoted to asserting Marston's claim to having founded the science of the detection of deception. Keeler had patented the polygraph machine, but this achievement Marston dismissed, arguing, "There never has existed, nor ever will exist a 'machine' which detects liars—it is a scientific test in the hands of an expert which does the lie detecting."[9] (When people asked Marston, "Where's the lie detector?" he liked to say, "*I'm* the lie detector!") Hoover's office charged an FBI agent with reviewing Marston's book. The agent reported, in a memo dated May 11, 1938, "The book is typical of all the work done by Doctor Marston in that it is written in an extremely egotistical vein and that the sole purpose of the book seems to be to establish the fact that Doctor Marston was the first to use the blood pressure test in the detection of deception."[10]

Marston's *Lie Detector Test* also includes a chapter about James A. Frye. "The Frye case proved an opening wedge for the later admission of deception test evidence into court procedure," Marston claimed. (Nothing could have been further from the truth; the Frye case closed the door on that evidence.) Marston also claimed that Frye had been convicted of second-degree murder, rather than first-degree murder, as a result of his having been given a lie detector test. "As far as Jim Frye was concerned, the test undoubtedly saved his life," Marston declared.[11] This wasn't true, either. Frye had been convicted of the lesser crime not because his lawyers tried and failed to get Marston introduced as an expert witness but because, in his confession, Frye had claimed that the gun with which the murder had been committed had gone off accidentally; nothing at the trial established that the murder had been premeditated, a requirement for conviction of murder in the first degree.

No one understood that better than Frye himself. After his conviction, Frye spent eight years in Leavenworth. He was then transferred to a federal penitentiary in Virginia, where he worked as a switchboard operator. All along, he maintained his innocence. In 1934, he requested a pardon. "My inability to prove an alibi was the sole cause of my conviction," he wrote in his application for clemency. This application was denied. Frye also believed that his appeal had been a failure because Mattingly and Wood had ignored other errors in the trial in favor of supporting Marston's attempt to have his evidence deemed admissible. As Frye pointed out, "There were more than one hundred exceptions made in the trial, yet only exceptions made in regard to the 'Lie Detector' were submitted to the higher Court." In a clemency application he filed in 1936, Frye included a copy of "Lie Detector," Olive Byrne's profile of Marston in *Family Circle*. This application, too, was denied. Frye was paroled on June 17, 1939, after serving more than eighteen years in prison. After his release, he filed repeated petitions for a presidential pardon. He regretted that his attorneys had rested their argument on Marston's credibility. He suspected that bias had contributed to his conviction, too: "This is Washington, and the

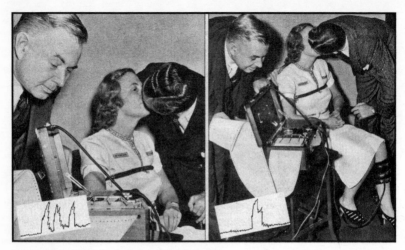

Marston's "love detector" tests, in *Look*, December 6, 1938

question of race plays an important part even in the Courts." His petitions were denied. Frye died in Washington in 1956. He is buried in Arlington National Cemetery.[12]

Much of *The Lie Detector Test* is about deception in matters of the heart. "Despite the fact that women resort to deception more frequently than men in social situations," Marston wrote, "I have found the more loving sex eager and anxious to abolish false pretenses which threaten intimate relationships or the welfare of their children."[13] He knew this, he said, from his experiments with the lie detector test, but also from his practice as a consulting psychologist. Patients came regularly to the house at Rye, to the children's annoyance. "Somehow, a raucous family house with a lot of people had to be converted into a quiet country preserve, like a rural rest home for those with bad nerves," Byrne Marston remembered. "Four kids were told that today Dad had a client coming and absolute quiet was necessary. A dark sedan would come up the driveway slowly and disengage a somber, depressed-looking middle-aged person who would then disappear into the library with Dad, who got all dressed up in a good suit for these occasions. After an hour or two the client was off and Dad was back in his sleeveless undershirt and the normal hollering started up."[14]

Most heartache Marston diagnosed as the product of deceit. "In a majority of cases which are brought to me as a consulting psychologist for love or marital adjustment, there are self-deceptions to be uncovered as well as attempts to deceive other people," he explained. "Beneath such love conflicts there is almost always a festering psychological core of dishonesty."[15]

Keen to sell his book, Marston engaged in a series of publicity stunts. He staged events for the press in which he administered "love detector" tests on pretty girls. He revisited his blondes-versus-brunettes experiments.[16] He took out a booth at the 1939 World's Fair in New York. Eleven-year-old Pete helped him build a contraption attaching the lie-detecting apparatus to a display. "You'd push a button and the light would go off," Pete said. "It was like a giant thermometer. My dad loved that."[17] He boasted to reporters that he intended to found a Truth Bureau, to be affiliated with the FBI.[18] He was in magazines. He was in newspapers. He was on CBS radio. He was so busy, "Olive Richard" told readers of *Family Circle,* that she could scarcely catch up with him:

> I offer my sincere apologies to those of you who have written and have received no help from Dr. William Moulton Marston, the FAMILY CIRCLE psychologist, or me. The past winter was an open season for influenza. (Dr. Marston had it at least twice.) However, the chief reason I haven't been able to catch up with him lately is that so many other people have beaten me to it.[19]

On November 21, 1938, Marston appeared in an advertisement in *Life* magazine, endorsing Gillette razor blades. Marston had a great appreciation for the power of advertising, if, as well, a great deal of cynicism about it. By the middle of the 1930s, the power of advertising had begun to make itself felt in the realm of politics. In 1934, after Upton Sinclair was defeated in his campaign to become the next governor of California, he labeled the advertising concern that

From "The Duke of Deception," *Wonder Woman #2* (Fall 1942)

defeated him a "lie factory." Marston took much the same view. One of Wonder Woman's most sinister adversaries, the Duke of Deception, runs an advertising firm called the Lie Factory. His workers—female slaves—operate a machine called a "Lieometer." Their job is to write "plots, deceptions, false propaganda, fake publicity and personality camouflage."[20]

The Gillette advertising campaign was Marston's idea. He'd approached Gillette early in 1938. The campaign was handled by Maxon's Inc., an advertising agency in Detroit. The idea was for Marston to conduct a series of tests on men while they were shaving. As the advertisement explained, "Not knowing which blade is which . . . each subject shaves one side of his face with a Gillette Blade . . . the other with a blade of competitive manufacture." The findings, the advertisement claimed, had been unequivocal: "9 out of 10 men tested by Dr. Marston express preference for Gillette blades."[21]

But, in fact, the findings had not been unequivocal at all, as a criminal investigator for the Detroit Police Department reported to the FBI in 1939. Marston had been asked to repeat his shaving cream tests at the Detroit police headquarters, with police officers looking on; under these circumstances, his subjects favored the Gillette blades

LIE DETECTOR "TELLS ALL"..
REVEALS STARTLING FACTS ABOUT RAZOR BLADES!

Hundreds of Men from All Walks of Life Take Amazing Tests that Disclose Important Truths about Shaving

WHAT are the facts about razor-blade quality? That's what Gillette wanted to know. And that's why Gillette retained Dr. William Moulton Marston, eminent psychologist and originator of the famous Lie Detector, to conduct scientific tests that reveal the whole truth. Truck drivers, bank presidents... men in every walk of life... take part in this investigation. Strapped to the Lie Detector... the same instrument used by police... these men shave while every reaction is measured and recorded.

Results Are Amazing

Now, men, here are the facts. The Gillette Blade is proved superior in every respect to various blades competitively tested. You get shaves that are: (1) Easier. (2) Faster. (3) Free from emotional disturbances that can upset and irritate you for hours to come.

Read the whole story. Weigh the evidence. Then see for yourself. Try the Gillette Blade and learn what a big difference it makes when you shave with a blade that's precision-built to fit your razor exactly.

Dr. William Moulton Marston

ACTUAL RECORD OF ONE MAN'S SHAVE AS RECORDED BY LIE DETECTOR

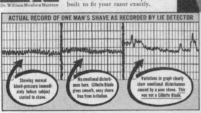

Showing normal blood-pressure immediately before subject started to shave.

No emotional disturbances here. Gillette Blade gives smooth, easy shave free from irritation.

Variations in graph clearly show emotional disturbances caused by a poor shave. This was not a Gillette Blade.

---

9 OUT OF 10 MEN TESTED BY DR. MARSTON EXPRESS PREFERENCE FOR GILLETTE BLADES. Not knowing which blade is which, each subject shaves one side of his face with a Gillette Blade... the other with a blade of competitive manufacture, while the *Lie Detector* accurately charts the reactions. In more than 9 out of every 10 cases, the shaver chooses Gillette as the superior blade. At the same time the Lie Detector proves this blade is far easier on the face.

DR. MARSTON PROVES CONCLUSIVELY that a Gillette Blade is easier on your face and shaves you in much less time. The critical eye of the camera reveals that this blade also gives you a much cleaner shave. Shown above (left) is a section of a man's face shaved with a Gillette Blade in a Gillette Razor, (right) another section shaved by another method. Now decide for yourself which gives the clean, close, long-lasting shave you want.

GILLETTE'S NEW BRUSHLESS SHAVING CREAM is better in five ways! (1) Softens whiskers double quick. (2) soothes the skin. (3) stays moist on your face. (4) speeds shaving and (5) never clogs razor or drains! Men say it is the finest shaving cream they have ever tried. You'll like it, too. Ask your dealer for Gillette Brushless—made with peanut oil. A large tube costs only 25¢!

ATTENTION! CONSUMER ORGANIZATIONS AND MEN EVERYWHERE

Dr. William Moulton Marston's scientific shaving tests are being conducted to reveal the truth about razor-blade quality. Gillette invites consumer organizations and individuals to observe—and participate in—this research. Address your inquiries to Gillette Safety Razor Company, Boston, Mass.

Now Let Dr. Marston Give You the Benefit of this Sweeping Investigation

"In conducting exhaustive shaving tests for Gillette I have discovered that the quality of a man's shave has a marked effect upon his mood and general attitude for hours to come. I cannot too strongly emphasize the psychological importance of this.

Bad Shaves Upset Nerves!

"Many subjects who came to me in a cheerful frame of mind actually went out grouchy and irritable because they had shaved one side of their faces with inferior razor blades. This shows how vital it really is to use the best blades obtainable. The results of my study make it possible for me to state flatly...and back my statement with positive proof ...that Gillette Blades are far superior in every respect to competitive blades tested."

Gillette
Blades
PRECISION-MADE TO FIT YOUR GILLETTE RAZOR EXACTLY

Marston's lie detector in *Life* magazine, November 21, 1938

only 50 percent of the time. Another polygraph expert, John Larson, a colleague of Keeler's, was called in to attempt to replicate Marston's initial, pro-Gillette results. He could not. Larson alleged that Marston then attempted to bribe him to fake his results, telling him "he stood to make around thirty thousand dollars for his part in the entire scheme." An FBI agent investigated the case and sent a report to Hoover. At the bottom of the report, Hoover scratched a note: "I always thought this fellow Marston was a phony & this proves it."[22]

FEMININE RULE DECLARED FACT

ON NOVEMBER 10, 1937, Marston held a press conference and issued a prediction: women would one day rule the world. The story was picked up by the Associated Press, wired across the continent, and printed in newspapers from Topeka to Tallahassee. "Women Will Rule 1,000 Years Hence!" announced the *Chicago Tribune*. The *Los Angeles Times* reported, "Feminine Rule Declared Fact."[1]

The idea had hardly come out of nowhere. Betty Boop ran for president in a film released in 1932. Other campaigns were more serious.

From *Wonder Woman #7* (Winter 1943)

"The women of America could convert this country to a matriarchy if they wanted to assert their power," a lawyer named Lillian D. Rock told reporters in 1935, the year she founded the League for a Woman President and Vice President. And she wasn't talking about a thousand years distant. A woman would be elected president of the United States within twenty years, Rock said. "I'm certain of it." These, after all, were the days of Eleanor Roosevelt. In 1935, three years before Superman appeared in comic books, Rock referred to the women she thought most eligible to run for president as "super women." She thought Mary Woolley, president of Mount Holyoke, would make an especially strong candidate. A female American president might be twenty years away, Rock thought, but she expected Americans "to elect a woman Vice-President in 1936 or 1940."[2]

She wasn't alone. "During the next decade," Franklin D. Roosevelt's secretary Louis Howe wrote in the *Woman's Home Companion* in 1935, "not only the possibility but the advisability of electing a woman as President of the United States will become a very seriously argued question. And if the issues continue to be as they are now— humanitarian, education, etc.—it is not outside the bounds of possibility that a woman might not only be nominated, but elected, on the ground that women better understand such questions than men."[3]

Marston was stagier. He made his announcement at a two-hour press conference held at the Harvard Club of New York and said so much about his qualifications as one of the world's most influential psychologists that the *New York Times* identified him, wrongly, as "former director of the psychological laboratory at Harvard."[4]

A matriarchy, Marston said, was inevitable. "Neglected Amazons to Rule Men in 1,000 Yrs., Says Psychologist," the *Washington Post* reported. "Women have twice the emotional development, the ability for love, than man has," Marston explained. "And as they develop as much ability for worldly success as they already have ability for love, they will clearly come to rule business and the Nation and the world." There would be a new race of Amazons: "The next 100 years will see the beginning of an American matriarchy—a nation of amazons in the psychological rather than the physical sense," he predicted. "In 500 years, there will be a serious sex battle. And in 1,000 years women will definitely rule this country."[5]

Marston's arguments about women's superiority drew on centuries of women's writing and borrowed especially heavily from the philosophy of the nineteenth-century women's movement, with its emphasis on women's moral superiority—their "angelic" natures. When Carrie Chapman Catt explained why women deserved the right to vote, she said, among other things, that women were more loving, because maternal, and ought to vote because they brought a distinct vantage to social problems.[6] In the 1930s, that was Louis Howe's thinking, too. But twentieth-century feminists had tended to turn away from arguments for rights that rested on ideas about difference, rather than on ideas about equality. In 1933, when the National Woman's Party's Inez Haynes Gillmore, author of *Angel Island*, wrote an account of a century of women's political activism, she called it *Angels and Amazons*.[7] Gillmore's point, and sometimes Marston's point, too, was that being an angel was horrible. (When Steve Trevor calls Wonder Woman "angel," she's irked. "What's an angel?" she asks. "I'd rather be a woman.")[8]

But one twentieth-century feminist who kept on making nineteenth-century-style arguments based on women's supposed superiority was Margaret Sanger. "She said women were very very great, she felt they were the strength of the future," her granddaughter later said. "Those are the words she used, 'Women are the strength of our future.' They take care of culture and tradition and roles and they preserve what's good. Men usually destroy."[9] Women were the future of the race, Sanger thought. So did Marston.

The press conference during which Marston predicted a matriarchy was part of the promotion for a new book, *Try Living*, a collection of self-help essays that he'd earlier printed in popular magazines like the *Rotarian*.[10] "Finished typing 'TRY LIVING,'" Olive Byrne wrote in her diary on July 10, 1937. "Looks good."[11] The book was released on October 1.[12] Marston's argument, in *Try Living*, is that happiness can be found in doing what you love. At his matriarchy press conference, he listed six successful and famous people whose lives illustrated this formula; the *Times* reported, "They are—in the order of the importance of their contributions to humanity in general, in his opinion—Henry Ford, Mrs. Margaret Sanger, President Roosevelt, Thomas E. Dewey, Helen Hayes and Mayor La Guardia."[13]

In the 1930s, Margaret Sanger was the best-known feminist in the world. "When the history of our civilization is written, it will be a biological history and Margaret Sanger will be its heroine," H. G. Wells predicted in 1935. In London, she met with Jawaharlal Nehru; in India, she debated Mahatma Gandhi. In 1937, she was featured in *Time* and the *Nation*; in *Life*, her life story was told in a four-page photo spread. She

Left to right: Byrne, O.A., Marston, Donn, and Pete, at Cherry Orchard
in 1938

achieved what she called the "greatest legal VICTORY in the birth
control movement": after attending a conference in Zurich, she'd
arranged to have Japanese pessaries—diaphragms—sent to the United
States; they were seized and destroyed by U.S. customs officers, a
decision that was appealed. In *United States v. One Package of Japanese Pessaries,* the Second Circuit Court of Appeals ruled that contraception did not violate obscenity laws if prescribed by a physician;
the ruling effectively removed contraception from the category of
obscenity. In 1937, the American Medical Association at last endorsed
birth control.[14] A matriarchy, Marston announced to reporters, was
inevitable.

The year Margaret Sanger won her greatest victory yet and William
Moulton Marston held a press conference about Amazonian rule, Olive
Byrne was typing his books and raising his children, and Sadie Eliza-

beth Holloway was supporting him.[15] A matriarchy Cherry Orchard was not.

Holloway worked all day. She took the seven o'clock train into the city in the morning, and the seven o'clock train home at night. Marston, for all his energy and all his writing, brought in little income, and none of it was regular. What Olive Byrne earned from *Family Circle* could not have been much. Counting Huntley, Holloway had seven people to support. In 1936, she filled out a Mount Holyoke alumnae survey:

"Do you administer the household?"

"Yes."

"Is it your chief occupation?"

"No."

"How do you spend your time: do you volunteer, are you involved in church, the arts, sports?"

Holloway scribbled a two-word reply: "No leisure."[16]

One day, Olive Byrne asked all the children what they wanted to be when they grew up. Pete, who was eight years old, said he wanted to be a writer. Byrne, five, wanted to be a psychologist. Donn, four, wanted to be a mother. And O.A., three, wanted to be a doctor.

One week later, Marston asked O.A. whether she was a boy or a girl. O.A. said, "Oh a boy, I s'pose."[17]

The kids knew which of the women was their mother—Pete and O.A. belonged to Holloway (they called her Keets), and Byrne and Donn to Olive (Dots). All of them were told that Byrne and Donn's father was a man named William Richard and that he was dead. Not all of them believed it. Donn, who looked just like Marston, had his suspicions. And Pete once walked into Olive's bedroom when his father and Olive were having sex. They told him that Daddy was sick and Dotsie was helping him feel better.[18] When the census taker came by, he was told that Huntley was a "lodger" and Olive was a "sister-in-law."[19]

If anyone asked about the family arrangements, the children were supposed to change the subject. ("The whys and wherefores of the family arrangements were never discussed with the kids—ever,"

Pete said.)[20] Everyone understood very well that Olive was Byrne and Donn's mother, but Holloway, who had adopted them, was their mother, too.[21] "This got a little confusing," O.A. said, not least because she and Donn were in the same grade at school. "How can he be your brother when he's only six months older than you?" kids would ask her.[22] The story that Olive was a servant—the family's housekeeper—is one that Holloway's children stuck with, for decades. "She was the housekeeper," O.A. insisted in an interview, as late as 1999, "and took care of the menial jobs like shopping and things like that."[23] They might have told that story. But that's not how they lived.

On November 4, 1937, the week before Marston announced to the world the inevitability of Amazonian rule, O.A., age four, said to Olive Byrne, "I wish I was your child."

"You are."

"Then you wash me every night & Keetie do Pete."[24]

Once, angry with Holloway, O.A. yelled at her, "Oh I wish I had never come out of you—I'd rather come out of Dotsie!"[25]

It couldn't have been easy.

"What are Mommies, Daddies, and Keeties for anyway?" O.A. asked.

Olive said, quietly, "I can't quite say myself."[26]

Marston spent most of his time in the study on the second floor. He kept his lie detector there, and a brass ashtray. He mainly worked lying on a daybed, wearing nothing but his underwear, a sleeveless undershirt, and slippers. He liked to nap there. When it was cold, he wore a faded blue wool sweater, stained with cigarette burns, and baggy linen pants. He had grown gigantic. He weighed more than three hundred pounds. (Holloway bought him a copy of a dieting book called *Eat and Reduce;* it didn't do any good.)[27] When he got up, the floorboards creaked. He smoked Philip Morris cigarettes, from cans of fifty—the kids used the cans to make forts for toy soldiers. He drank rye and ginger ale, morning and night. The piano, on the first floor, was just below his study. If anyone played it, he'd bang the floor and holler, "I'm writing!"[28]

He wrote for *Esquire*. He wrote for the *Rotarian*. In 1939, he wrote an article for *Your Life* called "What Are *Your* Prejudices?" It's an argument against intolerance. "Tolerant people are the happiest," he insisted, so "why not get rid of costly prejudices that hold you back?" He listed the "Six Most Common Types of Prejudice":

1. Prejudice against foreigners or races supposed to possess despicable characteristics.
2. Religious prejudices.
3. Class prejudices.
4. Prejudice against sexual frankness.
5. Male prejudice against successful men, and female prejudice against alluring women.
6. Prejudice against unconventional people and non-conformists.[29]

The kids would slip notes under his study door. Marston had a pad of memo paper engraved "Memorandum From the Desk of Dr. W. M. Marston." He used it to arbitrate disputes. On one piece of memo paper, written in red crayon, he negotiated a truce between nine-year-old Byrne (whose nickname was Whoopsie Doodle, or Dood for short, because he used to love falling off a rocking horse and crying out, "Whoopsie Doodle!") and seven-year-old Olive Ann (whose nickname was Doggie, because she once played a dog in a school play).

Memorandum From the Desk of Dr. W. M. Marston:
Dear Dood—I do not care who did what. I only wish that our Doggie shall be made happy by sitting on the couch as she wishes. Please accommodate! Yours, Daddy.

On the back of the memo, Byrne wrote back:

Okay! If you will tell her to stop arguing with Pete and quit bothering me. Byrne Marston.[30]

Marston wrote a poem for Pete: "Moulton Marston hurried home / An hour late for dinner / Dotsie said, 'You're just in time / To get a little thinner.'"[31]

The Marston children were fiercely loved. Olive doted on them; Holloway was proud of them. Huntley's incense-filled room in the attic was a place they could go when they needed quiet. Marston made the rules.[32] His diaries and letters are filled with stories of birthday parties, presents, and trips to schools, watching Byrne turn somersaults at the age of six and play the trumpet at age eight. He carried O.A. around on his shoulders.[33] "Seven good night hugs OOOOOOO and one good night kiss X," Marston wrote, signing off a letter to Byrne, away at summer camp. "I'm whispering, 'I love you.' "[34]

"Spent evening putting together O.A.'s dolls house," Marston wrote in his diary on Christmas Eve 1938. In the morning, the children woke up at seven and opened their stockings, hung in the library. After breakfast, they opened their presents, under the tree. "Pete likes his skiis best," Marston wrote in his diary, "Dood his puppets, Donn his farm animals (and his punching bag almost equally) and O.A. paid not the slightest attention to her dollhouse. Happy day."[35]

Marston was devoted and passionately affectionate, maybe too affectionate. Every night, he insisted that O.A. enter his study, say, "Goodnight Daddy," and kiss him on the mouth. Every night, she refused. "For Christ's sake," Olive would say, "just run in there and kiss him quick and get it over with."[36]

On weekends, Holloway worked in the garden or took O.A. to the city, shopping, or to the ballet. "Keets is plugging along at learning to ride a bike and she uses O.A.'s only she forgets that she's putting on the brakes and she took a looper Saturday," Olive wrote to Byrne one summer.[37]

Sundays, Marston held what he called the Sunday Five Club. Instead of sending the kids to church, they debated the meaning of life.[38] Marston convened the first meeting of the Sunday Five Club on June 23, 1935, when the children were seven, four, three, and two, but only the oldest, Pete and Byrne, said anything.

"Asked them what God was," Marston wrote in his diary.

Byrne: "A great big sprocket."

Pete: "All the laws there are."[39]

This went on for years. "We all hated it," Byrne later wrote. "The women rounded us up and pushed us, dragging our feet into Dad's study." It was less debate than indoctrination. "The purpose of the meeting was to instill Dad's principles and theories, especially the love vs. force one," Byrne said. The kids, naturally, fought and hit each other, and their father's insistence that they should love one another—that O.A. ought to answer a poke in the ribs with a kiss—didn't go over well.[40] Still, they took it in, his hodgepodge of Aquarianism and psychology and feminism. "It was the philosophy that the laws of the planet earth are forces bound by love, and love is bound by wisdom," O.A. said, and that "women could have more control by using force with love around it or love with wisdom around it."[41]

Marston administered IQ tests to each of his children. "IQ 173!" he wrote about Byrne in his diary. He promptly informed the children of their scores, which descended, by rank, from Byrne to Donn to Pete to O.A. and caused everyone no end of grief. He decided Byrne ought to skip two grades.[42]

The children defended themselves from these forces of division by forging a bond. In the summer of 1939, when they were eleven, eight, seven, and six, they started a family newspaper called the *Marston Chronicle*. Pete was the editor in chief, Byrne was the arts editor and staff artist, and Donn and O.A. covered the news. (Olive Byrne did the typing.) The lead stories were reported by Donn:

BYRNE LOSES TOOTH

Rye, July 18. Byrne lost a front lower tooth and he is hoping the fairies will leave ten cents under his pillow tonight.

DOG FIGHT

Lucky, our new dog got bitten in a dog fight by some dog. We took him to the Vet's who said the wounds are slight.

Pete wrote a story called "First Come, First Served," about a kid who wants to go to the World's Fair; O.A. contributed a cartoon. And Byrne wrote a comic strip, of twelve frames; "The Adventures of Bobby Doone" featured his alter ego, a boy who goes on a car trip to his grandmother's house in Massachusetts, where he plays with his great-grandfather's bayonet and gets into very big trouble when he breaks it.[43] That would be Captain Moulton's Civil War bayonet, kept

Sheena, Queen of the Jungle, in *Jumbo Comics #20* (October 1940), printed by Fiction House, where Olive Byrne's brother, Jack, was an editor

in a closet in William Moulton Marston's childhood home, in Cliftondale.

They were growing up in the golden age of comic books. Comic *strips,* or "funnies," had begun appearing in the pages of newspapers in the 1890s. But comic *books* date only to the 1930s. They'd been more or less invented by Maxwell Charles Gaines (everyone called him Charlie), a former elementary school principal who was working as a salesman for the Eastern Color Printing Company, in Waterbury, Connecticut, when he got the idea that the pages of funnies that appeared in the Sunday papers could be printed cheaply, stapled together, and sold as magazines, or "comic books." In 1933, Gaines started selling the first comic book on newsstands; it was called *Funnies on Parade.*

At first, comic books were just cut-and-pasted strips; soon they got to be something else. Gaines understood comic books as a wholly new art form whose relationship to the newspaper comic strip was not unlike that of the early motion pictures to photographs.[44] Comic books were a kind of motion picture, too.

Detective Comics first appeared in 1937. Superman, written and drawn by Jerry Siegel and Joe Shuster, made his debut in *Action Comics #1* in June 1938. Superman was unstoppable; soon, a million Superman comics were being sold every month.[45]

At Fiction House, Olive Byrne's brother, Jack, started printing comics, too, beginning with *Jumbo Comics* in September 1938. Its inaugural issue included a character created the year before, in London, by Will Eisner and S. M. Iger: Sheena, Queen of the Jungle, a female Tarzan. Jack Byrne's Fiction House became known for its powerful, invincible female heroes. At a time when many publishers had no women artists, Fiction House employed more than twenty.[46]

The popularity of comics soared. Gaines, who did not tend to hire women to do anything except secretarial work, began publishing *All-American Comics* in 1939. That same year, Superman became the

From "Amazona, the Mighty Woman," *Planet Comics #3*
(May 1940), also printed by Jack Byrne's Fiction House

first comic-book character to have an entire comic book all to himself; he could also be heard on the radio.[47] The first episode of Batman
appeared in *Detective Comics #27*, in May 1939. Three months later,
Byrne Holloway Marston, staff artist for the *Marston Chronicle*, drew
the first installment of "The Adventures of Bobby Doone."

By 1939, almost every kid in the United States was reading comic
books. A form of writing that hadn't existed just a few years earlier
seemed to have taken over the country. Comic books were cheap—
usually ten cents an issue—and children could pay for them with
their own money. They were sold everywhere: at grocery stores,
newsstands, and drugstores. Kids traded them. They read them by the
dozens. Their parents were dumbstruck.

In March 1940, Jack Byrne's Fiction House published "Amazona,
the Mighty Woman," in *Planet Comics*. It tells the story of a "woman
of surpassing strength and unmatched beauty" named Amazona:
"She and her people are the last survivors of a super race that per-
ished during the period of the last ice age." She is discovered by an

American reporter named Blake Manners, the lone survivor of a polar expedition. She falls in love with him: "Amazona, fascinated by the handsome stranger, does not want him to leave." But he wants to go back to the United States. "She finally convinces Blake to take her back with him to civilization." She frees his ship by using her "amazing strength" to lift the ice away from its hull. In America, she turns out to be ferocious and easily irritated. When a cabdriver calls her a "sweet gal," she clouts him, then leaves his cab a wreck, telling him, "I'll show you how sweet a 'babe' I am!"[48]

"I know from observation in my own household that children read the so-called funnies morning, noon, and—unfortunately—night," wrote Olive Byrne. She counted eighty-four different comic books that the kids read and traded.[49]

Reading comics was a way to have a moment of quiet at Cherry Orchard; quiet was usually hard to find. Marston was big and he was loud and he drank and he thundered when he was angry. One night at the dinner table, frustrated, he shouted, "At least I can still get an erection!"[50]

He was the loudest person in the house, but he was also the most ridiculous. "Now, Bill," Holloway would say when Marston got started on a rant. And then she would wait, in silence, for him to shut up.

The kids read the comics. Holloway earned the money. Huntley burned incense in the attic. Olive took care of everyone, stealing time to write for *Family Circle*. And William Moulton Marston, the last of the Moultons of Moulton Castle, the lie detector who declared feminine rule a fact, was petted and indulged. He'd fume and he'd storm and he'd holler, and the women would whisper to the children, "It's best to ignore him."[51]

★ **PART THREE** ★

PARADISE
ISLAND

From "America's Wonder Women of Tomorrow,"
Wonder Woman #7 (Winter 1943)

SUPREMA

IT BEGAN WITH A GUN. On September 1, 1939, the German army invaded Poland. Two days later, Britain and France declared war on Germany. In the October 1939 issue of *Detective Comics,* Batman killed a vampire by shooting silver bullets into his heart. In the next issue, Batman fired a gun at two evil henchmen. When Whitney Ellsworth, DC's editorial director, got a first look at a draft of the next installment, Batman was shooting again. Ellsworth shook his head and said, Take the gun out.[1]

Batman had debuted in *Detective Comics* in May 1939, the same month that the U.S. Supreme Court issued a ruling in *United States v. Miller,* a landmark gun-control case. It concerned the constitutionality of the 1934 National Firearms Act and the 1938 Federal Firearms Act, which effectively banned machine guns through prohibitive taxation, and regulated handgun ownership by introducing licensing, waiting period, and permit requirements. The National Rifle Association supported the legislation (at the time, the NRA was a sportsman's organization). But gun manufacturers challenged it on the grounds that federal control of

From "The Batman Wars Against the Dirigible of Doom," *Detective Comics #33* (November 1939)

gun ownership violated the Second Amendment. FDR's solicitor general said the Second Amendment had nothing to do with an individual right to own a gun; it had to do with the common defense. The court agreed, unanimously.[2]

With war devastating Europe, the disarming of the dark knight was *Detective Comics'* deferral to a cherished American idea about the division between civilian and military life. Superheroes weren't soldiers; they were private citizens. And so, late in 1939, one of Batman's writers drafted a new origin story for him: when Bruce Wayne was a boy, his parents had been killed before his eyes, shot to death. Not only did Batman not own a gun; Batman hated guns.[3] Hating guns is what made him Batman.

Batman's new backstory tempered his critics, but it hardly stopped them. On May 8, 1940, the *Chicago Daily News* declared war on comic books. "Ten million dollars of these sex-horror serials are sold every month," wrote Sterling North, the newspaper's literary editor. "Unless we want a coming generation even more ferocious than the present one, parents and teachers throughout America must band together to break the 'comic' magazine." Twenty-five million readers requested reprints of North's article, in which he'd called comic books "a national disgrace."[4]

In June 1940, Germany conquered France. Much of the comic-book trouble had to do, by then, with Superman, who'd begun to look to a lot of people like a fascist. Comic books would "spawn only a generation of Storm Troopers," the poet Stanley Kunitz predicted in *Library Journal*. In September 1940, the *New Republic* published an essay called "The Coming of Superman" by the novelist Slater Brown. "Superman, handsome as Apollo, strong as Hercules, chivalrous as Launcelot, swift as Hermes, embodies all the traditional attributes of a Hero God," Brown wrote, but in Germany, "it is not the children who have embraced a vulgarized myth of Superman so enthusiastically; it has been their elders." *Time* magazine would eventually ask the question Kunitz and Brown had circled around: "Are Comics Fascist?"[5]

In the heat of the controversy, Olive Byrne pitched an article to her editor at *Family Circle:* Who better to explain to American mothers whether comics are dangerous for children than Dr. William Moulton Marston? She got the assignment. Her article was published in October 1940. It begins, as her articles always began, with the fiction that she had traveled to Marston's house to interview him, in this case, troubled by "terrible visions of Hitlerian justice."

"Do you know anything about comics magazines?" she asked him.

Oh, he knew plenty. "He told me that he had been doing research in this field for more than a year—and that *he had read almost every comics magazine published during that time*!" There were more than one hundred comic-book magazines on the nation's newsstands, reaching forty to fifty million readers every month, he said.

"But do you think these fantastic comics are good reading for children?" she asked.

Mostly, yes, Marston said. They are pure wish fulfillment: "And the two wishes behind Superman are certainly the soundest of all; they are, in fact, our national aspirations of the moment—to develop unbeatable national might, and to use this great power, when we get it, to protect innocent, peace-loving people from destructive, ruthless evil. You don't think for a minute that it is wrong to imagine the fulfillment of those two aspirations for the United States of America, do you? Then why should it be wrong or harmful for children to imagine the same things for themselves, personally, when they read 'Superman'?"

"But what about other comics?" she pressed. "Some of them are full of torture, kidnapping, sadism, and other cruel business."

"Unfortunately, that is true," Marston admitted. "But there are one or two rules of thumb which are useful in distinguishing sadism from exciting adventure in the comics. Threat of torture is harmless, but if the torture itself is shown in the strip, it becomes sadism. When a lovely heroine is bound to the stake, comics followers are sure that the rescue will arrive in the nick of time. The reader's wish is to save the girl, not to see her suffer. A bound or chained person does not suffer even embarrassment in the comics, and the reader, therefore, is not being taught to enjoy suffering."

Convinced by the professor's every argument, "Olive Richard" leaves his house and, on her way to the train, picks up the latest copy of *Superman*.[6] Charlie Gaines at All-American Publications read Olive Byrne's article and was so impressed that he decided to hire Marston as a consulting psychologist.[7]

. . .

To defend himself against the assault on comics, Gaines needed experts. George Hecht, the publisher of *Parents' Magazine,* had announced his plan to publish *True Comics.* "Every page in this new comic maga-zine is filled with action and excitement," *Parents'* editor Clara Sav-age Littledale promised. "But the heroes are not impossible creatures. They are real." Its first issue included stories about Winston Churchill and Simón Bolívar. But what really set *True Comics* apart was that it was overseen by an editorial advisory board of experts: professors, especially historians, educators, and even the public-opinion pollster George Gallup.[8]

Gaines decided to form his own editorial advisory board. " 'Doc' Marston has long been an advocate of the right type of comic maga-zines and is now a member of the Editorial Advisory Board of all 'D.C. Superman' Comics," Gaines announced in a memo to his staff in 1940, enclosing a copy of Olive Byrne's *Family Circle* article.[9] DC also decided to stamp all comic books in which Superman and Batman appeared with a logo reading, "A DC Publication" or "A Superman-DC Publica-tion." In October 1941, in a message in *More Fun Comics,* the publish-ers told readers (and their parents) that the company's logo—a circle containing the letters *DC,* short for *Detective Comics*—ought to be considered a stamp of quality, a mark of the endorsement of the board, whose members included Robert Thorndike, a professor of educational psychology at Columbia; Ruth Eastwood Perl, another psychologist; C. Bowie Millican, who taught literature at NYU; Gene Tunney, a U.S. Navy lieutenant commander and director of a Catholic youth organi-zation; and Josette Frank, an expert on children's literature and the executive director of the Child Study Association of America (she'd worked with Holloway at *Child Study* in the 1920s).[10] Though Gaines had initially appointed Marston to the board, Frank asked Gaines to remove him, since Gaines had also signed Marston on as a writer.[11]

As consulting psychologist, Marston convinced Gaines that what he really needed to counter the attack on comics was a female super-hero. In some versions of the story, this was Holloway's idea. "Come on, let's have a Superwoman!" she'd told Marston, according to her son Pete. "Never mind the guys."[12] But Holloway herself was more likely to say she never had anything to do with Wonder Woman: "I've always had my own work and pay which meant there was no time left over for Wonder Woman nor was it necessary," she wrote. A female superhero might have been Olive Byrne's idea, though she'd have been the last person in the world to take credit for it. In any case, Marston, who at a press conference in 1937 had predicted that women would rule the world, and had named Margaret Sanger as the second-most-important person on the planet (second only to Henry Ford), as measured by "contributions to humanity," knew very well who he had in mind for a female superhero.[13]

At first, Gaines had objected. Every female pulp and comic-book heroine, he told Marston, had been a failure. "But they weren't *super-women*," Marston countered. "They weren't superior to men." A female superhero, Marston insisted, was the best answer to the critics, since "the comics' worst offense was their bloodcurdling masculinity." He explained,

A male hero, at best, lacks the qualities of maternal love and tenderness which are as essential to a normal child as the breath of life. Suppose your child's ideal becomes a super*man* who uses his extraordinary power to help the weak. The most important ingredient in the human happiness recipe still is missing—*love*. It's smart to be strong. It's big to be generous. But it's sissified, according to exclusively masculine rules, to be tender, loving, affectionate, and alluring. "Aw, that's girl's stuff!" snorts our young comics reader. "Who wants to be a *girl*?" And that's the point; not even girls want to be girls so long as our feminine archetype lacks force, strength, power. Not wanting to be girls they don't want to be tender, submissive, peaceloving as good women are. Women's strong qualities have become despised because of their weak ones. The obvious remedy is to create a feminine character with all the strength of Superman plus all the allure of a good and beautiful woman.[14]

In making this argument, Marston braided together more than a century of women's rights rhetoric, his own very odd brand of psychology, and, inevitably, his peerless hucksterism. Gaines was sold.

"Well, Doc," Gaines said, "I picked Superman after every syndicate in America turned it down. I'll take a chance on your Wonder Woman! But you'll have to write the strip yourself. After six months' publication we'll submit your woman hero to a vote of our comics readers. If they don't like her I can't do any more about it."[15]

In February 1941, Marston submitted a typewritten draft of the first installment of "Suprema, the Wonder Woman." For an editor, Gaines assigned Marston to Sheldon Mayer, who edited Superman. Mayer, who'd grown up in Harlem, had drawn since he was a little boy. He once wrote the story of his life as an aspiring comic-book artist in a comic book called *Scribbly*. He'd been working for Gaines since 1936, pasting newspaper strips into comic books. Mayer and Gaines would regularly work all night, then shave together in the office bathroom in the morning. Even after Gaines made Mayer an executive editor, he still sent him out to buy cigarettes. Mayer was small and rangy; he wore glasses and smoked a pipe, but he still looked like a kid.[16]

Mayer was twenty-four; Marston was forty-eight. Most of the writers and artists Mayer worked with were even younger than he was. He counted Marston's age, not to mention his Harvard degrees, against him. "When we first started Wonder Woman," Mayer later said, "I seriously hoped it wouldn't last more than 20 minutes." He found it easier "to take a former haberdashery salesman with a flair for writing" and teach him about comics than to work with "a guy who was already a writer." But the more Mayer got to know Marston, the better he liked him.[17] Marston was always disarming.

In a letter Marston sent Mayer with his first script, he explained the "under-meaning" of the story:

Men (Greeks) were captured by predatory love-seeking females until they got sick of it and made the women captive by force. But they were afraid of them (masculine inferiority complex) and kept them heavily chained lest the women put one over as they always had before. The Goddess of Love comes along and helps women break their chains by giving them the greater force of real altruism. Whereupon men turned about face and actually helped the women get away from domestic slavery—as men are doing now. The NEW WOMEN thus freed and strengthened by supporting themselves (on Paradise Island) developed enormous physical and mental power. But they have to use it for other people's benefit or they go back to chains, and weakness.

It might sound like a fantasy, Marston admitted, but "all this is true," at least as allegory, and, really, as history, because his comic was meant to chronicle "a great movement now under way—the growth in the power of women." He didn't mind Mayer editing it, though he preferred to be consulted. "I hope you'll call me up about any changes in the story, names, costumes or subject-matter," he told Mayer. "That's your business." But about the story's feminism, he was unmovable. "Let that theme alone," he told him, "or drop the project."[18]

Mayer made one change: he nixed "Suprema." Better to call her just "Wonder Woman." As for the rest, it sounded like a lot of crap to Shelly Mayer, but he figured, What the hell.

23

AS LOVELY AS APHRODITE

WHAT WOULD SHE LOOK LIKE? Botticelli's Venus? The Statue of Liberty? Greta Garbo?

"I am sending Peter, the artist, a carbon," Marston wrote to Mayer when he mailed him the first script. "Let me know when you want him and I'll send him down."[1]

Marston had hired his own artist: Harry G. Peter.[2] Peter was sixty-one, an antique by comic-book standards. "Harry seemed like quite an elderly gentleman to me," Mayer said.[3] Mayer didn't approve; he also thought Peter's drawings were awful. But he couldn't get Marston and Gaines to agree to accept anyone else.[4] When Marston hired Peter, Peter's only experience in comics was having drawn panels for George Hecht's *True Comics*. (In the spring of 1941, Peter would begin drawing a superhero named Man o' Metal, a flammable foundry worker, for *Reg'lar Fellers Heroic Comics*—but that came after Wonder Woman.)[5] Gaines must have liked the idea of swiping an artist from George Hecht; he hated him. In 1941, Gaines wrote a letter to Hecht inviting Hecht and *True Comics'* editorial advisory board to have lunch with Gaines and DC Comics' editorial advisory board, in order to stage a public debate about comics, pitting Gaines's experts against Hecht's. "I will be glad to underwrite the expense," Gaines told Hecht. Meanwhile, though, he hired one of Hecht's artists to draw Wonder Woman.[6]

Marston liked to say that Wonder Woman was meant to be "psy-

From Tarpé Mills, *Miss Fury*, Strip 285

chological propaganda for the new type of woman who should, I believe, rule the world," but neither he nor Gaines seem to have given much thought to hiring a woman to draw her. Fiction House employed dozens of women artists, but Gaines only ever hired one: Elizabeth Burnley Bentley. (Her work was uncredited, but she did lettering and backgrounding for *Superman* and *Batman*.)[7] It wasn't for a lack of choices. There were experienced editorial cartoonists, like Lou Rogers; in 1940, she was illustrating children's books. There were women who drew daily newspaper strips. Dalia Messick, using the name Dale Messick, began drawing *Brenda Starr* in 1940. And there were experienced comic-book artists. June Tarpé Mills, who'd studied at the Pratt Institute, paying her tuition by working as a fashion model, started drawing comics for *Reg'lar Fellers Heroic Comics* in the late 1930s. She was the first woman artist to create her own action hero. Early in 1941, a newspaper syndicate hired her to write and draw a daily comic strip called, at first, *Black Fury* and, later, *Miss Fury*. Miss Fury, sleek and glamorous, is a socialite named Marla Drake who fights crime while dressed as a black panther. Mills published using the name "Tarpé Mills." ("It would have been a major letdown to the kids if they found out that the author of such virile and awesome characters was a gal," she said.) By 1942, *Miss Fury* was appearing in her own comic book, published by DC's chief rival, Timely Comics (later Marvel Comics).[8]

Instead of hiring a woman artist who'd worked on comics, Mar-

Left to right: Marston, Harry G. Peter, Sheldon Mayer, and Charlie Gaines, 1942

ston hired a man. He said he liked that Peter knew "what life is all about."[9] But Peter's age also meant that he had lived through the suffrage movement.

Henry George Peter was born in San Rafael, California, in 1880. He was very likely named after the San Francisco newspaper editor and reformer Henry George, whose most famous work, *Progress and Poverty,* a wildly popular inquiry into economic inequality, was published in 1879. Henry George was an early and ardent advocate for women's education and for female suffrage. "In all questions of politics," George wrote, "women have as direct and vital an interest as men."[10] If Henry George Peter was named after Henry George, his parents were radicals. Both Peter and his older brother became artists. By the time Peter was twenty, he was working for a newspaper.[11] He signed his work "H. G. Peter"; sometimes people called him Harry; sometimes they called him Pete. He may have worked for the San Francisco *Bulletin.* By 1906 he was a staff artist for the *San Francisco Chronicle,* the newspaper that, in 1907, published the first daily comic strip, *Mutt and*

Jeff. Marston later claimed that Peter had worked on *Mutt and Jeff,* but it's not clear that he really had. He did, though, draw for the *Chronicle* during the years when its pages closely covered the suffrage movement in the state, led by the California Equal Suffrage League. The woman Peter eventually married was a newspaper artist, too, and, very probably, a suffragist.[12]

A Gibson girl, pen and ink drawing by Charles Gibson, c. 1891

Adonica Fulton was a staff artist for the San Francisco *Bulletin.*[13] She studied at the Mark Hopkins Institute of Art. Both Peter and Fulton were much influenced by the American illustrator Charles Gibson; he'd introduced the Gibson girl in the 1890s. She wore her haired piled on top of her head. She was wealthy, elegant, fashionable, and full of disdain. Her mouth was pouty, her eyes half-lidded, her breasts heavy, her waist pinched. Gibson's influence can be seen in Peter's work and in Adonica Fulton's early drawings of women, too.

In San Francisco, both Peter and Fulton were members of the Newspaper Artists' League, an organization limited to "the leading men and women employed upon the local newspapers and magazines." In 1904, they both had work displayed in San Francisco at a newspaper artists' exhibition, where Fulton's twenty drawings were singled out as among the most distinguished.[14]

Peter and Fulton moved to New York in about 1907, following friends and fellow newspaper artists Rube Goldberg and Herbert Roth. Peter started drawing for the *New York American.* By 1908, he was making pen and ink illustrations for *Judge.* In 1912, Peter and Fulton married. Their

Adonica Fulton, pen and ink drawing, 1904. From *The Newspaper Artists' Exhibit, San Francisco Call,* October 9, 1904

Harry G. Peter, "Seeing Miss America First," *Judge*, February 27, 1915

courtship had been unusually long. The year they married, they both turned thirty-two.[15]

At *Judge*, Peter met the feminist cartoonist Lou Rogers. Between 1912 and 1917, both Peter and Rogers contributed illustrations to *Judge*'s regular pro-suffrage feature "The Modern Woman." Rogers's work was better known than Peter's. In 1915, her name appeared in a *Judge* advertisement on a list of "the kind of writers of *real* humor and the distinctively skillful artists whom our readers choose"; Peter's name is not included.[16]

In 1920, Peter began working for the commercial art firm Louis C. Pedlar, Inc., with offices at 95 Madison Avenue. "He has been added to our staff because of his wide experience as a black and white artist, and a colorist of infinite imagination," the company announced.[17] By 1925, Peter and Fulton were living in a house they'd bought on Staten Island. It doesn't seem as though they ever had any children, nor is it certain whether Adonica Fulton Peter continued to work as an artist.[18] In the 1930s, commercial art, like every other business, fell slack. Hard times led Peter to comic books. To Wonder Woman he brought, among other things, experience drawing suffrage cartoons.

.   .   .

THE MODERN WOMAN

Curbside Comments

By OREOLA W. HASKELL

The Elderly

IN A BRIEF article written for a leading magazine, Jane Addams takes up the cudgels for the woman over fifty, citing many examples of those who are engaged in arduous public work of much benefit to the country. Few women realize that this coming of the elderly woman out of the shadow of the chimney corner is one of the most significant signs of the times. It means that to-day woman is valued far more than her sex activities, since in former times man considered her useless when the years of motherhood were over and so relegated her to the joys of knitting and nodding. And there is no hope of thrusting her back, for among many other changes the fireplace has become the steam radiator, the house an apartment, and there is no room for grandma to vegetate.

Chat Between an Old and New Woman

Old woman— Dear me, how much more interesting a son is than a daughter!

New woman— Why, what's the matter with yours? Both seem good to me.

Old woman— Not a bit of it! Jack is all for his business—has plunged in heart and soul to make a success of it—thinks of nothing else. But Helen—well, her head is just full of dresses, parties and beaus. And now she's going West to visit relatives in a town where, as she says, there are more men.

New woman— How can you be so blind? Don't you see Helen's attending to business just as much as Jack? You wouldn't let her become a wage-earner, held out marriage as the only occupation for a woman, so why shouldn't she try to be successful in the only line of work open to her?

Old woman— But woman was meant to be the pursued, not the pursuer; to wait delicately to be wooed——

New woman— Yes; but she can't be seen, wooed or pursued unless she comes out into the open where the wooers and pursuers range. Why tell a girl to marry and scorn

her for taking means to do it? If men were given matrimony as their only work, they'd rush for it in mobs, write letters, seek interviews and go into house-to-house canvassing. If the grown-ups find boys more interesting than girls, it's because they head one toward the ledger and the other toward the altar, and they themselves dote on the ledger. As for me, the altar seems just as useful and certainly more romantic. So if you disapprove of what you yourself have made Helen do, take her from the matrimonial warpath and set her face toward the glories of the counter and the cash box.

Many women would be pleased to be as popular as a car window.

HOUSE CLEANING DAY

What Is It To Be Feminine?

By ETHEL B. PEYSER

WE'RE cautioned to be "feminine,"
    To keep our "girlish ways,"
To think and speak like innocents,
    To fritter all our days.

And yet we hear, if women read
    New books of serious kinds
Or speak with force in public halls,
    "Those women have men's minds!"

We hear it said, if women
    In the business world succeed
And take adversity with grit,
    "They've got men's nerve, indeed!"

We hear it said, if women make
    A hat—"the dernier cri"—
"These women plan like men modistes:
    Their touch is just as free!"

If all the worthy, finer traits
    Are classed as masculine,
Why is it we should still be urged
    To do the artful feminine?

Suffrage Snapshots

By IDA HUSTED HARPER

THE WAY women will lose the respect of men when they get a vote was illustrated in Arizona, where, as soon as women were enfranchised, the men nominated the president of the Suffrage Association for State senator, and she received six hundred more votes than any other candidate on the ticket.

☐

The 135,000 members of the Woman Suffrage Party in New York City are balloting for their officers in the different districts. The Anti-Suffrage State Society announces that it is increasing at the rate of one thousand a month. This proves that in one hundred and thirty-five months, mor or less, it will catch up with the city party, provided the latter doesn't add any new members. Or at least it proves that New York women know there is a movement for the suffrage under way.

☐

The superintendent of the Cleveland public schools has just been awarded a fine and jail sentence for discharging some women teachers for organizing a union. Ohio women didn't get a vote, but they don't seem entirely destitute of rights.

☐

Why don't the antis get a sewing society somewhere to pass a resolution against woman suffrage? It is growing terribly monotonous to have all the women's organizations in the country declaring in favor.

☐

Indiana women have formed a council to work with the Legislature "for the uplift of women and children." Wouldn't it be of greater benefit to the State if they would work for the uplift of the legislators?

☐

In many States the suffragists' grievance is that they are kept on a political level with the convicts, but not so in South Carolina. Governor Blease took the convicts out of the penitentiary, put ballots in their hands and placed them on a political plane much higher than that of the women.

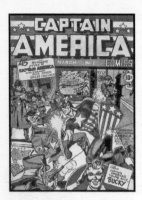

Captain America Comics #1 (March 1941)

Right when Marston and Peter must have been meeting with Gaines and Mayer to talk about what Wonder Woman ought to look like, a new superhero made his debut; Captain America.[19] He quickly became Timely Comics' most popular character.

Marston wanted his comic book's "under-meaning," about "a great movement now under way—the growth in the power of women," to be embodied in the way Wonder Woman carried herself, how she dressed, and what powers she wielded. She had to be strong, and she had to be independent. Everyone agreed about the bracelets (inspired by Olive Byrne's): it helped Gaines with his public relations problem that she could stop bullets with them; that was good for the gun problem. Also, this new superhero had to be uncommonly beautiful; she'd wear a tiara, like the crown awarded at the Miss America pageant. Marston wanted her to be opposed to war, but she had to be willing to fight for democracy. In fact, she had to be superpatriotic. Captain America wore an American flag: blue tights, red gloves, red boots, and, on his torso, red and white stripes and a white star. Like Captain America—because of Captain America—Wonder Woman would have to wear red, white, and blue, too. But, ideally, she'd also wear very little. To sell magazines, Gaines wanted his superwoman to be as naked as he could get away with.

Peter got his instructions: draw a woman who's as powerful as Superman, as sexy as Miss Fury, as scantily clad as Sheena the jungle queen, and as patriotic as Captain America. He made a series of sketches. Then he sent them to Marston.

"Dear Dr. Marston, I slapped these two out in a hurry," Peter wrote, sending along sketches, in color pencil, of Wonder Woman wearing a tiara; bracelets; a short skirt, blue with white stars; sandals; and a red bustier with an American eagle spread across her breasts. He explained, "The eagle is tough to handle as when in perspective or in profile he doesn't show up clearly—the shoes look like a stenographer's. I think the idea might be incorporated as a sort of Roman contraption. Peter."

Marston wrote back, adding his notes to the drawing. "Dear Pete—I think the gal with hand up is <u>very</u> cute. I like her skirt, legs, hair. Bracelets okay + boots. These probably will work out." Drawing an arrow to the fussy, delicate sandals, he added, "<u>No</u> on these!" Eyeing her bare midriff, he asked, "Don't we have to put a red stripe around her waist as belt?"[20]

A Fourth of July Varga Girl, Alberto Vargas, *Esquire*, July 1942

Later, it seems, Marston made another suggestion. What if Wonder Woman were to look more like a Varga girl, one of the pin-up girls drawn by Alberto Vargas that appeared every month in *Esquire* (a magazine Marston regularly wrote for). The Varga girl, introduced in *Esquire* in October 1940, was long-legged, slender, and open-mouthed. She wore her hair down, her nails polished, her legs bare, and barely any more clothing than what a swimsuit covers. Wonder Woman, with her kinky boots, looks as though she could have been on a page of *Esquire*'s annual pin-up calendar. The Varga girls were just this side of allowable, by the standards of the 1940s: in 1943, the U.S. Post Office declared that *Esquire* contained material of an "obscene, lewd, and lascivious character."[21] Wonder Woman would run into the same kind of trouble.

Peter sent Marston another drawing, in pen, ink, and watercolor. Wonder Woman, carrying her lasso, wears red boots instead of sandals, blue short shorts instead of a skirt, a tight-fitting red halter top with white lapels, and a belt marked "WW." Marston liked the boots and the short shorts. But he had doubts about the top. "This collar may become dated," he wrote on the drawing.[22] Her costume is very close to that

Harry G. Peter, Wonder Woman design, 1942

From "The Origin of Wonder Woman,"
Wonder Woman #1 (Summer 1942)

worn by the Fourth of July Varga girl from 1942.[23] Wonder Woman, as Peter eventually drew her, looks very unlike any of his earlier drawings of women. She's less a Gibson girl than a Varga girl, with a great deal of Lou Rogers added in: the suffragist as pin-up.

Peter worked under Marston's direction. Marston's control over the final product is suggested in the scripts themselves. Marston dictated page layouts, panels, and color choices. Below a caption to read, "Captain Steve Trevor, brilliant young officer in the Army Intelligence Service, crashes while flying over lonely seas and disappears in a smother of mist and foam," Marston explained what Peter should draw: "Trevor's plane nose diving into a sea covered with heavy mist, a fountain of water splashes up where the plane hits. Trevor's figure thrown clear of the plane, is falling head down, arms and legs waving helplessly, beside the plane into the sea." The final panel shows exactly that. (Marston suggested that Trevor should cry out, as he falls, "No hope of rescue here—this is the end!" That was cut, either by Peter or by Mayer.)[24] Marston's scripts include instructions, too, for the other artists working with Peter, letterers and colorists, like this one: "W.W. is tossing him a *purple* bottle of tablets—*color artist* take note!"[25]

Once Marston and Gaines agreed on Wonder Woman's look and Mayer approved the script, Peter set to work drawing a nine-page story called "Introducing Wonder Woman." From the start, she was a woman of mystery: "With a hundred times the ability and strength of our best male athletes and strongest wrestlers, she appears as from nowhere to avenge an injustice or right a wrong! As lovely as Aphrodite—as wise as Athena—with the speed of Mercury and the strength of Hercules—she is known only as Wonder Woman, but who she is, or whence she came, nobody knows!" (Marston hid his own identity, too, publishing Wonder Woman under the name "Charles Moulton," a pseudonym made up of Maxwell Charles Gaines's middle name and his own.)

In "Introducing Wonder Woman," Marston and Peter covered their character's backstory in a two-page spread. To the kids who read comic books, it was an entirely new story. But it came straight out of the pages of the feminist utopian fiction of the 1910s. Hippolyte recounts for her daughter, Diana, the history of the female race:

In the days of Ancient Greece, many centuries ago, we Amazons were the foremost nation in the world. In Amazonia, women ruled and all was well. Then one day, Hercules, the strongest man in the world, stung by taunts that he couldn't conquer the Amazon women, selected his strongest and fiercest warriors and landed on our shores. I challenged him to personal combat— because I knew that with my MAGIC GIRDLE, given to me by Aphrodite, Goddess of Love, I could not lose.

Hercules, defeated, contrives to steal Hippolyte's magic girdle, and all of the Amazons become the slaves of men, shackled and fettered, until, with Aphrodite's aid, they escape, flee Greece, and settle on Paradise Island. "For it was Aphrodite's condition that we leave the man-made world and establish a new world of our own!" Hippolyte tells Diana. "Aphrodite also decreed that we must always wear these bracelets fashioned by our captors, as a reminder that we must always keep aloof from men."

Their peace is interrupted when Captain Steve Trevor crashes his plane onto the island. "Danger again threatens the entire world," Aphrodite tells Hippolyte. "The Gods have decreed that this American army officer crash on Paradise Island. You must take him back to America—to help fight the forces of hate and oppression." Athena, the goddess of wisdom and war, agrees. "Yes, Hippolyte, American liberty and freedom must be preserved! You must send with him your strongest and wisest Amazon—the finest of your wonder women!"

Hippolyte stages a tournament to find the strongest and wisest Amazon. Diana wins. "And so Diana, the Wonder Woman, giving up her right to eternal life, leaves Paradise Island to take the man she loves back to America—the land she learns to love and protect, and adopts as her own!" Her mother stitches for her a red, white, and blue costume.[26]

In Wonder Woman, Marston created a character to answer every one of the comic-book critics' objections. She's strong, but she's not a bully: "At last, in a world torn by the hatreds and wars of men, appears a *woman* to whom the problems and feats of men are mere child's play." She hates guns: "Bullets never solved a human problem yet!" She's relentless, but she always spares her victims. "Wonder Woman never kills!" Above all, she believes in the United States: "America, the last citadel of democracy, and of equal rights for women!"[27] Wonder Woman left Paradise Island to fight fascism with feminism.

Wonder Woman made her debut in "Introducing Wonder Woman" in *All-Star Comics #8*, which appeared on newsstands in the fall of 1941 and stayed there through the end of its cover date of December 1941–January 1942, just when the United States was entering what would become the most fatal war in the history of the world. On December 12, 1941, five days after the bombing of Pearl Harbor, Marston wrote a letter to FDR. "Dear Sir," he began. "I have the honor to offer you my services in any military or civilian capacity where my training and experience as a lawyer and psychologist may be of use, for the duration of the war." He felt he could contribute in a number of ways: "I respectfully suggest that my most useful qualification in the present emergency is that of an expert in lie detection." Marston, who had conducted research for the army during the First World War, wanted to sign up to serve in the second. He enclosed with his letter to the president a copy of his 1938 book, *The Lie Detector Test,* along with his entry in *Who's Who.* He added, "I am also a lawyer, writer, public speaker, advertising and personnel adviser and am experienced in writing and directing publicity." He didn't mention that he was the creator of Wonder Woman. He signed off: "With my personal pledge of loyalty and devotion to the greatest cause on earth."[28]

The White House forwarded Marston's letter to the FBI. No one ever called on Marston to serve. Instead, Leonarde Keeler and his commercial polygraph were put to use in the war effort, first in the interrogation of POWs and then in the screening of American staff and scientists working on the atomic bomb. During the Second World War, passing a lie detector test became an essential step in obtaining U.S. national security clearance, a de facto loyalty oath. Between police interrogation, employee fidelity tests, prisoner-of-war interrogations, and security clearances, deception tests were given to millions of people in the United States over the course of the war, despite the fact that the test wasn't used anywhere else in the world and doesn't actually detect deception, as had been the conclusion of a study conducted by the National Research Council as early as 1941.[29]

Marston fought the war not with his lie detector but on the pages of his comic books. In "Who Is Wonder Woman?," published in *Sensation Comics* in January 1942, Wonder Woman leaves Paradise Island and flies to the United States in her invisible plane, bringing the injured and bandaged Steve Trevor along in a stretcher. In Washington, she fights off gangsters and outraces automobiles. To keep an eye on Steve, she trades places with a nurse in a military hospital. The nurse, "drab Diana Prince," happens to look exactly like her. (In another version of this backstory, Wonder Woman complains about being a nurse: "In Amazonia, I'm a doctor.")[30] Then Diana Prince leaves off nursing and becomes a secretary at U.S. military intelligence. She takes excellent dictation and is an extremely fast typist. "Diana types with the speed of lightning!"[31]

Olive Byrne was a super-fast typist, too. Wonder Woman wore her bracelets. And in the big, noisy house at Cherry Orchard, it was Olive Byrne who pounded out Marston's early scripts.

"Typed article for Bill," she wrote in her diary in 1941. "Super woman 48 pages!!!"[32]

She is known only as Wonder Woman, but who she is, or whence she came, nobody knows!

24

THE JUSTICE SOCIETY OF AMERICA

IT SEEMED TO CHARLIE GAINES like so much good, clean, superpatriotic fun. But in March 1942, the National Organization for Decent Literature put *Sensation Comics* on its blacklist of "Publications Disapproved for Youth." The list was used in local decency crusades: crusaders were supposed to visit news dealers and ask them to take titles off their shelves.[1] Wonder Woman was banned.

Censoring children's literature, like banning the discussion of contraception, had been among the many crusades waged by Margaret Sanger's nemesis, Anthony Comstock. In 1884, when Comstock was campaigning against obscenity, he also attacked dime novels in a book called *Traps for the Young*. "Our youth are in danger," Comstock warned. "Mentally and morally they are cursed by a literature that is a disgrace to the nineteenth century."[2] In the 1930s, in much the same spirit, a committee of Catholic bishops had formed the Legion of Decency to protest sex, nudity, and violence in motion pictures, printing lists of church-approved films. But just as one evil was suppressed, another cropped up: comic books, a medium that borrowed its forms of storytelling from cinema. In 1938, the committee of Catholic bishops founded the National Organization for Decent Literature, whose position was that comic books were a disgrace to the twentieth century.[3]

In 1942, when the latest list came out, Gaines wrote a letter to Bishop John F. Noll. "While I am pleased to see that comic magazines as a whole have been eliminated from this N.O.D.L. list," Gaines wrote, "I

am, of course, rather concerned that 'Sensation Comics' was included."
He reminded the bishop of the impeccable credentials of the members
of his editorial advisory board. He had just one question.

"Would you be good enough to advise me, at your earliest convenience, which of the five points in your 'Code for Clean Reading' has
been violated by anything which appears in 'Sensation Comics'?"[4]

"Practically the only reason for which 'Sensation Comics' was
placed on the banned list of the N.O.D.L. was that it violates Point
Four of the Code," the bishop wrote back. "Wonder Woman is not
sufficiently dressed."[5]

Gaines didn't much mind that objection; nor did it require much of
a response. He wasn't about to put more clothes on Wonder Woman.
And he was determined not to abandon her. Instead, he had plans for
her to join the Justice Society.

The Justice Society of America, a league of superheroes, held its first
meeting in *All-Star Comics #3*, in the winter of 1940, with nine founding members: the Flash, Hawkman, the Spectre, the Sandman, Doctor
Fate, Hourman, Green Lantern, and the Atom. "Each of them is a hero
in his own right, but when the Justice Society calls, they are only
members, sworn to uphold honor and justice!"[6]

The Justice Society was a good way to both promote established
superheroes and try out new ones before giving them more pages or
their own titles. Superman and Batman were honorary members; they
didn't have to show up unless the situation was dire. In the summer
of 1941, in *All-Star Comics #6*, the Flash was promoted to honorary
Justice Society membership, too, making way for Johnny Thunder
to become a regular.[7] Wonder Woman's debut, "Introducing Wonder
Woman" in *All-Star Comics #8*, came in an issue that included a Justice Society story in which Green Lantern became an honorary member; Hourman took a leave of absence; Dr. Mid-Nite and the Starman
became members; and Hawkman was elected chairman.[8]

There was a lot of turnover at the Justice Society, but there had
never been a female member. As soon as Wonder Woman made her
debut, Gaines ordered his writers and artists to find a place for her
in the next adventure of the Justice Society. Wonder Woman makes

her first appearance not as an elected member but "as a guest star in a national emergency," in *All-Star Comics #11*. The national emergency is, of course, the entry of the United States into the war: once the Japanese bombed Pearl Harbor, all the members of the Justice Society decided to join the armed services.

"I'm going to enlist in the U.S. Army!" announces Hawkman. "You'll have to get another chairman!"

Hawkman enlists as his alter ego, an archaeologist named Carter Hall. Eventually, though, he decides to reveal himself to his commanding officer. "I'm the Hawkman and part of your squadron!" Then he flies to a steamship en route to the Philippines, where he meets Diana Prince; he recognizes her instantly.

"Diana Prince—why, you must be Wonder Woman!"

"Why, how did you know?"

"The Justice Society manages to learn many things!"

Diana changes into her Wonder Woman costume and joins the fight. "Wonder Woman reporting for duty, sir!" she tells a U.S. Army officer after capturing some enemy soldiers. "Here are some Japs I caught!"[9]

Gaines had more plans for his girl star. In *Sensation Comics #5*, he included a special offer: free copies of the next issue of the magazine to the first thousand readers who filled out a ballot and mailed it to the editor. Influenced by the rise of public-opinion polling, Gaines conducted this sort of survey all the time, both to gauge his audience and to promote his comics. The survey asked which of six superheroes ought to be part of the Justice Society: Wonder Woman, Mr. Terrific, Little Boy Blue, the Wildcat, the Gay Ghost, or the Black Pirate?[10]

The results of the Justice Society readers' poll, taken in 1942

	U10 B*	U10 G	10–12 B	10–12 G	O12 B	O12 G	TOTAL BOYS	TOTAL GIRLS	TOTAL
WONDER WOMAN	37	27	128	123	112	73	277	223	500
MR. TERRIFIC	1	0	12	6	5	0	18	6	24
BOY BLUE	5	0	12	4	5	2	22	6	28
WILDCAT	1	0	15	4	1	4	17	8	25
GAY GHOST	1	0	12	2	6	2	19	4	23
BLACK PIRATE	1	0	6	2	7	0	14	2	16
TOTAL	46	27	185	141	136	81	367	249	616

*U10 B, boys under ten years old; U10 G, girls under ten; 10–12 B, boys ten to twelve; 10–12 G, girls ten to twelve; O12 B, boys over twelve; O12 G, girls over twelve.

Justice Society readers' poll. From *Sensation Comics #5* (May 1942)

In March 1942, Gaines's staff tabulated the results of the votes cast, sorting them by age and sex: Wonder Woman was the first choice of every group.[11] Gaines wanted to include Wonder Woman in the Justice Society; he got exactly the result he wanted. On the ballot, Wonder Woman's face is nearly double the size of the faces of the other contestants, and her face, and no other character's, appears twice. Gaines had rigged the vote. Still, it didn't stop the critics.

Lauretta Bender, with her husband, Paul Schilder, and their two sons, about 1939

For all of Wonder Woman's success, Gaines was still worried about the National Organization for Decent Literature's "Publications Disapproved for Youth." He'd hired Marston, a psychologist, in order to steer clear of censorship, only to encounter more of it after hiring Marston as a writer. He needed another expert.

In the winter of 1942, he arranged to have copies of his exchange with Bishop Noll sent to Lauretta Bender, MD.[12] Bender, forty-five, was a senior psychiatrist at Bellevue Hospital, where she was director of the children's ward. She was also an associate professor of psychiatry at NYU's medical school. She was an expert on emotionally disturbed and aggressive children; she specialized on children under the age of twelve, and she was especially interested in whether they could be either distressed or helped by reading. She herself hadn't learned to read until fourth or fifth grade; she was profoundly dyslexic, a disability that, she later said, accounted for her interest in studying what children get out of what they read. Delivering the valedictorian address at her high school graduation in Los Angeles in 1916, she spoke about the importance of educating girls: "We have hands that must work, brains that must think, and personalities that must be developed." When she decided she wanted to go to college, her mother denounced her, telling her, "A woman's place is in the home," but Bender ignored her and went to Stanford, and then to the University of Chicago, for a graduate degree in pathology. She earned her MD in Iowa in 1926. During a year at the Henry Phipps Psychiatric Clinic at Johns Hopkins, she met Paul Schilder, a Viennese psychoanalyst and colleague of Freud's. In the spring of 1930, Schilder left Baltimore to become director of clinical psychiatry at Bellevue Hospital in New York; Bender joined him there that fall. Four years later she was named director of the hospital's children's ward, and, two years after that, in 1936, she and Schilder married.[13]

Between 1930 and 1940, Bender observed the cases of some seven thousand children brought to Bellevue. In 1936, Bender and two colleagues published a study involving eighty-three children admitted to Bellevue for behavioral problems; the psychiatrists had shown the children scenes of aggression in Flash Gordon and other comic strips and asked them questions like "Is it right to hit somebody who insults you?"[14]

In 1940, Schilder, fifty-four, was killed by a car on his way home from visiting Bender and their eight-day-old daughter in the hospital. Bender, left with three children—Michael, three; Peter, two; and the baby, Jane—soon became painfully interested in studying how children cope with the traumatic loss of a parent.[15] Watching her own young children, she observed that there were stories they simply could not bear. "The oldest boy cannot tolerate anything in the way of a story, even of Peter Rabbit, who, if you recall your Peter Rabbit, went into a garden where his father got into an accident at the hands of a hoe of a farmer and had been put in a rabbit pie. I had to take him screaming out of the puppet show on that picture." Her second son, though, had found comfort in comic books, especially those containing stories of children losing parents. Bender explained, "I think for him it is an effort to find a solution of the mystery of life and death and how it can happen that a child's father can leave him even before the child knows the father." Her daughter, who never had any chance to know her father, began writing her own comic books as soon as she was old enough to write. She wrote one murder story, Bender said, "in which the bloody head of the person who had been attacked would lie on the lap of the beloved person, whoever it was, and an effort would be made to soothe it." This worried Jane's teacher, but Bender thought it was just fine: "It is her way of solving her problem."[16]

Gaines knew none of this. But what he did know—probably from Marston—was that in 1941 Bender had written a very interesting journal article with Reginald Lourie, a medical resident under her supervision, called "The Effect of Comic Books on the Ideology of Children." Bender and Lourie reported the results of a study they had conducted in the wake of the public debate that had begun in 1940, when Sterling North called comic books a national disgrace. As pediatric psychiatrists, they were, naturally, fascinated by comic books. "Anyone in contact with children of school age, and particularly those working closely with children, sooner or later becomes conscious of the extent to which the constant reading of comic books has invaded their thinking, daily activities, and play," they explained. They wanted to know whether comic books affected children's behavior. "Do they lead to anxiety?" they asked. "Do they lead to aggression?"

Bender and Lourie addressed these questions by recounting four cases of children brought to Bellevue Hospital for behavioral problems. All had suffered massive childhood trauma. Tessie, age twelve, had witnessed her father, a convicted murderer, kill himself. Her mother was dying of cancer. She had decided to call herself Shiera, after a comic-book girl who is always rescued, at the last minute, by the Flash. Bender and Lourie decided that reading comics was a form of self-therapy: "This overwhelmed child was attempting to find, via the comic books, a method of clarifying her confusing personal problems," they wrote. "By identifying herself with the heroine who is always rescued from perilous situations, she temporarily achieved an escape from her own difficulties." Kenneth, age eleven, had spent most of his life in foster homes. He had also been raped. He believed he was going to die. He was frantic unless medicated, or unless he was "wearing a Superman cape." He felt safe in it—he could fly away if he wanted to—and "he felt that the cape protected him from an assault in the rear." Bender and Laurie, who wrote with marked compassion, approved of comic books with considerable enthusiasm. "Comic books can probably be best understood if they are looked upon as an expression of the folklore of this age," they explained. They offered children a way to play, a kind of fantasy, entirely normal—a way, even, to solve problems. Sure, there was mayhem everywhere—murder, bondage, shootings. But it was resolved. "Aggression is dealt with in most of the stories," they observed, "but its purpose as carried out by the hero is to prevent hostile and noxious aggression by others." They concluded, "The comics may be said to offer the same type of mental catharsis to its readers that Aristotle claimed was an attribute of the drama." They were troubled, though, that "male heroes predominate."[17] Weren't women ever strong?

Gaines had one way to respond to the comic-book controversy—reaching out to Bender; Marston had another. It was probably at Marston's urging that *Family Circle* reported on Bender and Lourie's study in April 1942, with a reassuring tagline: "Heroes capable of any wonderwork—born of fantasy but related to reality—are but today's counterparts of what you yourself thrilled to as a child."[18]

Meanwhile, Marston did his best to rein in his excesses. "Enclosed find a wonderful script by the best writer in the business," he wrote to Mayer in June 1942. "If you send roses in token of your appreciation, make them large white ones indicating the purity of this script, the nice clean socking, blood, war and killing which you and our Catholic friends regard as nice, clean entertainment for youngsters and especially the absence of all electric chairs and needles, even knitting needles, being excluded from this extraordinarily virtuous script."[19]

Tidied up or not, Wonder Woman sold like crazy. No one, aside from Superman and Batman, even came close. Gaines didn't need any more convincing. Just to be sure, though, he conducted one more poll. He included a one-page questionnaire in *All-Star Comics #11*. It included the question "Should WONDER WOMAN be allowed, even though a woman, to become a member of the Justice Society?" Gaines, reporting the returns to Bender, remarked, "It is surprising to note (or is it?) that there is very little antipathy to the encroachment of a female into what was a strictly masculine domain." Of the first 1,801 questionnaires returned, 1,265 boys and 333 girls said "Yes"; 197 boys and just 6 girls said "No."[20]

Wonder Woman joined the Justice Society in the August–September 1942 issue of *All-Star Comics*. It was not quite the triumph it might have been. She was named the society's secretary.

25

THE MILK SWINDLE

MAKING WONDER WOMAN the Justice Society's secretary wasn't Marston's idea; it was Gardner Fox's idea. Wonder Woman's adventures as a member of the Justice Society were written not by Marston but by Fox, who'd worked on Batman, created Hawkman, and had helped launch the Flash and the Sandman. Like Marston's Wonder Woman stories, Fox's were edited by Sheldon Mayer and published by Charlie Gaines. But Fox's Wonder Woman is useless and helpless. She hardly ever leaves Justice Society headquarters. In the summer of 1942, when all the male superheroes head off to war, Wonder Woman stays behind to answer the mail. "Good luck, boys," she calls out to them. "I wish I could be going with you!"[1]

From Gardner Fox, "The Black Dragon Menace," *All-Star Comics #12* (August–September 1942)

In December 1942, when the men are about to leave on a mission to feed war-ravaged Europe, Wonder Woman stays at headquarters, explaining, "I have to remain behind but I'll be with you in spirit!" Two months later, no one but Wonder Woman turns up for a Justice Society meeting; the men are too busy. Bored, Wonder Woman decides to round up "all the girlfriends of the Justice

Society members," to go looking for the boys. "This is the opportunity of a lifetime for us girls!" But in the end, they don't rescue anyone; instead, they get trapped and need rescuing themselves.[2]

On the rare occasion that any real action takes place at Justice Society headquarters, Fox gets rid of Wonder Woman before anything interesting happens. "Gentlemen!" she cries out at the beginning of a story from the summer of 1943. "The minutes of all past Justice Society meetings have been *stolen*!"

"Are you sure you didn't take the record book home to type up the latest minutes?" asks Hawkman.

"Absolutely!" Wonder Woman bursts out. "But just to be on the safe side I'll go home and check on it."

And then she heads out the door and is gone for the rest of the episode. The story runs for fifty pages; Fox dispenses with Wonder Woman in two panels.[3]

Marston was furious. In April 1942, he complained to Mayer, and when Fox submitted his next script, Marston insisted on rewriting it. "I ask you to note the universal truth in my script re war and women taming men so they like peace and love better than fighting," Marston wrote to Mayer, handing in his own script, in which Wonder Woman rides a rocket through space.[4]

Fox's Wonder Woman was a secretary in a swimsuit. Marston's Wonder Woman was a Progressive Era feminist, charged with fighting evil, intolerance, destruction, injustice, suffering, and even sorrow, on behalf of democracy, freedom, justice, and equal rights for women. In 1942, when Fox's Wonder Woman was typing up the minutes to meetings of the Justice Society, Marston's Wonder Woman was organizing boycotts, strikes, and political rallies.

In a story published in *Sensation Comics* in July 1942, Wonder Woman discovers that the International Milk Company has been charging outrageous prices for milk, leading to undernourished American children. The story came straight out of a Hearst newspaper that Harry G. Peter had worked for in the 1910s. In 1919, and again in 1926, Hearst had used his papers to attack the politician Al Smith as "one of the milk crooks" for conspiring with "the milk trust" to raise the

Inez Milholland Boissevain, leading a suffrage parade in Washington, D.C., March 3, 1913

price of milk, a form of profiteering that was killing American babies.[5] "It *can't* be legal to deprive poor children of milk!" Diana Prince cries when she confronts Alphonso De Gyppo, president of the International Milk Company, in 1942. Kidnapped by Al De Gyppo's henchman, Diana is left to drown in a giant tank of milk. ("What a waste of good baby-food!" she thinks.) After she escapes, she changes into her Wonder Woman costume and organizes a "gigantic demonstration against the milk racket." Thousands of poor mothers and their children march through the streets, led by Wonder Woman and the girls from Holliday College, who carry a banner that reads, "THE INTERNATIONAL MILK COMPANY IS STARVING AMERICA'S CHILDREN!!" In composing a panel in which Wonder Woman, riding a white horse, leads the charge, Peter borrowed from a famous series of photographs of a suffrage parade held in Washington in 1913; Inez Milholland Boissevain led the procession, wearing a golden tiara and riding a white horse.

Marston updated the Progressive Era story about the milk trust by making it part of a secret German plot (itself an echo of the story from the 1910s) led by Baroness Paula von Gunther, a Nazi agent. "I have spent seven million dollars to take milk from the mouths of American children!" the baroness tells Wonder Woman after she's chained her to a train stock car filled with ten thousand gallons of milk. "Your

Wonder Woman leads a political rally. From "The Milk Swindle," *Sensation Comics #7* (July 1942)

rising generation will be weakened and dwarfed! Germany, in twenty years, will conquer your milk-starved youths and will rule America!" Wonder Woman frees herself from the chains that bind her, stops the milk-tank car from running off the tracks ("This will save thousands of gallons of good milk for American children!"), and captures the baroness. The price of milk drops.[6]

Wonder Woman's next adventure was inspired by Progressive Era labor activism, too, including a textile workers' strike in Lawrence, Massachusetts, in 1912. (Margaret Sanger had been involved in that strike and, likely, so had Ethel Byrne. Sanger went to Washington to testify before Congress about the damage done by the textile industry to the lives of women and children. Sanger had also helped organize restaurant and hotel workers in New York and silk workers in Paterson, New Jersey.)[7] In *Sensation Comics #8* (August 1942), Wonder Woman finds out that women working at Bullfinch's Department Stores, owned by the fabulously wealthy Gloria Bullfinch, are being underpaid. "We Bullfinch girls only make eleven dollars a week," Diana's friend Molly complains. Fifty girls have been fired for insubordination. The rest have gone on strike. At the picket line in front of the store, they carry signs reading, "OUR TOIL MAKES GLORIA GLAMOROUS," "BULLFINCH

The Lawrence textile strike of 1912

STORES UNFAIR TO GIRLS," and "WE STARVE WHILE GLORIA BULLFINCH DINES AT THE 400 CLUB!" The strikers are fired. Wonder Woman visits Gloria Bullfinch at her mansion and ties her up with her magic lasso. Using the hypnotic powers of the lasso, Wonder Woman tells Gloria Bullfinch that she is really a girl named Ruth Smith and instructs her to go get a job at Bullfinch's Department Stores. Meanwhile, Wonder Woman discovers that the fiend behind the store's exploitation of its workers is Gloria Bullfinch's fiancé, Prince Guigi Del Slimo. Gloria, after working in her own department store as Ruth Smith, is awakened to Del Slimo's perfidy, and slugs him, shouting, "I only wish I could punch like *Wonder Woman*!" Then she takes over management of the store and issues an announcement: "Girls, starting now your salaries are doubled!"[8]

Next, in a *Sensation Comics* story from September 1942, Wonder Woman tackles heartless husbands. The real Diana Prince—Wonder Woman's look-alike—returns to Washington, married to a man named Dan White and newly a mother. Her husband is a jealous brute. He is also out of work. In one panel, Diana White, wearing an apron, is

Diana Prince helps striking department store workers. From "Department Store Perfidy," *Sensation Comics #8* (August 1942)

cooking in the kitchen while the baby gurgles in a bassinet in the living room. When she tells her husband she'd like to go back to work, he storms across the room threateningly.

"Please let me go to work, Dan!"

"No! My wife doesn't *have* to work."

"But Dan, we're down to our last dollar and the baby *must* have food."

Then she leaves the apartment, dressed in her army nurse's uniform, to look for work. She goes to see Diana Prince, asking for her identity back—and her job. Wonder Woman, after obliging, visits the Whites' apartment, only to be mistaken by Dan White for his wife.

"Well? Did you get a job? If you did, I'll—"

"My, but you're tough! No, I haven't any job now, but—"

"You won't get any job—I'll fix that! You'll stay right in this room from now on."

"What are you going to do—keep me locked up?"

And then he chains her to the stove, telling her, "I'm going to chain you like this every time I go out!"

Much melodrama ensues, including the kidnapping of Diana White by Nazi agents who have also plotted to destroy Dan White's career. In the end, Wonder Woman rescues everyone, and the marriage is saved. Diana Prince, who's gotten her job back, tells Diana White, "But I envy you yours, as wife and mother."[9]

Wonder Woman had not one secret identity, in this episode, but two. She was Diana Prince, working woman, and also Diana White, her look-alike, wife and mother: Elizabeth Holloway and Olive Byrne, both. Marston went on record, more than once, advocating employment for women. "The truest kindness to any woman," he wrote in *Tomorrow* magazine in 1942, "is to provide her with an opportunity for self-expression in some constructive field: to work, not at home with cook-stove and scrubbing brush, but outside, independently, in the world of men and affairs."[10]

Wonder Woman cherishes her independence. She can't marry, according to Amazonian law, but she doesn't want to, either, despite Steve Trevor's repeated proposals. "Blistering blazes!" Trevor cries. "Why will that beautiful gal always invite trouble? If she'd only married *me,* she'd be home cooking my dinner right now!"[11] But Wonder Woman is very glad not to be home cooking dinner. She has other work to do. She is also careful about letting men have any kind of power over her. She knows that if she lets a man weld chains to her bracelets, she'll lose all her strength. When that happens, she succumbs to despair. "These bracelets—they're an Amazon's greatest strength and weakness! What a fool I was to let a man weld chains upon them! It just makes a girl realize how she has to watch herself in this man's world."[12] On the other hand, she needs her bracelets. The danger, illustrated in a story called "The Unbound Amazon," is that without her bracelets, Wonder Woman is wildly, terrifyingly violent. When the villainous Mavis removes her bracelets, Wonder Woman goes on a rampage. "I'm completely uncontrolled! I'm free to *destroy* like a *man*!"[13]

During the war, the villains in Wonder Woman were often German, like the fiends who cry, "*Vonder Voman*—bullets dond't hurt her!" They were also often Japanese. The racism of Wonder Woman is the racism pervasive in comic books from the 1940s. Blacks and Mexicans speak in dialect. "Dis suitcase show am heaby!" complains one Pullman porter.

"Si, si! Old mine, muy pronto!" cries Pancho, a Mexican. In spite of Marston's own writings condemning prejudice, including anti-Semitism, his comic books often featured greedy, hooked-nosed villains, like the blind Mole Men, who build a secret prison beneath Paradise Island where they use Amazons as slaves.[14]

But what the king of the Mole Men and all villains in Wonder Woman share is their opposition to women's equality. Against each of them, Wonder Woman fights for a woman's right to work, to run for political office, and to lead. When Wonder Woman discovers the lost world of the Incas, she tells

From "Grown-Down Land," *Sensation Comics #31* (July 1944)

the chief's daughter that she should gain the throne: "It's time those lost Incas were ruled by a *woman*!"[15]

In May 1942, FDR created the Women's Army Auxiliary Corps. One hundred and fifty thousand women joined the army, filling noncombat jobs and freeing men for combat. "The Women's Army Auxiliary

From "The Girl with the Gun," *Sensation Comics #20* (August 1943)

Corps appears to be the final realization of woman's dream of complete equality of men," Margaret Sanger wrote. But she thought it was a mixed success. "The government, however, authors this honor with a string attached." Sanger was outraged that the government refused to provide contraceptives for WAACs and adopted a policy of dismissing any woman who got pregnant. Still, she thought that was useful, because it was so illuminating. "This new women's Army is a great thing," Sanger declared, "a real test of the woman's movement. Never before has the fight for woman's equality narrowed down to the real issue, sex."[16]

At the time, Sanger was dismayed at the direction in which the Birth Control Federation of America was headed. In 1942, and over Sanger's strenuous objection, the organization changed its name to the Planned Parenthood Federation of America, on the grounds that the phrase "birth control" was simply too radical. "We will get no further because of the title; I assure you of that," Sanger warned. "Our progress up to date has been because the Birth Control movement was built on a strong foundation of truth, justice, right, and good common sense." During the Second World War, the leaders of Planned Parenthood argued that limiting family size was part of winning the war. Sanger, though, believed the best argument for contraception had to do with women's rights. "One democratic right which greater numbers of women are enjoying during this war and which was denied to most during the last," Sanger wrote in 1942, "is to decide for themselves whether they shall have babies or not."[17]

During the war, Sanger struggled to get that message across. The men who ran Planned Parenthood in the 1940s didn't want to hear about women's rights. But Marston, explaining why he had created Wonder Woman, carried forth the feminist argument Sanger had made in *The Pivot of Civilization*: "The only hope for civilization," he said, "is the greater freedom, development and equality of women."[18]

26

THE WONDER WOMEN OF HISTORY

ASIDE FROM SUPERMAN AND BATMAN, none of DC's superheroes was anywhere near as popular as Wonder Woman. She was the lead feature in *Sensation Comics;* she appeared regularly in *All-Star Comics;* and in *Comic Cavalcade,* a quarterly, she was, far and away, the star: she was on every cover, and hers was, in every issue, the lead story. In July 1942, she became the first female superhero to have her own comic book. "The reaction to my new feature, 'WONDER WOMAN,' in 'Sensation Comics,' has been so good," Gaines wrote to Lauretta Bender, "that I am publishing a 'WONDER WOMAN QUARTERLY' containing all episodes of that character, just like 'Superman' and 'Batman.' "[1]

It was a good time for Amazons. *By Jupiter,* Richard Rodgers and Lorenz Hart's longest-running musical comedy, opened on Broadway in June 1942. Based on a farce called *The Warrior's Husband,* it's the story of Greek warriors sent to steal Diana's sacred girdle; Ray Bolger plays Hippolyte's hapless husband. "We're here to fight the Amazons!" the men sing. "They're only women but we hear / they wield a mighty wicked spear!" Marston took Holloway to see it. He thought it was very funny.[2] It also didn't hurt sales of his comics.

With the launch of *Wonder Woman,* Marston decided that the time had come to make a splash, by revealing a secret. He drafted a press release titled "Noted Psychologist Revealed as Author of Best-Selling 'Wonder Woman' ":

With the announcement yesterday that the popular comics heroine, "Wonder Woman," will now rate a whole magazine to herself beginning July 22, M. C. Gaines, publisher of *All-American Comics* at 480 Lexington Avenue, also revealed officially for the first time that the author of "Wonder Woman" is Dr. William Moulton Marston, internationally famous psychologist and inventor of the widely-publicized "Lie Detector" test.

In the press release, Marston explained that Wonder Woman was meant as an allegory: "Like her male prototype, 'Superman,' 'Wonder Woman' is gifted with tremendous physical strength—but unlike Superman she can be injured." Marston went on, " 'Wonder Woman' has bracelets welded on her wrists; with these she can repulse bullets. But if she lets any man weld chains on these bracelets, she loses her power. This, says Dr. Marston, is what happens to all women when they submit to a man's domination." *Wonder Woman* was a form of feminist propaganda, Marston insisted: " 'Wonder Woman' was conceived by Dr. Marston to set up a standard among children and young people of strong, free, courageous womanhood; and to combat the idea that women are inferior to men, and to inspire girls to self-confidence and achievement in athletics, occupations and professions monopolized by men."[3] She wasn't meant to be a superwoman; she was meant to be an everywoman.

The first issue of *Wonder Woman* dwelled on her origins. "I think I got EVERYTHING in but the cat's tail," Marston wrote to Mayer, sending him the first script.[4] Also introduced in the first issue of *Wonder Woman* was a regular four-page centerfold feature called "Wonder Women of History": feminist biography.[5]

It started when Gaines met twenty-nine-year-old Alice Marble, the top women's tennis player in the world. Marble had won the U.S. Open women's singles in 1936, 1938, 1939, and 1940; the women's doubles every year from 1937 through 1940; and mixed doubles in 1936, 1938, 1939, and 1940. Then she retired from competition. Introduced to Gaines at a cocktail party where everyone was talking about the

Alice Marble, in *Wonder Woman #1* (July 1942)

crazy popularity of Superman and Wonder Woman, Marble asked a question.

"Why don't you do real-life wonder women, the women who have made history?"

"Such as?"

"Clara Barton, Dolley Madison, Eleanor Roosevelt."

Gaines asked Marble to do some research and write some scripts. Then he gave her a desk, and a title: associate editor. He put her photograph in the first issue of *Wonder Woman*. He also paid her a great deal of money. She later said she'd earned fifty thousand dollars writing the "Wonder Women of History."[6]

Each installment of Marble's "Wonder Women of History" profiled a different woman. One point of the series was to celebrate the lives of heroic women and explain the importance of women's history. Another was to promote *Wonder Woman*. In July 1942, Gaines sent to prominent women all over the country packages containing the first issue of *Wonder Woman;* Marston's press release; a self-addressed, stamped envelope; and a letter, under Marble's signature, seeking nominations for subjects to profile. "As you have probably found in your own experience," Marble wrote, "even in this emancipated world, women still have many problems and have not yet reached their fullest growth and development. 'WONDER WOMAN' marks the first time that daring, strength and ingenuity have been featured as womanly qualities. This cannot help but have its lasting effect upon the minds of those who are now boys and girls."

The first Wonder Woman of History was Florence Nightingale, Marble explained, and Clara Barton was up next. But as for who else to include, Marble said, that was up to the women of America: "I am conducting a nationwide poll of leading women in business and in public and professional life, to ascertain what famous women of ancient and modern times should be included."[7]

By its third issue, *Wonder Woman* was selling more than a half million copies.[8] How many responses Marble received to her nationwide poll is not known, but the women whose biographies appeared in the pages of *Wonder Woman* in the 1940s were scientists, writers, politicians, social workers, doctors, nurses, athletes, and adventurers: Sojourner Truth, Abigail Adams, Madame Curie, Evangeline Booth, Lillian D. Wald, Madame Chiang Kai-shek, Susan B. Anthony, Joan of Arc, Jane Addams, Julia Ward Howe, Helen Keller, Lucretia Mott, Elizabeth Blackwell, Sarah Bernhardt, Amelia Earhart, Maria Mitchell, Carrie Chapman Catt, Dolley Madison, Sacagawea, Elizabeth Barrett Browning, Dorothea Dix, Nellie Bly, Jenny Lind, and Fanny Burney. It was Hecht's *True Comics*—comic books as history books— but, here, women's history. Gaines had the feature separately stapled as a stand-alone four-page comic book and distributed hundreds of thousands of copies to public schools.[9] Magazine advertisements for *Wonder Woman* featured its celebration of women's history: one ad pictured a pigtailed girl lying on the floor, reading *Wonder Woman* and dreaming of what she might become when she grows up; busts of twelve Wonder Women of History are arrayed around the border of the ad, representing the newly expanded range of her imagination.[10]

Who wrote "Wonder Women of History" is hard to say. Although Marble was listed on *Wonder Woman*'s masthead as "associate editor," she couldn't have written the "Wonder Women of History" for long.[11] She married an army captain in 1942, just before he was sent to the front. In 1944, when she was five months pregnant, she was struck by a drunk driver and lost the baby. Soon afterward, she received word that her husband had been killed in a plane crash over Germany; she tried to kill herself. In 1945, she left the country, to serve as a U.S. spy in Switzerland.[12] Alice Marble helped launch the "Wonder Women of History," and she let Gaines use her name and her likeness, but much more she could not have done.

Marston had at least some hand in it. He chose which biography appeared in which issue. "Will switch from Joan d'Arc to Mme. Kaishek for WW6," he told Gaines in 1943.[13] He might also have chosen which women to profile. And he might even have written at least some of their biographies. Marston, who, as a freshman at Harvard, had found history dreadfully boring, had grown fascinated by women's history. He explained his change of heart in a Wonder Woman story called "The Ordeal of Queen Boadicea."

"Who cares about those old gezaboes that lived 1900 years ago?" a high school boy named Bif asks Diana Prince. "And especially *women*—they're all sissies!"

"Women seem sissies because you don't know their true strength," she answers. And then she turns into Wonder Woman, takes him on a trip into the past, and convinces him that history is fascinating.[14]

There's a good chance that "Wonder Women of History" was written by Dorothy Roubicek, DC's first woman editor.[15] She was born in 1913, in the Bronx, to Czech and Russian immigrants. She grew up on Long Island. She married a man named Irving Taub right after graduating from high school. They moved to Florida, where she gave birth to a son when she was twenty-three. Later, she returned to New York with her baby but without her husband and moved in with her parents. She found work as a stenographer before Mayer hired her as an editor in 1942, when she was twenty-nine. She went by "Miss Roubicek"; even during the war, it was difficult for married women to get work. She worked closely with Gaines and especially with Mayer, including on Superman. She began working on Wonder Woman when Wonder Woman joined the Justice Society. Roubicek is generally credited with coming up with the idea for kryptonite in 1943. As the story has it, Roubicek thought Superman ought to be more vulnerable. She might have gotten that idea from her work on Wonder

From "The Ordeal of Queen Boadicea," *Sensation Comics #60* (December 1946)

Woman, which involved conferring, often and at length, with Lauretta Bender.[16]

Whoever wrote it, "Wonder Women of History" was entirely consistent with Marston's hope, in creating Wonder Woman, "to combat the idea that women are inferior to men, and to inspire girls to self-confidence and achievement in athletics, occupations and professions monopolized by men."[17] The biographies cast Wonder Woman as the latest in a line of women fighting for women's equality. The Wonder Woman of History in the June–July 1943 issue of *Wonder Woman* is Susan B. Anthony. One panel pictures her holding a key, about to unlock the shackles of a woman bound in chains. The caption reads, "America has three great emancipators. George Washington welded four million colonists into a United States of America. Lincoln freed four million Negroes from slavery. And Susan B. Anthony struck the shackles of legal, social, and economic bondage from millions of American women. Brave, daring, generous, sincere, this Wonder Woman led her sex to victory and became 'The Liberator of Womankind.'" Anthony's four-page biography explains how the women's rights movement grew out of women's work as abolitionists. Anthony is shown speaking at Seneca Falls in 1848, in front of a banner reading, "WOMEN'S RIGHTS"; she is declaring, "Negroes must be freed but still another form of slavery remains. The old idea prevails that woman is owned and possessed by man! Most wrongs and conflicts of modern society grow out of this false relationship between man and woman!"[18]

The suffrage campaign, from 1848 to 1920, is often thought of as the "first wave" of the women's movement, and women's liberation, in the 1960s and 1970s, as the "second wave." In between, the thinking goes, the waters were still.[19] But there was plenty of feminist agitation in the 1940s in the pages of *Wonder Woman*.

The issue of *Wonder Woman* that contained a biography of Susan B. Anthony, calling her "the Liberator of Womankind," contained, too, a Wonder Woman story titled "Battle for Womanhood." It opens with Mars, the god of war, angry that so many American women are helping with the war effort. Both the story and the drawings borrow heavily from suffragists' use of the god of war as a stock character in cartoons from the 1910s, in which Mars appears regularly, shackling women to the misery of war. In the First World War, suffragists suggested that war was keeping women in a state of slavery. In the Second World War, Marston suggested that women's contributions to the war effort were helping emancipate them, much to Mars's dismay.

"There are eight million America women in war activities—by 1944 there will be eighteen million!" reports one of Mars's female slaves, dragging a ball and chain.

"If women gain power in *war* they'll escape man's domination completely!" Mars thunders. "They will achieve a horrible independence! . . . Women are the natural spoils of war! They must remain at home, helpless slaves for the victor! If women become warriors like the Amazons, they'll grow stronger than men and put an end to war!"

He commands the Duke of Deception to put a stop to it. The duke

From "Wonder Women of History: Susan B. Anthony," *Wonder Woman #5* (June–July 1943)

enlists the aid of Dr. Psycho, who, by means of tools he's developed in his psychological laboratory, conjures a trick in which George Washington rises from the dead and addresses a spellbound audience.

"I have a message for you—a warning!" Washington says. "*Women will lose the war for America!* Women should not be permitted to have the responsibilities they now have! Women must not make shells, torpedoes, airplane parts—they must not be trusted with war secrets or serve in the armed forces. *Women will betray their country through weakness* if not treachery!"

Wonder Woman, watching in the wings, cries out, "He's working for the Axis!" To defeat Dr. Psycho, she breaks into his laboratory, dropping in through a skylight. Captured, she's trapped. Dr. Psycho locks her in a cage chained to a wall. Eventually, she's rescued by Etta

Candy, after which she frees Psycho's wife, Marva, whom he has blindfolded and chained to a bed.

"Submitting to a cruel husband's domination has ruined my life!" an emancipated Marva cries. "But what can a weak girl do?"

"Get strong!" urges Wonder Woman. "Earn your own living—join the WAACs or WAVES and fight for your country!"[20]

Etta Candy takes that advice to heart. In the summer of 1943, in the lead story in *Comic Cavalcade*, Etta Candy and the Holliday College girls put on WAAC uniforms and

From "Battle for Womanhood," *Wonder Woman #5* (June–July 1943)

become special army intelligence agents. "Aux-iliary Etta Candy reporting for duty," Etta says, saluting General Wonder Woman.[21] "Women are gaining power in the man's world!" Wonder Woman reports to Hippolyte at the end of 1943. Hippolyte, pleased, shows Wonder Woman what lies ahead: Etta Candy will discover the secret to eternal life, for which she will be awarded an honorary degree and become professor of public health at Wonder Woman College, and a woman will be president of the United States. This, though, will lead to a battle of the sexes (the battle of the sexes that Marston described in 1937, when he held a press conference and predicted the rule of women). Unable to bear rule by women, a cranky professor named Professor Manly founds a new political party, the Man's World Party, in the year 3000.

"The men of this country are fed up with woman's oppression!" Senator Hemann warns the president in a meeting at the White House. "The Man's World Party demands male rights!"[22]

"Thousands of men are joining Professor Manly's new political party," a future Steve Trevor tells a future Diana. "They're going to elect a *man* president—he'll put more *strength* into government!"

The Man's World Party nominates Steve Trevor as its candidate. Diana runs as his opponent. Trevor wins, only to find out that Profes-

From "America's Wonder Women of Tomorrow," *Wonder Woman #7*
(Winter 1943)

sor Manly has rigged the election. Trevor is then kidnapped and has
to be rescued by Wonder Woman, after which Diana Prince becomes
president.[23]

Marston wanted the kids who read his comics to imagine a woman
as president of the United States. In this, he was considerably ahead
of public opinion. In 1937, when Gallup asked Americans, "Would
you vote for a woman for president?" only 33 percent of Americans
said yes.[24] Marston's promotion of Wonder Woman as a form of feminist literature led to a small but strident conservative political reaction
from writers wanting to put Wonder Woman back in a woman's place.
"A Wife for Superman" was the title of an editorial that appeared in
the *Hartford Courant,* in response to the press release in which Marston had revealed that he was the creator of Wonder Woman. "No less
a figure than the discoverer of the famous lie detector, Dr. William
Moulton Marston of Harvard, has emerged from the nebulous regions
where psychologists are supposed to hang their hats, to create a new
comic-book character," the editors remarked. What, they wondered,

From "The Amazon Bride," *Comic Cavalcade #8* (Fall 1944), here and on the next page

would Wonder Woman do with her days? "She would be, of course, the type to attack the day with vigor, stir up a hearty breakfast, breeze the children into their school regalia, slick up the house and herself be off downtown to pursue her man-size job." And "at the end of the day she would have lost little if any of her pep. After the dishes were done she would be ready to accompany her husband to a movie or lecture, where she would scintillate with ideas and conversation all the evening." Sure, "a man with her for a wife would be lucky. The only question is, could he stand the pace?"[25]

Marston had an answer for that. In "The Amazon Bride," a story in *Comic Cavalcade* in the fall of 1944, Wonder Woman loses her Amazonian strength. Steve Trevor, sensing her weakness, persuades her to marry him.

"I seem to be weak!" she cries after Steve defends her from a villain.

"Beautiful, you're only a *woman*, after all," he answers, lifting her off her feet. "You need a man to protect you!"

"No," she protests. "Aphrodite forbids us Amazons to let *any* man dominate us. We are our own masters." Suddenly, she weakens. "But I confess—I *love* to have *you* boss me!"

"You do? Why—I'd always wanted you to say that! Darling, marry me!"

Back at the office, she begs him to let her serve him in other ways. "Steve, dear," she says, "now that we're going to be married, won't you *please* let me be your secretary?"

"Well—maybe," Trevor answers, leaning back in his chair, puffing at his pipe. "Sit down at that machine and let's see how fast you can type. Every woman's place is in the home and girls should not try to do the work of men. They should be busy keeping house for their husbands!"

He gets a marriage license. "I'm ready to be your docile little wife!" she cries, bowing before him.

Fortunately, all of this turns out to have been a bad dream, from which Wonder Woman at last awakes.[26] And then she goes back to work, making the world safe for equality.

SUFFERING SAPPHO!

"**NOTED PSYCHOLOGIST REVEALED** as Author of Best-Selling 'Wonder Woman,'" Marston had headed his press release in the summer of 1942. Olive Byrne arranged to place a puff piece in *Family Circle*. In the August 14, 1942, issue of the magazine, "Olive Richard," worried about the war, tells about how she'd come across an issue of *Wonder Woman* and vaguely recalled hearing that the Amazonian princess had been created by her favorite psychologist.

"'Well,' I thought. 'If Marston is whipping up comics stories while Rome burns, there must be a reason.'"

Curious to find out more, she travels to his house in Rye.

"The Doctor hadn't changed a bit," she reports. "He was reading a comics magazine, which sport he relinquished with a chuckle and rose gallantly to his feet, a maneuver of major magnitude for this psychologic Nero Wolfe."

"Hello, hello, my Wonder Woman!" he calls out to her.

"What's the idea of calling *me* Wonder Woman?" she wants to know. (It gave them a great deal of pleasure, their game of hide-and-seek.)

He explains to her that her bracelets were the inspiration for Wonder Woman's bracelets. He hands her a copy of *Wonder Woman*. She is dazzled.

"I opened the book to read, 'This amazing girl, stronger than Hercules, more beautiful than Aphrodite,' and so on, and I remembered that my sons had argued as to whether she could lick the whole Japanese

From "America's Guardian Angel," *Sensation Comics #12* (December 1942)

army all at once or whether she'd have to take them a few thousand at a time. The Doctor beamed when I told him this and said, 'That's right, the kids love her.'" (Her sons, *his* boys, their children.)

"Boys, young and old, satisfy their wish thoughts by reading comics," he tells her. "If they go crazy over Wonder Woman, it means they're longing for a beautiful, exciting girl who's stronger than they are."

Wonder Woman, Marston tells her, is a New Woman. "The one outstanding benefit to humanity from the first World War was the great increase in the strength of women—physical, economic, mental," he says. "Women definitely emerged from a false, haremlike protection and began taking over

Lou Rogers, in *Why Should Women Vote?*, 1915, a collection of suffrage cartoons

men's work. Greatly to their own surprise they discovered that they were potentially as strong as men—in some ways stronger." No harem master, he.

Says Olive, "I feel like Wonder Woman already."[1]

The strength of women was one theme of Wonder Woman. The bondage of women was another. (For *Family Circle*, Olive Byrne once wrote an account of Marston's advice about happiness in marriage. It's called "Fit to Be Tied?")[2] Not a comic book in which Wonder Woman appeared, and hardly a page, lacked a scene of bondage. In episode after episode, Wonder Woman is chained, bound, gagged, lassoed, tied, fettered, and manacled. She's locked in an electric cage. She's winched into a straitjacket, from head to toe. Her eyes and mouth are taped shut. She's roped and then coffined in a glass box and dropped into the ocean. She's locked in a bank vault. She's tied to railroad tracks. She's pinned to a wall. Once, so that she can be both entirely bound and movable, her

From "The Disappearance of Tama," *Sensation Comics #33* (September 1944)

fettered feet are welded to roller skates. "Great girdle of Aphrodite!" she cries. "Am I tired of being tied up!"[3]

And it isn't only Wonder Woman. *Every* woman in the *Wonder Woman* comic books is bound. Diana Prince is chained to a kitchen stove. The girls of Paradise Island are blindfolded. So are the gay girls of Holliday College. Shackles are welded onto their wrists. They are tied to chairs. Underground, they are enslaved in lairs. Aboveground, they're hog-tied and dragged. They crawl across floors, leashed like dogs. They always escape. But first, they're tied up. And while it's true that much of this same iconography holds a prominent place in feminist and suffrage cartoons and protests from the 1910s—in which women are chained and roped and gagged, as an allegorical representation of their lack of rights and liberties—there's more to it than that.

In his original scripts, Marston described scenes of bondage in careful, intimate detail, with utmost precision, so that Peter would draw them exactly to his specifications: "The Amazon captives are marching along driven by the Greeks," he wrote in one early script. "The women wear massive chains on ankles and wrists and between, also their necks are chained together for marching. The Greek slave driver swings a whip. Another Greek pricks a prisoner with his spear. The women are bowed with blows, etc."[4] In the first story in *Wonder Woman #2*, Wonder Woman travels "to a ravaged country where Mars's men are collecting prisoners." She, too, is taken prisoner. In the script, Marston paid especial, almost loving attention to the work of describing Wonder Woman's bondage, giving Peter detailed instructions for the panel in which Wonder Woman is taken prisoner:

Closeup, full length figure of WW. Do some careful chaining here—Mars's men are experts! Put a metal collar on WW with a chain running off from the panel, as though she were chained in the line of prisoners. Have her hands clasped together at her breast with *double* bands on her wrists, her Amazon bracelets and another set. Between these runs a short chain, about the length of a handcuff chain—this is what compels her to clasp her hands together. Then put another, heavier, *larger* chain between her wrist bands

This panel and the two that follow are from "The God of War," *Wonder Woman #2* (Fall 1942)

which hangs in a long loop to just above her knees. At her ankles show a pair of arms and hands, coming from out of the panel, clasping about her ankles. This whole panel will lose its point and spoil the story unless these chains are drawn *exactly* as described here.

Later in the story, Wonder Woman is forced to do battle with another female prisoner during a tournament of slaves. In the script, Marston's painstaking attention to detail continues, with great insistence, as if he had encountered some resistance on this subject before: "Only here both girls have their hands tied behind them, don't forget." After defeating the female prisoner, Wonder Woman is hitched to a post: "Show WW chained by one ankle to a stout post. The ankle chain is long but very massive." Then, still chained to the post, she is attacked by one of Mars's warriors. Marston describes, for Peter, how to depict her beating: "Closeup of WW still lying face down. The paddle is just hitting her buttocks. The Martian does *not* show in this panel, only the spanker. Show the descent of the paddle with action lines and stars, etc." (Peter obliged, omitting only the stars.) After the beating, Wonder Woman defeats the Martian warrior, only to be imprisoned yet again. "Show WW in chains as at beginning of sequence. A chain runs from her metal collar to a ring bolt in the wall,

which is all steel." Straining to overhear a conversation in the next room, through the amplification of "bone conduction," she takes her chain in her teeth: "Closeup of WW's head shoulders. She holds her neck chain between her teeth. The chain runs taut between her teeth and the wall, where it is locked to a steel ring bolt."

Near the end of the story, Wonder Woman is given her own slave. "Be sure to whip her every day!" Mars tells her. The girl hands Wonder Woman a whip. Wonder Woman says, "Don't be absurd—I wouldn't whip you! Tell me your story!" The girl explains, "Women on Mars have no rights." Wonder Woman frees her. "Curse you Wonder Woman!" Mars cries. Quite how this story embraces women's rights is difficult to figure.[5] It's feminism as fetish.

"Marston's idea of feminine supremacy was the ability to submit to male domination," Mayer said.[6] He tried, without much success, to rein Marston in. Predictably, the bondage soon led to trouble with the editorial advisory board and, in particular, with Josette Frank, who'd worked with Holloway at *Child Study* in 1925 and who was now staff adviser to the Children's Book Committee of the Child Study Association of America.

At a time when plenty of librarians and schoolteachers were alarmed by comic books, Frank's Children's Book Committee generally gave favorable reports of the hundred or so comic books it reviewed every year, suggesting that, as "easy reading," comic books served as a bridge, carrying young readers to more sophisticated literature.[7] Sidonie Gruenberg, the director of the Child Study Association, rather liked comic books; she thought critics like Sterling North were cranks, and ill-informed.[8] Frank felt more or less the same way, except that she could not abide Wonder Woman. In February 1943, she sent Gaines a letter.

"As you know, I have never been enthusiastic about this feature," she reminded him. "I know also that your circulation features prove that a lot of other people *are* enthusiastic. Nevertheless, this feature does lay you open to considerable criticism from any such group as ours, partly on the basis of the woman's costume (or lack of it), and partly on the basis of sadistic bits showing women chained, tortured, etc. I wish you would consider these criticisms very seriously."[9]

Gaines forwarded the letter to Marston.

"For heavens sake," Marston wrote Gaines. "Don't let a person of her standing (or lack of it so far as such matters go) who is an avowed enemy of the Wonder Woman strip, of me and also of you in so far as she predicted this strip would flop and you rubbed it into her that it hadn't, rock the boat!" Frank, he said, was a lightweight. "For every criticism she makes," he promised Gaines, "I will get you half a dozen from real authorities, parents, teachers, educators, psychologists of national standing . . . , big-shot journalists like Pitkin, etc. who consider Wonder Woman a remarkably wholesome and constructive story strip, good for kids in every way."

Dorothy Roubicek had objected to Wonder Woman's binding, too. Bah, said Marston. "The secret of woman's allure," he told Gaines, is that "women *enjoy* submission—being bound."[10]

(For the record, Marston's son Byrne is really pretty certain that when Marston talked about the importance of bondage, he meant it only metaphorically. "I never saw anything like that in our house," Byrne Marston told me when I asked. "He didn't tie the ladies up to the bedpost. He'd never have gotten away with it.")[11]

Marston was irritated. As he saw it, he understood, as an "internationally famous psychologist," that the secret of a woman's allure is that she enjoys submission and bondage. Hadn't he already explained that to Gaines? So what if women like Josette Frank and Dorothy Roubicek didn't understand that? Why did he have to answer to them? What did *they* know?

"Of course I wouldn't expect Miss Roubicek to understand all this," Marston went on. "After all I have devoted my entire life to working out psychologist principles. Miss R. has been in comics only 6 months or so, hasn't she? And never in psychology."

As for the charge of sadism: "Binding or chaining the fair heroine, in comics strips, or the hero like Flash Gordon et al, is *not* sadism

Dorothy Roubicek, sketch, 1943

because these characters do not suffer or even feel embarrassed." Wonder Woman teaches the enjoyment of submission to loving authority: "This, my dear friend, is the one truly great contribution of my Wonder Woman strip to moral education of the young. The only hope for peace is to teach people who are full of pep and unbound force to *enjoy* being bound—*enjoy* submission to kind authority, wise authority, not merely tolerate such submission. Wars will only cease when humans *enjoy being bound*."[12]

Gaines was troubled. He asked Roubicek what she thought; no doubt he'd hired her so that he could ask a woman on staff what she thought. Roubicek said she thought it would be a good idea to keep Wonder Woman away from Paradise Island, where much of the kinkiest stuff tended to happen. She thought Wonder Woman ought to be more like Superman and, in just the way that Superman can't go back to the planet Krypton, Wonder Woman ought not to be able to go back to Paradise Island.

"I believe it would be to our eventual advantage to play up WW as a female SUPERMAN and give her the same type of escapade to play around with," Roubicek told Gaines. She could fight thugs and Nazis, not ancient Greek gods. Roubicek also suggested that some of Josette Frank's concerns might be alleviated if Wonder Woman would wear a skirt. She warned Gaines, "There has been a tendency in the past to play up WW as a rather sexy creature, and I think this should be avoided at all times—she should rather be shown as the All-American girl type. Her costume may be one of the reasons why she creates this impression, and attached is a sketch of the type of clothes I would suggest—feminine and yet not objectionable—as those short, tight panties she wears might be." Roubicek had sketched a possible outfit; it looks almost exactly like the skirt Wonder Woman wore in her first appearance, in *All-Star Comics*. Gaines sent it to Marston, with a note reading, "Doc: She did this without even knowing how close she came to the original costume!"[13] Wonder Woman kept her mini-shorts.

Days after Roubicek sent that memo to Gaines, Alice Marble received a letter from a twenty-six-year-old, college-educated Pittsburgh man named Francis J. Burke. Burke professed himself a fan of Marble's tennis career. "But I did not write you to talk about tennis," he went on. "Your acting as associate editor of Wonder Woman surprised me because I would have thought you to be a 'woman of the world,' and, as such, capable of perceiving sex perversion when it stood unveiled before your eyes." He was referring, he explained, to the representation in *Wonder Woman* of "characters in chains and bonds, particularly with characters who are chained and bound *by pretty girls*." Burke confessed that he was among those "readers who are themselves obsessed with chains-and-bonds images and fantasies," but he questioned whether this was the kind of thing that belonged in a comic book for children. He proceeded to give an elaborate account of a high school girl of his acquaintance—he gave her the name "Violet"—who, inspired by *Wonder Woman,* dressed up like Wonder Woman and led a secret society of high schoolers who called themselves the "Wonder Girls"; they dressed up in elaborate costumes, then tied boys up and beat them.[14]

Gaines decided that he had better solicit the opinion of Lauretta Bender. Unlike Josette Frank, who didn't have either an MD or a PhD, Bender, one of the most accomplished psychiatrists in the country, could not be so easily waved aside by Marston as lacking in expertise. Bender dismissed Burke's letter as a "mash note." Gaines also sent Bender a complete set of *Wonder Woman,* asking her for "any suggestions that you might have to eliminate any undesirable features."[15] He gave her a couple of weeks to read the comics, and then he sent Roubicek to Bellevue Hospital to interview her about the whole gamut of both Josette Frank's concerns and Marston's claims.

In a memo to Gaines, Roubicek reported Bender's reaction: "She does not believe that Wonder Woman tends to masochism or sadism. Furthermore, she believes that even if it did—you can *teach* neither perversion to children—one can only bring out what is inherent in the child. However, she did make this reservation—that if the women slaves wore chains (and enjoyed them) for no purpose whatsoever, there would be no point in chaining them." Really, she was tremendously approving. Bender *liked* Wonder Woman, as well as the way Marston was playing with feminism. Plus, Roubicek noted, "she thinks that Wonder Woman's costume is perfectly all right." Most of all, "she believes that Dr. Marston is handling very cleverly this whole 'experiment' as she calls it. She feels that perhaps he is bringing to the public the real issue at stake in the world (and one which she feels may possibly be a direct cause of the present conflict) and that is that the difference between the sexes is *not* a sex problem, nor a struggle for superiority, but rather a problem of the relation of one sex to the other." Roubicek summed up: "Dr. Bender believes that this strip should be left alone." Bender also wrote Gaines a letter, telling him she found Wonder Woman fascinating, since the psychological implications of the character's adventures "strike at the very heart of masculinity and femininity and of aggression and submission."[16]

Bender's view of Wonder Woman aligned with her ideas about comic books and fantasy generally. Bender believed that fantasy "is a constructive aspect of the child's experimental exploration of reality, or his progressive relating of himself to reality, of his trial-and-error attempts to solve his reality problems." And she believed that comic books, "like the folklore of other times, serve as a means to stimulate the child's fantasy life and so help him solve the individual and sociological problems inherent in his living." As for Wonder Woman, Bender had this to say: "She is an ordinary but good human being until she puts on her costume, when she can overcome all physical resistances. She can help people in need. She can change the direction of a warship or a bomb in flight. She can make herself little and offer herself for play to a lonely child. Her power to attract and hold lies in a lariat, which her author, William Moulton Marston, says represents 'love appeal.' One is not always convinced by his symbols, perhaps because he is too conscious of them. But 'Wonder Woman' represents a good try at solving the very timely problems of the girl's concept of herself as a woman and of her relationship to the world."[17]

Gaines was hugely relieved. Nevertheless, not everyone on Gaines's editorial advisory board agreed with Bender. W.W.D. Sones, a professor of education at the University of Pittsburgh's School of Education, wrote to Gaines that, while he was unconcerned by Wonder Woman's costume (she had "athletic" rather than "Hollywood" legs, in his view), he found there to be rather an excess of "chains and bonds," even though, "true enough, cruelty and suffering seem not to be involved." Still, he thought Marston's explanation—the mumbo jumbo about submission—was hogwash. "The social purpose which he claims is open to very serious objection," Sones wrote. "It is just such submission that he claims he wants to develop that makes dictator dominance possible. From the standpoint of social ideals, what we want in America and the world is cooperation and not submission."[18]

Gaines decided to keep Frank and Sones at bay, and placed his trust in Marston and Bender. Then, in September 1943, Gaines got the letter he'd been dreading. It came from John D. Jacobs, a U.S. Army staff sergeant in the 291st Infantry, stationed at Fort Leonard Wood, Missouri. It was addressed to "Charles Moulton." Gaines opened it. "The comic magazine, Wonder Woman, interests me as no other 'reading material' which I have ever been able to find in such volumes," Jacobs began. "I am one of those odd, perhaps unfortunate men who derive an extreme erotic pleasure from the mere thought of a beautiful girl, chained or bound, or masked, or wearing extreme high-heels or high-laced boots,—in fact, any sort of constriction or strain whatso-ever." He wondered, "Have you the same interest in bonds and fetters that I have?" He wanted to know, too, whether the creator of Wonder Woman himself had in his possession any of the items depicted in the stories, "the leather mask, or the wide iron collar from Tibet, or the Greek ankle manacle? Or do you just 'dream up' these things?"[19]

Gaines forwarded the letter to Marston, with a covering note.

"This is one of the things I've been afraid of, (without quite being able to put my finger on it)," he wrote. Something had to be done. He therefore enclosed, for Marston's use, a memo written by Roubicek containing a "list of methods which can be used to keep women con-fined or enclosed without the use of chains. Each one of these can be varied in many ways—enabling us, as I told you in our conference last week, to cut down the use of chains by at least 50 to 75% without at all interfering with the excitement of the story or the sales of the books."[20]

Marston wrote Gaines right back.

"I have the good Sergeant's letter in which he expresses his enthu-siasm over chains for women—so what?" As a practicing clinical psy-chologist, Marston said, he was unimpressed. "Some day I'll make you a list of all the items about women that different people have been known to get passionate over—women's hair, boots, belts, silk worn by women, gloves, stockings, garters, panties, bare backs, sweats, breasts, etc. etc.," he promised. "You can't have a real woman charac-ter in any form of fiction without touching off a great many readers' erotic fancies. Which is swell, I say."

Cut down on chains and ropes by 50 or 75 percent? Marston refused. He was sure he knew what line not to cross. Harmless erotic fantasies are terrific, he said. "It's the lousy ones you have to look out for—the harmful, destructive, morbid erotic fixations—real sadism, killing, blood-letting, torturing where the pleasure is in the victim's actual pain, etc. Those are 100 per cent bad and I won't have any part of them." He added, in closing, "Please thank Miss Roubicek for the list of menaces."[21]

.　　.　　.

Four months later, Josette Frank resigned from the editorial advisory board.

"Recent issues have omitted whippings, tortured women in chains, and other objectionable features," she told Gaines, but "I have come to the reluctant conclusion that it is the basic theme of the strip that is offensive, rather than its detail, or in addition to its details." That is, "the theme of men against women and women against men is hardly a suitable one for children's story material." Not to mention that the whole thing was "full of significant sex antagonisms and perversions." There was nothing for it but to quit.[22]

Once again, Gaines sent Frank's complaints to Marston. And once again Marston dismissed them. He pointed out that no one is ever actually whipped or tortured in his comic books. And as to the comic's *perversions,* "Frankly, I don't know what she means," Marston insisted. "Probably my basic idea of women fighting male dominance, cruelty, savagery and war-making with love control backed by force is what she means by 'sex antagonism.'" As for bondage: "My whole strip is aimed at drawing the distinction in the minds of children and adults between love bonds and male bonds of cruelty and destruction; between submitting to a loving superior or deity and submitting to people like the Nazis, Japs, etc.," he explained. "If this is wrong or vicious my entire career as a consulting psychologist is based on malice and misconception."[23] That, really, got exactly to the heart of the matter: Was his entire career as a psychologist based on a misconception?

Gaines turned once more to Bender. He arranged to have five hundred copies of DC comic books sent to the children's ward at Bellevue Hospital: a gift for the patients.[24] (Bender usually brought a copy or two home to her own children.)[25] And then he sent Roubicek to Bellevue to interview Bender again.

"Essentially she agrees with Dr. Marston that the strip cannot possibly be harmful to children and that he is merely presenting them with a solution to a social problem current in the world today—i.e., the struggle between man and woman to clarify their respective positions in the world," Roubicek reported. "She says it is not a sexual struggle in the genital sense, and no doubt Miss Frank reads into the strip some of her own confusion with regard to these problems, as no

Wonder Woman gets a newspaper strip. From "Wonder Woman Syndication," *Independent News*, April 1944

doubt many people will do if they have such problems." But, Bender was sure, "CHILDREN do not read any such sexual meanings into the strip." Roubicek concluded that, happily, "she thinks we shouldn't let this controversy bother us at all."[26]

Gaines wanted to understand what influence comic books have on the children who read them, but neither psychology nor psychiatry had a definitive answer to that question. He probably didn't mind not getting to the bottom of the problem. He was in no position to abandon Wonder Woman. The day Josette Frank resigned, Gaines and Marston signed an agreement for Wonder Woman to become a newspaper strip, syndicated by King Features. Out of the hundreds of comic books published, no other comic-book superhero, aside from Superman and Batman, had ever made the gigantic jump from comic books to newspaper syndication, with its vast daily circulation. To celebrate, Gaines had his artists draw a panel in which Superman and Batman, rising out of the front page of a daily newspaper, call out to Wonder Woman, who's leaping onto the page, "Welcome, Wonder Woman!"[27]

Gaines had another kind of welcome to make, too. He asked Lauretta Bender to take Frank's place on the editorial advisory board. She accepted.[28]

From *Editor and Publisher*, May 6, 1944

Marston wrote the newspaper strip stories himself; Harry G. Peter did the drawing.[29] The strips were tamer than the comic books, but Wonder Woman was still, as ever, fit to be tied. In an ad King Features ran to persuade newspapers to pick up the strip, her name is written in rope.

28

SUPERPROF

IN THE SPRING OF 1944, Marston was enjoying unbridled success for the first time since his student days at Harvard. Wonder Woman had ten million readers. Flush with cash, he rented offices on the fourteenth floor of a building at 331 Madison Avenue, at Forty-third Street. The sign on the door read MARSTON ART STUDIO.[1]

He had so much work, writing for *Sensation Comics, All-Star Comics, Comic Cavalcade, Wonder Woman,* and now for a daily newspaper strip, that he needed an assistant. He decided to hire a student in a psychology class he was teaching at the Katharine Gibbs School. The final, take-home exam required students to write eight short essays answer-

Joye Hummel, c. 1945

ing prompts about Marston's theory of emotions. The questions suggest that most of what Marston taught the young women studying at the Gibbs school was how to be more assertive at work. (Question 6: "Advise Miss F. how to overcome her fear of talking with the company Vice President who is in charge of her Division and whom she has plenty of opportunities to contact if she chooses; also tell Miss F. why these contacts are to her advantage.") Olive Byrne graded the exams. One of them proved to be so good that she thought Marston himself could have written it. She handed it over to him. The exam had been written by a very pretty young woman named Joye E. Hummel.[2]

In March 1944, a few weeks before Hummel was scheduled to graduate, Marston invited her to tea with him and Holloway at the Harvard Club in New York. He told her he wanted to hire her to help write scripts. Hummel was nineteen years old. He thought she could help him write slang. She was astonished and delighted. "I always did have a big imagination," she said.[3]

Marston installed Hummel at the office at Forty-third and Madison, where he himself "personally handled every aspect of the production up to the point of sending to the printer," according to Holloway. All of this work, Holloway later said, was overseen by Marjorie Wilkes Huntley, who "was office executive for the Art Studio, knew every phase of the work plus the background and history."[4] Hummel doesn't remember Huntley being there very often. But Harry G. Peter was there every day, and Hummel got along well with him. Peter smoked a pipe; he always had it hanging out of the corner of his mouth.[5] He was a famously sloppy dresser. Hummel once had to fish him out of a charity ward at Bellevue Hospital; he'd been taken for an indigent after being treated for getting a chicken bone caught in his throat.[6] Hummel and Peter were rarely alone in the office. Peter employed three artists: a colorist named Helen Schepens and a married couple who did the lettering. Marston was often there, too, and so were his kids. Huntley would bring O.A. into the studio; O.A. loved to watch Peter work. "He would put me on a stool and say that if I was a good little monster, I could watch him draw," O.A. said. "I could have sat there for eight hours." Peter hardly spoke. "He was more Thurberesque," Byrne Marston said. "Witty but not very many words."[7]

At first, Hummel typed Marston's scripts. Soon, she was writing scripts of her own. This required some studying. To help Hummel understand the idea behind Wonder Woman, Olive Byrne gave her a present: a copy of Margaret Sanger's 1920 book, *Woman and the New Race*. She said it was all she'd need.[8]

Life at Cherry Orchard was louder than the quiet of Marston Art Studio. Marston loved to hold parties at his house. Pete Marston, once he was old enough to get a driver's license, was given the job of ferrying the drunks home. Holloway never drank. Instead, she carried around a highball glass filled with water and a tiny bit of scotch and pretended to sip it. Olive Byrne drank till she collapsed. She and Marston once went to an Alcoholics Anonymous meeting together. (AA was founded in 1935.) They did not join.[9]

Whenever he had guests, Marston would pull out his lie detector. "One of the things they did to you when you came to visit at their house was to take a lie detector test," Sheldon Mayer said, "not because they didn't trust you but they wanted to have fun with you." At DC Comics, Mayer and Marston "fought like hell," but "once you went to his home," Mayer said, "you were the guest and he was the most delightful host, the most remarkable host, with a lovely bunch of kids from different wives and all living together like one big family—everybody very happy and all good, decent people. And what I liked about those kids is they used to love the way I played the piano, which was very bad, but it didn't matter to them because they were all tone-deaf."[10]

Mayer and his wife moved out to Rye. He spent a lot of time at Cherry Orchard. He'd draw cartoons for the kids. He once made O.A. a flipbook. He'd sing them dirty songs. To the tune of "Sing a Song of Sixpence," he sang, "The king was in his counting house, counting out his money. The queen was in her parlor, eating bread and honey. The maid was in the kitchen, explaining to the groom, 'The vagina, not the rectum, is the entrance to the womb!'"[11]

Gaines, for all his troubles with the bondage in Wonder Woman, had grown fond of Marston, too, and of the whole family, which was one of the reasons he put up with the chains and ropes. Like Mayer, Gaines was perplexed by Marston's family arrangements, but he adored Marston's kids. When O.A. got appendicitis, Gaines visited her in the hospital and brought her a stuffed monkey; she named it Charlie.[12]

At Cherry Orchard, counting Marston, Holloway ("Keets"), Olive ("Dots"), Huntley ("Yaya"), and the four kids, there were eight residents, not including pets. "We now have six cats and a dog!" Marston reported to thirteen-year-old Byrne in the summer of 1944, when Byrne was away at summer camp. "Dots wanted to dispose of the new kits before you kids came home but I thought you'd want to

The family in 1946. Left to right: Huntley, Byrne, O.A., Pete, Marston, Olive Byrne, Donn, and Holloway

see them so we're keeping them for you until then. If you know any kids at camp from near here who want kittens, better promise them one." Also: "Hedy Lamarr's litter are pretty big now," Marston wrote Byrne. "Fuzzy hasn't been around for several days—Yaya thinks he's dead. Molecat is about to have another family."[13]

Hedy Lamarr, Fuzzy, and Molecat were rabbits. They'd had pet rabbits at Cherry Orchard for years. "We had a domestic crisis in the family today, which is in the nature of a grave reflection on me, your niece," Olive Byrne once reported to Margaret Sanger. "Four weeks ago we had two rabbits, three weeks ago the number was increased, via blessed event, to eight. Father rabbit was hurriedly removed from mother's vicinity and has lived a solitary life since. However, today we were presented with ten more—father apparently made an affectionate good bye."[14]

With regret, in 1944 Marston reported to his son Byrne, "I had to put poor little Limpy the paralyzed rabbit out of his misery"; he assured him that he'd done the job quickly. "The other rabbits are thriving," he went on. "Hedy Lamarr got out yesterday and made for the garden but Pete soon recaptured her; she's a very tame rabbit and she kept licking little Limpy's sore parts up to the very last—a fine mother." (Marston wrote a whole script about Wonder Woman and a rabbit; it was never published.)[15]

When O.A., age eleven, was at Camp Po-Ne-Mah in Connecticut, Marston drove everyone out to visit her. "Donn and Pete went (with both Mommies and poor old Dad)," he reported to Byrne, adding that O.A. had become an expert Ping-Pong player. Marston wrote to Byrne every few days and sent him care packages—including comics. "Wonder Woman is going very well—they've sold her to a lot of new papers including one in Honolulu and one in Rio de Janeiro, Brazil. Will send you more comic books if you want and the camp permits. (But you don't have to read WW if you don't want to—say which books you want.)" For the first time in his life, Marston was writing stuff his kids might actually want to read. He loved asking their opinions. He conducted his own informal readers' polls. "Sometime when you think of it," he asked Byrne, "write me what you and other boys prefer about other books as contrasted to the D-C comics (not WW but the other D-C books)."[16]

Marston adored his life of nonconformity, a family life with "both Mommies and poor old Dad." The older the kids got, the more Marston wanted to tell Donn and Byrne that he wasn't only their adoptive father but their biological father. Olive Byrne refused. She said she'd kill herself if anyone told them.[17]

"Olive Richard has been hectoring me for years," Marston wrote in an article for *Family Circle* in 1943. "I decided something must be done about it." He and "Olive Richard" switched places. The next time "Olive Richard" stops by his house, he hectors her. He tells her she's a loafer.

"I'm going to tell you a few things, Mr. Psychologist!" she replies. "Do you really imagine that I write articles just to pass the idle hours? I have two children—you've psyched them, and you say they have high I.Q.'s and are marvelously well adapted to their school and home environment. Do you suppose that nice adaptation just happened? Or do you think I've worked my head off to bring it about?"

"You fascinate me," Marston says.

"You think I'm lying, do you?"

The real point of the article was to give Marston a chance to shower Olive Byrne with affection, in print: "This young woman is a truly remarkable mother. I hate to admit it publicly because it will make her unbearably cocky when she interviews me again. But the fact is that she has everything it takes."[18]

But if Marston had everything he wanted—a house tumbling with children and animals, exactly the number of women he wanted, and a runaway best seller—he also felt, keenly, the sting of censure. And he wanted something more: he wanted academic acclaim. He wanted the world to know—he wanted scholars to know, he wanted *Harvard* to know—that Wonder Woman was a work of scholarship. He sat down in his study on the second floor of his house in Rye and tried to explain. He wrote an article called "Why 100,000,000 Americans Read Comics." It was published early in 1944 in *American Scholar,* the journal of the Phi Beta Kappa Society.

"The phenomenal development of a national comics addiction puzzles professional educators and leaves the literary critics gasping," Marston began. "Comics, they say, are not literature—adventure strips lack artistic form, mental substance, and emotional appeal to any but the most moronic of minds." But, he wondered, "Can it be that 100,000,000 Americans are morons?" No, of course not. Readers of comics weren't morons, and neither were the writers. They were brilliant! And comics were brilliant; they were the highest form of art: "The picture-story fantasy cuts loose the hampering debris of art and artifice and touches the tender spots of universal human desires and aspirations, hidden customarily beneath long accumulated protective coverings of indirection and disguise."[19]

This explanation did not sit well with literary scholars. In particular, it outraged New Critics. Cleanth Brooks and Robert Heilman, who, at the time, were both teaching at Louisiana State, objected to Marston's presumption in presenting himself as a scholar and Wonder Woman as a scholarly project. They objected to Marston's feminism.

Above all, they objected to Marston's argument that the popularity of a comic book, or of anything, was a measure of its quality. In a response published in *American Scholar*, Brooks and Heilman offered a satire of Marston's own bloated and pretentious essay. They purported to celebrate Marston's marriage of the academic and the popular, high and low: "Here is no ivory tower, no intellectual attic: here is the common touch: here the high realm of scholarship is married to daily actuality." They said they'd conducted a Marston-inspired experiment in their own lecture halls: "In all our classes we now have the aid of two alluring young things clad as 'Wonder Woman.' Part of the time they stand, gracefully poised, on either side of the lecture desk. At least once during each hour we pause while the two beauties do a modern dance routine, and you have no idea how it livens things up. Our class enrollments are truly marvelous. Our joint seminar in Vedic Mysticism has grown in size from two to 367. Who dares to say that 367 American university students can be wrong?"

They added that, in their class on Vedic Mysticism, "The climax of each hour comes when our two lovelies reach over and tap us on the head with charming pearl-handled hammers, and as the bell of dismissal rings we fall cold (not really, of course). Thus is the enemy vanquished; thus do our Wonder Women add, to their allure and their altruistic homilies, a convincing demonstration of power. All in all, we have helped remove the shackles of MAN'S SUPERIORITY, PREJUDICE, AND PRUDERY from lovely woman." (Marston's article had been illustrated by a drawing made by Harry Peter of Wonder Woman breaking chains that bind her hands and feet. The chains are labeled PREJUDICE, PRUDERY, and MAN'S SUPERIORITY.) The professors had become wildly popular: "the students here voted forty-to-one for us in a popularity contest in which we ran against a professor who has been using male athletes to give gymnastic exhibits during his lectures." A colleague of theirs, they said, had done Marston one better, having created "a new comic, 'Superprof.' "[20]

On August 11, 1944, a Friday night, Marston, Holloway, and Olive Byrne went to dinner at the Harvard Club and then to the theater.

They saw *School for Brides,* a farce about a much-married man, at the Royale on West Forty-fifth Street. The play was very funny, Holloway remembered; she remembered everything about that night: the dinner, the play, and yelling at Marston to wait up and not run so fast along Forty-fourth Street. "Our last date," she called it.[21] She remembered the running because he never ran again.

Two weeks later, on August 25, Marston, carrying a briefcase and lugging a suitcase, took the train from Rye into the city and walked from the station to his office at Forty-third and Madison. Just before five, Joye Hummel walked him back to Grand Central to catch a train to Boston; he had banking business to do there. On the train, he worked on *Wonder Woman,* writing a week's worth of the newspaper strip. When Marston got to Boston, Marjorie Wilkes Huntley, who'd been visiting Ethel Byrne on Cape Cod, was waiting for him at the station. Marston and Huntley wrestled his bags to Carolyn Marston Keatley's apartment, but only with difficulty; Marston was unsteady and in pain. When he woke up the next morning, his left leg was "unaccountably lame and wobbly." Before the end of the day, he'd been admitted to the Deaconess Hospital. He could no longer move his left leg. On August 28, he was taken by ambulance to the Lenox Hill Hospital in New York. He had contracted polio.[22]

He spent a month in the hospital and went home to Cherry Orchard on September 25. As best he could, he went back to work that same night. "When pain began around midnight, I concentrated on revising a WW daily," he wrote in his diary.[23]

At first, Marston used braces and crutches—braces make an appearance in a Wonder Woman story called "The Case of the Girl in Braces"—but before long, he was confined to a wheelchair. Holloway had a ramp installed out front and a hand-driven pulley on the stairs inside, so Marston could get from a car into the house, and from the first to the second floor. A nurse, Annette Trainor, visited nearly every day. The children called her Misty (for "Miss T").[24]

Joye Hummel had been working for Marston for only five months when he was struck ill. He couldn't possibly travel to New York to supervise the production of *Wonder Woman.* Hummel worked in Marston Art Studio with Peter all week. On weekends, she took the train

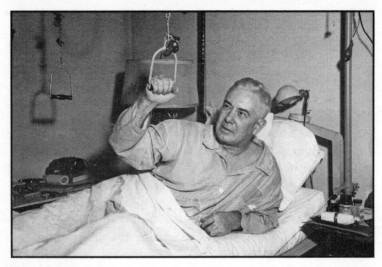

Marston after polio

up to Rye to meet with Marston at his house. She had no idea about the family arrangements. She was told that Olive Byrne was Marston's widowed sister-in-law.

The daily newspaper strip was canceled in 1945. It's possible that it hadn't been picked up by enough newspapers; more likely, Marston simply could no longer produce it quickly enough.

The weaker Marston became, the more of the writing Hummel handled.[25] "The Winged Maidens of Venus," the first story written by Hummel, appeared in *Wonder Woman #12*, with a cover date of Spring 1945. She was paid $50 a script. Marston kept on writing his own scripts, too. Together, he and Hummel would talk through story ideas. "He would write his scripts," Hummel said. "And I would write my scripts. I would type all of my scripts. And take them to the editor Sheldon Mayer. He always okayed mine faster because I didn't make mine as sexy."[26]

Hummel's stories were more innocent than Marston's. She also started writing *Wonder Woman* just at the moment when the censure of the Catholic bishops, the fan mail from fetishists, and Josette Frank's resignation had led Gaines to request even more oversight from the editorial advisory board. "We had a group of people who were psychologists or professors, whatever, who oversaw what I wrote," Hummel said. "We had ten restrictions. Things that we could not put in a comic strip. And then at the end of it Mayer would say, Now, I dare you to write a good story."[27]

The most concerted attack on Wonder Woman came just after V-E Day. Walter J. Ong, a Jesuit priest who had written a master's thesis under the supervision of Marshall McLuhan, and who was at the very beginning of what would be a long career as a literary theorist, had read Marston's *American Scholar* essay and found it both foolish and contemptible. He wrote a response called "Comics and the Super State." He sent the manuscript to the *Atlantic Monthly, Harper's,* the *Commonweal,* the *Yale Review,* and the *Kenyon Review.* Everyone rejected it.[28] Finally, Ong placed his article in the inaugural issue of a new journal called the *Arizona Quarterly.* It appeared in the spring of 1945.

"In the 25,000,000 comic books which are produced in this country monthly, each to be read by an average of four or five individuals, and in the 6,000,000,000 comic strips which appear every month in the United States newspapers, there is at work a squirming mass of psychological forces," Ong wrote. "What all these forces are, no one knows. Not many people care." But Ong did care, as a priest, as a literary theorist, and as a citizen of a democracy. He believed that Superman and Wonder Woman comics, specifically, had a great deal in common with the Third Reich, not least Hellenism, paganism, and totalitarianism.

"The very title 'superman'—as well as its earlier and unsuccessful form, 'overman'—is an importation brought into English by George Bernard Shaw out of Nietzsche, the herald of Nazism and the new order," Ong wrote. Wonder Woman was worse: "The companion female-hero piece which has recently appeared is in a way more symptomatic than *Superman* himself." For this, he blamed Marston: "Its calculated conception in the mind of an American educational psychologist as an ideal comic strip shows the fertility of the superman ideology outside Germany." Ong found Marston's explanation for Wonder Woman as a remedy for what ailed comic books to be entirely unconvincing. "Indeed, although he says she is designed to counteract the 'blood-curdling masculinity' of the other comics and to introduce 'love' into the comic field, Wonder Woman is dubbed by her enthusiastic creator an Amazon, while the ambit of her activities excludes the life which most normal women might desire." Ong's deepest problem with Wonder Woman was that she was too much like a man: "She is incapable of sustaining womanly standards in the face of the demand for total leveling in the monolithic state ideology. She therefore exists entirely by the standards of males, supplying on the score of her womanhood only the sexiness which the herd of males demands. This is, of course, not a healthy sex directed toward marriage and family life, but an anti-social sex, sex made as alluring as possible while its normal term in marriage is barred by the ground rules from the start."

Ong had read Wonder Woman comics carefully. And he'd read the work of both her critics and her defenders. He quoted the remarks made about "chained women" by Josette Frank in a report she wrote for the Child Study Association of America. He repeated Lauretta Bender's contention that comic books are modern-day folklore and dismissed it as ridiculous: "Only say that the comics are like folk tales, and all misgivings vanish. The taut muscles of the mind relax." Anyone who believed that was just plain gullible, Ong maintained: think of how the works of Wagner were "snapped up as props for the official civilization of the Third Reich," and it becomes clear that "the defense of the comics, which adopts as the ultimate criterion of worth an indiscriminating enthusiasm for mass likes and dislikes, is in the same tradition." Undoubtedly, 100,000,000 Americans read the comics; it didn't follow that the comics were brilliant, or even folklore. No: they were fascist propaganda.[29]

Harry Behn, the editor of the *Arizona Quarterly,* had decided to run Ong's essay in his inaugural issue because he figured it would draw the attention of the press. "Your article on the Comics promises to be the most exciting grenade we have yet tossed out!" Behn wrote to Ong, letting him know that he was pitching a write-up in *Time* and a reprint in *Reader's Digest. Time* published a condensation titled "Are Comics Fascist?" Ong received congratulations from Catholic intellectuals across the country. "I got a big laugh when I read that Moulton [*sic*] has an A.B., LL.B. and a Ph.D., and that he has resorted to such low and despicable means to convince an unsuspecting public," Aldo

Notarianni wrote from Catholic University. "Even should publication of Superman and Imitators continue, it has now definitely been proclaimed that the Catholic mind has not been lulled into accepting what is in reality an insult to man."[30]

By the time Ong's piece appeared, it was mostly obsolete. Wonder Woman had weakened. With the war over, and Marston confined to his bed, many Wonder Woman stories were being written by Joye Hummel, and those written by Marston had grown domestic.[31] He started putting his children in them. In a story Marston wrote in 1946, when Donn was thirteen, a thirteen-year-old boy named Don struggles with his impulsive nature in "The Battle of Desires," in *Comic Cavalcade #16*. Donn Marston had a famously bad temper. Also, he was reckless. He and his brother Byrne made some pipe bombs, which almost got them both arrested when the police came to the house in Rye.[32] In "The Battle of Desires," Don, who can't control his anger, keeps getting into trouble. Lately, he's been blowing things up. "Your desire for dominance is too strong," Wonder Woman tells him. "It controls your good desires. I'll show you what's happening inside your own mind: a battle of desires." Then she attaches him to her Introspection Machine. It shows Don that there's a battle going on in his head, between a giant, ugly caveman called Dominance and a

From "The Battle of Desires," *Comic Cavalcade #16* (August–September 1946)

From "The Bog Trap," *Sensation Comics #58* (October 1946)

beautiful winged angel called Love. Dominance captures Love and gets out a pair of scissors. "Oh let me keep my wings!" she begs him. He refuses: "I don't trust you, Love. Your wings must be clipped!" (This scene comes straight out of Inez Haynes Gillmore's *Angel Island*.) Wonder Woman races to the rescue, but Don has learned a lesson. "Thanks, Wonder Woman, for teaching me to control my dominance."[33]

In another story Marston wrote in 1946, when pigtailed Olive Ann Marston was twelve, Wonder Woman meets a pigtailed girl of just that age, also named Olive, who is being tormented by her older brothers. The splash page reads, "Poor Olive! The boys wouldn't let her play with them. They said she was a mere girl—a sissy. But after Wonder Woman took Olive to Paradise Island and gave her Amazon training, she showed strength and courage which amazed her former tormentors and even saved one of them from a horrible death! The boys had to admit, then, that girls are something!" In the story, Olive is playing baseball with her brothers but keeps striking out. Wonder Woman tells her, "You can be strong as any boy if you'll work hard and train yourself in athletics, the way boys do."[34]

Marston was dying. He had surgery, at home, for the removal of a mole that turned out to be malignant. He was never told that he had cancer. "The family swore everyone to secrecy," Hummel said. "If he knew, he would have gone into a deep depression." There was some worry, too, that he'd become violent and difficult to handle; Marston's temper could be terrifying. He was in nearly constant pain.[35]

The cancer metastasized to the lymph nodes in his armpits. He was put on morphine. Two days before he died, he was working on Wonder Woman.[36] "The night before he died, he really couldn't talk much," Byrne Marston wrote.[37] Marston died on May 2, 1947.

O.A. was getting dressed for school when Joye Hummel came to her room on the third floor to tell her that her father was dead. Olive Byrne told her sons. Byrne Marston's mothers sent him to New York to deliver Marston's obituary to the *New York Times*.[38]

"Dr. W. M. Marston, Psychologist, 53," was the headline. "He had been most active in the last five years as the originator, writer and producer of 'Wonder Woman,'" the obituary read, but it chiefly identified Marston as "the originator in 1915 of the systolic blood pressure deception test, popularly known as a lie detector test." It included a lie about the Frye case, the story Marston told himself, the story he wanted to believe: "Dr. Marston, on one occasion, aided in saving the life of a Negro accused of murder." It listed his survivors: "He leaves a widow, Mrs. Elizabeth Holloway Marston; three sons, Moulton, Byrne H. and Donn R. Marston, and a daughter, Miss Olive Marston." It made no mention of Olive Byrne.[39]

R.I.P., Superprof.

29

THE COMIC-BOOK MENACE

IN JANUARY 1948, seven months after Marston's death, Holloway sent a three-page letter to Jack Liebowitz, DC's publisher. "Hire me," she told him.[1]

Liebowitz was in a bind. Wonder Woman had been orphaned. Marston had died in May 1947. In August, Charlie Gaines had been killed in a boating accident while vacationing at Lake Placid. That same month, Joye Hummel married a widower with a four-year-old daughter; Hummel adored her. "I resign," Hummel told Sheldon Mayer when she got back from her honeymoon. "I cannot leave this child."[2] Mayer was desperate to quit, too, but he felt responsible for Marston's family. "I inherited his kids, I really did," he said later. "All of a sudden I became a member of the family because, well there's several reasons, but mainly while I didn't approve of his approach to Wonder Woman, it became my job to replace the writing, to find someone else. And I was the only person who really understood what he was trying to do."[3]

But, as Holloway attempted to point out to Liebowitz in January 1948, Mayer was not, in fact, the only person who knew what Marston was trying to do.[4] "Remember I have known Bill since the age of 12," Holloway reminded Liebowitz. "I suggested the original Lie Detector experiment and cooperated with him in his laboratory work at Harvard. My training is the same as his—A.B., Mt. Holyoke; LLB, Boston University and M.A., Radcliffe. The main difference is that I insisted that he complete work for a PhD which I was too lazy to do. Remember also that I have been editing all my life and have helped materially in the mechanical production of Bill's books."

Since her husband's death, she told him, she'd been studying Wonder Woman from an editorial and business vantage point, making "a careful review of our progress since June first." She was not impressed. The Wonder Woman comics that appeared in the months following Marston's death were produced from story ideas and half-written scripts left behind by Marston and Hummel. Most have since been credited to Robert Kanigher, because, decades later, he took credit for them, but actually not Kanigher but a hodgepodge of writers—Holloway thought they were very bad writers—had worked Marston's and Hummel's materials into scripts. "Frankly the results show as rank a display of incompetence as it has ever been my discomfort to sit on the side-lines and watch," Holloway told Liebowitz. Wonder Woman stories had gotten shorter and the printed pages had gotten more expensive to produce. The production schedule was chaotic, "four episodes behind schedule with only eight pages of new script in questionable readiness for the artists."

There was more to worry about, too. "At this point we also have to meet the competition of Moon Girl," Holloway warned Liebowitz. "It is being written by a very intelligent, well educational professional writer on a share basis, whose wife, for a short time at least, was editor of Wonder Woman."[5] Dorothy Roubicek had married a comic-book writer named William Woolfolk in 1947; she'd quit DC Comics when she was three months pregnant.[6] *Moon Girl* made its debut in the fall of 1947, published by Charlie Gaines's EC Comics (after Gaines's death, EC was run by his son, William). Neither Woolfolk nor Roubicek are listed on the masthead, but *Moon Girl* was their creation. "As a team they are equipped to turn out a quality product and a strong runner-up for Wonder Woman," Holloway told Liebowitz. "The one thing they don't have is the Marston psychology of living which was injected into every page of WW."[7] Moon Girl is, nevertheless, remarkably similar to Wonder Woman. With her long black hair and tight blue shorts, she is "a woman of sensational strength, superhuman speed and endurance and surpassing loveliness." She is the princess of the moon, sent to the United States by her mother, the queen, to join the man she loves. She's got a moon rocket and her magic moonstone

From Dorothy Roubicek Woolfolk and Bill Woolfolk, *Moon Girl #3*
(Spring 1948)

allows her to stop bullets and gives her "the powers of ten ordinary men." She looks like Wonder Woman, and she sounds like her, too; she's forever saying things like "Pluto, aid me!" and "Jupiter protect us!" Her alter ego, Clare Lune, is a history teacher. In the second issue, published in the winter of 1947, "Future Man," a harassed, henpecked husband who lives three thousand years in the future, goes to the library to watch films made in the twentieth century and there falls in love with Moon Girl. He travels through time to meet her; he wants to marry her. She clobbers him, but he captures her after he manages to steal her moonstone. Then, just as he's making away with her, his nag of a wife appears, having followed him through time to bring him back home, using her "husband pacifier."[8]

Holloway made a strong case that Liebowitz should hire her as the editor of *Wonder Woman*. "Jack, I *know* I can get writers," she promised. "I *know* I can get stories and can put over a high quality Wonder Woman with all the characteristics given it by Bill, *if I have your 100 percent backing.*" The only way to save *Wonder Woman,* she insisted, was to keep it in the family. "Jack, if the Marston family doesn't work on Wonder Woman," she told Liebowitz, "I give it two years—one to run on Bill's stuff, the second to peter out."[9]

But Liebowitz didn't give Holloway his 100 percent backing; he didn't give her any backing at all. Instead, he hired Kanigher, over not only Holloway's objections but also Mayer's. Mayer had never liked Kanigher's Wonder Woman stories. The first time Kanigher gave Mayer a Wonder Woman script, Kanigher said, "I brought it in and he threw it on the floor and jumped up and down on it. I picked it up, went home, and came back with another Wonder Woman story. He went into his routine of throwing it on the floor and jumping up and down on it. The third time I came in he went through his routine. So I said, 'Fuck you.'" But that night, according to Kanigher, Mayer called him and told him Liebowitz wanted to meet with him. "I said, 'What for?' He said, 'About taking over Wonder Woman.'" Kanigher came in for a meeting. Liebowitz offered him a position as both writer and editor, with complete control over Wonder Woman. When Holloway protested, Whitney Ellsworth, DC Comics' editorial director, told Kanigher, "Take the old lady out for lunch."[10]

After that, Holloway was altogether cut out of all editorial conversations. Determined to pass along Marston's vision, she sent Kanigher a long document titled "Information for Wonder Woman Scripts." It explains Wonder Woman's origins, her motivation, her favorite sayings, and each of her special tricks and toys. ("WW's plane is invisible. It is not a robot plane.") It lists each of the recurring characters, including villains, and their backstories. ("Paula has secret laboratories in Washington; at Holliday College near Washington, under the steam plant.") It explains the story structure: Wonder Woman must appear by page 2 or 3, the menace by page 4. It includes a list of curses:

FEMININE (Preferred)	MASCULINE (Avoid)
Merciful Minerva	Poseidon's Beard
Great Hera	Zeus' Thunderbolt
Suffering Sappho	Vulcan's Hammer
Athena's Shield	Great Caesar's Ghost
All-wise Athena	Hammers of Hephaeastus (my favorite)
Aphrodite aid me, etc.	Phaeton's Chariot

"Bill used feminine expletives for the most part," Holloway instructed Kanigher. "This is a detail which helps to build the 'woman' atmosphere."[11]

"You, Daughter, must become the women's leader," the Duke of Deception tells Lya in a Wonder Woman story written by Kanigher in 1948. "You must persuade them that they don't want any political rights and that everything I dictate they vote for."

Lya smiles. "That'll be easy!"[12]

Kanigher filed Holloway's instructions away. Then he did with Wonder Woman whatever the hell he wanted.

Mayer quit. Holloway was all but forbidden from ever coming to the office again. According to one of her grandchildren, "The guys at DC would hide under their desks when she showed up."[13]

Holloway sent Kanigher that set of instructions in February 1948. The next month, in *Winters v. New York,* the U.S. Supreme Court declared unconstitutional a section of the New York State Penal Code banning printed material that appears to glamorize crime. The court found that terms used in the code, like "indecent" and "disgusting," had no "technical or common law meaning." Critics of comic books believed that the ruling made a specious distinction between obscenity (which was not then protected by the First Amendment) and violence (which was). To protest the ruling, a psychiatrist named Fredric Wertham organized a symposium called "The Psychopathology of Comic Books." One speaker, Gershon Legman of the Association for the Advancement of Psychotherapy, said that *Winters v. New York* meant that naked women could not be tortured on the pages of a comic book but "if they were being tortured to death with all their clothes on, that would be perfect for children." He attacked both Marston, for having created, in Wonder Woman, a character who "lynches her victims," and Lauretta Bender, for providing "the standard psychiatric justification for these comic books."[14]

In May, an indictment of comics written by Wertham appeared in the *Saturday Review of Literature.* Working with children in Queens and Harlem, Wertham had grown worried about what comic-book characters like Wonder Woman did to little girls. He told a story about a four-year-old girl living in an apartment building where all the other children were boys; they'd gotten the idea, from comic books, that it would be fun to hurt her: "The boys in the building, from about three to nine years old, hit her, beat her with guns, tie her up with rope whenever they get a chance. They hit her with whips which they buy at the circus. They push her off her bicycle and take her toys away. They handcuff her with handcuffs bought with coupons from comic books. They take her to a vacant lot and use her as a target for bow and arrow. They make a spearhead and scare her. Once, surrounding her in this way, they pulled off her panties to torture her (as they put it). Now her mother has fastened the child's panties with a string around her neck so the boy can't pull them down."[15]

Wertham, born in Nuremberg in 1895, received his MD in Germany in 1921; the next year, he immigrated to the United States. He was a liberal, an especially ardent supporter of racial equality, and an advocate of gun control. In the 1930s, Wertham worked closely with Clarence Darrow; in criminal cases, Wertham often testified on behalf of indigent blacks. In 1930, Margaret Sanger established a birth control clinic in Harlem, with the support of W.E.B. DuBois. ("Those who would confine women to childbearing are reactionary barbarians," DuBois said.)[16] Two years later, Wertham began setting up mental health clinics nearby. In 1934, he started working at Bellevue Hospital. Between 1936 and 1940, Lauretta Bender's husband, Paul Schilder, director of Bellevue's Mental Hygiene Clinic, was Wertham's boss. In 1938, Wertham argued in John Henry Wigmore's *Journal of Criminal Law and Criminology* that psychiatry had a great deal to contribute to the law because psychiatrists could understand the forces that contaminated children's minds and turned them into criminals. By that he meant, in part, that psychiatrists ought to decide what kind of children's reading should be banned. The year Schilder died, 1940, Wertham left Bellevue Hospital to become director of psychiatric services at Queens Hospital, where he started what came to be called the Hookey Club, a therapy group for delinquent children. In 1946 he founded the Lafargue Clinic in Harlem.[17]

The racism, the sexual exploitation of women, and the glorification of guns in comic books bothered Wertham more than anything else, although he was also obsessed with what he considered the comics'

Frederick Wertham inspecting the comics

promotion of forms of sexual "perversion," including homosexuality. No small part of his animus against comics, though, had to do with Lauretta Bender, who was Wertham's professional rival, and also his bête noire. When he called comic-book industry advisers "psycho-prima donnas," he was referring, quite specifically, to Bender: "The fact that some child psychiatrists endorse comic books does not prove the healthy state of the comic books," he said. "It only proves the unhealthy state of child psychiatry." Even the troubled children in the Hookey Club could see that anyone who served on a comic-book publisher's editorial advisory board was untrustworthy. "If you got a thousand dollar check for these funny books, would you talk against them?" he said a fourteen-year-old boy had pointed out. "They give some people side money, so they write, 'Approved by Dr. So-and-So: Good Reading Matter for Children.'"[18]

By the end of the 1940s, laws banning or restricting the sale of comic books had been passed in dozens of cities and states. In 1950, Congress held a set of hearings on juvenile delinquency, chaired by Estes Kefauver. The hero in comic books is almost always "an athletic, pure American white man," Wertham pointed out, while "the villains on the other hand, are foreign-born, Jews, Orientals, Slavs, Italians, and dark-skinned races."[19] Very few people interested in shutting down the comic-book industry were as troubled by the racism in comics as was Wertham. Kefauver's interest was, instead, in the relationship between comic books and juvenile delinquency. "It is my belief that comics do not excite children to criminal activity," Lauretta Bender wrote to Kefauver before the hearings began. "I have found a relationship between comics and delinquency in children but that the relationship is a positive one in that comics can be and are used by children as a means of relief from conflict, confusion, frustration, anxiety and may prove also to be a vicarious release of aggression. In this way, children's use of comics may be compared to adults' use of literature of all kinds, art, music, theater, movies etc., as these help us all to a better understanding of life, of other people's problems, of social concepts and bring all people closer together in a mutual understanding."[20]

Wertham tried to discredit Bender by pointing out, during his testimony, that "the comic book experts who have become most known to the public have admitted to the United States Senate Crime Committee that they have been employed by the crime comic book industry."[21] In his final report, Kefauver was unable to demonstrate that comics caused children to commit acts of violence. Wertham was furious, calling Kefauver's conclusions "the greatest advertisement the crime comic book industry has had to date."[22] Bender was pleased, writing to Whitney Ellsworth at DC Comics to tell him that she felt that Kefauver's hearings had proved nothing so much as that, regarding the relationship between comic books and juvenile delinquency, "there is clearly no evidence that the influence is a negative one."[23]

Wertham decided that the only way he could prevail in his fight against the comic-book industry was to discredit Bender. He compiled a list he titled "Paid Experts of the Comic Book Industry Posing as Independent Scholars." First on the list, as the comic-book industry's lackey #1, was Bender. "On crime comics payroll since 1941," Wertham wrote. "Boasted privately of bringing up her 3 children on money from crime comic books."[24]

"Dr. Wertham is at large again," a friend wrote to Bender in October 1953. "He has written a book."[25] That book, *Seduction of the Innocent,* was published in the spring of 1954. In 1951, Wertham had testified on behalf of the National Association for the Advancement of Colored People, in a school desegregation case in Delaware. In a study he'd conducted at the Lafargue Clinic, Wertham found that school segregation was psychologically harmful. (Wertham's work, along with his testimony for the NAACP, was cited, in 1954, in *Brown v. Board of Education.*)[26] In *Seduction of the Innocent,* he revisited this argument in his case against comics. He related, from his case notes, the stories of children he worked with in his clinic in Harlem, quoting, for instance, a twelve-year-old black girl who read seven or eight comic books a day, including *Wonder Woman*. She said,

> I don't think they make the colored people right. The way they make them I never seen before—their hair and big nose and the English they use. They never have an English like we have. They put them so dark—for real I've never seen anybody before like that. White kids would think all colored people look like that, and really they aren't.

Wertham paid special attention to the three most popular superheroes. "This Superman-Batman-Wonder Woman group is a special form of crime comics," he explained. One of his chief arguments was that comics promoted homosexuality. Batman and Robin live together ("it is like a wish dream of two homosexuals"); they love each other. "Sometimes Batman ends up in bed injured and young Robin is shown sitting next to him." Even their house is gay: "They live in sumptuous quarters, with beautiful flowers in large vases." They share furniture: "Sometimes they are shown on a couch, Bruce reclining and Dick sitting next to him, jacket off, collar open, and his hand on his friend's arm." It wasn't just that Bruce and Dick were lovers; it was that they turned boys gay. "The Batman type of story may stimulate children to homosexual fantasies," Wertham charged.[27] The Amazonian princess, he thought, was worse. "The Lesbian counterpart of Batman may be found in the stories of Wonder Woman," Wertham asserted, taking the opportunity to attack Bender: "The *Psychiatric Quarterly* deplored in an editorial the 'appearance of an eminent child therapist as the implied endorser of a series . . . which portrays extremely sadistic hatred of all males in a framework which is plainly Lesbian."[28]

Wertham told the story of Edith, fourteen, a juvenile delinquent. "Her ideal was Wonder Woman," he explained. "There was no question but that this girl lived under difficult social circumstances. But she was prevented from rising above them by the specific corruption of her character development by comic-book seduction. The woman in her had succumbed to Wonder Woman." For Wertham, Wonder Woman was quite possibly the worst comic-book character of all. She could be vicious; her comic books were racist; she was a lesbian Batman, and the Holliday College girls were "gay." Bender had written that Wonder Woman comic books display "a strikingly advanced concept of femininity and masculinity" and "women in these stories are placed on an equal footing with men and indulge in the same type of activities." Wertham found the feminism in Wonder Woman repulsive. "As to the 'advanced femininity,' what are the activities in comic books which women 'indulge in on an equal footing with men'? They do not work. They are not homemakers. They do not bring up a family. Mother-love is entirely absent. . . . Even when Wonder Woman adopts a girl there are Lesbian overtones."[29]

Seduction of the Innocent was published on April 19, 1954. Two days later, the Senate Subcommittee on Juvenile Delinquency, headed by Kefauver, convened hearings in New York.[30] William Gaines testified on the first day of the hearings. After his father's death, Gaines had launched a run of horror comics, including *The Vault of Horror* and *Tales of Terror*. In 1952, he'd started publishing *Mad* magazine. "What are we afraid of?" Gaines asked during the hearings. "Are we afraid of our own children?" On the second days of the hearings, Wertham testified and said exactly what he was afraid of, revisiting each of the arguments he had made in *Seduction of the Innocent*. "Hitler was a beginner compared to the comic-book industry," he said.

Bender testified the next day. Like William Gaines, Bender, who was forever underestimating Wertham, had a hard time taking his criticism of comics seriously. She said she found horror comics "unspeakably silly." She tried, unsuccessfully, to turn the committee's attention from comic books to film and television by pointing out that she'd seen children at her clinic who'd been driven into a panic by watching animated Walt Disney films. If anything in American popular culture was bad for girls, Bender thought, it wasn't Wonder Woman; it was Walt Disney. "The mothers are always killed or sent to the insane asylums in Walt Disney's movies," she said.

"Would you consider that excessive reading of crime and horror comics is symptomatic of emotional maladjustment?" she was asked.

Only if the evidence was contrived, she answered: "It is conceivable, and I am sure if enough research work is done, sooner or later someone or other can find an incident in which a child can be got to say that he got the idea from such and such a comic book." But she thought Wertham had extracted what amounted to false confessions.[31]

It didn't much matter what Bender said or didn't say. She'd been set up. In a letter written to Kefauver in 1950, answering a questionnaire he'd sent her, Bender had disclosed to him her role as a member of DC Comics' editorial advisory board and her monthly fee, which, by then, was $150.[32] Urged by Wertham, Kefauver's aim in calling Bender to testify was to discredit her, turning the best-credentialed champion of the comic-book industry into a "paid apologist" for the industry because she had been accepting money from DC Comics since 1944.[33]

In the aftermath of the hearings, the Comics Magazine Association of America adopted a new code, closely based on the Hays Code. Under its terms, comic books could contain nothing cruel: "All scenes of horror, excessive bloodshed, gory or gruesome crimes, depravity, lust, sadism, masochism shall not be permitted." There could be nothing kinky: "Illicit sex relations are neither to be hinted at nor portrayed. Violent love scenes as well as sexual abnormalities are unacceptable." There could be nothing unconventional: "The treatment of love-romance stories shall emphasize the value of the home and the sanctity of marriage." And there could be nothing homosexual: "Sex perversion or any inference to same is strictly forbidden." Jack Liebowitz disbanded DC Comics' editorial advisory board and formed a new one; Bender was not on it.[34]

Most superheroes didn't survive either peacetime or the code. The Justice Society closed its doors in 1948. *Sensation Comics* was canceled in 1953. Wonder Woman lived on, but she was scarcely recognizable. Robert Kanigher hated the character he called "the grotesque inhuman original Wonder Woman."[35] And he didn't like Harry G. Peter's art, either; he began easing him out. The first *Wonder Woman* cover drawn by someone other than Peter appeared in 1949. It featured Steve Trevor carrying a smiling, daffy, helpless *Wonder Woman* over a stream. Instead of her badass, kinky red boots, she wears dainty yellow ballerina slippers.[36] Peter died in 1958.

In the 1950s, Wonder Woman followed the hundreds of thousands of American women who had worked during the war only to be told, when peace came, that not only was their labor no longer needed but it threatened the stability of the nation, by undermining men. By the end of the Second World War, the number of American women working outside the home had grown by 60 percent; three-quarters of these women were married, and one-third were mothers of young children. Women's work had been crucial during wartime. "There are practically no unmarried women left to draw upon," *Fortune* magazine had reported in 1943. "This leaves, as the next potential source of industrial workers, the housewives." At the end of the war, three-quarters of working women hoped to keep their jobs; very few were able to. They were told to quit, to make room for men returning from military service. Women's pay was cut. Factories that had provided child care during the war cut those services. Unmarried women were told to marry; married women were told to have children. Working women went to the altar and to the maternity ward.[37]

Wonder Woman became a babysitter, a fashion model, and a movie star. She wanted, desperately, to marry Steve. She gave advice to the lovelorn, as the author of a lonely-hearts newspaper advice column. In 1950, Kanigher killed off Etta Candy. ("Etta Candy! Jesus Christ!" he

From Robert Kanigher, "Wonder Woman, Romance Editor,"
Wonder Woman #97 (March 1950)

said.) He also abandoned "Wonder Women of History"; he replaced it with a series about weddings, called "Marriage a la Mode."[38]

Women went home. Women's rights went underground. And homosexuals were persecuted. Is there a "quick test like an X-ray that discloses these things?" U.S. Senator Margaret Chase Smith asked in hearings about homosexuality in 1950. At the State Department, a former FBI officer was put in charge of purging the civil service of homosexuals by administering lie detector tests. Those who failed were required to resign. Between 1945 and 1956, one thousand alleged homosexuals employed by the State Department and as many as five thousand employed by the federal government lost their jobs.[39]

Marston, Holloway, and Byrne had led a secret, closeted life. It had its costs.

30

LOVE FOR ALL

OLIVE BYRNE AND ELIZABETH HOLLOWAY MARSTON lived together for the rest of their lives. They were inseparable.[1]

Their four children tell very different stories about their family, the way the children in any family do. Pete says his father was like an express train and his mother was like a bulldozer. Byrne says his mother was a lot like Jane Eyre. Donn never forgave any of them for lying. O.A. would rather not say what she thinks.

Olive Byrne never told her children that Marston was their father. She hinted, though, at some things. "You had a curious upbringing," she wrote to her son Byrne in 1948, when he was a freshman at Harvard. Even if she admitted to nothing more, she admitted this much: it hadn't been easy living the experimental life of William Moulton Marston. "I tried very hard to minimize his fanaticisms as far as you kids were concerned," she told him. But there was only so much she had been able to do. "All this is by way of saying we must be tolerant with ourselves and allow ourselves some deviations from the straight line we set up to follow. Even more we must allow others the same prerogative."[2]

In 1948, unable to prevail on DC Comics to hire her, Holloway, who'd taken time away, for bereavement, went back to her job at Metropolitan Life Insurance. Olive Byrne found another kind of work. "I am working for our local 'Maternal Health Center' clinic," she wrote to Margaret Sanger, "and am most amused when they speak of you. Somehow they think you are a contemporary of Florence Nightingale." It was as if Sanger had lived in another century, a Wonder Woman of History. Olive Byrne tried to explain to the people at the clinic that Sanger was alive and well, but she never told anyone at the clinic that she was Sanger's niece. "I'm afraid they'll expect too much of me!"[3]

Pete, who'd gone to Harvard but quit after freshman year, married young and started a family. So did O.A, who dropped out of junior college. Both Byrne and Donn Marston graduated from Harvard; Margaret Sanger helped pay for their education. Their mothers were inseparable, but the children grew apart. Olive Ann dropped "Olive" from her name; Byrne Holloway Marston dropped "Holloway."

In 1952, Holloway and Olive Byrne—"the ladies," the children called them—moved out of the house in Rye. "So you are leaving the nest," Sanger wrote to her niece when she heard the news. "It is what we all must do. But it was a wonderful basis & roots for those children to develop in."[4] Olive Byrne and Holloway settled into an apartment in New York City. Marjorie Wilkes Huntley lived with them, every once in a while. During the stretches when all three of them lived together, Holloway and Huntley shared one bedroom; Olive slept in another.[5]

In the 1950s, Sanger turned her attention to the question of how she would be remembered. She'd been sorting through her papers, preparing them for the Library of Congress and for Smith College, deciding what to keep and what to throw away.[6] One thing Sanger was keen to do was to write her sister Ethel out of the story of her life. In 1952, Sanger sold the rights to a film based on her autobiography. She then wrote a letter to Ethel Byrne, claiming that the scriptwriter wished to make a slight alteration to the facts of the founding of the birth control movement, regarding the trials the two women had faced in 1917. In the film, Sanger told her sister, "I should be the Hunger Strikee." Ethel Byrne would not be mentioned; it would be as if she had never existed. Sanger asked her sister to sign a release stating that she agreed that the film would not "portray me or any part of my life" and that, in the film, it would appear "that Mrs. Sanger engaged in the famous hunger strike instead of myself." Ethel Byrne thought the release was "the funniest thing in the world," according to Olive. She never signed it. The film was never made.[7]

In much the same way that Sanger wished she could erase from the historical record the fact that Ethel Byrne, and not she, had gone on a hunger strike, she kept well hidden her ties to the comic-book superhero created by William Moulton Marston. Maybe she thought it was unimportant. Maybe she found it embarrassing. Maybe never mentioning it was among the things Sanger did to help keep Olive Byrne's family arrangements secret, in order to avoid scandal for Olive and the children and harm to Sanger's cause. Whatever the reason, in no part of the story of Sanger's life, as she told it—as she saved it—did she ever mention Wonder Woman.

Ethel Byrne died in 1955. In the last years of her life she lived with her son, Jack.[8] Olive felt little but bitterness about her. "I could not bring myself to forgive Mother for leaving Jack and me," she told Sanger. The funeral was gruesome. "The undertaker didn't know her," Olive wrote to Sanger, "so he frizzled her hair and painted her up so she didn't look like anybody we know." She scattered her mother's ashes in Truro.[9] Then she selected papers of her mother's to give to her aunt, to include in the papers Sanger was preparing to donate to Smith College. Very few of Ethel Byrne's papers survive.[10]

In 1953, Olive Byrne took a job at Victor Chemical Works, in New York. "The job is not a world beater and requires very little intelligence," she wrote Sanger. "This last I rather like since it is a change from being brilliant over a kitchen sink." Sanger suggested that Olive consider trying to get a job at *Life, Time,* or *Reader's Digest*.[11] Olive said she thought she'd rather work for Dr. Abraham Stone, the director of the Margaret Sanger Research Bureau in New York. The bureau was the clinical research arm of Planned Parenthood; a diaphragm-and-jelly contraceptive regime had been developed there in the 1930s.[12] In the 1950s, Sanger and Stone were pressing for the development of an oral contraceptive.[13] Olive Byrne never ended up taking a job at the bureau; instead, in 1955, Sanger hired her as her personal secretary.[14]

In the 1950s, Planned Parenthood's clinics provided mainly marriage counseling. Sanger had little to do with the organization she and Ethel Byrne had founded in 1916. Sanger had lost patience with it, ever since 1942, when it stopped calling itself the Birth Control Federation of America. "If I told you or wrote you that the name Planned Parenthood would be the end of the movement," Sanger wrote to Planned Parenthood's former national director in 1956, "it was and has proven true. The movement was then a fighting, forward, no fooling movement, battling for the freedom of the poorest parents and for woman's biological freedom and development. The P.P.F. has left all this behind."[15]

Nevertheless, Sanger had a great many arrangements to manage and a great deal of mail to answer. In 1955, Olive Byrne and Elizabeth Holloway Marston went for an extended visit to Tucson, to stay in Sanger's house so that Olive could handle Sanger's affairs while she was traveling in Asia. "I am so happy your friend Betty Marston is there with you and doubtless you will return with her to New York," Sanger wrote to Olive. Every time Sanger traveled, Olive and Holloway went to Tucson and stayed at her house. Sanger was most particular about the sleeping arrangements: "You and Betty can come and stay here in the room with two beds—not in my room."[16]

In 1956, Olive wrote to Sanger to tell her that her son Byrne had gotten engaged.

"Does he know about birth control?" Sanger asked. "He and his bride should go hand in hand to Dr. Stone's office or the M.S. Bureau and get well grounded in contraceptive technique."[17]

"I am fairly certain that Byrne is fully acquainted with BC," Olive wrote, amused.[18] (Byrne Marston was studying to become an obstetrician.)

The night before the wedding, Olive and Holloway gave the rehearsal dinner.[19] Sanger's son Stuart and his wife and their two teenage daughters, Margaret and Nancy, lived in Tucson, too, right next door to Sanger's house. Olive Byrne's son Donn, visiting his mothers in Arizona, met Margaret Sanger's granddaughter Margaret (his second cousin), and they fell in love. Donn Marston was studying law. "I can quite appreciate your Clarence Darrow," Sanger wrote to Olive, on hearing the news. "It's time we had something of the kind in our family."[20]

In 1957, Sanger, who'd grown ill, and difficult, and obsessed with her legacy, appeared on television in an interview with Mike Wallace. It proved devastating to her reputation. Sanger came across as paranoid, hostile, and weak-minded—intimated by Wallace and flummoxed by his questions. Repeatedly, Wallace steered the conversation away from Sanger's work and toward her personal life. Hadn't she abandoned her first husband? Hadn't she abandoned her children? And for what? He pressed her: "Could it be that women in the United States have become too independent—that they have followed the lead of women like Margaret Sanger by neglecting family life for a career?"[21]

Sanger's health worsened. Holloway retired in 1958. The next year, she and Olive Byrne moved to Tucson to take care of Sanger. "It is a wonderful idea that of you & 'Bet' to come here & find a house," Sanger wrote Olive.[22]

In 1960, the Pill, the product of Sanger's decades-long advocacy of birth control research, was released to the public; it hardly ended the national debate about what, at the start of Sanger's career, was called "voluntary motherhood." But Ethel Byrne hadn't gone on a hunger strike and nearly died in vain. And Olive Byrne, despite her bitterness toward her mother, was proud of the fight her mother had waged. In 1965, the Supreme Court ruled in *Griswold v. Connecticut* that the banning of contraception is unconstitutional. In Tucson, Olive Byrne sat down at her typewriter and composed a letter to Justice William O. Douglas.

Dear Sir:
In writing the majority opinion invalidating Connecticut's
birth control laws you put an end to a most vicious disregard
of individual liberty. It is of especial satisfaction to me because
my mother, Ethel Byrne and Margaret Sanger (her sister)
opened the first birth control clinic in Brooklyn 40 years
ago. They were arrested at that time and persecuted and
defiled for years afterwards by religious and political groups.
I am sure Mrs. Sanger, who is very ill, would rejoice in this
pronouncement which crowns her 50 years of dedication to

the liberation of women from enslavement born of bigotry.
All women, everywhere, must rejoice in this final victory over
ignorance and intolerance.

Very truly yours, Olive Byrne Richard (Mrs.)[23]

Margaret Sanger died in September 1966, days before her eighty-seventh birthday. The *New York Times* called her "one of history's great rebels."[24]

Olive Byrne's son Donn and Margaret Sanger's granddaughter Margaret Sanger were married in Tucson on March 25, 1961. The marriage announcement referred to the groom as the "son of Mrs. William Kendall Richard of Tucson." The bride took her husband's name.[25]

Margaret Sanger Marston wasn't willing to put up with the Marston family's secrets. Donn Marston still didn't know who his father was. His wife thought this was ridiculous and set for herself the task of convincing one of the ladies to tell her the truth. At last, she succeeded.

"We have good news on the Father discussion," she wrote to Byrne Marston and his wife, Audrey, in 1963. "While Dots and Betty were here I got Betty to tell me the entire story. She said she would if Donn & Byrne would lay off Dots & not ask her any more questions about their father. She said that Dots would never never tell the truth and said if they tried to make her tell that she would take morphine that she has tucked away. And that would be the end of that."

Byrne and Donn's father was William Moulton Marston, Holloway said. Keeping the boys' father's identity a secret had been Olive Byrne's idea; Holloway and Marston had opposed it but felt the decision was hers. Living as a threesome had been Marston's idea, Holloway said, insisting "that W.M.M. was 100 years ahead of himself" and "that some day everyone will be living like this." Holloway went on for a while in that vein, about how in the future everyone would live the way the Marstons had lived at Cherry Orchard, in one of the stranger corners of America between the wars. At the bottom of the letter, there's a postscript: "Her thinking (E.H.M.'s) is so way out on the subject of W.M.M. that it is almost impossible to record."[26]

Much about any life is impossible to record. Every marriage, each love, is ineffable. And the ways of mothers and fathers remain, to every child, mysterious.

They had been immensely happy together, Holloway said. "W.M.M. really loved Dots & she loved him," Margaret Sanger Marston reported. "And Betty loved him too." Their passion had never weakened. "The affair went on until his death," according to Holloway, "with love making for all." Margaret Sanger Marston was relieved. "At last the truth is out!!"[27]

Holloway had one request: no one was ever to speak of it again.

EPILOGUE

GREAT HERA! I'M BACK!

Ms. magazine, July 1972

"I'M ELIZABETH MARSTON and I know all about Wonder Woman," she said when she charged into the offices of *Ms.* magazine in New York in the spring of 1972. She was nearly eighty years old, pale as paper, thin as bone, and hard as flint. In Virginia, where she was living with Olive Byrne, who was sixty-eight, she'd gotten a letter from an editor at *Ms.,* telling her that the magazine was planning to run a cover story about Wonder Woman in its first regular issue. Holloway, as unstoppable as ever, flew to New York. She pored over the text; she peered at the art. She met the magazine's staff. "All were on the young side, very much in earnest," she reported to Marjorie Wilkes Huntley. "I told them I was 100% with them in what they are trying to do and to 'charge ahead!' " Huntley, thrilled, rushed to send in a money order for a subscription, signing herself, at the age of eighty-two, "Marjorie Wilkes Huntley (Ms.)."[1]

Ms. was meant to be an organ for a revived feminist movement. Betty Friedan's *Feminine Mystique* was published in 1963. The National Organization for Women was founded in 1966. In 1969, Ellen Willis and Shulamith Firestone started the Redstockings of the Women's Liberation Movement. Firestone's manifesto, *The Dialectic of Sex: The Case for Feminist Revolution,* was published the next year, along with Kate Millett's *Sexual Politics* and Robin Morgan's anthology *Sisterhood Is Powerful.* A revolution was being waged, too, in the world of magazines. In March 1970, forty-six women working at *Newsweek* sued the magazine for discrimination. At the *Ladies' Home Journal,* more than a hundred women staged an eleven-hour sit-in, demanding day care, the hiring of female senior editorial staff, and a special issue of the magazine to be called the *Women's Liberated Journal.* Firestone, standing on the editor's desk, tore up copies of the *Ladies' Home Journal* in front of him.[2]

Wonder Woman was part of that revolution. In July 1970, the Women's Liberation Basement Press, in Berkeley, California, launched

From "Breaking Out," *It Aint Me Babe*, July 1970

an underground comic book called *It Aint Me Babe*. The cover of its first issue featured Wonder Woman marching in a rally protesting stock comic-book plots. Inside, Supergirl tells Superman to get lost, Veronica ditches Archie for Betty, Petunia Pig tells Porky Pig to cook his own dinner, and when Iggy tells Lulu "No girls allowed!" she has only one thing to say: "Fuck this shit!"[3]

A nationwide Women's Strike for Equality was held on August 26, 1970, the fiftieth anniversary of the passage of the Nineteenth Amendment. A young writer named Joanne Edgar helped organize the work stoppage at Facts on File. Patricia Carbine went on strike at *Look*. A year later, they were both at *Ms.*, Edgar as an editor, Carbine as publisher.[4] *Ms.* was meant to be a "women's magazine"—like one of the Seven Sisters, like *Family Circle*—but also a critique of them: a women's magazine, liberated. It was also an offshoot of the National Women's Political Caucus, founded in July 1971 by a group of women that included Friedan, Gloria Steinem, Bella Abzug, and Shirley Chisholm, the first black woman elected to Congress. A preview issue of the magazine went on sale in December 1971; it sold out in eight days. An up-and-coming conglomerate agreed to invest a million dollars in the magazine while owning only 25 percent of its stock. "Warner Communications has helped create the first large national magazine controlled by its staff," Steinem said.[5]

By the beginning of 1972, when the editors of *Ms.* were planning the magazine's first regular issue, the women's movement seemed on the verge of lasting, breathtaking success. In January, Chisholm announced that she was running for president, seeking the Democratic Party's nomination. In March, the Equal Rights Amendment, first introduced to Congress in 1923, passed the Senate. In June, Richard Nixon signed into law Title IX, ensuring that "no person in the United States shall, on the basis of sex, be excluded from participation in, be denied the benefits of, or be subjected to discrimination under any education program or activity receiving federal financial assistance." Nineteen seventy-two was a legislative watershed. "We put sex discrimination provisions into everything," Abzug said. "There was no opposition. Who'd be against equal rights for women?"[6]

When the July 1972 issue of *Ms.* appeared on newsstands in June, Chisholm was still in the race. She didn't concede the nomination to George McGovern until the Democratic National Convention, held in Miami the second week of July. Even as delegates made their way to Florida, they saw, in airports, on the cover of *Ms.*, the drawing Holloway saw when she visited the magazine's offices: a giant Wonder Woman striding across a city beneath a banner reading, "WONDER WOMAN FOR PRESIDENT." (Holloway didn't like it: it was "done by a man who had no feeling for what he was doing," she wrote to Huntley.)[7] In running Wonder Woman for president, *Ms.*'s editors were attempting to stake out political terrain: theirs would be a magazine of politics. They also wanted to bridge the distance between the feminism of the 1910s and the feminism of the 1970s with the Wonder Woman of the 1940s, the feminism of their childhood.[8]

"Looking back now at these Wonder Woman stories from the '40s," Steinem said, "I am amazed by the strength of their feminist message." Steinem, born in Ohio in 1934, had loved the original Wonder Woman as a girl. She'd also had something to do with comics as a grown-up. In the 1960s, while working for Harvey Kurtzman, who'd helped William Gaines create *Mad*, she'd gotten to know Dorothy Roubicek Woolfolk, who'd returned to DC Comics to edit a line of romance comics.[9] For the July 1972 issue of *Ms.*, Steinem was supposed to write both the cover story about Wonder Woman and a feature story about women voters. She handed the cover story over to Joanne Edgar. Edgar, born in Baton Rouge in 1943, grew up reading comics, too. The kids on her street, mostly boys, used to stack their comic books up and down the sidewalk, for trading. For one *Superman*, Edgar could get three issues of *Wonder Woman*.[10]

"Wonder Woman had feminist beginnings, but like many of us, she went into a decline in the 'fifties,'" Edgar explained in her cover story.

Marston died in 1947, but Wonder Woman lived on. The new writers didn't understand her spirit, however, and she lost some of her original feminist orientation. Her superhuman strength remained, but her violence increased. Rather than proving her superiority over men, she became more and more submissive.

Edgar, like Steinem, was troubled that, beginning in 1968—during what is known as the "Diana Prince Era," when she wasn't even called Wonder Woman anymore—Wonder Woman had lost both her costume and her superpowers. But, according to Edgar, with a renewed women's rights movement, all this was about to change. In 1971, DC Comics named Roubicek Woolfolk as *Wonder Woman*'s new editor, and Edgar reported that she planned to bring back Marston's Wonder Woman: "Ms. Woolfolk also plans to decrease violence in the plots and return our heroine to the feminism of her birth. And maybe to politics, too?"[11]

The founders of *Ms.* placed great faith in Wonder Woman's ability to launch the magazine. The July 1972 issue featured not only "WONDER WOMAN FOR PRESIDENT" on the cover and Edgar's article inside but also a four-page pullout, a reproduction of "Introducing Wonder Woman" from the December 1941–January 1942 issue of *All-Star Comics*. Steinem, Edgar, and Carbine also decided to publish a stand-alone anthology of *Wonder Woman* comics from the 1940s as a way to build publicity and gain subscribers for *Ms.* Steinem picked out which of Marston's original stories to include, steering clear of the bondage theme as best she could.[12] *Wonder Woman: A "Ms." Book,* appeared in the summer of 1972 as a *Ms.* publication, distributed by Warner. "The *Ms.* cover story on Wonder Woman in July, 1972, brought so many requests for these vintage and out-of-print stories, that they have been collected in one irresistible book," the magazine's editors claimed. (This was disingenuous; the book had been typeset even before the first issue of the magazine was printed.) Profits went to the magazine; order forms encouraged fans of Wonder Woman to subscribe to *Ms.*[13]

"Lovely and Wise Heroine Summoned to Help the Feminist Cause," the *New York Times* announced. The *Los Angeles Times* declared Wonder Woman "The Movement's Fantasy Figure." In November 1972, during the week of the presidential election, wire-service stories about the return of Wonder Woman were published all over the country.[14] By May 1973, *Ms.* and Warner were wondering, together, whether they might manufacture and market a Wonder Woman doll.[15] In July 1973, a women's health collective in Los Angeles featured Wonder Woman wielding a speculum on the cover of a newsletter dedicated to teaching women how to conduct their own vaginal exams.[16]

In 1973, the year Wonder Woman was named a "symbol of feminist revolt," the Supreme Court issued a ruling legalizing abortion. But the aftermath of *Roe v. Wade* didn't bolster the feminist move-

From a 1973 feminist newsletter

ment; instead, it narrowed it. If 1972 was a legislative watershed, 1973 marked the beginning of a drought. Some gains were lost; others proved illusory. Even the idea that DC Comics was hiring Dorothy Roubicek Woolfolk to edit a new Wonder Woman comic book and "return our heroine to the feminism of her birth" turned out to be wrong.

Dorothy Roubicek Woolfolk did edit one issue of *Wonder Woman* in 1971, and another early in 1972; those issues are no different from any published during the Diana Prince Era.[17] About that time, Steinem, visiting DC Comics to pick out old Wonder Woman stories to reprint in the Wonder Woman *Ms.* book, saw some of the Diana Prince Era issues and said, "What's happened to Wonder Woman? You've taken away all her super-powers. Don't you realize how important this is to the young women of America?"[18] Roubicek Woolfolk sided with Steinem—she wanted Wonder Woman to get her superpowers back— for which she was fired, right about when the July 1972 issue of *Ms.* appeared on newsstands.

"I've just heard that you're no longer with National Publications and I wanted to say that I think it's a damn shame," *Glamour* staff writer Flora Davis wrote to Roubicek Woolfolk on June 23. Davis had been writing an article about Wonder Woman. *Glamour* killed it. "I enjoyed working with you on the Wonder Woman article," Davis told Roubicek Woolfolk. "I had hoped it would be a piece about how comics were quietly—and at long last—becoming healthy reading for kids, especially for girls. It's disappointing to have to retract that. Whatever you do now, I wish you luck in your new career. You are one of the most articulate women's-lib spokespeople I've ever met."[19]

In July, out of work, Roubicek Woolfolk wrote to Steinem to tell her that she'd gone on a public speaking tour, talking about "women's liberation and the role of comics," and in every city she visited, *Ms.* was a sellout: "I got the feeling the lively Wonder Woman cover didn't hurt sales a bit."[20]

Roubicek Woolfolk had no hand in it, but in December 1972, DC Comics published a "Special! Women's Lib Issue" of *Wonder Woman,* edited by Dennis O'Neil and written by a science-fiction writer named Samuel R. Delany. It was meant to be the first installment of a six-part storyline; in each installment, Diana Prince was supposed to battle a male chauvinist.[21] In the first story (a recycling of a story from the

From Samuel R. Delany, "The Grandee Caper," *Wonder Woman #203* (December 1972), the special "women's lib" issue

1940s), Diana defeats a department store owner who is underpaying women workers. "Another villain was a college advisor who really felt a woman's place was in the home," Delany later explained. "It worked up to a gang of male thugs trying to squash an abortion clinic staffed by women surgeons." The abortion clinic story was killed. Only the first of Delany's six "women's lib" stories was ever published.[22]

The comic-book industry found it nearly impossible to respond to the women's movement. In 1972 and 1973, Marvel Comics, keen to hitch its wagon to the women's movement, produced three "women's comics"—*Night Nurse, Shanna the She-Devil,* and *The Cat;* all failed after fewer than half a dozen issues.[23] DC Comics abandoned Delany's Diana Prince stories. Instead, in early 1973, Wonder Woman returned, in costume and with all her superpowers restored, in DC's "New Adventures of the Original Wonder Woman," written and edited by Robert Kanigher, who, to say the least, wasn't known for his sympathy with the women's movement. ("Bob Kanigher was a very wild chauvinist," his assistant later said.)[24] The first thing Kanigher did, in "New Adventures," was to have a barely fictionalized Dorothy Roubicek Woolfolk murdered. A panel pictures her dead at her desk, slumped over a typewriter. The caption reads: "The sniper's first bullet fells Dottie Cottonman, woman's magazine, editor."[25]

From Robert Kanigher, "The Second Life of the Original Wonder Woman," *Wonder Woman #204* (February 1973)

．　　．　　．

"Who'd be against equal rights for women?" Bella Abzug asked in 1972. A lot of people. In the late 1970s and 1980s, the women's movement stalled. Wages never reached parity; social and economic gains were rolled back; political and legal victories seemingly within sight were never achieved.[26] Then, too, feminists were divided, radicals attacking liberals and liberals attacking radicals in a phenomenon so widespread it even had a name: "trashing."[27] As early as 1970, the founder of the New Feminist Theater warned, in a letter of resignation from the Congress to Unite Women, that feminist "rage, masquerading as a pseudo-egalitarian radicalism," was becoming "frighteningly vicious anti-intellectual fascism."[28]

In that battle Wonder Woman wasn't caught in the crossfire; Wonder Woman was the ammunition. In 1967, William Dozier, who'd launched a *Batman* TV series on ABC in 1966, filmed a screen test for a super-campy Wonder Woman series called *Who's Afraid of Diana Prince?;* the show was never produced.[29] But *Ms.*'s revival of Wonder Woman made ABC take another look. In March 1974, Cathy Lee Crosby starred in an ABC-TV Wonder Woman movie. It had little to do with the 1940s Wonder Woman; it was set in the 1970s, and it was a flop.[30] But the next year, ABC launched *The New Original Wonder Woman.* Set in the 1940s, it was based very closely on Marston's comics, as was its theme song:

> *Wonder Woman! Wonder Woman!*
> *All the world is waiting for you*
> *And the power you possess.*
> *In your satin tights,*
> *Fighting for your rights,*
> *And the old red, white, and blue.*

> *Wonder Woman! Wonder Woman!*
> *Now the world is ready for you,*
> *And the wonders you can do:*
> *Make a hawk a dove,*

Stop a war with love,
Make a liar tell the truth.

Wonder Woman!
Get us out from under, Wonder Woman!
All our hopes are pinned upon you![31]

The New Original Wonder Woman ran for four years. To radical feminists, it looked like a sellout of everything the feminist movement stood for. In 1968, the Redstockings of the Women's Liberation Movement had protested the Miss America pageant in Atlantic City, chucking high heels and issues of *Playboy* into a Freedom Trash Can and crowning, as Miss America, a sheep. The star of *The New Original Wonder Woman* was Lynda Carter, a beauty pageant winner who'd represented the United States in the Miss World contest in 1972. But the battle over Wonder Woman predated Carter's debut as Wonder Woman. As early as July 1972, Betty Friedan distanced herself from Gloria Steinem by accusing her of telling women they had to be "superwomen."[32]

In May 1975, six months before ABC aired its pilot starring Carter, the Redstockings held a press conference to announce the release of a sixteen-page report. It purported to prove (1) that Gloria Steinem was a CIA agent; (2) that *Ms.* was both a capitalist manifesto and part of a CIA strategy to destroy the women's movement; and (3) that Wonder Woman was a symbol of the ruination of feminism.[33] The report, printed as a broadside, was illustrated by a drawing of Wonder Woman with Steinem's head.[34] The Redstockings indicted *Ms.* for its relationship with Warner Communications, citing the terms of the original deal—in which Warner provided most of the funding but was not a majority stockholder—and asking, "What possible interest could this mammoth conglomerate have in women's liberation that would lead them to agree to such unbusiness-like terms?" The Redstockings wanted to know: Why would Warner spend a million dollars to fund a feminist magazine, unless it was part of a secret plan to sabotage the feminist movement? Even the fact that Diana Prince is "an army intelligence officer" seemed to the Redstockings to be evidence that

RADICAL FEMINISTS WON'T BE MSLED

data sheets to their subjects, requesting them to furnish the details.

The 1968-69 edition was the first issue ever mentioning Steinem and at the time she was listed as: "Director, educational foundation, Independent Research Service, Cambridge, Mass., NYC, 1959-62, now member Board of Directors, Washington."

By the 1970 edition of Who's Who, this entry was shorted to "Director, educational foundation...1959-60." No mention of her position in Washington on the Board of Directors appears and the abbreviated bar form of employment with the Independent Research Service to one year. The censored version appears in each successive edition of Who's Who.

There does seem to be an attempt, on Steinem's part, to mislead Ms. readers and conceal parts of her past. For instance, her bio-blurb in the June, 1973, Ms. is even vaguer: "Gloria Steinem has been a free-lance writer all her professional life...Ms. magazine is her first full-time, salaried job."

Then there is Gloria Steinem's mysteriously swift rise to national prominence so soon after the 1967 exposures. It is a common complaint among ex-CIA agents that past involvement with the Agency often impedes their ability to find other forms of employment. This was not the case for Steinem. Again, according to the Redstockings:

'Her career skyrocketed a year after the 1967 exposures. Much of the credit for this must go to Clay Felkner, publisher of New York magazine. Recently in the news for his acquisition of the Village Voice, Felkner immediately fired its two remaining founders from their jobs as publisher and editor.

"Felkner was Steinem's editor at Esquire where her first free-lance pieces were published. He hired her as contributing editor to New York magazine in 1968 and booked publicity spots for her on radio and TV talk shows. Felkner put up the money for the preview issue of Ms. in January 1972, a large part of which appeared as a supplement to the 1971 year-end issue of New York magazine.

"In effect, it was Felkner who made Steinem famous by giving her a platform from which to establish her women's liberation credentials. These facts are all part of the public record. What has not been widely known up to this time are the earlier political roots of the Steinem/Felkner collaboration. Felkner was with Steinem at the Helsinki Youth Festival, editing the English language newspaper, put out by the CIA-financed delegation."

In addition to Steinem's initial boost from Clay Felkner, the Redstockings were able to determine two other major sources of funds for the then fledgling Ms. magazine. One resource was Katherine Graham, owner and publisher of the Washington Post and Newsweek. She bought $20,000 worth of stock before the first issue of Ms. was ever published. According to perfect Ms. "ideology," Graham was recently featured on the magazine's cover, depicted by the headline as "The Most Powerful Woman in America." (10/74.)

'It should be noted in conjunction to this fact, that Newsweek became the most enthusiastic mass circulation magazine promoting the Independent Research Service and later Gloria Steinem as an individual. (See early article of 5/10/65 and cover story of 8/16/71.)

The second major money source for Ms. was Warner Communications, Inc. They purchased $1 million worth of Ms. stock, after the preview issue appeared. Warner's allegedly put up nearly all the money and only took 25% of the actual stock holdings. Even the Ms. editors admitted that this was a trifle odd: "We are especially impressed that they took the unusual position of becoming a major investor, but minority stockholder; thus providing all the money without demanding the decision vote in return." (Ms. Reader, p. 226)

Warner Communications is a mammoth operation, now owning Warner Brothers movies and records besides having large holdings in cable TV, publishing, building maintenance and construction, parking lots

and other companies. What was their vested interest in women's liberation which inspired them to make such an unlikely business deal with Ms? Well, Warner is also the owner of National Periodical Publications, which publishes the Wonder Woman comic book.

Warner bought the Ms. stock in May 1972. In July 1972, the first regular issue of Ms. appeared on the stands, featuring a cover story on Wonder Woman. Wonder Woman as a feminist heroine, no less. The truth is that Wonder Woman was an army intelligence officer, working "for America, the last citadel of democracy, and equal rights for women." The Ms. story also announced that Wonder Woman comics, which had been on the wane since the 1940's, would be reborn in 1973 with a woman editor.

Next January's issue of Ms. told readers that the magazine would soon publish a book on Wonder Woman: "It is the first Ms. book. (In fact, we hadn't planned to do one so soon; it just grew out of readers queries about how to find these comics. . .)"

Elitism

This exemplifies the fraudulent relationship Ms. has with its readers. It seems obvious, once the facts of financing are known, that commercial interests and politics are coinciding in the Ms. empire.

The 1973 version of Wonder Woman was to be more pacifistic, in adherence to the general line pushed by Ms. In both her old and new model, Wonder Woman's guiding incentive is "patriotism" -- a stance provocative of American ruling class interests.

The promotion of this comic strip heroine is also an indication of the anti-people attitude of liberal feminists who glorify mystical "models," while they ignore or actually denigrate the real achievements of down-to-earth women. The Redstocking investigators point out that this practice, "leads to an individualist line that denies the need for a mass movement, and implies that when women don't make it, it's their own fault."

The elitist line is actually one of Ms.' biggest selling points in attracting advertisers. In order to get ads, Ms. has sold out the ordinary woman. From a Ms. ad in the New York Times of March 19, 1974: "...a standard market survey shows the Ms. audience of 1,400,000 as having the best education, living in higher income households, holding more managerial/professional jobs than any other woman's magazine readers, and 54% of them are between 18 and 34."

The ad policies of Ms. are an equally important indicator of the magazine's financial and political backing, especially in view of the frequently stated Ms. claims of extreme selectivity regarding which ads they will accept. This stance makes any ad they choose amount to an endorsement.

Blatantly sexist ads are most often rejected, along with ads for cosmetic and fashion products. However, Ms. seems to have no moral problem accepting public relations and job recruitment ads for large corporations. ITT is one of the most regular advertisers in Ms., along with non-product ads from Ortho pharmaceuticals, Exxon Oil, Chemical Bank, Bell Telephone, Singer Aerospace, Shearson-Hamill stockbrokers, Gulf and Western Oil and Merrill-Lynch stockbrokers.

In their special "Human Development" section each month, Ms. runs a series of advertisements for careers in companies like these. A letter in September 1973, from Amy Swerdlow of Women Strike for Peace questioned what the recruiting of women for ITT had in common with human development. "Let's have a Ms. story on all ITT activities around the world. Then let the reader decide what talented women will find at ITT headquarters," she submitted.

Ms. editors replied that in the light of all the unemployed women and women on welfare, they could not be too selective about job ads. As if welfare mothers are all headed towards ITT careers. There is much controversy over whether Ms. magazine is a commercial or a political enterprise. Elements of both seem to exist, as ingre-

The Redstockings' attack on *Ms.*, 1975, with Steinem as Wonder Woman

Steinem was a CIA puppet, a willing and knowing participant in a conspiracy to destroy the women's liberation movement. Furthermore: "Wonder Woman also reflects the anti-people attitude of the 'liberal feminists' and the matriarchists who look to mythical and supernatural heroines and 'models' while ignoring or denigrating the achievements and struggles of down-to-earth women. It leads to the 'liberated woman,' individualist line that denies the need for a movement, and implies that when women don't make it, it's their own fault."[35]

Steinem rebutted each of these charges.[36] "It's really crazy, isn't it?" Edgar wrote to the head of Warner, enclosing the Redstockings' statement.[37] But this rift, like so many others, proved impossible to close.[38] And, while the Redstockings' conspiracy theory really was crazy, they did have a point about Wonder Woman. Who needs consciousness-raising and equal pay when you're an Amazon with an invisible plane?

One tragedy of feminism in the twentieth century was the way its history seemed to be forever disappearing. In 1969, Shulamith Firestone and a group of young feminists visited eighty-four-year-old Alice Paul in Washington, D.C. Paul had founded the National Woman's Party in 1916, had gone on a hunger strike in 1917, and had drafted the Equal Rights Amendment in 1923. She brought her visitors into her parlor, where the walls were covered with oil portraits of suffragists. When she asked them to identify the women in those portraits, they couldn't name a single one.[39]

In the late 1970s and 1980s, between feminists trashing one another, the reduction of a struggle for equality to the defense of abortion, and the rise of the New Right, the women's movement floundered. The "woman's dilemma" described in 1926—"Can a Woman Run a Home and a Job, Too?"—was hardly any closer to a solution, a half century later.[40] The constitutional amendment introduced by Alice Paul in 1923 was never ratified; by 1982, the fight for the ERA had been abandoned.

Meanwhile, a generation of women historians dedicated themselves to never again forgetting the names of the women whose portraits hung on the walls of Alice Paul's parlor. Women's history exploded: brilliant, passionate scholars studied everything from the shape of

David Levine caricature of Margaret Sanger, 1978

women's lives to the history of their political struggles. In 1970, Anne Firor Scott published a reader, *Women in American Life.* The first edition of *Notable American Women,* a biographical dictionary, appeared in 1971. So did Gerda Lerner's landmark textbook, *The Woman in American History.* Nancy Cott's documentary history, *Root of Bitterness,* was published in 1972. Linda Gordon's history of the birth control movement, *Woman's Body, Woman's Right,* came out in 1976. Elizabeth Pleck and Nancy Cott published *A Heritage of Her Own,* a six-hundred-page history of American women, in 1979.

This scholarship shed little light on Wonder Woman. Her debt to Greenwich Village bohemianism, socialism, free love, androgyny, sex radicalism, and feminism; Holloway and Marston's relationship to suffrage; their family arrangements; Jack Byrne and Fiction House; Wonder Woman's ties to Olive Byrne, Ethel Byrne, and Margaret Sanger—this history hadn't been forgotten; it had been deliberately and carefully hidden. In 1978, the artist David Levine drew a caricature of Margaret Sanger dressed as Wonder Woman, leaping into the air from a giant diaphragm. He was trying to tie one era's feminism to another's. He had no idea that Sanger was an inspiration for Wonder Woman. How could he? The story of Wonder Woman's origins wasn't a neglected history, waiting to be written. It was a family secret, locked in a closet.

Sometimes, a secret or two slipped out through the keyhole. In the 1970s, Holloway boasted about how well she had known Sanger. "I spent a lot of time with M.S. both at her home and mine," she told Joanne Edgar. "Had the good fortune to know well in their later years Ethel Byrne and Margaret Sanger," she wrote to the Mount Holyoke Alumni Office in 1975, declaring them to be "two who didn't need any Women's Lib." But she never explained quite how she'd come to know them, because that would have required explaining about Olive Byrne. She did sometimes mention her "companion of many years," but she never called Olive Byrne by name or explained that she was Sanger's niece.[41] In 1974, when a Berkeley PhD student named Karen Walowit writing a dissertation about Wonder Woman asked Holloway about Wonder Woman's bracelets, Holloway wrote to her, "A student of Dr. Marston's wore on each wrist heavy, broad silver bracelets, one African and the other Mexican. They attracted his attention as symbols of love binding so that he adopted them for the Wonder Woman strip."[42] The bracelets were, of course, Olive Byrne's. And while it's true that Olive Byrne was once "a student of Dr. Marston's," she had at that point been living with Holloway for forty-eight years.

Olive Byrne, interviewed in the 1970s and 1980s by historians and biographers studying Margaret Sanger—interviewed often for hours at a time—never mentioned Marston or Wonder Woman.[43] That made it impossible for anyone outside the family to tie Sanger and Wonder Woman together. And when reporters or scholars asked Holloway about Wonder Woman, she told them to write to Marjorie Wilkes Huntley, to steer them away from Olive Byrne. "No one knows more about the production of Wonder Woman than Marjorie W. Huntley," she would say. "She is the person you should refer people to if there are any questions."[44]

In her nineties, Marjorie Wilkes Huntley moved to a nursing home in Massachusetts. She put up a poster on the wall of her room; it read, "When God made man She was only joking." In 1982, Huntley was interviewed by a reporter for a local newspaper. Drinking Guinness and rocking in a chair, she said that she had once worked for the man who created Wonder Woman; she didn't mention Elizabeth Holloway or Olive Byrne. Huntley died in 1986, one day after her ninety-seventh birthday. She'd left instructions. She wanted no ceremony at her cremation except for the reading of a poem: "Oh, my soul is not a timid spirit."[45]

For a long time, no one paid much attention to the fact that the creator of Wonder Woman was also the inventor of the lie detector test. This is partly because Marston had published his comics under a pseudonym, "Charles Moulton," but mainly it's because the people interested in the history of comic books are not the same as the people interested in the history of the polygraph. (And very few people in either group are also interested in the history of feminism.) By the 1980s, lie detector tests were being administered on two million Americans every year. The Reagan administration attempted to stop security leaks by ordering random testing: during his presidency, more than two hundred thousand government employees were required to take lie detector tests. Before the passage of the Employee Polygraph Protection Act of 1988, which limited the practice, one-quarter of all U.S. companies tested their employees. The use of the polygraph exploded after 9/11, when it became a feature of the interrogation of suspected terrorists and of tests given to American citizens applying for security clearance, in spite of a report released by the National Academy of Science in 2003 demonstrating that the polygraph does not work.[46]

No one ever gave Elizabeth Holloway Marston, Olive Byrne, and Marjorie Wilkes Huntley a lie detector test, and they never broke their silence. The veil of secrecy kept by the family over Wonder Woman's past proved impossible to lift. Joanne Edgar, writing a magazine piece about the history of Wonder Woman on a deadline in 1972, and even Karen Walowit, writing a doctoral dissertation in 1974, were hardly any better off than that newspaper editor, in a *Wonder Woman* comic strip from 1944, who, looking for "the exclusive story of Wonder Woman," finds the hunt so maddening that he has a nervous breakdown and ends up in a hospital. The secret history of Wonder Woman stayed secret.

That secrecy led to a distortion not only of Wonder Woman but also of the course of women's history and the struggle for equal rights. Wonder Woman didn't begin in 1941 when William Moulton Marston turned in his first script to Sheldon Mayer. Wonder Woman began on a winter day in 1904 when Margaret Sanger dug Olive Byrne out of a snowbank. The fight for women's rights hasn't come in waves. Wonder Woman was a product of the suffragist, feminist, and birth control movements of the 1900s and 1910s and became a source of the women's liberation and feminist movements of the 1960s and 1970s. The fight for women's rights has been a river, wending.

Olive Byrne died in 1990, at the age of eighty-six. She and Hollo-

Elizabeth Holloway Marston and Olive Byrne in 1985

way had been living together in an apartment in Tampa, near Olive's son Byrne. While Olive was in the hospital, dying, Holloway fell and broke her hip; she was admitted to the same hospital. They were kept in separate rooms. They'd lived together for sixty-four years. When Holloway, in her hospital bed, was told that Olive had died, she sang a poem by Tennyson: "Sunset and the evening star, / And one clear call for me! / And may there be no moaning of the bar, / When I put out to sea."[47]

Byrne Marston scattered his mother's ashes in the Pamet River in Truro. No newspaper ran an obituary.[48]

Elizabeth Holloway Marston died at her son Pete's house in 1993, with Wharton's *Sappho* resting on her nightstand.[49] An obituary ran in the *New York Times*. It was headed, "Elizabeth H. Marston, Inspiration for Wonder Woman, 100."[50] This was, at best, a half-truth.

AFTERWORD: THE HYDE DETECTOR

In the summer of 1941, Marston conducted one last experiment. At
the Astor Theatre in New York, he strapped his subjects up to his
lie detector during a screening of a new MGM film, *Dr. Jekyll and
Mr. Hyde*, starring Spencer Tracy, Ingrid Bergman, and Lana Turner.
(MGM's film was a remake of a very scary and incredibly racy pre-
code Paramount film that had been produced in 1931, while Marston
was still in Hollywood.)

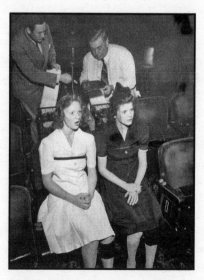

Marston, in shirtsleeves, conducting experiments
with his "Hyde Detector" at the Astor Theatre
in New York, 1941

"More than 100 girls from all walks of life took part in a series of psychological experiments to determine feminine emotional reactions to male aggressiveness," read the story in *The Hollywood Reporter*, under the headline, "MGM Tries Out 'Hyde Detector.'" Marston divided his subjects by hair color (blondes, brunettes, and redheads); marital status (single and married); and occupation ("secretaries, débutantes, and students"). He wanted to know which "love scenes" the women enjoyed more: Jekyll's tender embraces of his fiancée or Hyde's brutal rape of a prostitute. He also wanted to know what portion his subjects thought of every man, was a brute, as if this were merely a matter of mathematics. He concluded, "Average percentage of Hyde in every man, 34 percent."[1]

What, exactly, was the percentage of Mr. Hyde in Dr. Marston? While writing this book, I struggled with that question. Still, it was hard to know, honestly, what to make of him. He sometimes seemed so silly, his experiments so nutty, his showmanship so delightfully ridiculous. But then he sometimes seemed so creepy, his appetites so cruel, his recklessness so dangerous. I wished I had a Hyde Detector.

After the book was published, I heard from a lot of readers who asked the same question: how much Jekyll, how much Hyde?[2] But fascinating as I found Marston, the questions that haunted me after I'd finished writing didn't have to do with him; they had to do with the women in his life, whose lives were much more sparsely chronicled in the records the family left behind. In most instances, their silence had been their choice: what they left behind is what they had chosen to leave behind.

I'd tried to get around that constraint: I conducted the bulk of the research for this book outside the family papers, and above all, in university archives, partly because the family papers, while extraordinary, had been so carefully culled by the women the family has always called "the ladies." When Elizabeth Holloway and Olive Byrne moved out of Cherry Orchard in 1952, they left behind a vast collection of comic books in the attic: they considered that stuff rubbish. (I met the children of the family that moved in; they'd wanted to keep the comics but their mother threw them away; she thought they were rubbish, too.) In the 1950s, Byrne went through her mother's papers, and Margaret Sanger's papers, sorting, choosing what to save, and what to throw away. She would have gone through her own papers, too: her plan, it seems, was to all but erase herself from the historical record. In the 1960s, Holloway went through the Marston family papers. She must have thrown a great deal away, and then she gave a carefully chosen set of Wonder Woman materials to the Smithsonian Museum, and then she sorted the rest of what she had into four piles, and gave one pile to each of the four children: photo albums and folders of papers. When I wrote the book, I had seen two of the four collections and I was amazed at how different they were from one another. Holloway gave Byrne Marston one photo album, and Pete Marston another. Some photographs appear in both albums; most do not. She did the same thing with diaries, letters, and other papers. One set of photographs and documents tell one story, another set tells another. The same family photograph, plainly taken on the same day, has one group of people in one album (Marston, Holloway, and the four kids, while Olive Byrne takes the picture), and another group in another album (Marston, Olive Byrne, and the four kids, while Holloway takes the picture). From Marston's diary, she made extracts for each of the four kids: she transcribed only the entries that concerned *them*. Byrne, his birthday presents, Donn, his measles. Holloway had bequeathed to her children *different histories*. She and Olive Byrne also told their children and grandchildren entirely different—and irreconcilable—family stories.

After the book came out, I got the chance to look at a third set of family papers: the photographs and documents that Holloway had given to Donn Marston. When Donn Marston died in 1988, his wife, Margaret Sanger Marston, threw boxes and boxes of family papers into the trash. I'd heard they'd been destroyed. But, in fact, her daughters, Nan and Peg, pulled those boxes out of the trash. Days after my book was published, I met Nan and Peg in Washington, D.C., and they told me they still had those boxes. It turns out that the photographs and documents Holloway left Donn Marston tell yet another story. "Dear Donn, I am going over a batch of ADM's letters to WMM," she wrote him; she'd saved for him a sheaf of Marston's mother's letters, and much more, too.[3] Meanwhile, I'd stumbled onto some other new evidence on my own, and curators and archivists, on reading the book, sent me things they'd come across in their archives. It began to pile

up. All told, it isn't much—there's no Hyde Detector here—but it's
enough that I thought I had to write about it. Hence, this afterword.

He was, all along, his mother's boy. The first envelope I opened, in the
quiet kitchen of the warm house of one of Marston's granddaughters,
was a faded, peacock blue, about the size of a postcard, but thick, wad-
ded, even. Inside was a smaller envelope, white, but brown with age on
the back of which, in pencil, Marston's mother, Annie Dalton Marston,
had written: "My Baby's Hair." Inside was a visiting card. One side was
engraved: "Mrs. Frederick W. Marston." On the other side, Marston's
mother had written, "William Moulton Marston, Born May 9th, 1893.
First hair cut—June 25, 1894." Affixed to the visiting card by a rusted
paperclip was a strip of brown tissue paper, folded up. I unfolded it.
Inside was a lock of blond hair, as yellow as corn silk. I thought about
Marston's lifelong obsession with hair color. He'd concluded, from
his MGM experiments at the Astor Theatre, "Blondes have less resistance (more compliance) toward an aggressive male love-maker than
any other type."[4] But more, I thought about his mother, because inside
that white envelope within the blue envelope she had stuffed two more
locks of her son's hair, wrapped in paper, and carefully labeled, "Second Hair Cut," and "Third Hair Cut." And in the bigger envelope of
peacock blue, she had stuffed a bound notebook, in which she had kept
notes about her baby, from the moment of his birth "at 3:50 PM," on a
Tuesday. "Baby continued to thrive until Thurs. A.M. when some dis-
coloration upon cheek and ear developed in a manner quite alarming."[5]

"My dear Billie-boy," she addressed him in a sheaf of letters I found
in that kitchen.[6] She wrote him, it seems, every week, long, chatty letters, sending birthday wishes every May: "So farewell dear boy, my
little son so longed for and so welcome on May 9, 1893," she wrote to
him on his forty-eighth birthday, in 1941. "So dear and beloved. Be
good and keep an honorable name for the children."[7]

He was an only child who came to his parents late in their lives, and
I'd guessed he must have been petted, and indulged, by his childless
aunts. But this was something more. In the photographs in these new
albums, too, there were photographs I'd never seen before, in anyone
else's albums: Marston and his mother.

Marston and his mother on the grounds of Moulton
Castle, 1894

Holloway had sorted through the letters, and arranged them chron-
ologically. She'd made an index, too, a list, by date, of her favor-
ites, and their subjects: "8/13/42 comment on W.W.'s costume."[8]
Marston had sent her, that week, a copy of *Wonder Woman #1,* together
with a set of newspaper clippings. "The long article about Wonder
Woman in New York World Telegram, and your note, reached me while at
N. Scituate," she wrote him.

Both were read with great interest. I had just read an item in
the Boston Herald of Tues. Aug. 4, telling of your dropping the
pseudonym and admitting yourself to be the author of Wonder Woman. Great advertising—I imagine fellow psychologists
will be somewhat amazed at your theories but it may be you
are an advance herald of what is to come. Hope this great success will continue, and may have the effect upon the minds of
children that you prophesy. I read through the entire story of
Wonder Woman in the magazine you sent, and must admit that
it was quite absorbing. I do wish however that your artist would
lengthen her pants, even a wee bit. And how about an embroi-

Marston and his mother in front of the house in Cliftondale, 1897

dered scarf of red white and blue? It might save her from an attack of pneumonia.[9]

She wrote him every week, and he wrote back, sending word, in letter after letter, of his accomplishments, like a schoolboy. Did Marston do everything he did for his mother's approval? Had I missed that, entirely?

Marston's fascination with women began with his mother. "Here's one of Dr. Marston's favorite subjects, mothers," Olive Byrne wrote in an article for *Family Circle* that was never published; it's called "Mothers on Trial."[10]

I pawed through those boxes, and found much more. I unfurled a Harvard football banner made of felted, faded crimson that he must have waved from the stands, cheering the team he never played for.[11] In a photo album, I saw that there were Harvard banners all over the walls of his undergraduate room in Hollis Hall, too. I'd tried very hard to find a print of *Jack Kennard, Coward*, the silent film about a Harvard football player, whose script Marston had written in 1915. I never found one. And I'd been skeptical of his claim that he'd worked his way through Harvard by writing screenplays; I was wrong. After the book came out, the curator of film at the Museum of Modern Art in New York e-mailed me that he'd found a print of a one-reel film Marston had sold to Biograph in 1913. *Love in an Apart-*

Marston in his room in Hollis Hall at Harvard, 1914

ment Hotel was directed by D. W. Griffith, the year before Griffith made *Birth of a Nation*.[12] Biograph's story editor had apparently bought the film from Marston (identified, by his return address, as belonging to Harvard University) because he already had another writing credit to his name: in 1912 or 1913 he sold a script called "The Thief" to Solax, where it was filmed by director Alice Guy Blaché.[13] I went to see *Love in an Apartment Hotel* at MoMA, and *The Thief* at the Library of Congress. They have rather a lot in common with *Jack Kennard, Coward*. All three of the silent films that Marston is known to have written tell the story of a man who is falsely suspected of wrongdoing. In *Kennard*, the girlfriend of a dashing young Harvard student thinks he's a coward for quitting the football team, but, actually, he is very brave, and has made a brave sacrifice.[14] In *The Thief*, Colonel Spottiswood, a veteran of the Civil War—shades of Marston's maternal grandfather, Henry W. Moulton—is invited to a reunion dinner at Delmonico's, hosted by his very wealthy fellow veterans. But Spottiswood has fallen on hard times; he lives in a tenement with his wife, in rags, and a daughter, dying of hunger. He borrows a suit, goes to the dinner, and is wrongly suspected of stealing a piece of jewelry; in fact, he's taken only an apple or two, to try to save the life of his dying daughter. Most interesting of all is *Love in an Apartment Hotel*: the beautiful fiancée of a well-heeled gentlemen makes a surprise visit to his hotel room only to discover that a chambermaid is hiding in his closet. She assumes he has been unfaithful—foreshadowing of Elizabeth Holloway and Olive Byrne—but, actually, a burglar, not the gentleman, has hidden the chambermaid in the closet.

The climactic scene from *Love in an Apartment Hotel* (1913), in which the hero's fiancée confronts him after a maid emerges from his closet

Each of these is a story about a man who appears to have a dark secret, a Jekyll hiding his Hyde. But in each story, there really isn't any Hyde: Jekyll is only Jekyll, misunderstood, and falsely accused. What happened to Marston when he was at Harvard that he got so obsessed with telling this same story, over and over again?

Marston, having gained a great deal of weight, in the summer of 1916

By the summer of 1916, Marston was wildly overweight: huge, much earlier than I'd thought. It's hard to believe this wasn't related to some medication. Meanwhile, I'd speculated that Marston might have been with Münsterberg on the day that Münsterberg died, in November of 1916. I was wrong. Holloway had very carefully preserved a letter Münsterberg sent Marston on September 9, 1916, just before the semester began. It's a friendly note, professor to student, complimenting Marston on his work, and urging him on: "As to your new paper I do not understand

Marston with Marjorie Wilkes Huntley in Marblehead, Massachusetts, in 1927

exactly what you intend to bring out in it, but if you feel that you have the material for a printable paper, prepare it by all means."[15] On the envelope, Holloway has made an annotation: "Münsterberg was prof of psych at Harv when Bill was there. WWI caused him such stress (he was German) that he dropped dead during a lecture at Radcliffe. Harold Burt was there at the time, also one of Bill's pupils."[16] But not, as I had thought, Marston himself.

Marjorie Wilkes Huntley remains as mysterious as ever, though I found an earlier photograph of her, with Marston in 1927. The year that photograph was taken, Marston wrote an anonymous letter to the editor of the New York *World*, complaining about the newspapers campaign against pornographic magazines. At the time, Marston, Holloway, Byrne, and Huntley were living together in New York, while Holloway worked at Metropolitan Life Insurance, Byrne worked toward a Ph.D. at Columbia, and Marston worked at the university as a lecturer. They'd moved there after their time together in Boston, attending regular meetings of a cult of female sexual power at Marston's aunt Carolyn's apartment. When the *World* began campaigning against pornographic magazines, Marston, Holloway, Byrne, and Huntley together wrote a letter announcing that the family had cancelled its subscription to the *World*, in protest:

> Your campaign against what you call "obscene" magazines carrying pictures of female nudes is costing you this day one subscription to your paper. This family, including several women, can't stand your policy-inspired prudery. . . . Every member of this family, save one [Huntley], is a college-trained person, and two members [Marston and Holloway] have taught the biological sciences in large American universities. All believe that there is no worse crime possible to commit against civilization than suppressing and making abnormal the natural normal sex instincts.

It seems quite clear to those who have studied and done extensive research on the subject that the destruction expressions of sex are due to suggestions just like the ones you are now advocating. Why cannot some great and powerful paper like yours act like a mentally grown-up person, and run a campaign to educate children, big and little, to feel reverence and respect for the nude female body? Instead, you join the opportunists and call woman's body "obscene" when photographed and displayed! The magazines you are attacking contain not a single suggestive caption or story, simply photographic nudes. This family believes they furnish splendid material with which to teach children that the most lovely and sacred thing in the world is a real woman's body.

The *World* printed the letter under the headline, "Defender of Sex Magazines Stops Reading The World," Holloway clipped it, and pasted it into a scrapbook. In the margin, she wrote drily, "This is one we failed to hide under the rug."[17]

Photographs and clippings from Marston's time in Hollywood from 1928 to 1931 suggest that among his duties, as Director of Public Relations for Universal Studios, was providing psychological treatment to actresses. Marston also kept careful records of the experiments he conducted in Hollywood: they survive in files crammed with lie detector graphs, the readings of blondes, brunettes, and redheads watching films. Apparently, he'd hoped to publish his work in Hollywood, in a book whose illustrations would have included still shots taken on the sets of four different films, to illustrate what he believed to be the four elemental emotions: compliance, submission, dominance, and inducement.[18]

Marston analyzing the actress Ruth Elder in Hollywood in 1929

A problem, for historians interested

in marriages, is that people don't often write letters to people they live with. Between 1931 and 1934, when Marston, Olive Byrne, and the children lived in Cliftondale with Marston's mother, there are no letters from her to him, though there are many photographs of the family, inside and outside the house on Avon Street.[19] Instead, the correspondence begins in the spring of 1935, when the Marstons moved to Cherry Orchard, right around the time Marston was courting the press with his attempts to give Bruno Hauptmann a lie detector test.[20] And there are so many pictures from those years: Marston playing football in the front yard with the boys; the kids in Halloween costumes, on a swing set, shoveling snow.

His mother was as close to Olive Byrne as she was to Elizabeth Holloway. She called Holloway her "Dearest Little Daughter" and Olive Byrne "my dear Bobby," a nickname she'd gotten in college.[21] (Marston, Annie Dalton Marston said, was "the best and the biggest of men" and Holloway "the smartest of women."[22]) And she was close to Marjorie Wilkes Huntley, too.[23] Marston's mother seems to have known all about the family arrangements, and about the lies that hid them: she read Olive Byrne's *Family Circle* articles. And after all, the family had lived with her in Cliftondale, and she spent weeks at a time visiting the house in Cherry Orchard, sleeping in O.A.'s bedroom. All the women in the house, and the children, too, regularly wrote to

The family in 1933, with Marston's mother holding Olive Ann, Marston holding Byrne, Olive Byrne holding Donn, and Elizabeth Holloway standing next to Pete

Marston's mother, letters filled with details—"Bobby wrote that Betty had a cough," for instance—and she knew, too, how Marston, Holloway, and Byrne liked to lie about who wrote and who did what. "I was immensely amused at your making a cake which took the prize under Bobby's name," Marston's mother wrote to him in 1939. "Congratulations."[24] She followed their doings, almost daily, writing to Marston in 1940, when Byrne, Donn, and O.A. were nine, eight, and seven. "Byrne's letter was delightful. Thanks to the dear boy, and to Donn for the nicely printed one sent by you. And Olive Anne for her special letter. Also Bobby's—always so welcome. Today came a good letter from Marjorie also Bobby's magazine article."[25] And when she visited Cherry Orchard, they doted on her: "I think of the long restful hours spent in the pleasant room at Rye," she wrote to Holloway after one visit. "William looking in every now and then, Bobby bringing the breakfast tray, Marjorie the newspaper, your evening calls, the children with their lively antics."[26] She was a devout Christian but she was made, in 1939, an "honorary member" of the Sunday Five Club: debating, with her son and her four grandchildren, the order of the universe.[27]

"Mrs. Margaret Sanger's love for her work has brought success to the birth control movement," a *Look* magazine ad for Marston's 1937 book, *Try Living*, read. "Her love for her family brings success at home. She advocates: 'Try living.'"[28] Marston, meanwhile, lived lavishly. He drank and he flirted. A friend wrote an "Ode to William Moulton Marston." It begins,

> *In the city of Rye lives a wonderful guy,*
> *Bill Marston, the savant and wit:*
> *The women all vie for a glance from his eye,*
> *Whether he's sober or lit.*[29]

He also kept tinkering with his theories about sex and emotions. Sometime after 1931, Marston wrote a book that was never published. I began to read the typewritten manuscript in his granddaughter's kitchen.[30] The title page is missing but the book is a condensation of Marston's ideas about personality, with much emphasis on the relationship between personality and hair and eye color: "Chapter VII:

The All Blond Type"; "Chapter IX: The Brown-Eyed Brunet Personality"; "Chapter XI: Those Inducive Red-Heads." ("My own hair, in early childhood, was tow color," he wrote, adding, "there are samples in existence."[31]) Marston's theories concern heredity, and they are largely derived from eugenics (he frequently cites, for instance, the eugenicist Charles Davenport), though there is a great deal, in the manuscript, about physiology, too. Most interesting is his discussion of sex in Chapter VI, "Men and Supermen," in which Marston explains what, if it had been written a few decades later, would have been called a theory of the relationship between sex and gender. "Contrary to popular belief," he begins, "every normal person is both male and female in some degree." What he calls "erotic emotions" are felt by all people, toward virtually all other people. The problem is that "people not trained to an analytical point of view fail to consider these more complex expressions of erotic feeling," and tend to regard them as abnormal. "Observing only the obvious physical contacts between males and females, they assume, accordingly, that erotic emotion exists as a result of the separation of humanity into two sexes." They therefore wrongly confuse and conflate gender and sexuality and, for instance, decide that "all love affairs between women are 'Lesbian' despite the fact that such affairs went on for thousands of years before the island of Lesbos was inhabited." Gender and sexuality, Marston insists, are not so exclusively attached: "There is every reason to believe that erotic relationships would continue unabated if everybody in the world belonged to the same sex." In short, "Erotic emotion is part of the warp and woof of human nature. It is in no sense a product of, or dependent upon sex."[32] The personality traits deemed "masculine" or "feminine," Marston argues, are neither physiological nor psychological but purely cultural. In fact, "The traits of courage and self-reliance which are stressed in moral admonitions to 'be a man' are common to both sexes. Victorian timidity was largely a pose which women practiced to produce certain desired effects on men. Actually, women are far more 'manly' than men in certain situations that appeal to them, and always have been."[33] There are, he believes, very few differences between men and women: "the natural personality differences of the sexes are small and their abnormally superimposed differences great."[34] Sorting out men and women into personalities and calling them natural is an artifice, he argues, and it leads, grotesquely, "to the creation of a sex difference which is nothing less than a matched pair of psychological deformities."[35]

He turns, next, to the prospects for change. As a matter of history, these deformities stand a chance of being eliminated, Marston suggests, because since the First World War, "the social taboos against love and erotic relationships have substantially decreased in strength and strictness," and there has been a rise in "tolerance of free love relationships."[36] One day soon, he predicts, the natural similarities of men and women may be freely expressed, and the contrivances of artificial traits overthrown. "This prophetic glimpse into the psychological future of the sexes may seem fantastic," Marston wrote. "But so did the submarine envisaged by Jules Verne, legalized birth control sponsored and foretold by Annie Besant in the midst of the Victorian era, . . . and equal political right for women." Imagine, he thought, a world in which "it becomes the usual thing instead of the exception to have women senators, women legislators, women governors, and a woman president."[37]

Miss Elusive, by George Petty, for *True* magazine, 1945

By the late thirties, Marston had taken on another writing assignment: providing the copy for the centerfolds in a new monthly magazine called *True: A Man's Magazine*; it began publishing in 1937. The centerfolds, pinups, were painted by an artist named George Petty, who, like Marston, had first worked for *Esquire*, whose centerfolds included not only Varga girls, but also Petty girls.[38]

The Petty girls in *True* were more or less the same as the Petty girls in *Esquire*: big-breasted, tiny-waisted, blond, and talking on the phone. Marston gave them each a name, and wrote accompanying text, each with the subheading, "An Analysis by Dr. Wil-

Miss Bewitching, by George Petty, for *True* magazine, 1945

liam Moulton Marston, Noted Author and Lecturer on Female Psychology." Miss Elusive wears a pink negligée whose purple strap has slid down her arm. "Miss Elusive is afraid of love," Marston writes, in his diagnosis. "A secret fear of men and moments amorous was implanted in her submissive subconscious during childhood or early adolescence, perhaps by inhibiting instruction, or maybe by shocking experience."[39] Miss Heartsnatcher (for a Valentine's issue) wears nothing but a see-through babydoll, and clutches a box of chocolates to her chest. Marston: "You're a fascinating, clever, yet frankly ruthless man-huntress, my heart-enslaving young friend."[40] "Miss Bewitching," in a black witch's hat, for Halloween. "You keep a private prison—the more bewitched prisoners, the merrier amusement for their bewitching captoress."[41] "Miss Career Girl" wears a red bathing suit: "You'll go on working after you're married? Then you are a career girl! You've got what it takes—energy, initiative, persistence, poise, and most essential of all, self-reliance."[42] In nothing but a cellophane raincoat, but carrying an Easter bonnet, "Miss Girl of Tomorrow" is, for Marston, the future of the race. "If, my fellow trouser-wearers, you should marry Miss Girl of Tomorrow, don't take your pants too symbolically. . . . Accept your Girl of Tomorrow's frivolity, her inconsequence, and her refusal to freeze ebullient femininity

Miss Girl of Tomorrow, by George Petty, for *True* magazine, 1945

into Victorian repression, with a grin, and a hug."[43] Each of the Petty girls has a name, and a costume. There was Miss She-Wolf, Miss Paddy-Whack (who liked to be spanked), Miss Bashful, Miss Clinging Vine, and Miss Chummy Bunny, a clear predecessor of Hugh Hefner's Playboy Bunny. (Hefner's middle name, incidentally, was Marston.) Miss Pixie, Miss Wrong Number. Marston described at least sixteen—during the very same years that he was writing Wonder Woman. They're like a league of soft-porn superheroes.

Miss Chummy Bunny, by George Petty, for *True* magazine, 1945

In the context of his work for *True*, Marston's defense of comic books looks somewhat different. In the fall of 1939, he wrote an article for *Your Life* called "What Comics Do to Your Children." His defense of comics was not unlike his defense of pornography, in that anonymous letter to the editor of the New York *World* in 1927: on behalf of his family. "I like comics," Marston wrote. "I like them the same way and for the same

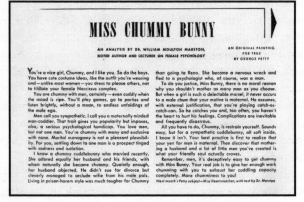

Marston's analysis of Miss Chummy Bunny, for *True* magazine, 1945

reasons my youngsters like them and I know that they produce in me the same general effects they cause in children." They allowed him to fulfill his wishes.[44] Marston loved nothing so much as fantasy.

From the time he was a very little boy, a golden-haired toddler, Marston had presented his work to his mother for her approval. She was a Victorian schoolmarm who was raised in a castle and longtime spinster who married down—a salesman—and who had lost baby after baby (miscarriages and stillbirths) until she had given birth, at last, and so late, to this one beautiful son. She offered him her approval with a prim and pinched precision. She loved all three of the women he lived with, and she loved all four of the children. She admired his books; she read his articles. He and Olive Byrne sent her Olive Byrne's *Family Circle* articles, too ("Bobby has a pleasing style and makes an interesting story," with a nod of approval).[45] Marston's mother was not unaware of the tangle of lies that constituted her son's family ties. Her own news was of bridge parties and sewing guilds and Bible study groups and literature classes and women's clubs. She was a woman of tremendous energy. ("I fear the time will never come when I for one, and you, for another, can take life seriously and placidly," she wrote him.[46]) Marston never sent his mother Miss Paddy-Whack or Miss She-Wolf. But, in 1942, when he was forty-nine, and she was eighty-three, he did write to tell her about Wonder Woman.

"How amazing that Wonder Woman should make such a record," she wrote back. "You are certainly to be congratulated upon your success in the invention of such a popular heroine. To surpass Superman is an achievement." Gold star, check plus, A. Still, she didn't *quite* approve. "Although my knowledge of comics is decidedly limited, I do know that Superman has taken the highest place in that variety of literature (?)." She underlined "literature" and added a question mark. She was not keen: "Sometime I should like to see those stories so famous, but I doubt if I should have a chance to read them."[47]

He sent her *Wonder Woman #1*, and she read it. She didn't approve of the costume, she wrote him, but she did think the associate editor was a catch: "A great card to have Miss Marble on the editorial staff."[48] By now, he'd begun to grow ill. "Of course you are doing too much," she chided him. "A psychologist knows the need of regular hours of rest. <u>Do</u> be careful, and drop some of these extras." By which she meant: the comic books. He sent her the clipping about Wonder Woman in the Phi Beta Kappa *Key Recorder*. "If Wonder Woman is the cause of breaking down your health, I shall begrudge her getting that Phi Beta Kappa key."[49] And again, in 1943 when he was, more and more, on the radio: "Rather hope you will not take on a weekly broadcast and regret your having taken on the management of production of W.W.: too much."[50] He told her, selectively, about Wonder Woman's successes. Nothing of the scandal over the bondage, or of the banning by the National League for Decent Literature, but much of his writing an article about comics for the learned *American Scholar*. "Should like very much to read it," she wrote back. "Of course you could not refuse to prepare it for Phi Beta Kappa magazine when requested to do so."[51]

He sent her flowers, he sent her letters, he sent her gifts.[52] He remembered to call her, despite the long-distance charges. She visited Cherry Orchard, for the last time, in the spring of 1944.[53] "How lovely Cherry Orchard must look, with the cherries all abloom," she wrote when she got home. "Had many thoughts of the Sunday school," she added, about the Sunday Five Club. "Will try and send a message for next session."[54] In her last letter to her son, in May 1944, she told him not to visit. "Nothing you can do," she wrote. "I have a nice comfortable bed, and sleep a good deal. No need for anyone to worry . . . Much love to all. With deep affection, Mother."[55] She died shortly afterward, at the age of eighty-five.[56] She'd been born one year before the Civil War began, and died one year before the Second World War ended. Weeks after his mother's death, Marston contracted polio, and began his own, horrible decline.[57] She had been a doting mother, he a dutiful son. And also Mr. Hyde?

"We always expected, when Gram died, that she'd have left a letter," Donn Marston's daughters, Nan and Peg, told me. "You know, a letter in an enveloped labeled 'To Be Opened After My Death.'" Olive Byrne never left that letter or, if she did, either no one ever found it, or else someone found it, and destroyed it. But the reason her granddaughters thought she might leave one is that, apparently, their father asked her to. Donn Marston married Margaret Sanger's granddaughter, Margaret Sanger, in 1961. Peg was born in 1962. At about that time, Peg and Nan told me, their father, who was a lawyer, threatened to bring his mother to court, to force her to tell him the truth. He intended to sue her. I hadn't known that. But that helped explain why, in 1963, Holloway finally told the truth—or at least, what I had taken for the truth.

"Did you ever read the letter your mother wrote to your uncle Byrne and your aunt Audrey?" I asked Nan and Peg. They had not. They'd never heard of it. I opened up my computer, and they read it, together, aloud, smiling at their mother's handwriting, and turns of phrase.

FEB. 27, 1963

Dear Byrne and Audrey,

We have good news on the Father discussion. While Dots and Betty were here I got Betty to tell me the entire story. She said she would if Donn & Byrne would lay off Dots & not ask her any more questions about their father. She said that Dots would never never tell the truth and said if they tried to make her that she would take the morphine she has tucked away and that would be the end of that. Donn said he wouldn't say anything to Dots [added by Donn: "also she wanted Byrne not to say anything"] if she didn't bring the subject up. If she did, he wouldn't promise Betty anything. And he asked Betty if she would try to talk Dots into writing down the truth to be opened at her death. Betty said she would try. Anyway, the story is this.

Both Donn & Byrne are the sons of Bill Marston. Olive met him while she was in college and came to live with them at the age of 21. YaYa had already been living with W.M.M. for two or three years. Betty knew what was going on. In fact Bill came to her and told her this was the way he wanted to live. He needed more than one woman to live. No affair took place with YaYa. It was "mental" love, to quote E.H.M. Betty gave her consent

and so—O.B. became W.M.M.'s mistress. Five years later Byrne
was born, after they tried for a long time. It was difficult for
her to conceive, and 18 mo's. later Donn was born. Keets said
they were both very much wanted by both O.B. & W.M.M. and
there was never any regret.

The name William Richard is Bill's name. William being
his first name & Richard was a nickname that they called
Bill—coming from some Greek name which was difficult to
pronounce and was shortened to Richard. The name Kendall is
new to Betty. The first time she heard about it was at Audrey
and Byrne's wedding. The photograph of the 'Bill Richard'
was an old one of YaYa's which Dots picked up. Bill & Betty
always wanted to tell both you boys—but O.B. said no—and
Keets says it's very very wrong & this is the reason she told the
story. But she warned that she would protect O.B. to the end &
doesn't want any harm to come to her.

Betty always wants to go to visit you when O.B. goes but
Dots says no because she would take over and be another
grandmother & she would be pushed into the background.
Betty said she would have loved to see Byrne graduate from
Medical School but let O.B. go alone. And as a result cried &
cried—what a woman!!! She loves you both so very very much
and feels that she sacrificed her own children to make D. & B.
feel loved and wanted.

But she said that W.M.M. really loved Dots & she loved him.
And Betty loved him too, and explains that W.M.M. was 100
years ahead of himself to rationalize the whole thing in her mind.
And said that some day everyone will be living like this. The
human energy needs to be released to create instead of destroy.

The affair went on until his death, with love making for
all. Pete walked in on O.B. & Bill once—and was ushered out
quickly, with the explanation that his Dad was sick & Dots was
taking care of him.

I don't think I've left out anything. At last the truth is out!!
Dots of course denies the entire thing. I didn't ask her anything
but she tried to explain her made up story & said that some people
thought W.M.M. was B. & D.'s father—it wasn't true. She wouldn't

do that to her children. She had such a miserable childhood & she wouldn't do anything to hurt her boys. So that's that.

> Either hide this well or destroy it. . . .
>
> Love, Margaret[58]

Either hide this well or destroy it. It was the family motto.

Wonder Woman returns as "The Liberated Lady," by Edward Sorel, in *New York* magazine, 1969 [with permission of Edward Sorel]

The Marston family story stayed hidden throughout the 1960s and 1970s. Wonder Woman, meanwhile, was resurrected as a feminist icon. In 1967, she appeared in the pages of *New York*—Gloria Steinem was on the magazine's staff—in a drawing by Edward Sorel called "The Liberated Lady": she's fighting rapists. By 1974, on behalf of the National Women's Political Caucus, she had infiltrated Nixon's cabinet.

Holloway kept on working her way through the family history, sorting papers, and photographs and, finally, furniture. In 1975, after she'd divided up the family letters and photo albums and scrapbooks and given a different set to each of the four children, she made, too, an inventory of the "Family Mementos." One section is titled "Furniture History." To each object, she attached a story. A little rocking chair: "Used to be in the kitchen at 36 Avon. F.W.M. was sitting in it while A.D.M. washed dishes when he keeled over with a fatal cerebral hemorrhage." (Marston's father died on January 17, 1923.) The

In a flyer printed by the National Women's Political Caucus, Wonder Woman joins Richard Nixon's cabinet, 1974

house in which the Marstons had lived was a curiosity shop of family heirlooms. Holloway's inventory, room by room, includes a kitchen table of Huntley's, "given to her by a friend"; a cookie pail that Marston's mother had "used to hold raspberry jam"; a dining room table of Ethel Byrne's; a chest of drawers that "used to be in W.M.M.'s room at 36 Avon Street"; a nest of tables "given by E.H.M. to Carolyn Keatley one Christmas"; and Marston's mother's desk ("Desk has a secret panel"). Then there was the art: a painting of the railroad bridge, over the Pamet River in Truro, painted by Olive Byrne; a sampler "stitched by some one in M.W.H's family"; a seascape "given to us by Harry Peter."[59]

At family dinners, Nan and Peg told me, Holloway would tell long stories about her life with Marston. And then, after dinner, clearing up in the kitchen, Olive Byrne would whisper to her granddaughters, "Those stories were about *me*."[60]

In 1975, Holloway inventoried, too, the contents of the family's

China cabinet: "Doll's Tea Set belonged to A.D.M. as a child"; a set of Sandwich glass plates, found on the beach by O.B.R.; a "Hob Nail Mug"—"history lost in the mists of time." And a gift: "For-get-me-not Mug, Given to E.H.M. by O.B.R.," who did not, in the end, wish to be so entirely forgotten.[61]

NOTES

ABBREVIATIONS USED IN THE NOTES

ADM	Annie Dalton (Moulton) Marston
BHRM	Byrne Holloway Richard Marston
EHM	(Sadie) Elizabeth Holloway Marston
JE	Joanne Edgar
JHMK	Joye Hummel Murchison Kelly
JHW	John Henry Wigmore
LB	Lauretta Bender
MCG	Maxwell Charles Gaines
MM	Moulton ("Pete") Marston
MS	Margaret Sanger
MSML	Margaret Sanger Marston Lampe
MWH	Marjorie Wilkes Huntley
OBR	Olive Byrne "Richard"
WMM	William Moulton Marston
WW	Wonder Woman

A Note Regarding Abbreviating Women's Names

In the notes I have used abbreviations for married women's latest married names rather than for any earlier names, regardless of how I refer to them in the text. For example, in the text, I call Joye Hummel Murchison Kelly by her maiden name, "Joye Hummel," before 1947, when she married Dave Murchison. After her first husband's death, she married Jack Kelly. In the notes I abbreviate her name as "JHMK" throughout. Similarly, in the text I refer to Donn Marston's wife, during their marriage, as "Margaret Sanger Marston," but because after his death she married a man named Lampe, I consistently use the abbreviation "MSML" in the notes. Olive Byrne never married, but she did use the name "Olive Richard" professionally, and she used the initials "OBR" in her own papers. Sadie Elizabeth Holloway Marston dropped the name "Sadie" after her marriage, and she used the initials "EHM" in her own papers. Their children most often refer to these two women either by these preferred initials, OBR and EHM, or by Marston's pet names for them, Dotsie (or Dots) and Keetsie (or Keets). I therefore use the initials in the notes, and in the text I refer to OBR as "Olive" and to EHM as "Holloway"—an imperfect solution, but this seemed the best way to avoid confusion with other Marstons and Byrnes.

A Note Regarding DC Comics as an Abbreviation

The invention of "DC Comics" as a brand is inseparable from the creation of Wonder Woman. DC Comics, Inc., traces its origins to the founding, in 1934, of National Allied Publications. National was soon absorbed by Detective Comics, Inc., founded in 1937; the company had close ties to All-American Publications, founded in 1938, by Maxwell Charles Gaines and Jack Liebowitz. Superman debuted in *Action Comics* in 1938; Batman debuted in *Detective Comics* in 1939. In 1940, attempting to fend off critics who charged that his best-selling comics were bad for children, Gaines hired William Moulton Marston as a consulting psychologist and also appointed him to a newly formed editorial advisory board. " 'Doc' Marston has long been an advocate of the right type of comic magazines and is now a member of the Editorial Advisory Board of all 'D.C. Superman' Comics," Gaines wrote in a memo. Also in 1940, DC decided to stamp comic books in which Superman and Batman appeared with a logo reading, "A DC Publication" and, later, "A Superman-DC Publication." ("DC" was short for "Detective Comics.") The logo was meant to serve as a stamp of quality. Meanwhile, Marston convinced Gaines that another way to fend off critics would be to create a female superhero. Gaines reluctantly agreed to give it a try. Marston submitted his first Wonder Woman script in February 1941. In October 1941, the publishers announced to readers, "The 'DC' at the top of our magazine covers is your guide to better magazines." Wonder Woman made her debut that same month, in an issue of *All-Star Comics* with a cover date of December 1941–January 1942. Hiring Marston, introducing the logo as a stamp of approval, forming an editorial advisory board, and creating Wonder Woman were part of a single, simultaneous effort: to defend the comics against critics. In 1944, Detective Comics and All-American Publications, along with other concerns, merged to become National Periodical Publications. In 1977, National Periodical Publications officially changed its name to DC Comics, Inc., the name it had been known by, informally, for decades. For the reader's sake, I have elected to refer to the publisher of Superman, Batman, and Wonder Woman comics as "DC Comics" from the start, which is also how, beginning in 1940, the publisher of these comic books was popularly known.

All citations to Wonder Woman comic strips and comic books are to stories written by WMM, unless otherwise indicated.

1. IS HARVARD AFRAID OF MRS. PANKHURST?

1. Henry W. Moulton, *Moulton Annals,* ed. Claribel Moulton (Chicago: Edward A. Claypool, 1906), 13–14, 310, 324–27, 405–6; Sir Walter Scott, *Tales of the Crusaders,*

ed. J. B. Ellis (1825; repr., Edinburgh: Edinburgh University Press, 2009), vol. 3, *The Talisman,* chapter 6, pp. 56–58. Annie Moulton taught primary school in Amesbury in 1876; a certificate of appointment is in the possession of MM. WMM's grandfather, Henry William Moulton, died in 1896. Moulton Castle was demolished by the property's new owners in around 1900. WMM's father, Frederick W. Marston, was the eldest son of Frederick A. Marston and Theresa Maria Cotton. He was born in Stratham, New Hampshire, on December 10, 1860. He died on January 23, 1923. "Summary of Marston Genealogy," unpublished papers of BHRM.

2. Marston's first prize was a book he won at the age of seven: Jacob Abbott, *Rollo in Switzerland* (New York: Mershon, 1898), inscribed "William Moulton Marston, June 30, 1899, Prize book," in the possession of MM. WMM's library is filled with books given to him by his aunts, including Jacob Abbott, *Rollo's Tour in Europe* (New York: Burst, n.d.), inscribed "William Moulton Marston. From Aunt Claribel, May 9, 1896," in the possession of MM.

3. BHRM, "Memories of an Unusual Father," unpublished typescript, 2002, in the possession of BHRM, 2.

4. WMM, *Try Living* (New York: Thomas Y. Crowell, 1937), 2–3.

5. EHM, "Tiddly Bits: The Tale of a Manx Cat," unpublished typescript, in the possession of MM.

6. WMM's high school career can be followed in the 1910 and 1911 volumes of the *Oracle,* published by the Malden High School Literary Society and housed in the Malden Public Library, Malden, Massachusetts. The meeting of the literary society in which a paper titled "Woman Suffrage" was read was held on September 23, 1910.

7. WMM, Undergraduate Record File, Harvard University Archives, USIII 15.88.10.

8. WMM, *Try Living,* 2–3.

9. Ibid., 2. WMM tells this same story, with embellishments, in OBR, "To Be or Not," *Family Circle,* January 21, 1938.

10. Harvard University, *Harvard University Catalogue, 1911–1912* (Cambridge: Published by the University, 1911), 328, 401. During his freshman year, Marston lived at 185 Hancock Street (p. 94).

11. Charles Homer Haskins, "History: One of a Series of Lectures Given to the Freshman Class in Harvard College," *Historical Outlook* 16 (1925): 195–97. For a similar contemporary effort, see Allen Johnson, *The Historian and Historical Evidence* (New York: Charles Scribner's Sons, 1926, 1930).

12. WMM, *Try Living,* 3.

13. The chemical itself is not mentioned, but the men who find the body smell kernels—that is, nuts or almonds: "Right in the midst there lay the body of a man sorely contorted and still twitching. They drew near on tiptoe, turned it on its back and beheld the face of Edward Hyde. He was dressed in clothes far too large for him, clothes of the doctor's bigness; the cords of his face still moved with a semblance of life, but life was quite gone; and by the crushed phial in the hand and the strong smell of kernels that hung upon the air, Utterson knew that he was looking on the body of a self-destroyer." Robert Louis Stevenson, *Strange Case of Dr. Jekyll and Mr. Hyde* (London: Longmans, Green, 1886), 84.

14. A detailed physical description of Palmer, later in life, is in W. A. Macdonald, "George Herbert Palmer at 90," *Boston Evening Transcript,* March 19, 1932. And see George Herbert Palmer, *The Life of Alice Freeman Palmer* (Boston: Houghton Mifflin, 1908), and Ruth Bordin, *Alice Freeman Palmer: The Evolution of a New Woman*

(Ann Arbor: University of Michigan Press, 1993). Bordin dismisses Alice Freeman Palmer's commitment to suffrage as slight (p. 6), but the National Woman Suffrage Association counted on her support and printed, as a pamphlet, an essay of hers called "The Progress of Equal Suffrage." NWSA, *Handbook of the National Woman Suffrage Association* (Washington, DC: Stormont and Jackson, 1893), 60, 84.

15. George Herbert Palmer, preface to *The Odyssey of Homer* (1884; rev. ed., Boston: Houghton Mifflin Company, 1921), v. This preface was written for the 1891 edition. Palmer hired James, but James considered Palmer a prig, and Jane Addams found Alice Freeman Palmer's style of reform patrician. See Louis Menand, *The Metaphysical Club: A Story of Ideas in America* (New York: Farrar, Straus and Giroux, 2001), 358, 312–15.

16. "What constitutes the teacher is the passion to make scholars," Palmer thought, "and again and again it happens that the great scholar has no such passion whatever." George Herbert Palmer, *The Ideal Teacher* (Boston: Houghton Mifflin, 1910), 9. George Herbert Palmer, *The Autobiography of a Philosopher* (Boston: Houghton Mifflin, 1930), 131–36; the quotation is from p. 133. And on Dewey and this principle, see Steven Fesmire, *John Dewey and Moral Imagination: Pragmatism in Ethics* (Bloomington: Indiana University Press, 2003). For more on Palmer, see recollections of his younger colleagues in *George Herbert Palmer, 1842–1933: Memorial Addresses* (Cambridge: Harvard University Press, 1935). WMM, *Try Living,* 3.

17. A complete set of notes for Palmer's Philosophy A in the fall of 1911 was taken by a fellow student of WMM's, a junior named Arthur McGiffert. Arthur McGiffert, AB 1913, student notes, 1911–1913, Harvard University Archives, HUC 8911.400. Passages quoted above come from the following lecture dates (page references are to the pages in McGiffert's notebook): October 10, 1911, p. 7; October 14, 1911, p. 10; November 9, 1911, p. 33; December 19, 1911, pp. 67, 71.

18. "The Declaration of Sentiments," 1848, in Elizabeth Cady Stanton, *A History of Woman Suffrage* (Rochester, NY: Fowler and Wells, 1889), 1:70–71.

19. Paula Bartley, *Emmeline Pankhurst* (London: Routledge, 2002), 98.

20. G. K. Chesterton, "The Modern Martyr," *Illustrated London News,* February 8, 1908.

21. John Reed, "The Harvard Renaissance," unpublished manuscript, John Reed Papers, Houghton Library, Harvard University, MS Am 1091: 1139, pp. 57, 62–65; "Woman Suffrage Movement," *Harvard Crimson,* November 2, 1911; "Harvard Men's League for Woman Suffrage," *Harvard Crimson,* December 2, 1911; Harvard Men's League for Woman Suffrage, records, Harvard University Archives, HUD 3514.5000. No membership list survives. And see Christine Stansell, *American Moderns: Bohemian New York and the Creation of a New Century* (New York: Metropolitan, 2000), 229. On the prominence of the suffrage debate on college campuses during these years, see Barbara Miller Solomon, *In the Company of Educated Women: A History of Women and Higher Education in America* (New Haven, CT: Yale University Press, 1985), 111–12.

22. "Mrs. Kelley on 'Suffrage,'" *Harvard Crimson,* November 1, 1911. On Kelley, see Kathryn Kish Sklar, *Florence Kelley and the Nation's Work: The Rise of Women's Political Culture, 1830–1900* (New Haven, CT: Yale University Press, 1995).

23. "Woman Suffrage Movement," *Harvard Crimson,* November 2, 1911.

24. Reed, "Harvard Renaissance," 66.

25. "Is Harvard Afraid of Mrs. Pankhurst?" *Detroit Free Press,* December 1, 1911; "Harvard and the Suffragettes," *Atlanta Constitution,* December 11, 1911; and Editorial,

"Disorder at Harvard," *New York Times,* December 5, 1911. See also "Harvard Boys Will Hear Mrs. Pankhurst," *San Francisco Chronicle,* December 1, 1911; "Harvard Is Split over Mrs. Pankhurst," *Atlanta Constitution,* December 1, 1911; and "Harvard Bars Suffragette," *New York Times,* November 29, 1911. "Must our University assume towards this newer phase of the battle for political freedom the same blind, reactionary attitude to which it held—to its disgrace—throughout the struggle for the abolition of human slavery in America?" asked Harvard alum Oswald Garrison Villard in a letter sent to the Harvard Corporation. Villard was the son of Fanny Garrison Villard, a founder of the Woman's Peace Party, and the grandson of the abolitionist William Lloyd Garrison. He was also the editor of the *New York Evening Post.* "A Graduate's View of the Discussion over Mrs. Pankhurst," *Harvard Crimson,* December 4, 1911, and "Villard Criticises Harvard," *New York Times,* December 4, 1911.

26. "Harvard Split on Suffrage," *New York Times,* November 30, 1911. See also "Harvard and Mrs. Pankhurst," *Boston Daily Globe,* December 5, 1911.

27. "A Graduate's View," *Harvard Crimson,* December 4, 1911; "Villard Criticises Harvard," *New York Times,* December 4, 1911; "Mrs. Pankhurst's Lecture," *Harvard Crimson,* December 6, 1911; "Students Fight to Hear Mrs. Pankhurst," *New York Tribune,* December 7, 1911; and "Jeers for Mrs. Pankhurst," *New York Times,* December 7, 1911.

28. "Crowd to Hear Her," *Boston Daily Globe,* December 7, 1911. And see "Growth of Woman Suffrage," *Harvard Crimson,* December 7, 1911.

29. WMM, *Try Living,* 3.

30. Arthur McGiffert, AB 1913, student notes, 1911–1913, Philosophy A, undated, mid-year examination, p. 98.

31. WMM, *Try Living,* 3. Writing in 1937, Marston was remarkably accurate in recollecting his grades at Harvard in 1911. He did indeed earn an A in the fall of 1911, in Philosophy A: The History of Ancient Philosophy, taught by George Palmer. He was one of a tiny handful of students to excel in this difficult course. The course average appears to have been a C–. Final Return of Grades in 1911–1912, Philosophy A (Professor George Herbert Palmer), Faculty of Arts and Sciences, Final Return Records, 1848–1997, Harvard University Archives, UAIII 15.28, box 85. According to the final returns, he got a B+ in History 1 (a B on the transcript).

32. "Introducing Wonder Woman," *All-Star Comics,* December 1941–January 1942. "Dr. Poison," *Sensation Comics,* February 1942. The parenthetical is from *Wonder Woman,* newspaper strip, August 1944.

2. THE AMAZONIAN DECLARATION OF INDEPENDENCE

1. EHM to the Mount Holyoke College Alumni Office, February 26, 1987, Mount Holyoke College Archives. EHM, "Tiddly Bits."

2. "Introducing Wonder Woman," *All-Star Comics #8* (December 1941–January 1942). And "Wonder Woman Comes to America," *Sensation Comics #1* (January 1942).

3. "A Spy in the Office," *Sensation Comics #3* (March 1942).

4. A copy of John Ruskin, *Sesame and Lilies* (New York: A. L. Burt, n.d.), inscribed "Sadie E. Holloway from her Mother, May 8, 1909," is in the possession of MM. The

quotation is from the chapter "Of Queens' Gardens." Much evidence suggests that EHM was born on May 8, 1893, although EHM sometimes reported that she had been born in February of that year.

5. "Amazonian Declaration of Independence," July 4, 1851, in a folder called MHC Student Life, General, Political Activities Through 1930s, Mount Holyoke College Archives. The declaration subsequently appeared in the *Springfield Republican* and in the *Boston Evening Transcript,* July 11, 1851. Among its complaints: "They will not allow us to vote for any of our civil rulers, even though we should submit to the humiliation of promising to vote for *men,* which most certainly our self-respect and inalienble 'woman's rights' would not allow us to do, till we have had our turn in governing them, as long as they have tyrannized over us." And see also Arthur C. Cole, *A Hundred Years of Mount Holyoke College* (New Haven, CT: Yale University Press, 1940), 49–52.

6. Cynthia Eller, *Gentlemen and Amazons: The Myth of Matriarchal Prehistory, 1861–1900* (Berkeley: University of California Press, 2011).

7. Elizabeth Cady Stanton, "The Matriarchate, or Mother-Age" (1891), reprinted in *Elizabeth Cady Stanton, Feminist as Thinker: A Reader in Documents and Essays,* ed. Ellen DuBois and Richard Candida Smith (New York: New York University Press, 2007), 268.

8. Nancy F. Cott, *The Grounding of Modern Feminism* (New Haven, CT: Yale University Press, 1987), 40–41, and Sara M. Evans, *Born for Liberty: A History of Women in America* (New York: Free Press, 1989), 147. The fullest accounts of women's education in this period are Helen Lefkowitz Horowitz, *Alma Mater: Design and Experience in the Women's Colleges from Their Nineteenth-Century Beginnings to the 1930s* (1984; repr., Amherst: University of Massachusetts Press, 1993) and Solomon, *In the Company of Educated Women.*

9. Entry for EHM in *The Llamarada 1916* (South Hadley, MA: Mount Holyoke College, Published Yearly by the Junior Class, 1916), 51. About field hockey: "I was no shining light," she confessed. EHM, "Tiddly Bits."

10. Mary Woolley's 1906 speech before the NWSA is reprinted as "Miss Woolley on Woman's Ballot," *Political Equality Series,* 2 (1909). A copy of the tract is in the Mount Holyoke College Archives. See also Anne Carey Edmonds, *A Memory Book: Mount Holyoke College, 1837–1987* (South Hadley, MA: Mount Holyoke College, 1988), 97.

11. Kathryn M. Conway, "Woman Suffrage and the History of Rhetoric at the Seven Sisters Colleges, 1865–1919," in *Reclaiming Rhetorica: Women in the Rhetorical Tradition,* ed. Andrea A. Lunsford (Pittsburgh: University of Pittsburgh Press, 1995), 219.

12. The April 1913 lecture is mentioned in the Lebourveau Papers, Mount Holyoke College Archives. Jeannette Bickford Bridges Papers, 1914–1986, Mount Holyoke College Archives, box 1, folder 2. "Equal Suffrage League Notes," *Mount Holyoke* 23 (May 1914): 606–8. See the documents, including the league's constitution, in the Mount Holyoke College Records, National College Equal Suffrage League, 1912–1919, box 26, folder 3. The college's catalog for 1914–15 lists a total of 768 students. Support for suffrage grew during Holloway's time in South Hadley. Earlier, it had been more limited. In 1909, the Debating Society held a debate on the question of woman suffrage; when, at the end, the vote was taken for or against, it was a tie that had to be broken by the incoming president, who voted in the affirmative. Helen W. King

to her mother, April 18, 1909: "At debating Society last evening we had debate informal on Woman Suffrage, and then took vote as to those who favored it and who did
not and it came out a tie until the president voted which gave it to the affirmative."
Helen W. King Papers, Mount Holyoke College Archives, box 1, folder 2.

13. Jeannette Marks, *Life and Letters of Mary Emma Woolley* (Washington, DC: Public
Affairs Press, 1955), 79.

14. Inez Haynes Gillmore, "Confessions of an Alien," *Harper's Bazaar*, April 1912, 170.

15. Quoted in Cott, *Grounding of Modern Feminism*, 14, 48. As Cott explains, "By the
early twentieth century it was a commonplace that the New Woman stood for self-
development as contrasted to self-sacrifice or submergence in the family" (p. 39).
And see Evans, *Born for Liberty*, 161–62.

16. EHM to JE, November 16, 1983, in the possession of JE.

17. EHM to JE, January 11, 1972, in the possession of JE.

18. EHM, "Tiddly Bits."

19. "The College Girl and Politics," *New York Evening Post*, November 16, 1912.

20. Although her thirty-fifth Mount Holyoke reunion report says she majored in both
Greek and psychology, I cannot tell, from her transcript, whether Greek was a major
or a minor; she certainly took a lot of courses in Greek. Sadie Elizabeth Holloway,
Transcript, Office of the Registrar, Mount Holyoke College, as filed with EHM's
graduate student records at Radcliffe. "Mount Holyoke College required a course in
either chemistry or physics," she remembered. "I knew if I chose chemistry I'd blow
the place up so I chose physics—which my roommate said I passed in spite of the
laws of learning and because I liked the professor's dog." EHM, "Tiddly Bits."

21. Sappho, *Memoir, Text, Selected Readings and a Literal Translation by H. T. Wharton*
(London, 1885). Yopie Prins, *Victorian Sappho* (Princeton, NJ: Princeton University
Press, 1999); on Wharton, see 52–73. And see Terry Castle, "Always the Brides-
maid," *London Review of Books*, September 30, 1999. For a biographical study of a
romance that began on a college campus in this era, see Lois W. Banner, *Intertwined
Lives: Margaret Mead, Ruth Benedict, and Their Circle* (New York: Knopf, 2003).
Mead and Benedict met in an anthropology course at Barnard in 1922.

22. Lillian Faderman, *Odd Girls and Twilight Lovers: A History of Lesbian Life in
Twentieth-Century America* (New York: Columbia University Press, 1991), 13–18,
32–33, 52–54, and Anna Mary Wells, *Miss Marks and Miss Woolley* (Boston: Houghton Mifflin, 1978), 41, 56, 65–66, 134, 154. See also Marks, *Life and Letters of Mary
Emma Woolley*.

23. Wells, *Miss Marks and Miss Woolley*, 145.

24. *Mount Holyoke College: The Seventy-fifth Anniversary* (South Hadley, MA: Mount
Holyoke College, 1913), 176, 195–96. "Mount Holyoke College: The Festival Procession, October 8, 1912: A Record." Scrapbook, with photographs. The ceremonies
were held on October 8 and 9, 1912.

25. EHM, "Tiddly Bits."

26. Sappho, *If Not Winter: Fragments of Sappho*, trans. Anne Carson (New York: Knopf,
2002), Fragment 31.

27. EHM to Robert Kanigher, February 4, 1948, DC Comics Archives, New York.

28. EHM, "Tiddly Bits."

29. EHM to Gloria Steinem, book inscription, Steinem Papers, Smith College. Holloway
also sometimes signed letters "Aphrodite with you." E.g., EHM to Jerry and Jean
Bails, April 28, 1969, in the possession of Jean Bails.

3. DR. PSYCHO

1. WMM, "The Search for the Holy Ghost," c. 1914–15, in the possession of BHRM. BHRM, "Memories of an Unusual Father," 3, 11–12. Writing a parody of "The Raven," like joining the Harvard Men's League for Woman Suffrage, was another way in which Marston's experience of Harvard followed John Reed's. "The Chicken," Reed's parody of "The Raven," written while he was at Harvard, is in the John Reed Papers, Houghton Library, Harvard University, MS Am 1091: 1280.

2. William James, "The Hidden Self," *Scribner's Magazine*, March 1890, 361–73.

3. William James, *The Principles of Psychology*, 2 vols. (New York: Holt, 1890), 2:452.

4. Dr. Psycho makes his first appearance in "Battle for Womanhood," *Wonder Woman* #5, June–July 1943.

5. On James and Münsterberg, see Bruce Kuklick, *The Rise of American Philosophy, Cambridge, Massachusetts, 1860–1930* (New Haven, CT: Yale University Press, 1977), 186–89, and on Münsterberg, see 196–214. And see Matthew Hale Jr., *Human Science and Social Order: Hugo Münsterberg and the Origins of Applied Psychology* (Philadelphia: Temple University Press, 1980).

6. William James to Hugo Münsterberg, February 21, 1892, in Margaret Münsterberg, *Hugo Münsterberg: His Life and Work* (New York: D. Appleton, 1922), 33.

7. Jutta Spillmann and Lothar Spillmann, "The Rise and Fall of Hugo Münsterberg," *Journal of the History of the Behavioral Sciences* 29 (1993): 325–26.

8. Münsterberg insisted that the building be shared with philosophy (rather than, as others suggested, with biology or physics). Spillmann and Spillmann, "The Rise and Fall of Hugo Münsterberg," 327.

9. Hugo Münsterberg, "The Psychological Laboratory in Emerson Hall," *Harvard Psychological Studies* 2 (1906): 34–39.

10. Solomon, *In the Company of Educated Women*, 54–55.

11. Bordin, *Alice Freeman Palmer*, 160, 212–14. As Helen Horowitz has pointed out, "The creators of Radcliffe College were masters of indirection. They devised a means to offer women a Harvard education at no expense to the university and without introjecting the unwanted women into male college life" (*Alma Mater*, 97–98).

12. Gertrude Stein, "In a Psychological Laboratory," December 19, 1894, Gertrude Stein Papers, Beinecke Library, Yale, box 10, folder 238, and quoted in Coventry Edwards-Pitt, "Sonnets of the Psyche: Gertrude Stein, the Harvard Psychological Lab, and Literary Modernism," senior thesis, History of Science Department, Harvard University, 1998, p. 98.

13. Münsterberg quoted in Hale, *Human Science and Social Order*, 63.

14. Editorial, *San Francisco Chronicle*, September 13, 1913.

15. Hugo Münsterberg, *The Americans*, trans. Edward Bissel (1904; repr., Garden City, NY: Doubleday, Page, 1914), 586–87, 572–75; and see, generally, chapter 22: "Self-Assertion of Women."

16. "It is the aim of experimental psychology, as it is of every other science, to be exact," Langfeld told his students. Langfeld coauthored a textbook based on the course: Herbert Sidney Langfeld and Floyd Henry Allport, *An Elementary Laboratory Course in Psychology* (Boston: Houghton Mifflin, 1916), vii.

17. In the second semester of freshman year, Marston had taken Philosophy B with Royce and gotten a B− (according to the final returns but recorded on the transcript as a B). The course average, though, appears to have been a D. Final Return of Grades

in 1911–1912, Philosophy B (Professor Josiah Royce), Faculty of Arts and Sciences, Final Return Records, 1848–1997, Harvard University Archives, UAIII 15.28, box 85. But, actually, Royce could not have taught Philosophy B in the spring of 1912 because he had a stroke on February 1, 1912. (See Josiah Royce to Frederick James Eugene Woodbridge, March 15, 1912, in Josiah Royce, *The Letters of Josiah Royce*, edited and with an introduction by John Clendenning [Chicago: University of Chicago Press, 1970], 563.) Although he is listed as the instructor, someone else taught it. Marston did study with Royce during his junior year, though: in 1913–14, he took two semesters of Philosophy 9: Metaphysics with Royce and received A's both terms.

18. Kuklick, *Rise of American Philosophy*, 242.

19. What Royce said in class is actually known: in 1915–16, a student in Philosophy 9, Royce's year-long course in metaphysics, took stenographic notes, and they have recently been published. Josiah Royce, *Metaphysics: His Philosophy 9 Course of 1915–1916, as Stenographically Recorded by Ralph W. Brown and Complemented by Notes from Bryon F. Underwood*, ed. William Ernest Hocking (Buffalo: State University of New York, 1998), 59. Royce's lectures on the social theory of truth run from pp. 59 through 90.

20. On the courses offered by the Department of Philosophy and Psychology, see the university catalog. As for when Marston began his research, he noted in his doctoral dissertation: "This thesis reports researches by the writer upon the problem of psycho-physiological symptoms of deception, which we began in the Harvard Psychological Laboratory in 1913 under Professors Munsterberg and Langfeld, and which have been carried on practically without interruption to date." WMM, "Systolic Blood Pressure and Reaction Time Symptoms of Deception and Constituent Mental States," PhD diss., Harvard University, 1921, Harvard University Archives. The research Marston conducted in his junior year earned him honorable mention from the Bowdoin Prize Committee: "5 Bowdoin Prizes Awarded," *Harvard Crimson*, May 20, 1914. Marston later published that research: WMM, "Reaction-Time Symptoms of Deception," *Journal of Experimental Psychology* (1920): 72–87; he described this study as reporting on experiments "performed in the Harvard Psychological Laboratory during the Academic Year 1913–1914. At that time the writer of the present article, at the suggestion and under the direction of Professor Hugo Munsterberg, began experiment upon what was then planned to be a series of psycho-physiological problems in the field of legal testimony" (p. 72).

21. On the popularization of science in this period, see Marcel C. LaFollette, *Making Science Our Own: Public Images of Science, 1910–1955* (Chicago: University of Chicago Press, 1990).

22. As Münsterberg remarked, "It has been said, and probably with truth, that more newspaper columns have been printed about the Haywood-Orchard trial than about any jury trial in the history of the United States." From Hugo Münsterberg, "Experiments with Harry Orchard," 1907, p. 2, Hugo Münsterberg Papers, Boston Public Library, folder 2450. "Machines That Tell When Witnesses Lie," *San Francisco Sunday Call*, 1907.

23. The best account of Münsterberg's role in the Orchard case is in Tal Golan, *Laws of Men and Laws of Nature: The History of Scientific Expert Testimony in England and America* (Cambridge, MA: Harvard University Press, 2004), 232–35; this quotation is from p. 232. See also Michael Pettit, "The Testifying Subject: Reliability in Marketing, Science, and the Law at the End of the Age of Barnum," in *Testimonial*

Advertising in the American Marketplace: Emulation, Identity, Community, ed. Marlis Schweitzer and Marina Moskowitz (New York: Palgrave, Macmillan, 2009), 51–78.

24. Clarence Darrow, "Darrow's Speech in the Haywood Case," *Wayland's Monthly,* October 1907, 6, 31, 24.

25. I suspect it was Wigmore who convinced Münsterberg to suppress the original essay, "Experiments with Harry Orchard." On August 20, 1907, Münsterberg wrote to Wigmore from Clifton, "On account of the acquittal of Haywood I have withdrawn my whole Orchard article which was already printed in many thousand copies. (This confidential.) I have substituted a harmless article in the September McClure and have in the October McClure a paper 'The First Degree' which introduces some experiments on Orchard." Hugo Münsterberg to JHW, August 20, 1907, Wigmore Papers, Northwestern University Archives, box 92, folder 16.

26. "The progress of experimental psychology makes it an absurd incongruity that the state should devote its fullest energy to the clearing up of all the physical happenings," Münsterberg wrote, "but should never ask the psychologist to determine the values of the factor which becomes most influential—the mind of the witness." Quoted in Golan, *Laws of Men and Laws of Nature,* 234. On Münsterberg fearing a lawsuit, see 233.

27. JHW, *A Treatise on the System of Evidence in Trials at Common Law* (Boston: Little, Brown, 1904–05). The *Treatise* is widely considered "the most complete and exhaustive treatise on a single branch of our law that has ever been written," according to a review quoted in William L. Twining, *Theories of Evidence: Bentham and Wigmore* (Stanford, CA: Stanford University Press, 1985), 111. Wigmore, who as a student had been one of the founders of the *Harvard Law Review,* was a man of such exhaustive energy and erudition that Louis Brandeis, not one to blanch at a stack of books, had been known to call on him for research assistance (see Wigmore's recollections as quoted in William R. Roalfe, *John Henry Wigmore: Scholar and Reformer* [Evanston, IL: Northwestern University Press, 1977], 15). Wigmore was also capable of great ferocity. In 1927, after Felix Frankfurter criticized the trial of Sacco and Vanzetti, Wigmore raged at him in an article that Brandeis called "sad & unpleasant," which indeed it was. (As Frankfurter liked to tell it, Abbott Lawrence Lowell, then Harvard's president, cried out, on reading Wigmore on Frankfurter, "Wigmore is a fool! Wigmore is a fool!") Louis D. Brandeis to Felix Frankfurter, Washington, DC, April 27, 1927, in *Letters of Louis D. Brandeis,* ed. Melvin I. Urofsky and David W. Levy, 5 vols. (Albany: State University of New York Press, 1978), 5:283, and Felix Frankfurter, *Felix Frankfurter Reminisces* (New York: Reynal, 1960), 215, 217.

28. These experiments were conducted in the United States as well, and not just at Harvard. At the University of Kansas, a professor staged a holdup in the middle of his psychology class. This experiment was originally reported by William A. M'Keever, "Psychology in Relation to Testimony," *Kansas Bar Association Proceedings* (1911), an excerpt of which appears in JHW, *The Principles of Judicial Proof, as Given by Logic, Psychology, and General Experience* (Boston: Little, Brown, 1913), 581–83. Münsterberg routinely conducted testimony experiments during his lectures. "Last winter I made, quite by the way, a little experiment with the students of my regular psychology course in Harvard," he explained. "Several hundred young men, mostly between twenty and twenty-three, took part. It was a test of a very trivial sort. I asked them simply, without any theoretical introduction, at the beginning of an ordinary lecture, to write down careful answers to a number of questions referring

to that which they would see or hear." The German experiments were more antic. In a lecture hall in Berlin, a professor arranged for two of his students to enter into a heated argument over a book. One drew a revolver; the other tried to grab it. The professor stepped between them; the revolver went off. Another fracas—this one involving "a clown in a highly coloured costume" and "a negro with a revolver"— was staged during a meeting of psychologists and jurists in Göttingen. After each of these scenes, experimenters stepped in, revealed that the action had been staged, and asked witnesses to write down everything they'd seen. Hugo Münsterberg, *On the Witness Stand: Essays on Psychology and Crime* (New York: Doubleday, Page, 1909), 20–21, 49–52.

29. JHW, "Professor Muensterberg and the Psychology of Testimony," *Illinois Law Review* 3 (1909): 399–445; the quotation is from p. 401. Wigmore's review is bizarre and bitter. Twining calls Wigmore on Münsterberg "uncharacteristically acerbic" and "an effective satire" (*Theories of Evidence*, 136). I disagree with both characterizations. Twining cites the belief that "this scathing attack discouraged a nascent interest in testimony among American psychologists with the result that progress was delayed for a generation," and although he considers that to be "probably an exaggeration" (*Theories of Evidence*, 136), I don't think it is.

30. Münsterberg quoted in Hale, *Human Science and Social Order*, 59, 61–63.

31. Spillmann and Spillmann, "The Rise and Fall of Hugo Münsterberg," 328, 332–34, and see Hale, *Human Science and Social Order*, 172–83; Hugo Münsterberg, *American Traits from the Point of View of a German* (Boston: Houghton, Mifflin, 1901); Hugo Münsterberg, *The Americans* (New York: McClure, Phillips, 1904).

4. JACK KENNARD, COWARD

1. Display advertisement, Olympia Theatre, *Cambridge Chronicle*, March 29, 1913; display advertisement, Scenic Temple, *Cambridge Sentinel*, February 24, 1912; Russell Merritt, "Nickelodeon Theaters, 1905–1914," in *The American Film Industry*, ed. Tino Balio (Madison: University of Wisconsin Press, 1976), 59–79. Merritt demonstrates the dramatic expansion in the number of theaters in Boston in this era, from thirty-one in 1907 to forty-one in 1914. This change also affected the outlying neighborhoods: "The Boston theater district, which in 1910 was restricted to two downtown thoroughfares, gained considerable new ground by the outbreak of World War I. New movie theaters opened in virtually every major residential neighborhood surrounding the city. By the end of 1913, Dorchester, Roxbury, Cambridge, Somerville, Newton, Belmont, and Watertown had all succumbed to the rising movie fever and had permitted construction of motion picture theaters on their main streets" (Balio, ed., *American Film Industry*, 98–99). The era also marked a rise in the status of movies, from cheap working-class entertainment to legitimate, middle-class outings: "The climax came on November 23, 1914, when B. F. Keith announced that the Boston, the city's oldest, largest, and most prestigious playhouse, would henceforth become a full-time movie theater" (p. 100).

2. Most of the digging was done by Irish laborers with the help of mules, who were worked so hard that their treatment occasioned an underground visit by the Society for the Prevention of Cruelty to Animals. "Mules in Cambridge Subway Never See

Light of Day," undated clipping, probably 1911, in Boston Elevated Railway Company Scrapbook, Cambridge Historical Commission.

3. "Third Rail Kills Terminal Employee," *Boston Post,* March 11, 1912.

4. "Open Subway to Cambridge," *Boston Post,* March 23, 1912; "Harvard and the Hub," *Duluth Herald,* March 4, 1911.

5. "Tremont Temple," *Cambridge Sentinel,* April 27, 1912.

6. "From One Prize Winner," *Moving Picture World,* April 17, 1915, 387.

7. Herbert Case Hoagland, *How to Write a Photoplay* (New York: Magazine Maker, 1912). WMM did not name the book, but only two other books available in 1912 also fit his description: Epes W. Sargent, *Technique of the Photoplay* (New York: Motion Picture World, 1913), and M. M. Katterjohn, *How to Write and Market Moving Picture Plays: Being a Complete Mail Course in Picture Play Writing Prepared in the Form of a Book and Containing Twenty Complete Articles* (Boonville, IN: Photoplay Enterprise Association, 1912). These seem less likely to have been available in Cambridge than Hoagland's book.

8. Hoagland, *How to Write a Photoplay,* 6, 10–11, 13–14, 44, 61, 63, 67, 75. WMM could also have learned about the market by reading motion picture company requests in the *Photoplay Author,* which ran a regular column called "The Photoplay Market." See, e.g., the column for February 1914, p. 61, in which the New York Motion Picture Company advises, "We are in the market for both double- and single-reel stories. We prefer plausible, short-cast, tensely dramatic scenarios with big themes carefully worked out with original business and careful characterization. All stories should have a well developed love or heart interest. Our greatest demand is for Indian-Military stories. We are also in the market for straight dramatic, Puritan and Spanish Stories."

9. "From One Prize Winner," *Moving Picture World,* April 17, 1915, 387.

10. WMM first applied for a scholarship on May 26, 1913. The file includes two letters of support, one from the principal of Malden High School, Thornton Jenkins, dated June 3, 1913, stating that Marston is rugged and steadfast, and another from the pastor of the First Congregational Church in Cliftondale, Harry C. Adams, dated June 2, 1913: "He is an only son and yet my impression is that he is in large part helping himself through College. He is a member of my church and is I am sure worthy of any assistance he may receive from the College." Marston endeared himself to professors and deans as easily as he had to his principal and pastor. See, e.g., Marston's correspondence with B. S. Hurlbut, dean of the college. See WMM, Application for a Scholarship, May 13, 1913; WMM to B. S. Hurlbut, January 12, 1915, and B. S. Hurlbut to WMM ("Dear Marston"), January 18, 1915; and WMM, Application for a Scholarship, Harvard College, April 27, 1914, all in WMM, Undergraduate File, Harvard University Archives, UAIII 15.88.10. Also in the file are WMM's addresses: as a sophomore he lived in Weld 5, and as a junior, at 64 Dunster Street.

11. WMM, *The Lie Detector Test* (New York: Richard D. Smith, 1938), acknowledgments.

12. "I . . . wrote the episodes used in the experiments and mailed them to him," EHM wrote to JE, January 11, 1973. And again: "I was at Mt Holyoke and supplied the 'true' stories used in the experiment." EHM to JE, November 16, 1983, both in the possession of JE. And see EHM, autobiographical statement, Mount Holyoke Alumni Office, submitted August 18, 1986.

13. The whole of his life, Marston relied on women to help him with work that he published under his name alone. This wasn't uncommon; the girlfriends and wives of

scholars and scientists and writers helped them in their work all the time, in everything from typing to research to editing. Lillian Moller Gilbreth, who earned a PhD in psychology at Brown in 1915, not only edited most of the books published under the name of her husband, Frank Gilbreth but, it appears, wrote most of them, too. She was also a mother of twelve. (Her life was later the subject of the film *Cheaper by the Dozen,* based on a memoir written by two of her children.) She used the weeks after childbirth to work on her husband's books. In 1911, after giving birth to Frank Jr., she edited *Motion Study* and wrote *The Primer of Scientific Management.* Both books are credited only to her husband. Lancaster, *Making Time,* 117, 164–65. And see Lepore, *The Mansion of Happiness: A History of Life and Death* (New York: Knopf, 2013), chapter 6.

14. WMM, "Systolic Blood Pressure Symptoms of Deception," *Journal of Experimental Psychology* 2 (1917): 117–76. This work is cited by WMM's former professor Herbert Sidney Langfeld in "Psychophysical Symptoms of Deception," *Journal of Abnormal Psychology* 15 (1921): 319–28.

15. "The Rubber Barons," *Wonder Woman #4,* April–May 1943. For another scene in which Diana Prince administers a lie detector test, see "The Girl with the Gun," *Sensation Comics #20,* August 1943.

16. Hugo Münsterberg, "Why We Go to the Movies," *Cosmopolitan,* December 15, 1915, 22–32.

17. Hugo Münsterberg, *The Photoplay: A Psychological Study* (New York: D. Appleton, 1916), 38, 39, 43. A modern reprint, which includes the *Cosmopolitan* article, along with a valuable introduction, is Hugo Münsterberg, *Hugo Münsterberg on Film: "The Photoplay: A Psychological Study" and Other Writings,* edited and with an introduction by Allan Langdale (New York: Routledge, 2002).

18. Münsterberg, *Photoplay,* 99, 112.

19. "$100 Offered for 'Movies' Scenario," *Harvard Crimson,* May 21, 1914.

20. "From One Prize Winner," *Moving Picture World,* April 17, 1915, 387.

21. "Colleges Fail in the Test," *New York Dramatic Mirror,* February 24, 1915, 25; display advertisement, "The Prize Play of the Edison College Contest," *Moving Picture World,* May 1, 1915, 693; "Scenario Prize Won by Senior," *Harvard Crimson,* February 25, 1915; and "Harvard Senior Wins Movie Prize," *Boston Daily Globe,* February 25, 1915. And see Edwin H. McCloskey, "Harvard Man Wins Edison Scenario Prize," *Moving Picture World,* March 13, 1915, 1641: "It is claimed that when this photoplay is released that it will give the famous Cambridge educational institution the largest amount of gossip matter that it has had for many years. The author has worked his way through college by selling scenarios. He claims that the prize play deals directly with the adventures of star football players who are now in college. He also declares that the play has been written so that the students of the institution will recognize the men at whom the thrusts are directed." McCloskey was the Boston correspondent for the *Moving Picture World,* but it appears that he got his information from the story about Marston in the *Boston Evening Record,* rather than from interviewing him; at least, his story does not go beyond that one.

22. "Exposes Harvard Gambling: Movie Scenario a Sizzler," *Boston Evening Record,* February 26, 1915.

23. BHRM, "Memories of an Unusual Father," 3. The drawing appears as an illustration for "A PBK Writes Comics," *Key Reporter,* Autumn 1942, p. 5. That WMM was the president of his PBK chapter is mentioned in Herbert Langfeld to Robert Yerkes,

October 8, 1917, folder titled "Ex Com: Committee on Psychology. Projects: Deception Test, 1917," National Research Council Papers, National Academy of Sciences.

24. "Exposes Harvard Gambling," *Boston Evening Record,* February 26, 1915.

25. "From One Prize Winner," *Moving Picture World,* April 17, 1915, 387.

26. Joe Bertagna, *Crimson in Triumph: A Pictorial History of Harvard Athletics, 1852–1985* (Lexington, MA: Stephen Greene Press, 1986), 16–17. The coach from 1908 through 1916 was Percy Haughton. There was no one on the team during Marston's senior year with a name especially close to "Jack Kennard," although both Stan Pennock and Tack Hardwick come close. Hardwick seems unlikely to have inspired WMM's scenario, though. A three-time All-American, a plaque was later placed in his honor in front of the Dillon Field House, engraved: "Inspiring leader, eager competitor, loyal sportsman." "'Sock 'Em' is Latest Football Cry," *Harvard Crimson,* September 25, 1950.

27. John J. Reidy Jr., "Twenty Years of Harvard-Yale . . . a Day for Harvard Greats," *Harvard Crimson,* November 20, 1937.

28. WMM liked to be known as a high school football star. The announcement of his wedding, in September 1915, referred to him as "a graduate of Cliftondale High School where he took part in athletics, especially in football, in which he starred." *Whitman (MA) Times,* September 15, 1915, in Clippings file, WMM, Quinquennial File, Harvard University Archives. I can't find any evidence that WMM ever tried out for the football squad or practiced with it. He does not appear on the roster of players; nor is he listed as those who will receive an *H* for playing, as per Minutes, December 4, 1912, the Committee on the Regulation of Athletic Sports, Athletic Committee Minutes, 1882–1951, v. 2, pp. 785–86. The only controversy I can find in these minutes involves faculty and alumni concern about the roughness of play on the field. There is, in 1913, a remark about "The case of A. Fleisher, '15, a member of the second team squad [that is, the JV], whose tickets were sold at a premium," Minutes, December 16, 1913, p. 815. In the fall of Marston's senior year, the Committee on the Regulation of Athletic Sports voted to prohibit members of any team from writing signed articles "about a team or crew or squad of which he is a member"; moreover, "the question of the advisability of a rule to forbid a man's rowing and playing football in the same year was discussed but no action was taken." Minutes, October 6, 1914, p. 843. And: "Letters of protest at alleged unfair tactics of the Yale team at the football game on November 21st were submitted by the Chairman, and the matter was discussed. No action was taken." Minutes, December 1, 1914, p. 847.

29. WMM, *March On! Facing Life with Courage* (New York: Doubleday, Doran, 1941), 36–37. Also: "He played a little college football," Marston's son Byrne later wrote, "but he was more interested in psychology." BHRM, "Memories of an Unusual Father," 3.

30. Display advertisement, "The Prize Play of the Edison College Contest," *Moving Picture World,* May 1, 1915, 693; "Releases of the Week After," *Motion Picture News,* May 1, 1915; "CHARLES M. SEAY. Current Edison Releases. JACK KENNARD, COWARD—May 5. AN INNOCENT THIEF—May 11. Address care SCREEN CLUB." This is a classified ad printed in the *New York Dramatic Mirror,* May 12, 1915. A description of the film had been sent to distributors at the end of April. "A single reel story of college life, written by William Marston, prize winner of the Edison College Contest, featuring Julia Calhoun, Harry Beaumont, Olive Templeton, and Marie La Manna. A college student in financial difficulties borrows money from a supposed friend, who uses the debt as a club to make his fiancée believe that he is a coward. He

proves his physical bravery in a dramatic manner by rescuing a girl from being run over by a subway train, and the interrupted course of true love again runs smoothly. Directed by Charles Seay." "Licensed Films," *New York Dramatic Mirror,* April 28, 1915. I have been unable to find a print of the film.

31. I have found evidence of the film being played in Ohio, Missouri, Pennsylvania, Illinois, and Massachusetts: display advertisement, Royal Theatre, *Mansfield (OH) News,* June 9, 1915; display advertisement, Jefferson Theatre, *Daily Democrat-Tribune* (Jefferson City, MO), June 19, 1915; display advertisement, Walters Theatre, *Star and Sentinel* (Gettysburg, PA), September 1, 1915; "Movie Directory" (listing for the Harvard Photo Play House), *Chicago Daily Tribune,* May 13, 1915; and "Agreed," *Moving Picture World,* September 11, 1915, 1824. Regarding the Cambridge screening, I believe the film was shown when it was released, in May; this story, "Agreed," published on September 11, 1915, includes, as an illustration, two programs from Durrell Hall, one of which lists *"Jack Kennard, Coward."* The programs are undated; the story concerns the typesetting on theatrical programs. The Durrell Hall programs submitted by the proprietor, E. B. Thomas, would have been sent to the editors of the *Moving Picture World* some weeks before the story was published.

32. Review of "Jack Kennerd [*sic*], Coward," *Moving Picture World,* May 22, 1915, 1259.

33. "Drape Kaiser's Gift: Harvard Students Commemorate the 'Lusitania Massacre,'" *New York Times,* May 10, 1915.

34. Josiah Royce to Lawrence Pearsall Jacks [June, 1915?], in *Letters of Josiah Royce,* 627–28. On the Harvard dead, see "War Exacts Death Toll," *Harvard Crimson,* December 13, 1917, and Mark Antony DeWolfe Howe, *Memoirs of the Harvard Dead in the War Against Germany,* 5 vols. (Cambridge, MA: Harvard University Press, 1920), 1:33.

35. Edward Estlin Cummings, "The New Art. Commencement Part, 1915," in General Information About Harvard Commencement and Class Day, 1911–1920, Harvard University Archives, box 1, HUC 6911. "The Commencement Celebration," *Harvard Alumni Bulletin,* June 30, 1915, 710–20, as filed in General Information about Harvard Commencement and Class Day, 1911–1920, Harvard University Archives, box 2, HUC 6911. The commencement program, *Alvmos Conlegi Harvardiani Ornatissvmos, Concelebranda, Ad Sollemnia Academica* (Cambridge, MA: Harvard University, 1915), is filed in General Information About Harvard Commencement and Class Day, 1911–1920, Harvard University Archives, box 2, HUC 6911. On the use of Latin on the diplomas, as well as the use of sheepskin, see Mason Hammond, "Official Terms in Latin and English for Harvard College or University," *Harvard Library Bulletin* 35 (1988): 294. At the time, Marston's advisers considered him with the set of their graduate students. "All our men are placed with the exception of Feingold and Kellogg," Langfeld wrote to Yerkes. "Marston got his degree magna cum laude." Herbert Langfeld to Robert Yerkes, June 17, 1915, Robert M. Yerkes Papers, Yale University Manuscripts and Archives, box 30, folder 565.

5. MR. AND MRS. MARSTON

1. William Ernst Hocking, a member of Harvard's philosophy department, delivered Mount Holyoke's commencement address. He spoke about the philosophy and psy-

chology of power. True power is calm, he said. Hocking's commencement address is printed in "Diplomas for 147 Seniors," an unidentified 1915 newspaper clipping in the Mount Holyoke College Archives.

2. "Vogue of Bobbed Hair," *New York Times,* June 27, 1920.

3. A copy of Vachel Lindsay, *The Congo and Other Poems* (New York: Macmillan, 1915), inscribed, "May 8th, She's Twenty-Two! Bill," is in the possession of MM. "The Mysterious Cat" is on p. 38.

4. "The Sphinx Speaks of the Class of 1915, Mount Holyoke College: A Biographical History . . . for our Thirty-second Reunion, June 1947" (South Hadley, MA: Mount Holyoke College, 1947), n.p., and "The Riddle of the Sphinx in Your Living Room, 1915–1970" (South Hadley, MA: Mount Holyoke College, 1970), 13.

5. *The Llamarada 1915* (South Hadley: Mount Holyoke College, 1915), 174.

6. EHM to JE, November 16, 1983, in the possession of JE.

7. Solomon, *In the Company of Educated Women,* 120.

8. See the marriage notice in the *Whitman (MA) Times,* September 15, 1915, in Clippings file, WMM, Quinquennial File, Harvard University Archives.

9. EHM to JE, January 20, 1974, in the possession of JE.

10. EHM, "Tiddly Bits." EHM to Caroline Becker (Alumnae Office), February 26, 1987, EHM Alumnae file, Mount Holyoke College Archives.

11. "Mr. and Mrs. Marston are living at 12 Remington Street, Cambridge, Mass." *Harvard Bulletin,* in Clippings file, WMM, Quinquennial File, Harvard University Archives. 12 Remington Street was a development called Remington Gables; see the Remington Street folder, Cambridge Historical Commission: "At Remington Gables we have a suite consisting of Living room, Dining room, Reception hall, two chambers, Kitchenette and Bath, rent of which is $37.50 per month." Newhall and Blevins to Robert J. Melledge, November 26, 1911. And: "Suite 102—To sublet from April 1th for remainder of lease—Oct. 1, 1914—Rent $42.50 per mo. Suite consists of Living room, Dining room, 2 Chambers, kitchenette, bath and piazza." Newhall and Blevins, Revised Renting List, Remington Gables, Cambridge, April 13, 1914.

12. Holloway quoted in Andrew H. Malcolm, "Our Towns: She's Behind the Match for That Man of Steel," *New York Times,* February 18, 1992.

13. *First Report of the Class of Nineteen Hundred and Fifteen of Mount Holyoke College* (South Hadley, MA: Mount Holyoke College, 1916), n.p. A copy of Fannie Merritt Farmer, *Boston Cooking-School Cook Book,* rev. ed. (Boston: Little, Brown, 1918), inscribed by WMM's mother, is in the possession of MM.

14. Solomon, *In the Company of Educated Women,* 51. EHM to JE, April 19, 1974, in the possession of JE.

15. WMM, *Try Living,* 8.

16. WMM, transcript, Harvard Law School, class of 1918, Harvard Law School Registrar: Student Permanent Record Cards, 1893–1972, Harvard University Archives, call number 14258. Faculty members are not listed on the transcript, but I have consulted the law school's course catalog. On Thayer and Wigmore, see Twining, *Theories of Evidence,* 7–9. James Bradley Thayer, *Select Cases on Evidence at Common Law* (Cambridge, MA: C. W. Sever, 1892).

17. Theodore Roosevelt said that Wilson's campaign slogan ("He kept us out of war") was an "ignoble shirking of responsibility." Wilson countered. "I am an American, but I do not believe that any of us loves a blustering nationality," he said in one campaign speech. "We love that quiet, self-respecting, unconquerable spirit which

doesn't strike until it is necessary to strike, and then it strikes to conquer." Quoted in A. Scott Berg, *Wilson* (New York: Putnam's, 2013), 412, 404–5.

18. Berg, *Wilson*, 417. John Milton Cooper, ed., *Reconsidering Woodrow Wilson: Progressivism, Internationalism, War, and Peace* (Baltimore: Johns Hopkins University Press, 2008), 126.

19. A. Lawrence Lowell to Alfred C. Lane, November 2, 1916, Harvard University Archives, HUA 734.26.

20. Münsterberg's address is given as 7 Ware Street in "Cosmopolitan Clubs to Convene During Recess," *Harvard Crimson,* December 22, 1915. That the class was Elementary Psychology is reported in "H. Munsterberg, Psychologist, Is Fatally Stricken," *San Francisco Chronicle,* December 17, 1916. See also "Munsterberg Dead," *Washington Post,* December 17, 1916. That Münsterberg had, in the last years of his career, been chiefly regarded as a popularizer is well illustrated by the many mixed tributes of this sort: "Nowadays, when our magazines are loaded with ignorant expositions of Freud and Jung and every whiffler is driveling about the 'sex-complex' and the theory of dreams, it is well to remember that Professor Münsterberg was never a mere caterer to prurient curiosity or the vulgar love of wonders" ("Hugo Munsterberg," *New York Tribune,* December 17, 1916).

21. Splash page, *Wonder Woman #5,* June–July 1943.

6. THE EXPERIMENTAL LIFE

1. On the suffrage movement during Wilson's presidency, see Christine A. Lunardini, *From Equal Suffrage to Equal Rights: Alice Paul and the National Woman's Party, 1910–1928* (New York: New York University Press, 1986).

2. Berg, *Wilson,* 438. And see Jill Lepore, "The Tug of War: Woodrow Wilson and the Power of the Presidency," *New Yorker,* September 9, 2013.

3. The best account is Lunardini, *From Equal Suffrage to Equal Rights,* chapter 7. But see also Catherine J. Lanctot, " 'We Are at War and You Should Not Bother the President': The Suffrage Pickets and Freedom of Speech During World War I," Villanova University School of Law Working Paper Series, 2008, Paper 116.

4. A list of the members of this group appears in a visitor logbook kept by the Psychological Laboratory: Experimental Group, April 5–7, 1917, "Visitors to the Psychological Laboratory" (pp. 11–12), Department of Psychology, Harvard University Archives, UA V 714.392.

5. Robert M. Yerkes, "Psychology in Relation to the War," *Psychological Review* 25 (1918): 85–115; quote on 94. See also Robert M. Yerkes, ed., *The New World of Science: Its Development During the War* (New York: Century, 1920), 354.

6. WMM, Class Note, *Harvard College Class of 1915: Decennial Report* (Cambridge: Printed for the Class of 1915, 1926), 178–79.

7. WMM, draft card, Cambridge, Massachusetts, June 5, 1917, World War I Draft Registration Cards, 1917–1918 (Provo, UT: Ancestry.com, 2005). According to WMM's Harvard Law School transcript, his last day in residence during the 1916–17 academic year was June 21.

8. "Is there a chance to be commissioned as Chief Examiner in regular army service like the medics, or is the only opportunity open, in case the work is extended, a

civil appointment as assistant examiner?" and "Is there any opportunity or need for research work, like Mr. Troland's etc., which can be done in the Harvard Lab.?" WMM to Robert Yerkes, September 11, 1917, National Research Council Papers, National Academy of Medicine.

9. WMM to Yerkes, September 20, 1917, NRC Papers.

10. E. L. Thorndike to Yerkes, October 1917 (on National Research Council letterhead), NRC Papers.

11. Herbert Langfeld to Robert Yerkes, October 8, 1917 (on Harvard Psychological Laboratory letterhead), NRC Papers.

12. WMM to Yerkes, from Cambridge, October 9, 1917, with 12-page typewritten enclosure titled, "Report on Deception Tests," NRC Papers.

13. Minutes of the Meeting of the Psychology Committee, National Research Council, October 13, 1917, NRC Papers. WMM reported: "In October, 1917, at the request of the Psychological Committee of National Research Council, tests of this type [systolic blood pressure] were conducted in the Harvard Laboratory, with a view to determining their value in government service during the war." WMM, "Psychological Possibilities in the Deception Tests," *Journal of Criminal Law and Criminology* 11 (1921): 552–53. He cites the report in the Psychological Committee files, under the date of November 13, 1917. "This opportunity for a practical try-out of these tests was made possible by the liberal and patriotic attitude of the court and the energetic efforts of Major Robert M. Yerkes and Dr. [James R.] Angell of the National Research Council," WMM later acknowledged (WMM, "Psychological Possibilities in the Deception Tests," 554). Robert M. Yerkes, "Report of the Psychology Committee of the National Research Council," *Psychological Review* 26 (1919): 85, 134.

14. Telegram, WMM, Harold E. Burtt, and Leonard T. Troland to Yerkes, November 13, 1917; and WMM to Yerkes, November 13, 1917, an eight-page letter signed by Harold E. Burtt and Leonard T. Troland below a postscript reading, "The above is a correct account of Marston's deception tests in which we have participated," NRC Papers.

15. Yerkes, "Report of the Psychology Committee," 134.

16. Herbert Langfeld to Robert Yerkes, October 16, 1917, Robert M. Yerkes Papers, Yale University Manuscripts and Archives, box 30, folder 565, and WMM, "Psychological Possibilities in the Deception Tests," 556, 566. How the study came to be authorized can be found in Yerkes to WMM, December 1, 1917, and WMM to Yerkes, December 4, 1917, NRC Papers.

17. "Demand Release of Pickets," *New York Times*, November 9, 1917, and "Suffragists Will Use Ballots to Resent Jailing of Pickets," *New York Tribune*, November 12, 1917.

18. WMM to Yerkes, December 12, 1917, NRC Papers; Yerkes to Mr. A. Bruce Bielaski, Chief of Bureau of Investigation, Dept. of Justice, January 15, 1918, and Bielaski to Yerkes, February 23, 1918, NRC Papers. That Hoover was at this meeting is also recalled by WMM in WMM to Albert L. Barrows, Executive Secretary of the NRC, July 29, 1935, NRC Papers. Yerkes to Major Nicholas Biddle, December 18, 1917; WMM to Yerkes, December 19, 1917, NRC Papers. WMM to Yerkes, December 19, 1917, NRC Papers.

19. WMM, "Systolic Blood Pressure and Reaction Time Symptoms of Deception and Constituent Mental States," 134–39; WMM to Yerkes, January 21, 1918, and WMM to Yerkes, February 23, 1918, NRC Papers. The investigation rekindled his avidity

for the law. "While engaged in deception testing of criminal and spy cases," he later wrote, "I became genuinely interested in the law." WMM, *Try Living*, 8–9.

20. Yerkes, "Report of the Psychology Committee," 135; Yerkes to WMM, March 5, 1918, NRC Papers; Yerkes to Dean Roscoe Pond, April 2, 1918, and Pond to Yerkes, April 5, 1918, NRC Papers. Marston was "deficient in one second-year course."

21. "Passed Bar Examinations," *Cambridge Chronicle*, August 3, 1918. EHM, "Tiddly Bits."

22. "October 22, 1918. Commissioned as a second lieutenant in the U.S. Army, Sanitary Corps; assigned to Psychological Division and stationed at Fort Oglethorpe, GA; transferred to Camp Upton, NY; to Camp Lee, VA; discharged May 9, 1919," U.S. Adjutant General Military Records, 1631–1976 (Provo, UT: Ancestry.com, 2011). This is at variance with Marston's account: he says he took a leave of absence from law school in his third year.

23. EHM, "Tiddly Bits."

24. "Battle for Womanhood," *Wonder Woman #5*, June–July 1943.

25. WMM, "Psychological Possibilities in the Deception Tests," 567.

26. "A sufficient psychological background probably exists to qualify an expert upon deception in court," he concluded. Ibid., 567–70.

27. Yerkes, "Report of the Psychology Committee," 135–36.

28. I haven't been able to locate letters between WMM and JHW from 1919 and 1920, but the later letters make clear that their correspondence began about this time. On March 15, 1921, WMM sent JHW a reprint of the article, "written at your suggestion for the Journal of Criminal Law and Criminology." WMM to JHW, March 15, 1921, Wigmore Papers, Northwestern University Archives, box 90, folder 12.

29. WW comic strip, June 10, 1944.

7. MACHINE DETECTS LIARS, TRAPS CROOKS

1. United States of America, Bureau of the Census, *Twelfth Census of the United States, 1900* (Washington, DC: National Archives and Records Administration, 1900), Atlanta Ward 7, Fulton, Georgia; Roll: 200; Page: 11A; Enumeration District: 0083; FHL microfilm: 1240200, as available at Ancestry.com, *1900 United States Federal Census* (Provo, UT: Ancestry.com, 2004).

2. "A Glimpse in Advance of a Section of the Suffrage Parade," *Chicago Herald*, May 18, 1916. Many thanks to Allison Lange for this clip and other references. And see Allison Lange, "Images of Change: Picturing Women's Rights from American Independence through the Nineteenth Amendment," PhD diss., Brandeis University, 2014.

3. EHM to JE, January 11, 1973, in the possession of JE.

4. "Mole Men of the Underworld," *Wonder Woman #4*, April–May 1943.

5. Brief sketches of Wilkes's life can be found in Donald W. Swinton, "Clinton Woman, 92, Believes It's Never Too Late to Vote," *Clinton Daily Item*, undated clipping, 1981 (in the possession of BHRM), and Mary Frain, "93 Years Old; She's Lived Every Day of Life," *Clinton Daily Item*, October 15, 1982, 183. My account of MWH is also much informed by BHRM, interview with the author, July 14, 2013.

6. Sue Grupposo, interview with the author, July 15, 2013.

7. EHM, "Tiddly Bits."

8. MWH to JE, June 14, 1972, Steinem Papers, Smith College, box 213, folder 5.

9. WMM, Graduate Record Card, Harvard University, Graduate School of Arts and Sciences, Harvard University Archives, HAIH63 UA1161.272.5. EHM, Graduate Record Card, Harvard University Graduate School of Arts and Sciences, Schlesinger Library, Radcliffe.

10. The birth and death dates for Fredericka Marston are given as January 7, 1920, on EHM's entry for Mount Holyoke College's *One Hundred Year Directory*, 1936, Mount Holyoke College Archives.

11. They are on a ship's passenger list as leaving Hamilton, Bermuda, and arriving in New York on August 9, 1920, Passenger Lists of Vessels Arriving at New York, New York, 1820–1897 (National Archives Microfilm Publication M237, 675 rolls); Records of the U.S. Customs Service, Record Group 36; National Archives, Washington, DC, as made available by Ancestry.com, Passenger Lists, 1820–1957 (Provo, UT: Ancestry .com, 2010).

12. Evans, *Born for Liberty*, 187.

13. Quoted in Cott, *Grounding of Modern Feminism*, 194.

14. EHM, Graduate Record Card, Harvard University Graduate School of Arts and Sciences, Schlesinger Library, Radcliffe. In 1920–21, EHM took two semesters of Psychology 20a and one semester of Psychology 20b. WMM took those same three courses as well (two semesters of Psych 20a and one of 20b), along with another psychology laboratory course.

15. EHM to Jack Liebowitz, January 5, 1948, DC Comics Archives.

16. EHM, "Tiddly Bits."

17. It is true that Holloway was not proficient in German; she took two semesters of it at Mount Holyoke and earned a D and a D+. EHM, Transcript, Office of the Registrar, Mount Holyoke College.

18. Solomon, *In the Company of Educated Women*, 127, 131.

19. EHM, autobiographical statement submitted to the Mount Holyoke College Alumni Office, August 18, 1986; EHM, "Tiddly Bits."

20. EHM, "Tiddly Bits."

21. "New Mass. Corporations," *Cambridge Chronicle*, March 27, 1920. WMM is listed as the incorporator of the Tait-Marston Engineering Company, of Boston, foundry and machine shop. Its offices are given as 60 State Street, Boston, in display advertisement, Tait-Marston Engineering Company, *American Machinist*, vol. 52 (June 24, 1920), 328. The company was dissolved in 1924, according to *Acts and Resolves of the General Court [Massachusetts]*, 1924.

22. "New Incorporations," *New York Times*, March 17, 1920.

23. Forte appears in a photograph in one of the Marston family photo albums, helping Marston do tests on the porch of a house on Lowell Street. On Fischer, see *Harvard Alumni Bulletin*, vol. 22 (April 29, 1920), 719; Boston Legal Aid Society, *The Work of the Boston Legal Aid Society: A Study of the Period Jan. 1, 1921 to June 30, 1922* (Boston, 1922), 28: Marston, Forte & Fischer donated fifty dollars to the society.

24. WMM, Class Note, *Harvard College Class of 1915: Decennial Report*, 178–79.

25. "Machine Detects Liars, Traps Crooks," *Philadelphia Inquirer*, May 14, 1921. The

publicity material was picked up by trade journals, too: see, e.g., "This Machine Detects Liars," *Science and Invention* 9 (1921): 618.

26. WMM, Class Note, *Harvard College Class of 1915: Decennial Report,* 178–79.

8. STUDIES IN TESTIMONY

1. The experiment is recounted in WMM, "Studies in Testimony," *Journal of Criminal Law and Criminology* 15 (May 1924): 5–31.

2. *American University: Announcement for 1922–1923, Graduate School of Arts and Sciences* (Washington, DC: American University, 1922), 12–13. This course catalog describes courses offered in the academic year 1922–23. WMM, however, had begun teaching at American University during the previous academic year, even though his courses were not then listed in the catalog; he was apparently a late addition to the faculty. In a letter dated March 30, 1922, he describes the experiments as "just concluded" (WMM to JHW, Wigmore Papers, Northwestern University Archives, box 90, folder 12). In academic year 1921–22, the winter term began on January 2, 1922, and ended on March 18, 1922. The spring term began on March 20 and ended on June 3. For the calendar, see *American University: Announcement for 1921–1922, Graduate School of Arts and Sciences* (Washington, DC: American University, 1921), 2.

3. WMM, "Studies in Testimony," 9.

4. WMM wrote Wigmore that the course was "based to a considerable extent upon your 'Principles of Judicial Proof'" (WMM to JHW, March 30, 1922). Wigmore's attack on Münsterberg notwithstanding, Wigmore was keenly interested in applying psychological research to the question of evidence: he hoped to found a science of evidence. *The Principles of Judicial Proof* is a compendium, consisting of case studies taken not only from the courts but also from the annals of literature. JHW, *Principles of Judicial Proof,* 168–70, 502–3. Above all, Wigmore drew from psychology. Explaining what constitutes proof of identity, for instance, he quoted William James's *Principles of Psychology;* on perception, he relied on Josiah Royce's *Outlines of Psychology.*

5. There is some evidence that Wigmore and Münsterberg had had some kind of rapproachement by the time of the latter's death. In 1913, Wigmore asked Münsterberg for permission to use some portion of his work in *The Principles of Judicial Proof.* When Münsterberg granted that permission, Wigmore wrote back, "Thank you heartily for your kind consent to my use of the passage from your book. You need not fear that I should attempt to take advantage of the occasion to continue the sarcastic controversy of three years ago. I am anxious, in this book, to see your views expounded fully to law students, and hence the desire for a quotation from your book. I shall merely append a few serious remarks on the other side of the question." JHW to Hugo Münsterberg, January 3, 1913, Wigmore Papers, box 92, folder 16.

6. JHW, *Principles of Judicial Proof,* 583–91.

7. WMM thought the scenes played in earlier experiments, using shams and "blood (or paint) smeared actors, shouting and gesticulating," skewed the results. He therefore devised, instead, a scene of utmost ordinariness, an incident "of such a character

that no one of the 18 witnesses suspected anything unusual had occurred until so informed by the experimenter." WMM, "Studies in Testimony," 7–8. Wigmore had suggested a modification to the standard experimental design: "include a jury (or judge of facts) in the experiment, and observe whether the findings of fact follow the testimonial errors or whether they succeed in avoiding them and in reaching the actual facts." Wigmore's Northwestern University Law School experiments are reported in his *Principles of Judicial Proof,* 585–91.

8. WMM to JWH, March 30, 1922.

9. Mississippi would be the last state to drop its ban on female jury service; that change didn't come until 1968. Holly J. McCammon, *The U.S. Women's Jury Movements and Strategic Adaptations* (Cambridge: Cambridge University Press, 2012); my count is derived from table 3.1, on p. 38. For the length of time from the beginning of women's activism on this issue to success, see table 3.2, on p. 51.

10. EHM, "Tiddly Bits."

11. WMM to JHW, March 30, 1922, and JHW to WMM, May 11, 1922. WMM, "Studies in Testimony," 16–17.

12. WMM, *March On!,* 235.

13. "President of the National Benefit Life Insurance Company Cowardly Murdered," *Philadelphia Tribune,* December 4, 1920; "Offer $1,000 Reward for Doctor's Slayer," *Chicago Defender,* December 18, 1920.

14. A useful account of the arrest and questioning and a faithful summary of the confession is "Mystery Finally Solved as How Prominent Physician Was Murdered Last Year," *Washington Tribune,* August 27, 1921.

15. James A. Frye, Statement Made to Inspector Clifford I. Grant, August 22, 1921. A copy is filed with *Curtis v. Francis,* National Archives, RG 21, Equity 40432, box 3060, 16W3/06/27/03.

16. Local coverage: "Negro Held in Charge of Slaying Physician," *Washington Bee,* August 27, 1921. National coverage: "Dr. Brown's Slayer in Law's Grip," *Chicago Defender,* September 3, 1921.

17. *United States v. Bowie, Frye et al.,* National Archives, RG 21, Criminal #38380, box 316, 16W3/08/21/06. Bowie was also tried separately for housebreaking and larceny and found guilty. *United States v. William N. Bowie,* 1921, National Archives, RG 21, Criminal #38310, box 316, 16W3/08/21/06.

18. Lester Wood, Student Record, October 8, 1921, Registrar's Office, American University.

19. "William N. Bowie and James Frye Convicted," *Washington Tribune,* November 12, 1921. Wood also filed a motion for a separate trial for Bowie, who, with Benjamin Grice, was also charged with larceny and housebreaking. *United States v. William N. Bowie,* 1921, Motion for a New Trial, filed by Lester Wood, attorney for the defendant, January 6, 1922, National Archives, RG 21, Criminal #38310, box 316, 16W3/08/21/06. *United States v. William N. Bowie,* 1921, Motion filed by Lester Wood, attorney for the defendant, December 21, 1921, National Archives, RG 21, Criminal #38310, box 316, 16W3/08/21/06. This is before the introduction of court-appointed attorneys for destitute defendants. Wood's serving as counsel in a case like this was volunteer work, and a common way to acquire legal training.

20. "New Trial Is Granted Bowie," *Washington Tribune,* December 10, 1921, and "Bowie and Frye Get Four Years in Penitentiary," *Washington Tribune,* December 31, 1921.

21. *United States v. Frye,* Docket Entries, National Archives, RG 21, Criminal #38325,

box 316, 16W3/08/21/06. O'Shea is listed as his attorney during the indictment in the full appeal trial record, *Frye v. United States,* National Archives, RG 276. Frye pled not guilty to murder just before Marston conducted his experiment in testimony at American University. In 1922, the spring term at American University began on March 20. Legal Psychology met twice a week. That messenger with a Texas twang must have knocked on the door of the lecture room during one of the very first class meetings, because on March 30 Marston wrote to Wigmore to tell him that he had "just concluded a very interesting experiment on testimonial evidence." WMM to JHW, March 30, 1922.

22. Richard V. Mattingly, Student Record, October 4, 1921, Registrar's Office, American University.

23. Only four scholars have ever investigated the Frye case. All four are historians of science. In 1982, J. E. Starrs, the first person to bother to dig up the trial records—by that time most of the police reports had been destroyed—speculated that Frye was probably guilty, despite his protestations to the contrary. J. E. Starrs, "A Still-Life Watercolor: *Frye v. United States,*" *Journal of Forensic Sciences* 27 (July 1982): 684–94. In 2004, Tal Golan situated the ruling within the history of expert testimony to argue that psychology is where Progressive Era law drew a line between what, of science, can enter the courtroom and what cannot. In 2007, Ken Alder placed the story within his fascinating history of lie detection: Ken Alder, *The Lie Detectors: The History of an American Obsession* (New York: Free Press, 2007), chapter 4, "Monsterwork and Son." That same year, in a Harvard dissertation, Seán Tath O'Donnell argued that the case could be understood only in the context of race relations in Washington, DC. O'Donnell, "Courting Science, Binding Truth: A Social History of *Frye v. United States,*" PhD diss., Harvard University, 2007. None of these scholars was especially interested in Marston, and none discovered that Frye's attorneys were Marston's students. Both Starrs and O'Donnell refer to Mattingly as "court-appointed"; O'Donnell adds that he was "appointed to the case at the last minute" (p. 196). Starrs and O'Donnell, unaware that Mattingly and Wood were Marston's students, assumed, instead, that the lawyers sought the expert out. "Mattingly found Marston employed as a lecturer at American University," writes O'Donnell (p. 12). And see also O'Donnell's discussion on p. 140, where he asserts that Mattingly, desperately hoping to corroborate Frye's recantation of his confession, discovered a professor at American University who might help him out.

24. WMM to JHW, June 3, 1922, Wigmore Papers.

25. Frye at some point also submitted to an intelligence test, administered by Major Harold C. Bingham of the National Research Council, who determined that his intelligence "was superior to that of the average draft negro." Memorandum of Scientific History and Authority of Systolic Blood Pressure Test for Deception, *Frye v. United States,* Briefs, #3968, National Archives RG 276, box 380, 14E2A/02/05/04, p. 4.

26. For Frye's recollection of Marston's visit to the jail on June 10, 1922, see Frye's 1945 application for executive clemency, National Archives, RG 204, stack 230, 40:14:2, box 1583, file 56-386, 12–13.

27. WMM to JHW, July 4, 1922, Wigmore Papers. WMM sent Wigmore more clippings on July 30, 1922, including a *Washington Daily News* clipping dated July 20, 1922.

28. McCoy was born in Troy, New York, on December 8, 1859. He graduated from Harvard in 1882. "In 1904 and 1908 he sat as New Jersey delegate in the National Democratic Conventions, also in many State conventions, before being elected, in 1911, to

the 62d Congress, from the Eighth New Jersey District. Service to the first Wilson Administration brought him into notice, and he was appointed, as Associate Justice, to the Supreme Court of the District of Columbia on October 5, 1914. When Chief Justice Covington resigned, on May 30, 1918, Associate Justice McCoy was promoted," notes John Clagett Proctor in *Washington: Past and Present* (New York: Lewis Historical, 1930), 1:234.

29. The criminal trial record, at least the part that survives, is *United States v. Frye,* National Archives, RG 21, Criminal #38325, box 316, 16W3/08/21/06. So far as I can discover, the transcript of the criminal trial is gone, except for those parts excerpted for the appeal. For the rest of the trial, I have relied on newspaper accounts.

30. Frye himself insisted, on the witness stand, that "not a word of the confession . . . was true." "Frye Convicted of Dr. Brown's Murder," *Washington Tribune,* July 22, 1922. He said that "on the Wednesday following the murder of Dr. Brown, he and Dr. John R. Francis Jr. got into an automobile and went to Southwest Washington, where Francis purchased cocaine and gin" and that Francis, while high on cocaine, "confessed to him that he (Francis) had killed Dr. Brown, giving the details as to how the climax of murder came after a failure to extort money from the slain man through a blackmail threat." From "Convict Slayer of Dr. Brown," *Chicago Defender,* July 29, 1922.

31. Richard V. Mattingly and Lester Wood, Request for Continuance, July 14, 1922, *United States v. Frye,* National Archives, RG 21, Criminal #38325, box 316, 16W3/08/21/06.

32. For Frye's recollection of Watson's illness and death, see Frye's 1945 application for executive clemency, National Archives, RG 204, stack 230, 40:14:2, box 1583, file 56-386, pp. 2–3. On Cox, see pp. 12–13, where Frye writes, "My lawyers Messrs. R.V. Mattingly and Lester Wood attempted several times to have this woman to give them a statement, such efforts met with no results. She was summoned to court as a witness, the Prosecuting Attorney stated that she was a defense witness and my attorneys said, she was a State's witness. I have never been able to learn the cause for her actions."

33. Their story went like this: Frye, having been arrested on the robbery charge, had been tricked into confessing to murder. He had been assured by both a police detective and by John R. Francis that if he said he had killed Brown, the robbery charge would be dropped; the murder charge wouldn't stick (because Frye had an alibi); and Frye would receive a portion of the $1,000 reward. The real murderer, Frye said, was Francis. In July 1922, immediately following Frye's conviction, Francis began pursuing the reward, filing suit with William H. Robinson. against the National Benefit Life Insurance Company and N. Pearl Curtis and Robbie Lofton, Brown's daughters, for the recovery of the reward, which was also claimed by Julian Jackson. See *Curtis v. Francis,* National Archives, RG 21, Equity 40432, and *Curtis, Lofton et al. v. Francis et al.,* box 3060, 16W3/06/27/03. In the fall of 1922, Robinson was convicted of dealing in narcotics. See *United States v. Robinson,* National Archives, RG 21, Criminal #39682, box 329, 16W3/08/22/02.

34. "Dr. Marston made a test of Frye's blood pressure yesterday. Frye stoutly maintains that he is innocent of the crime. While not disclosing the result of the test, Dr. Marston will make a supplementary test if Chief Justice and the jury so request." From "Lie-Detector Verdict Today," *Washington Post,* July 20, 1922. Meanwhile, WMM and several of his students and colleagues held a meeting at American Uni-

versity, where they founded the American Psycho-Legal Society; Marston and Wigmore were to be honorary co-presidents. WMM to JHW, July 30, 1922, and JHW to George Curtis Peck, November 16, 1922, Wigmore Papers.

35. That WMM took the stand, and that the courtroom was standing room only, is reported in "Holds Frye Guilty of Killing Doctor," *Washington Post,* July 21, 1922.

36. *Frye v. United States,* Transcript of Record, taken from the Bill of Exceptions submitted to the court by Mattingly and Wood on September 26, 1922, recording court proceedings during the criminal trial, held July 17–20, 1922, pp. 11–18, National Archives, RG 276, Briefs #3968, box 380, 14E2A/02/05/04.

37. Even McCoy, who was not a scientist, could see the flaws in Marston's methods in the study he'd conducted on convicted criminals in Massachusetts in 1917. In this study, published in Wigmore's *Journal of Criminal Law and Criminology,* WMM reported having conducted deception tests on twenty criminal defendants who had been recommended by the courts for medical and psychological evaluation; in every case, he noted, the judgment made by his blood pressure test, as to the defendants' guilt or innocence, was corroborated by subsequent events. As McCoy saw at a glance, the investigation was wildly unscientific: the cases were handpicked; there was no control group; and the blood pressure test itself might have affected the subsequent events. McCoy, therefore, lectured Mattingly about the scientific method:

> I happened to read one test that was made, and I believe it was stated—I could not make out whether it was when a man was on probation after conviction or on the witness stand before conviction. I could not tell that. He was on probation, and it was claimed that this test had been established either that the man—it must be that the man had lied about his case. The judge did something or other—I don't know what it was—but subsequent to the time the test was made it was found that the man had been guilty of some similar crime. Now, did the judge act upon the test, or did he act upon his additional information as to the perpetration of some other similar crime. As far as that test is concerned, Dr. Marston will admit that it was not scientific as far as his instrument was concerned, because, as he understands, as a scientist, he has to exclude everything except the constants before he can make a deduction. If there are a lot of variables, all he can say is that on the whole this is probably so.

38. "Rely on 'Lie Test' in Appeal," *Washington Post,* July 22, 1922.

39. In closing arguments, Bilbrey said Frye was "the most colossal liar that ever appeared in court"; Mattingly said the prosecution's chief witness, John R. Francis, was "nothing but a slick crook." From "Convict Slayer of Dr. Brown," *Chicago Defender,* July 29, 1922. On the length of the jury's deliberations, see "Holds Frye Guilty of Killing Doctor," *Washington Post,* July 21, 1922. On the sentencing: "Life-Sentence Penalty in Murder of Doctor," *Washington Post,* July 29, 1922.

40. WMM to JHW, July 30, 1922, Wigmore Papers.

41. "Offers New Law Course," *Washington Post,* July 30, 1922. Studying the philosophy of law, however, apparently included conducting lie detector tests on convicts:

> A last effort to win vindication for a crime which he is accused of committing twelve years ago led Dr. E. E. Dudding to undergo the nerve-racking test of

the sphygmomanometer, better known now as the 'lie detector,' last night, in the offices of the American university. The test was administered by Dr. William Marston, professor of legal psychology at the school, and Paul E. Haddick, secretary of the American Psycho-Legal society. Dudding was tried and convicted in February, 1910, of killing his uncle in Huntington, W.Va., following a quarrel growing out of a family feud, being found guilty by a jury of voluntary manslaughter, despite his continued declarations that the killing was done in self-defense. Sentenced to five years in the West Virginia penitentiary for that offense, he went off to prison steadfastly declaring that some day he would win vindication that would make truth prevail. His appearance before Dr. Marston and a corps of university students of psychology twelve years after the alleged crime was committed is the culmination of this fight for vindication. Following the tests, Dr. Marston said that he was convinced that the man was justified in committing the deed—he has never denied that he did the shooting—and that he had just cause for carrying the gun the day of the killing, which was September 6, 1909.

This story describes the test in some detail, provides the questions, too, and concludes: "The test last night, and the subsequent tests which will follow, are almost the direct result of an opinion rendered by Judge McCoy in Criminal court No. 2 about ten days ago in which he refused to allow the sphygmomanometer to be admitted." From "Lie Detector Said to Clear Dudding in Killing of Uncle 12 Years Ago," *Washington Post,* August 2, 1922.

42. Richard V. Mattingly, Transcript, Registrar's Office, American University. Lester Wood, Transcript, Registrar's Office, American University.

43. "Professor Marston is primarily an experimental psychologist, and arrangements have been made to open, at the American University this fall, what will probably be the only psycho-legal research laboratory in the United States." From "William Moulton Marston," *American University Courier,* October 1922.

9. FRYE'D

1. *Frye v. United States,* Brief for the Appellant, Briefs, #3968, National Archives RG 276, box 380, 14E2A/02/05/04. Mattingly and Wood listed eight assignments of errors in the criminal trial as grounds for appeal. Errors 4–8 involved Marston. *Frye v. United States,* Transcript of Record, Assignment of Errors (filed February 8, 1923), pp. 3–4, in National Archives, RG 276, Briefs #3968, box 380, 14E2A/02/05/04.

2. *Frye v. United States,* Brief for Appellee, prepared by Peyton Gordon, U.S. Attorney, and J. H. Bilbrey, Assistant U.S. Attorney, filed November 2, 1923, in National Archives, RG 276, Briefs #3968, box 380, 14E2A/02/05/04, pp. 1–2, 8. Zechariah Chafee, "The Progress of the Law, 1919–1921: Evidence," *Harvard Law Review* 35 (1922): 302–17; the quotations are from p. 309. In Marston's second year of law school, he was a student in Chafee's course on bills of exchange and promissory notes. Chafee began teaching at Harvard Law in 1916. In 1916–17, he taught Bills of Exchange and Promissory Notes, a.k.a., "Bills & Notes." Harvard Law School, *Law School of Harvard University, Announcements 1916–1917* (Cambridge, MA, 1916), 6.

In Bills & Notes, Marston earned a 72. WMM, transcript, Harvard Law School, class of 1918, Harvard Law School Registrar: Student Permanent Record Cards, 1893–1972, Harvard University Archives, call number 14258. As McCormick later pointed out ("Deception-Tests and the Law of Evidence," p. 500 n51), it was likely Chafee's printed remarks that doomed Frye's appeal.

3. *Frye v. United States,* Brief for Appellee, prepared by Peyton Gordon, U.S. Attorney, and J. H. Bilbrey, Assistant U.S. Attorney, filed November 2, 1923, in National Archives, RG 276, Briefs #3968, box 380, 14E2A/02/05/04, pp. 4–5.

4. *Frye v. United States,* 54 App. D.C. 46, 293 F. 1013, 34 A.L.R. 145.

5. "The Frye test has been accepted as the standard in practically all of the courts of this country which have considered the question of the admissibility of new scientific evidence," the Kansas Supreme Court observed in 1979. Quoted in Starrs, "Still-Life," 685.

6. On the leanness of the ruling, see O'Donnell, "Courting Science," 247–52.

7. "Arrest Inventor of Lie Detector," *Boston Daily Globe,* March 7, 1923.

8. "It is alleged that the defendant owes $2125. William M. Marston has been sued for $5000. In an action of contract by Edward Fischer, of Brookline. Papers have been filed by Attorney Edward G. Fischer, 60 Oliver Street, Boston. It is alleged that the defendant owes $3401.31." *Cambridge Chronicle,* January 14, 1922. "William M. Marston has been attached for $500 in an action of contract by Edward G. Fischer, of Brookline. Papers have been filed by Attorney F. L. Fischer, 60 Oliver Street, Boston." *Cambridge Chronicle,* May 6, 1922.

9. *United States v. William M. Marston,* December 1922, an indictment. *United States v. William M. Marston,* report of W. J. Keville, U.S. Marshal, by James M. Cunningham, Deputy; and warrant for the arrest of William M. Marston, both dated February 17, 1923, National Archives, Boston.

10. "Marston, Lie Meter Inventor, Arrested," *Washington Post,* March 6, 1923, and "Arrest Inventor of Lie Detector," *Boston Daily Globe,* March 7, 1923.

11. *United States v. William M. Marston,* indictment for using the mails in a scheme to defraud, December 1, 1922, National Archives, Boston.

12. *United States v. William M. Marston,* indictment for aiding and abetting in the concealment of assets from the trustee in bankruptcy, December 1, 1922, National Archives, Boston. The claimants in the case included a furnace tender who had worked for the Tait-Marston Engineering Company and said Marston owed him $100. Marston, it seemed, left a trail of debts wherever he went. Dateline Washington, DC, March 6:

> Dr. William Moulton Marston Jr., Professor of legal psychology at the American university and inventor of the sphygmomanometer or "lie detector," has made $3,000 bond and will be given a hearing March 16 on a charge he "lied by mail." Dr. Marston was arrested on a warrant charging use of the mail to defraud and was taken before United States Commissioner McDonald, who fixed the date of the hearing. He was indicted last November in Boston on complaint of a number of creditors who charged that as treasurer of the United Dress Goods, Inc. he misrepresented the financial condition of his firm and thus obtained considerable bills from them. Prominent among the complainants are A.D. Juliard & Co. and C. Babsen & Co. of New York. Another is his ex-furnace tender, of Boston, whom it is alleged he owes more than $100.

From "Will Give Hearing to Alleged Mail Defrauder," *Bridgeport Telegram*, March 7, 1923.

13. "William M. Marston, inventor of the 'lie detector,' professor of psychology in the American University at Washington, walked into the office of the United States Marshal in the Federal Building yesterday afternoon and was ushered into Judge Morton's chambers, where he was arraigned." From "Marston Held in $2600 for Trial," *Boston Daily Globe*, March 17, 1923.

14. *United States v. William M. Marston*, Recognizance of Defendant, March 16, 1923, National Archives, Boston.

15. "Hold 'Lie-Finder' Inventor," *Washington Post*, March 17, 1923; "'Lie Detector' Inventor Arraigned," *New York Times*, March 17, 1923; and "Marston Held in $2600 for Trial," *Boston Globe*, March 17, 1923.

16. Hale and Dorr, now WilmerHale, is still at 60 State Street, Boston.

17. American University: Announcement for 1922–1923, Graduate School of Arts and Sciences (Washington, DC: American University, 1922), 11–15.

18. JHW to WMM, November 20, 1923, Wigmore Papers, Northwestern University Archives.

19. Memorandum of Scientific History and Authority of Systolic Blood Pressure Test for Deception, *Frye v. United States*, Briefs, #3968, National Archives RG 276, box 380, 14E2A/02/05/04. The science brief, which had been misfiled, was discovered by O'Donnell, who came across it while searching through other Frye bins at the National Archives ("Courting Science," 264 n731). O'Donnell's discovery of the science brief is invaluable. O'Donnell argues that the science brief, which places Marston's work as just one piece of a larger endeavor—"the brief refocused the debate from the credentials of one scientist, Dr. Marston, to the work of many scientists" (p. 274)—is "telling about the extent to which the new science of experimental psychology was able to conceive of itself as a communal activity" (p. 265). But, having discovered that Marston was arrested for fraud, I believe that the motivation for the brief was to distance the case from Marston, whose widely publicized arrest and arraignment had devastated the prospects for a successful appeal.

20. WMM to JHW, December 31, 1923, Wigmore Papers.

21. Richard W. Hale to the President of American University, November 1, 1924, WMM, Faculty/Staff Personnel Records, American University Archives, American University Library, Washington, DC. By the time Hale wrote this letter, Marston had long since been fired. Hale knew there was no chance Marston would be reappointed; he wrote this letter, he said, simply to set the record straight, requesting that it be placed in Marston's dossier, which it was.

22. The nolle prosequi on the two bills of indictment is dated January 4, 1924.

23. JHW to WMM, January 9 and January 18, 1924, Wigmore Papers. Marston revisited the experiments he had conducted at American University in 1922 in an article he published in *Esquire* in 1937; it was excerpted in *Legal Chatter*. "The startling fact that a jury is never right has been proved beyond doubt by my work in the psycho-legal laboratory. No jury can be right—or anywhere near it—in its total reconstruction of facts." WMM, "Is the Jury Ever Right?" *Legal Chatter* 1 (1937–38): 30–35; quotation is from p. 30. Wigmore's *Principles of Judicial Proof* was, for the most part, forgotten. Apart from Wigmore's own classes at Northwestern and Marston's course in Legal Psychology at American University in 1922, only one other course in the country, offered at a law school in Idaho, seems ever to have used Wigmore's

Principles of Judicial Proof as its textbook. Outside of Northwestern University Law School, where Wigmore himself assigned it, Twining could find only one school, in Idaho, that ever adopted it (Twining, *Theories of Evidence*, 165). EHM, "Tiddly Bits."

24. For Lester Wood and Richard V. Mattingly's admission to the bar, see *Journal of the Supreme Court of the United States* 1923 (June 1924), p. 283. Lester Wood earned a doctorate in civil law from American University's Graduate School of Law and Diplomacy in 1923, having written a thesis about labor law. *The American University Ninth Convocation* (Washington, DC: American University, 1923), 4. Richard Mattingly dropped out. Three years after the appeal ruling, Mattingly left the law altogether. He went to medical school and spent the rest of his life working as a doctor. According to his son, interviewed by O'Donnell in 2003, Mattingly always said he withdrew from the legal profession, in part, because of his regret over the fate of James A. Frye. O'Donnell, "Courting Science," 18 n53.

25. In an unpublished memoir, EHM left out everything that happened between the years 1922 and 1927, never once mentioning Frye, Marston's arrest, or the scandal that ended his academic career. EHM, "Tiddly Bits"; there is a gap between 1922, when WMM began teaching at American University and EHM began working at the Haskins Information Service, and 1927, when, living in New York, she became pregnant.

26. WW comic strip, March 27–31, 1945.

10. HERLAND

1. My account of Olive Byrne's early years is taken chiefly from an unpublished memoir and a series of unpublished family histories she wrote in the 1970s and 1980s: OBR, "Mary Olive Byrne," "Ethel Higgins Byrne, 1883–1955," "310 East Tioga Avenue, Corning, New York," "John Frederick Byrne, 1880–1913," "Michael Hennessey Higgins, 1844–1929," "John Florence Byrne, 1851–1914 (approximately)," "Margaret Donovan Byrne (Gram), 1853–1914," and "John Lucas," all in the possession of BHRM.

2. OBR, "Mary Olive Byrne," 1–2. Ethel Byrne told OBR that it was Jack Byrne who threw her out, into the snow. But according to MSML, it was Ethel Byrne, not Jack Byrne, who tossed baby Olive into the snowbank (a story that must have come from MS, whose relationship with her sister had become strained). MSML, interview with the author, July 9, 2013.

3. OBR, "Mary Olive Byrne," 2.

4. MSML, interview by Jacqueline Van Voris, MS Papers, Smith College, 1977, box 19, folder 7, pp. 53–54.

5. "I do not like secret marriages," MS wrote. "They are so liable to cause comment." MS to Mary B. Higgins, [May?] 12, 1902, in MS, *The Selected Papers of Margaret Sanger*, ed. Esther Katz (Urbana: University of Illinois Press, 2003–10), 1:31. The published papers are in three volumes, hereinafter referred to as *Selected Papers of MS*. The bulk of Sanger's papers are available in three different microfilm collections.

6. MS said, "We have always been very near to each other. She took care of me when my children were born and I took care of her. She is younger than I. We have never been separated except when she was first married. After her husband died she came

home to me to live, and we have been together ever since." Part of Sanger's account here is untrue. Ethel Byrne left her husband in 1906, at which point she lived, on and off, with her sister; her husband didn't die until 1913. "Mrs. Byrne Gets 30-Day Jail Term," *New York Tribune,* January 23, 1917; "Mrs. Byrne Too Weak to Move," *New York Tribune,* January 27, 1917. The definitive biography of MS remains Ellen Chesler, *Woman of Valor: Margaret Sanger and the Birth Control Movement in America* (1992; repr., New York: Simon and Schuster, 2007). But see also David Kennedy, *Birth Control in America: The Career of Margaret Sanger* (New Haven, CT: Yale University Press, 1970), and Jean H. Baker, *Margaret Sanger: A Life of Passion* (New York: Hill and Wang, 2011).

7. OBR, "Ethel Higgins Byrne," 3–5, and OBR, "Mary Olive Byrne," 1.

8. Chesler, *Woman of Valor,* 62, and MS to Lawrence Lader, October 10, 1953, *Selected Papers of MS,* 3:334–35 and 335 n111. No evidence corroborates Ethel Byrne's claim, made later in life, that she tried to regain custody of the children in 1913.

9. OBR, "Ethel Higgins Byrne," 5–6.

10. OBR, "Mary Olive Byrne," 2–3, 6, and OBR, "Ethel Higgins Byrne," 4.

11. On Parker, see *Selected Papers of MS,* 1:104 n18. The apartment on West Fourteenth Street was Sanger's. OBR gives it as her mother and Parker's address in "Ethel Higgins Byrne," 8. She says MS lived there until she married J. Noah Slee, which was in September 1922. And when Sanger and Byrne faced trial in 1917, Byrne was described as living with Sanger at that address. Katz says that Byrne lived with Parker "from the 1910s through the early 1920s" (*Selected Papers of MS,* 1:104 n18). On the dissolution of Sanger's first marriage, see Chesler, *Woman of Valor,* 90–97.

12. On "sexual modernism," see Stansell, *American Moderns,* chapter 7. On sex radicalism and its relationship to both free love and feminism, see Joanne E. Passet, *Sex Radicals and the Quest for Women's Equality* (Urbana: University of Illinois Press, 2003).

13. Sanger considered some of Heterodoxy's priorities, like a woman's right to keep her name after marriage, frivolous. Judith Schwarz, *Radical Feminists of Heterodoxy: Greenwich Village 1912–1940* (Lebanon, NH: New Victoria, 1982), 14, 65. Stansell, *American Moderns,* 80–92.

14. Crystal Eastman (1920), as quoted in Evans, *Born for Liberty,* 168.

15. Lou Rogers, "Lightning Speed Through Life," originally published in the *Nation* in 1926 and reprinted in Elaine Showalter, ed., *These Modern Women: Autobiographical Essays from the Twenties* (New York: Feminist Press, 1978); the quotation is from p. 103. On Roger's anti-war cartoons, see Rachel Lynn Schreiber, "Constructive Images: Gender in the Political Cartoons of the *Masses* (1911–1917)," PhD diss., Johns Hopkins University, 2008, pp. 221–56. And on women as comic strip artists in this period, see Trina Robbins and Catherine Yronwode, *Women and the Comics* ([S.I.]: Eclipse, 1985), 7–18.

16. "Lou Rogers, Cartoonist," *Woman's Journal and Suffrage News* 44 (August 1913): 2. She also held meetings on street corners where she drew cartoons and gave lectures. See "Suffrage Cartoons for Street Crowds," *New York Times,* July 19, 1915. "A Woman Destined to Do Big Things in an Entirely New Field," *Cartoons Magazine* 3 (1913): 76–77; the quotation is from p. 77. Display ad, *New York Evening Post,* February 22, 1914; "Prize for Suffrage Films," *New York Times,* July 2, 1914; and "Cartoon Service by Lou Rogers," *Woman's Journal and Suffrage News,* November 14, 1914, p. 302: "The cartoons furnished by Miss Rogers may be used in newspaper articles,

and on flyers and campaign literature. They make excellent suffrage arguments and are eagerly sought by those who realize the advantage of illustrated propaganda." Alice Sheppard, *Cartooning for Suffrage* (Albuquerque: University of New Mexico Press, 1994), 52, 212; for more on Rogers's cartoons featuring chains, see pp. 32, 34, and 192.

17. Max Eastman, *Child of the Amazons and Other Poems* (New York: Mitchell Kennerley, 1913), 23. Eastman, a prominent advocate of suffrage, was invited to speak at Harvard in 1911: "Woman Suffrage Movement," *Harvard Crimson*, November 2, 1911.

18. Inez Haynes Gillmore, *Angel Island* (1914; repr., New York: New American Library, 1988), with an introduction by Ursula K. Le Guin; quotations are from pp. 61 and 308.

19. Charlotte Perkins Gilman, *Herland* (1915), in *Charlotte Perkins Gilman's Utopian Novels,* edited and with an introduction by Minna Doskow (Madison, NJ: Fairleigh Dickinson University Press, 1999), 205.

20. In the winter of 1914, MS went to see Charlotte Perkins Gilman speak in New York. Sanger was impressed. See MS's diary entry for December 17, 1914, in *Selected Papers of MS*, 1:106; and for her seeing Gilman speak in New York earlier that year, see p. 107.

11. THE WOMAN REBEL

1. The full series of Sanger's essays from the *New York Call* can be found in MS Papers, Collected Document Series, microfilm edition, C16: 24–62; the suppressed article is C16: 59–62. For an excerpt, see MS, "What Every Girl Should Know: Sexual Impulses—Part II," in *Selected Papers of MS*, 1: 41–46.

2. Chesler, *Woman of Valor,* 97–98.

3. MS, "Why the Woman Rebel?" *Woman Rebel,* March 1914, in *Selected Papers of MS*, 1:71.

4. *Selected Papers of MS,* 1:69–74, 41; Linda Gordon, *The Moral Property of Women: A History of Birth Control Politics in America* (Urbana: University of Illinois Press, 2002), 143; James Reed, *From Private Vice to Public Virtue: The Birth Control Movement and American Society Since 1830* (New York: Basic Books, 1978), 70, 73; and MS, *An Autobiography* (New York: Norton, 1938), 89.

5. On Reed's involvement, see Daniel W. Lehman, *John Reed and the Writing of Revolution* (Athens: Ohio University Press, 2002), 19, 61; and see John Reed Papers, Houghton Library, Harvard University, MS Am 1091: 1156. On Ethel Byrne taking care of Sanger's children: family histories suggest that Ethel Byrne, rather than William Sanger, cared for the Sangers' three children when MS left the country. Of Olive Byrne and Stuart and Grant Sanger (MS's sons), Stuart's daughter Nancy said, "They were all the same age and Ethel raised them essentially when Mimi was going off." Nancy Sanger, interview by Jacqueline Van Voris, MS Papers, Smith College, 1977, p. 20.

6. Havelock Ellis, *"The Erotic Rights of Women" and "The Objects of Marriage": Two Essays* (London: Battley Brothers, 1918). And see Baker, *Margaret Sanger,* 92–97.

7. *Selected Papers of MS,* 1:109. On MS's relationship with Ellis, see Chesler, *Woman of Valor,* 111–21.

8. MS, *Family Limitation* (New York: Review, 1914), 1.

9. Quoted in Chesler, *Woman of Valor*, 127.

10. OBR, "Ethel Higgins Byrne," 26–27.

11. Quoted in Chesler, *Woman of Valor*, 139.

12. "Noted Men to Aid Her," *Washington Post*, January 19, 1916; Chesler, *Woman of Valor*, 140.

13. MS, *Autobiography*, 216–17, 219; and see *Birth Control Review*, October 1918.

14. "Birth Controllers Up Early for Trial," *New York Times*, January 5, 1917, and "Mrs. Sanger's Aid Is Found Guilty," *New York Times*, January 9, 1917; Chesler, *Woman of Valor*, 152.

15. The best account is Lunardini, *From Equal Suffrage to Equal Rights*.

16. "Mrs. Byrne Gets 30-Day Jail Term," *New York Tribune*, January 23, 1917.

17. Cott, *Grounding of Modern Feminism*, 25–27.

18. On the extent and intensity of the coverage, see Chesler, *Woman of Valor*, 153–54.

19. Ethel Byrne quoted in MS, *Autobiography*, 227–29.

20. "Will 'Die for the Cause,'" *Boston Daily Globe*, January 24, 1917; "Mrs. Byrne, Sent Back to Prison, Starves On," *New York Tribune*, January 24, 1917; "Mrs. Byrne Fasts in Workhouse Cell," *New York Times*, January 25, 1917; and "Mrs. Byrne Weaker, Still Fasts in Cell," *New York Times*, January 26, 1917.

21. Chesler, *Woman of Valor*, 155; "Mrs. Byrne, Too Weak to Move, Fasts," *New York Tribune*, January 27, 1917; *Selected Papers of MS*, 1:194–5; Reed, *Private Vice, Public Virtue*, 106–7; Gordon, *Moral Property*, 156–57; MS, *Autobiography*, 215–21; and Kennedy, *Birth Control in America*, 82–88.

22. "Mrs. Byrne Sinking Fast, Sister Warns," *New York Tribune*, January 29, 1917. The *Tribune* got Olive's brother's name wrong and also reported that he was a girl. "Two little girls will learn to-day that their mother is in a prison hospital. Olive and Jessie [*sic*] Byrne are waiting for a letter from Mrs. Ethel Byrne. Instead of their mother's telling them that she has an apartment home all ready for them, as she had planned, they will be told of the jail sentence and their mother's refusal to take nourishment."

23. Baker, *Margaret Sanger*, 137–38.

24. OBR, "Mary Olive Byrne," 14–15, and OBR, "My Aunt Margaret," in "Our Margaret Sanger," vol. 2, pp. 236–37, MS Papers, Smith College, box 87.

25. "Mrs. Byrne to Have a Feeding Schedule," *New York Times*, January 29, 1917; "Hunger Strike Woman Passive: Mrs. Ethel Byrne Receives Food," *Boston Daily Globe*, January 29, 1917; "Mrs. Byrne Fed by Tube: Has 2 Meals," *New York Tribune*, January 28, 1917; and MS, *Autobiography*, 228.

26. "For State Inquiry into Birth Control," *New York Times*, February 1, 1917.

27. "Mrs. Byrne Pardoned; Pledged to Obey Law," *New York Times*, February 2, 1917, and "Mrs. Byrne, Set Free by Pardon, Defiant to End," *New York Tribune*, February 2, 1917.

28. Lou Rogers's name begins appearing on the masthead of the *Birth Control Review* in July 1918, with vol. 2, no. 6.

29. MS, *Autobiography*, 231.

30. "Guilty Verdict for Mrs. Sanger," *New York Tribune*, February 3, 1917.

31. MS to Ethel Byrne, February 14 and February 21, 1917, in *Selected Papers of MS*, 1:207, 209.

32. MS to Ethel Byrne, February 14, 1917, in *Selected Papers of MS*, 1: 207.

33. "Mrs. Sanger Is Freed," *Washington Post*, March 7, 1917.

34. Editorial note, *Selected Papers of MS,* 1:194–95. And see, especially, OBR, interview by Jacqueline Van Voris, MS Papers, Smith College, November 25, 1977, box 20, folder 4: "Oh, my mother was always jealous of her. She didn't like being put out of the birth control movement because she figured she was in it as much as Margaret was to begin with" (p. 21). And see OBR, "Ethel Higgins Byrne," 26:

> In the early days of the Birth Control movement they were close and worked hand in hand putting their efforts into establishing the first public clinic. When Ethel went on the famous hunger strike that brought the movement into the national public eye, Margaret promised the judge who presided over the case that her sister would no longer be associated with Birth Control if he would release Ethel from jail. Ethel was furious with that provision and wanted to go on as before. Margaret refused. The former assumed that Margaret was using that excuse to get rid of her, mainly she often asserted, because Margaret had gone 'uptown' with the Movement and had no use for the Village people who started things in the first place. All of this may have been true. The Village people were long on talk and short on cash, and Margaret knew where success came from—money, and the people who have it.

12. WOMAN AND THE NEW RACE

1. See, e.g., the Greenville, Pennsylvania, *Record-Argus,* July 13, 1917; the *Greenville Evening Record,* July 13, 1917; the Connesville, Pennsylvania, *Daily Courier,* June 26, 1917; the *Newark (OH) Advocate,* October 16, 1917; and the *Iola (KS) Register,* June 25, 1918. In OBR, "Mary Olive Byrne," 24, OBR says she wanted to sing in the chorus, but didn't; however, newspaper accounts of the performances suggest that she did.
2. OBR, "Mary Olive Byrne," 22–26, 35.
3. MS, Diary, *Selected Papers of MS,* 1:249–50. Chesler, *Woman of Valor,* 197, argues that Parker began ghostwriting Sanger's books only with *The Pivot of Civilization,* which appeared in 1922, but OBR's remarks during interviews and in her memoirs suggest otherwise. Interviewer: "After the first clinic was closed did she [Ethel] work with the movement at all after that?" OBR: "No, she worked as a nurse and she lived with Robert Allen Parker who wrote Margaret's books: he ghost wrote all her books." From OBR, Van Voris interview, 23. And see OBR, "Ethel Higgins Byrne," 7.
4. OBR, "Ethel Higgins Byrne," 6–8.
5. OBR, Van Voris interview, pp. 7, 21.
6. Havelock Ellis, "The Love Rights of Women," *Birth Control Review* 2 (June 1919): 3–5, with drawings by Lou Rogers.
7. H. G. Wells, *The Secret Places of the Heart* (New York: Macmillan, 1922). On the start of their affair, see Chesler, *Woman of Valor,* 186–92.
8. Gordon, *Moral Property,* 206–8; Chesler, *Woman of Valor,* 238.
9. Chesler, *Woman of Valor,* 192, 198.
10. MS, *Woman and the New Race,* 1–2, 217–18.
11. Gilman quoted in Cott, *Grounding of Modern Feminism,* 37.

12. MS, *Motherhood in Bondage* (New York: Brentano's, 1928), xi.
13. Cover, *Birth Control Review,* November 1923.
14. MS, *Woman and the New Race,* 5, 18, 10–11, 117, 162, 182.
15. Display advertisement, Brentano Books for Autumn, *New York Tribune,* October 17, 1920. Ellis also wrote the book's preface.
16. "A Spy in the Office," *Sensation Comics #3,* March 1942.
17. JHMK, interview with the author, January 12, 2014.

13. THE BOYETTE

1. On the relationship between free love and feminism, see Passet, *Sex Radicals.*
2. OBR, "Ethel Higgins Byrne," 23.
3. OBR, "Mary Olive Byrne," 48. According to the *1921–1922 Tufts College Catalogue,* the first day of regular class exercises in the fall of 1922 was Friday, September 22. On Slee paying for OBR's education: "Uncle Noah (as I called him) financed several young women through college on the basis that his investment be repaid. After finishing at Jackson I began sending him a monthly check. After four such re-payments he cancelled all my obligations." OBR, Van Voris interview, p. 13.
4. "OLIVE ABBOTT BYRNE, A O II. 'Bobby.' New York, NY. B.S. in English. Mount St. Joseph Academy. *Weekly* Staff (1); Class Basketball (1); Chairman Social Committee (1), (2), (3); Assistant Manager Basketball (2); Glee Club (1); Class Play (2); Liberal Club; Junior Prom; Asst. Mgr. Basketball (3)," in *The 1925 Jumbo Book* (Medford, MA: Published by the Senior Class of Tufts College, 1925), 177, Tufts University Archives. Harry Adams Hersey, *A History of Music in Tufts College* (Medford, MA: Tufts College, 1947), 151; "Liberal Club Forms and States Its Aims," *Tufts Weekly,* October 22, 1924, p. 3, Tufts University Archives; and OBR, Van Voris interview, 14–15. "Bobbie Strong" appears in "The Vanishing Mummy," *Wonder Woman #23,* May 1947.
5. OBR, "Mary Olive Byrne," 49–50. Olive Mary Byrne, transcript, Tufts University Archives. Byrne was given an academic warning on November 15, 1922. She was put on probation on December 14, 1922; probation continued in the spring semester of 1923; it expired on May 10, 1923.
6. "Siege of the Rykornians," *Wonder Woman #25,* September–October 1947, and "The Vanishing Mummy," *Wonder Woman #23,* May 1947. Starvard College is introduced in "The Million Dollar Tennis Game," *Sensation Comics #61,* January 1947.
7. "The Greatest Feat of Daring in Human History," *Wonder Woman #1,* Summer 1942.
8. Alpha Omicron Pi photographs in the Tufts University Archives. There are three, all taken in June 1923.
9. OBR, "Mary Olive Byrne," 52, 55.
10. *The 1925 Jumbo Book,* 177, and Olive Mary Byrne, transcript, Tufts University Archives.
11. Quoted in Chesler, *Woman of Valor,* 220.
12. "Liberal Club Officers for Next Year Chosen," *Tufts Weekly,* May 27, 1925, p. 1. Reviewing the activities of the club's first year: "It was also instrumental unofficially in having Miss Margaret Sanger speak within reach of the Hill students." (Tufts's Medford campus is known as the Hill.) "Some of us formed a club called the

Liberal Club. We thought we were very daring, and all the people with liberal ideas joined up. Margaret came to Boston to speak to some woman's group and I went over to see her (she stayed at the Copley), and I said, 'I wish you would come over to school and talk.' She said, 'I will.' She said she was going to be going someplace, and would be back at a certain time if I'd arrange it. Then the college wouldn't let her come there to speak. Undaunted, we searched around and found a Unitarian minister in Somerville who lent us his church." OBR, Van Voris interview, 14–15.

13. Cott, *Grounding of Modern Feminism,* 149–51.
14. OBR, Van Voris interview, 9, 30, 47.
15. "Jumbo Looks Back Again at the Great Class of '26, 25th Reunion," Class material, 1922–27, UA039/Classes, 1858-1997, box 7, folder 6, Tufts University Archives.
16. See Laura Doan, "Passing Fashions: Reading Female Masculinities in the 1920s," *Feminist Studies* 24 (1998): 663–770; the quotation from the *Daily Mail* is from p. 673.
17. Olive Mary Byrne, transcript, Tufts University Archives.

14. THE BABY PARTY

1. Cott, *Grounding of Modern Feminism,* 153–55.
2. WMM, "Sex Characteristics of Systolic Blood Pressure Behavior," *Journal of Experimental Psychology* 6 (1923): 387–419.
3. "On the Hill," *Tufts College Graduate,* September–November 1925, p. 44, Tufts University Archives. The announcement continued: "Much of his time has been spent at Harvard with Münsterberg and Langfeld, his degrees being A.B. in '15, LL.B. in '18, and Ph.D. in '21. He has taught at Radcliffe, and comes to Tufts after working with the National Committee on Mental Hygiene on two surveys, one on The Schools of Staten Island and the other on The Texas Prisons." No mention was made of his professorship at American University.
4. WMM is listed as Assistant Professor of Philosophy and Psychology, living at 440 Newbury Street, Boston, in *Catalogue of Tufts College, 1925–1926* (Medford, MA: Tufts University, 1925), 22. In this catalog, Marston is named as teaching a slew of courses: 16-3, Applied Psychology; 16-4, Applied Psychology; 16-5, Experimental Psychology; 16-6, Abnormal Psychology; 16-7, Comparative Psychology; 16-8, History of Psychology; and 16-9, Seminar in Psychology. He is also said to be co-teaching 16-1, Psychology of Human Behavior (pp. 102–3). Marston is not listed in the *Catalogue of Tufts College, 1925–1926* (Medford, MA: Tufts University, 1925).
5. On the date EHM started at *Child Study,* see, in EHM's alumni files, a clipping dated April 1926, Mount Holyoke College Archives. The first issue of the first volume of *Federation for Child Study Bulletin* appeared in January 1924 (the journal's name was abbreviated to *Child Study* in February 1925, with vol. 2, no. 3). "Elizabeth H. Marston" is listed as managing editor on the masthead of *Child Study* through the end of volume 3. Josette Frank's name appears as an editor beginning in March 1924 (1:4). "Elizabeth H. Marston" is first listed among the journal's editors (not as managing editor but as editor) in January 1926 (3:1); this continued for February 1926 (3:2), and March 1926 (3:3). She is listed as managing editor in April 1926 (3:4), and May 1926 (3:5). And then she disappears. Josette Frank has returned as an editor

by October 1926, by which time EHM is no longer working for the magazine. It may be that Marston and Frank were not compatible. On Josette Frank, see also "Josette Frank, 96, Dies; Children's Book Expert," *New York Times,* September 14, 1989. The Children's Book Award, founded in 1943, was renamed the Josette Frank Award in 1997, in her honor.

6. On the parent-education movement, see Jill Lepore, "Confessions of an Amateur Mother," in *The Mansion of Happiness,* chapter 7. And see Cott, *Grounding of Modern Feminism,* 167–71.

7. Faderman, *Odd Girls and Twilight Lovers,* 63–67.

8. "The Fun Foundation," *Sensation Comics #27,* March 1944.

9. "The Malice of the Green Imps," *Sensation Comics #28,* April 1944.

10. OBR, transcript, Tufts University Archives. These are the courses Olive Byrne took with Marston during her senior year: Applied Psychology: "A continuation of 16-3, with special emphasis upon vocational guidance and mental health problems. Prerequisite, 16-3"; Experimental Psychology: "An introductory course in methods of experimentation upon human subjects. Each student will act, in turn, as experimenter and subject, investigating vision, audition, temperature, pressure and other sensations of the human body. Brief experimental studies of higher thought processes such as memory, association, and imagination will also be undertaken"; Abnormal Psychology: "A study of the chief types of mental deficiency, with special reference to social maladjustment"; Seminar in Psychology: "Advanced work, theoretical or experimental, especially for graduate students. Individual experimental problems will be assigned to students who have satisfactorily passed in 16-5. Prerequisite, except by special permission, 12 credits in psychology." (Olive Byrne did not have twelve credits in psychology.)

11. WMM, *Emotions of Normal People* (London: K. Paul, Trench, Trubner; New York: Harcourt, Brace, 1928), 113–15, 249.

12. Ibid., 107–9, 299–301.

13. Ibid., 300.

14. Ibid., 299.

15. Seventieth Annual Commencement of Tufts College, June 14, 1926 (Medford, MA: Tufts University, 1926).

16. MSML, interview with the author, July 9, 2013.

15. HAPPINESS IN MARRIAGE

1. Years later, OBR was asked in an interview, "What happened to your medical training? You were going to college and thought of going to medical school." "I got diverted," she said. "I went into psychology instead." OBR, Van Voris interview, p. 29.

2. OBR to J. Noah Slee, September 5, 1926, MS Papers, Smith College, box 33, folder 4.

3. "The Brand of Madness," *Sensation Comics #52,* April 1946.

4. OBR to J. Noah Slee, September 18 and September 5, 1926, MS Papers, Smith College, box 33, folder 4.

5. Sheldon Mayer, 1975 DC Convention: Wonder Woman Panel, transcript in the DC Comics Archives.

6. MSML, interview with the author, July 9, 2013.

7. EHM to BHRM and Donn Marston, March 14, 1963, in the possession of BHRM.

8. BHRM, e-mail to the author, June 18, 2013. BHRM, interview with the author, July 14, 2013. Carolyn Marston was married to Robert J. Keatley; they are listed as living in Boston in the 1930 and 1940 U.S. censuses. In 1930, Robert Keatley was still living and the two of them are listed as living together, with no other occupants. United States of America, Bureau of the Census, *Fifteenth Census of the United States, 1930* (Washington, DC: National Archives and Records Administration, 1930), as made available by Ancestry.com, *1930 United States Federal Census* (Provo, UT: Ancestry .com, 2002). In 1940, Carolyn Marston Keatley was sixty-eight and listed as the head of the household at 166 Pilgrim Road, Boston, a property she rented; presumably her husband had died. She was still working full-time at the hospital. She was living with a sixty-five-year-old woman named Anne Shea. United States of America, Bureau of the Census, *Sixteenth Census of the United States, 1940* (Washington, DC: National Archives and Records Administration, 1940), as made available by Ancestry .com. *1940 United States Federal Census* (Provo, UT: Ancestry.com, 2012).

9. Keatley's copy of Levi Dowling, *The Aquarian Gospel of Jesus the Christ* (1907; repr., Los Angeles, 1928), marked, "Return to Mrs. Carolyn Marston Keatley," is in the possession of MM.

10. "Wonder Woman: The Message of Love Binding," typescript, dated April 5, 1943, but containing notes with dates given, in handwriting, from 1925 to 1926. This ninety-five-page, single-spaced document appears to have been typed by MWH in around 1970, from notes taken at meetings held in 1925 and 1926. Meeting dates are added in pencil; apparently, the group met on October 26, November 15, 18, 20, and December 13 and 17 in 1925, and on January 7, 17, 24, 28; February 14, 18, 21; March 1, 14, 16, 21; April 4; and May 9 and 26 in 1926. The typescript is unpaginated but divided into sections with titles like "What Is Wisdom?," "Messengership," "Love and Love Organs," "Dominance and Submission," "Adaptation," "The Difference Between Love Submission and Force Submission," "The Way in Which Love Binds Force or Power Under the Operation of the Divine or Eternal Love Law," and "Creation." I believe this manuscript is the document EHM refers to in a letter to Donn Marston and BHRM in 1963, in which she says everything is explained in a box of documents stored in a closet of Huntley's home in Charlestown, Rhode Island. O.A.'s daughter, Sue Grupposo, believes that Huntley destroyed this box. Grupposo told me, "Yaya had, in Charlestown, in the upstairs closet, in a hallway, a whole treasure. On a rainy day, we'd go visit and look at everything. . . . It was a lot of things of a spiritual nature, the spiritual stuff they were discussing. Much of it was based on *Emotions of Normal People*. She would have burned that box. 'The world isn't ready for this, and I have to destroy it,' she told me." Sue Grupposo, interview with the author, July 15, 2013. But I believe the ninety-five-page typescript of notes taken during the meetings in 1925 and 1926 may be from that box. A photocopy of the typescript is housed at the DC Comics Archives.

11. MWH to JE, Steinem Papers, Smith College, box 213, folder 5.

12. "Mystery of the Crimson Flame," *Comic Cavalcade #5,* Winter 1943. In another story, Wonder Woman destroys a "fiendish cult" led by a "purple priestess" who is duping women. Cries the priestess, "She has ruined my racket now, but someday I shall have my revenge!" From "The Judgment of Goddess Vultura," *Wonder Woman #25,* September–October 1947.

13. EHM to BHRM and Donn Marston, March 21, 1963, in the possession of BHRM. I

have wondered whether, when EHM said, in 1963, that the meetings in 1925 and 1926 were held at the apartment of Aunt Carolyn—Marston's father's sister—whether she was misremembering and that she in fact meant Aunt Claribel—Marston's mother's sister, who is listed among the five women to whom Marston dedicated *Emotions of Normal People*. There seems no way to be certain. As for her family arrangements: "The answers to all these relationships can be expressed mathematically," she wrote. "No mysteries, no fairy tales, just exact science." EHM to BHRM and Donn Marston, March 15, 1963, in the possession of BHRM.

14. BHRM, interview with the author, July 14, 2013.
15. MS, *Happiness in Marriage* (1926; repr., New York: Brentano's, 1928), chapter 7, pp. 123, 112.
16. EHM to BHRM and Donn Marston, March 14, 1963, in the possession of BHRM.
17. EHM to BHRM and Donn Marston, March 15, 1963, in the possession of BHRM. The tradition, in the Sanger family, of calling MS "Mimi" came from the grandchildren, to whom she used to say, "Come to me, come to me" (Chesler, *Woman of Valor,* 403).
18. Cott, *Grounding of Modern Feminism,* 181.
19. Eastman is quoted in a collection of *Nation* autobiographies called *These Modern Women: Autobiographical Essays from the Twenties,* edited and with an introduction by Elaine Showalter (Westbury, NY: Feminist Press, 1978), 5.
20. Helen Glynn Tyson, "The Professional Woman's Baby," *New Republic,* April 7, 1926, pp. 190–92.
21. Alice Beal Parsons, *Woman's Dilemma* (New York: Thomas Y. Crowell, 1926), iv, 247.
22. Suzanne La Follette, *Concerning Women* (New York: Albert and Charles Boni, 1926), quotation on p. 305. And see Cott, *Grounding of Modern Feminism,* 191–92.
23. Virginia MacMakin Collier, *Marriage and Careers: A Study of One Hundred Women Who Are Wives, Mothers, Homemakers and Professional Workers* (New York: Channel Bookshop, 1926), 9–10, 113. For an analysis of Collier's findings, with remarks about the strangeness of her sample, see Cott, *Grounding of Modern Feminism,* 196–97.
24. On the division of labor, see MSML, interview with the author, July 9, 2013.

16. THE EMOTIONS OF NORMAL PEOPLE

1. "I had the work all done for the Ph.D. but I never got the thesis written." OBR, Van Voris interview, p. 29.
2. OBR to J. Noah Slee, September 18, 1926, MS Papers, Smith College, box 33, folder 4.
3. OBR, "The Evolution of the Theory and Research on Emotions," MA Thesis, Columbia University, 1927, Columbia University Archives.
4. WMM's appointment as a lecturer in psychology began on July 1, 1927; he was appointed to teach at the university extension on November 7, 1927. His term expired on June 30, 1928. According to WMM, Appointment Record, box 38. A separate document, WMM, Nomination for Appointment, is dated July 26, 1927. Marston is listed as succeeding Harold E. Jones, at an annual salary of $2,000. His address is noted as 88 Morningside Drive. A. T. Poffenberger is named as hiring him, in his capacity as "Executive Officer of Department."
5. Robert S. Woodworth, *The Columbia University Psychological Laboratory: A Fifty-*

Year Retrospective (New York: Columbia University, 1942), in Historical Subject Files, box 46, folder 7, Department of Psychology, Columbia University Archives.

6. Cott, *Grounding of Modern Feminism*, 219.

7. Emilie Hutchinson, *Women and the Ph.D.* (Greensboro, NC: Institute of Professional Relations, 1929), 101, as quoted in Cott, *Grounding of Modern Feminism*, 227. For an assessment of the situation today, see Mary Ann Mason et al., *Do Babies Matter? Gender and Family in the Ivory Tower* (New Brunswick, NJ: Rutgers University Press, 2013).

8. Olive Byrne completed thirty-one credits in 1926–27 and twenty more in 1927–28, for a total of fifty-one. The PhD required sixty credits. Olive Byrne, Transcript, 1926–28, Registrar's Office, Columbia University. My thanks to Byrne Marston for permission to view his mother's transcript.

9. EHM, "Tiddly Bits."

10. The best brief account of the fourteenth edition is Harvey Einbinder, *The Myth of the Britannica* (New York: Grove, 1964), 52–53: "The *Encyclopaedia* lost much of its British character, since the fourteenth edition was freed of the restraining influence of the *Times*. This change was accentuated when separate editorial offices were established in London and New York. The new American influence was evident: nearly half of its 3,500 contributors were Americans—in contrast to the eleventh edition, whose 1,500 contributors had included only 123 Americans." See also Herman Kogan, *The Great EB: The Story of the Encyclopaedia Britannica* (Chicago: University of Chicago Press, 1958), chapter 18.

11. P. W. Wilson, "This Era of Change," in *The New Britannica, 14th Edition* (New York: Encyclopaedia Britannica, 1929), 5–6, and back page. Wilson was a critic for the *New York Times Book Review*.

12. EHM, "Tiddly Bits."

13. Molly Rhodes, "Wonder Women and Her Disciplinary Powers: The Queer Intersection of Scientific Authority and Mass Culture," in *Doing Science + Culture*, ed. Roddey Reid and Sharon Traweek (New York: Routledge, 2000), 102.

14. WMM, *Emotions of Normal People*, 389–91; emphasis mine.

15. OBR, review of *Emotions of Normal People*, by WMM, *Journal of Abnormal and Social Psychology* 24 (April 1929): 135–38.

16. WMM, C. Daly King, and EHM, *Integrative Psychology: A Study of Unit Response* (London: K. Paul, Trench, Trubner; New York, Harcourt, Brace, 1931).

17. E.g., WMM to Boring, April 2, 1928. EHM had her own secretary, as per "EHM/DIG," in, e.g., EHM to Boring, April 3, 1928, Edward Garrigues Boring Papers, Harvard University Archives, Correspondence, 1919–1969, box 39, folder 845, HUG 4229.5.

18. WMM to Edwin G. Boring, March 18, 1928, Boring Papers.

19. EHM's correspondence with Boring, which begins on November 30, 1927, and ends on September 22, 1928, is considerable. They exchanged dozens of letters; all of it can be found in the Boring Papers. EHM often mentions Pitkin in the correspondence. Boring contributed dozens of entries, but he also helped EHM identify possible contributors—e.g.: "I am stumped on two points. Who can I get to write the article on the PSYCHOLOGY OF SALESMANSHIP, and who should write SEX DIFFERENCES?" EHM to Edwin G. Boring, January 19, 1928. Only a very small part of the correspondence mentions WMM, and then only jokingly—e.g.: "P.S. Is your husband going to put the blond and brunette follies into the Britannica?" Edwin G.

Boring to EHM, February 2, 1928, Boring Papers. Marston's experiments with blondes and brunettes were conducted in January 1928, at the Embassy Theatre in New York, as described in the next chapter.

20. EHM to Boring, June 20, 1928, this letter from Darien, CT, Boring Papers.

21. WMM, "Emotions, Analysis of," *Encyclopaedia Britannica* (New York, 1929), 8:399–400. This entry on the analysis of emotions remained in the *Encyclopaedia Britannica* into the 1950s. Marston's name also appears as the author of the entries for Anger, Antipathy, Blood Pressure, Defence Mechanisms, and Synapse. EHM contributed the entry for Conditioned Reflex (6:221–22). Britannica.com Customer Service, e-mail to the author, June 18, 2013.

22. Boring also recommended Marston for a position teaching at the New Jersey School of Law (now Rutgers School of Law) in Newark. Marston did not get the job. Edwin G. Boring to WMM, March 22, 1928; WMM to Boring, April 2, 1928; and Boring to WMM, April 3, 1928, Boring Papers.

23. WMM, New York (Columbia) to the Harvard Appointments Bureau, April 2, 1928. WMM, Registration Form, April 14, 1928, Harvard Appointments Bureau, WMM Undergraduate File, Harvard University Archives, UAIII 15.88.10. On his registration form he says that he is a "university and consulting psychologist," that he smokes but doesn't drink often, that he is six feet tall and weighs 220 pounds, and that he plays tennis and football and swims. As far as college work, he also lists "Personality clinics for emotional readjustment of students." His list of references includes E. G. Boring, R. B. Perry, and L. T. Troland. For his vitae he lists "Psychology Assistant, Radcliffe, 1915; Professor of Legal Psychology, American University 1922–23; Assistant Professor of Philosophy and Psychology (in charge of psychology), Tufts College, 1925–26; Lecturer, Columbia University and N.Y. University, in Psychology, 1927 to date." For non-Harvard references he lists Professor A. T. Poffenberger, Columbia; Professor Sidney Langfeld, Princeton; and Professor E. S. Thorndike, Columbia.

24. A. T. Poffenberger (Columbia) to the Harvard Appointments Bureau, April 23, 1928.

25. Troland graduated from Malden High School in 1907, four years before Marston. Leonard T. Troland, Application for Admission to the Graduate School of Arts and Sciences, Harvard University, January 14, 1913, Harvard University Archives, UAV 161.201.10, box 107, HAoWKo. "Troland agrees to do his shorts on condition that he does the long article on psychophysiological opticks." From Boring to EHM, February 16, 1928; on the entry for the color black, see Boring to EHM, April 16, 1928, Boring Papers.

26. L. T. Troland (Harvard, Emerson Hall) to the Harvard Appointments Bureau, April 23, 1928.

27. E. G. Boring (Harvard, Emerson Hall) to the Harvard Appointments Bureau, April 23, 1928.

28. E. S. Thorndike (Columbia) to the Harvard Appointments Bureau, April 23, 1928.

29. Herbert S. Langfeld (Princeton) to the Harvard Appointments Bureau, April 23, 1928.

30. That MWH brought EHM to the hospital is recorded in a caption under a photograph in an album owned by MM. EHM wrote, "The rose covered cottage in Darien Conn where Pete was almost born but Zaz got me to New York on time."

31. "I quit on Tuesday," Holloway later wrote. "The baby was born on Friday at the

Lenox Hill Hospital in Manhattan. I was thirty-five years old." EHM, "Tiddly Bits."
See also Edwin G. Boring to EHM, September 22, 1928: "I write to congratulate you
on the advent of young Moulton, and to say that you are quite a sport to keep on
with your job as you did and then run off to New York to meet him." Boring Papers.

32. "I am commuting to New York and expect to keep on the job until the first of August
when I'll take a month off," she wrote to Boring from Darien on June 20, 1928.
EHM's last letter to Boring from the New York office is dated August 21, 1928. In it,
she directs him to send his remaining articles directly to her boss, Walter Pitkin.

33. EHM, Alumnae Association of Mount Holyoke College, Biographical Questionnaire,
June 13, 1960, Mount Holyoke College Archives.

34. OBR to J. Noah Slee, November 27, 1928, MS Papers, Smith College, box 33, folder 4.

17. THE CHARLATAN

1. [Carl Laemmle], "Watch This Column," *Saturday Evening Post,* July 21, 1928.

2. On Laemmle, see John Drinkwater, *The Life and Adventures of Carl Laemmle* (London: Windmill, 1931), and "Carl Laemmle Sr., Film Pioneer, Dies," *New York Times,* September 25, 1939.

3. "Carl Laemmle Digs the 'Doc,'" *Variety,* December 26, 1928.

4. "Brunettes More Emotional Than Blondes, Movie Experiments Prove," *Daily Boston Globe,* January 31, 1928.

5. "Proves Brunettes More Emotional Than Blondes," *Wisconsin Rapids Daily Tribune,* January 31, 1928.

6. A sample of the papers in which the story appeared: the *Kingsport (TN) Times,* January 27, 1928; the Danville, Virginia, *Bee,* January 28, 1928; the Helena, Montana, *Independent,* January 28, 1928; the *Newark (OH) Advocate,* January 31, 1928; the *Oelwein (IA) Daily Register,* January 31, 1928; the *Iowa (KS) Daily Register,* January 31, 1928; the *Olean (NY) Times,* January 31, 1928; the *Lowell (MA) Sun,* January 31, 1928; the *Lancaster (OH) Daily Eagle,* January 31, 1928; the Ironwood, Michigan, *Daily Globe,* January 31, 1928; the *Tipton (IN) Tribune,* January 31, 1928; the *Lebanon (PA) Daily News,* February 1, 1928; the *Edwardsville (IL) Intelligencer,* February 2, 1928; the *Port Arthur (TX) News,* February 4, 1928; the *Oakland (CA) Tribune,* February 6, 1928; the *Billings (MT) Gazette,* February 9, 1928; and the *Hamburg (IA) Reporter,* February 9, 1928. "Measure for Love," newsreel, 1928. A similar experiment was featured in another newsreel, "Preferred by Gentlemen," in 1931. Both newsreels are available at F.I.L.M. Archives, Inc., New York.

7. A useful biographical treatment is "Man Who Wrote 'Life Begins at 40' Dies at 74," *New York Herald Tribune,* January 26, 1953. Also useful is a profile of Pitkin written by Marston: WMM, "Energizer of the Aged," *Esquire,* August 1936, 66, 158, 161.

8. Byrne Marston believes Pitkin may have attended the meetings at Carolyn Marston Keatley's apartment in Boston. BHRM, interview with the author, July 14, 2013.

9. Walter B. Pitkin, *On My Own* (New York: Charles Scribner's Sons, 1944), 505.

10. Dorothy E. Deitsch, "Age and Sex Differences in Immediate and Delayed Recall for Motion Pictures," MA thesis, Columbia University, 1927.

11. Nicholas Murray Butler to Robert S. Woodworth, September 25, 1929: "I am for-

warding a self-explanatory letter from Mr. Will H. Hays." Central Files, 1895–1971, Office of the President, Columbia University, box 341, folder 17, Robert Sessions Woodworth.

12. John N. Howard, "Profile in Optics: Leonard Thompson Troland," *Optics Info Base,* June 2008, 20–21.

13. Carl Laemmle, "Watch This Column," *Saturday Evening Post,* February 9, 1929. "Possibly you will recall that several months ago I appealed, through this column, for America's most practical psychologist to assist UNIVERSAL in choosing the stories most apt to appeal to the general public. After months of patient search and the reading of hundreds of letters, <u>I have at last found the man</u>. He is no less than Dr. W. M. Marston, the eminent Doctor of Psychology of both Columbia and New York Universities, who is now under an indefinite contract to Universal with the title of Director of Public Service. His coming to our California Studios will mark a new and greater era in Universal Pictures and I hope you will watch them from now on." And see "Carl Laemmle Digs the Doc," *Variety,* December 26, 1928.

14. "Movie Psychology Dooms Cave Man: It's Jung Woman's Fancy That Turns to Love, Dr. Marston Avers," *New York Evening Post,* December 28, 1928.

15. Although WMM always listed NYU as a place where he had taught, his teaching there was quite limited; he appears to have been an adjunct, listed in the 1927–28 course catalog as an "instructor." Erin Shaw, NYU Archives, e-mail to the author, March 20, 2013.

16. Henry W. Levy, "Professor to Cure Scenarios with Wrong Emotional Content: Dabbled in Movies While at Harvard; Now Sought by Hollywood with Offer of Favorable Contract," *New York University Daily News,* January 8, 1929.

17. EHM, "Tiddly Bits."

18. Ibid.

19. "Noted Psychologist Employed to Improve Moving Pictures," *Universal Weekly,* January 5, 1929. "Carl Laemmle Digs the 'Doc,'" *Variety,* December 26, 1928.

20. Display ad for *The Man Who Laughs,* Universal Pictures, *Variety,* January 16, 1929; display ad for *The Man Who Laughs, Variety,* January 2, 1929; "Film Psychology," *Times of India,* February 22, 1929.

21. WMM relates this experiment in Walter B. Pitkin and WMM, *The Art of Sound Pictures,* with an introduction by Jesse L. Lasky (New York: D. Appleton, 1930), 154–55.

22. Esther L. Cottingham, "Dr. Marston Applies Psychology of Human Emotion to Films," *Hollywood Daily Screen World,* March 2, 1929.

23. Pitkin, *On My Own,* 504.

24. WMM, "Energizer of the Aged," *Esquire,* August 1936, 161.

25. Pitkin and WMM, *Art of Sound Pictures.* Although 1930 is given as the imprint date, the book was released in November 1929.

26. Pitkin and WMM, *Art of Sound Pictures,* vi.

27. Ibid., 127, 160–61.

28. Pitkin wrote a long chapter called "Your Story"—a reprise of his earlier book, *How to Write Stories,* adapted for sound pictures; Marston wrote a long chapter called "Feelings and Emotions," a reprise of his theory of domination, submission, inducement, and captivation, largely taken from *Emotions of Normal People.* Pitkin and WMM, *Art of Sound Pictures,* 53, 72–73, 79.

29. "New Books," *New York Times,* January 26, 1930; "Books and Authors," *New York*

Times, November 3, 1929. "Hollywood was dizzy," Pitkin explained. "We did publish the first book on talkie technique. But we would have gained much by having deferred it a full year." Pitkin, *On My Own,* 509.

30. Photographs of WMM testing audiences watching the rushes of *Dr. Jekyll and Mr. Hyde* are in the possession of MM.

31. Pitkin, *On My Own,* 506.

32. *The Charlatan* is the film Marston is on the set of, in the publicity shots I found in the Marston family photo albums. Many thanks to Josh Siegel for identifying this film from the still photograph. Regarding *Show Boat:* WMM himself said, "I went to Hollywood as personal adviser to the late Carl Laemmle in the production of motion pictures and was called upon to do everything I knew nothing about, from raising three million dollars to putting new music in 'Show Boat.' But I did have some congenial duties also, buying and supervising adaptation of stories for picture production, trying to out-guess the state censors as representative of the Hays organization in cutting pictures on the Universal lot and some work with color photography." Harvard College, *Class of 1915 25th Anniversary Report,* 481.

33. The work of Larson and Keeler is excellently chronicled and analyzed in Alder, *Lie Detectors.*

34. WMM, "Energizer of the Aged," *Esquire,* August 1936, 158.

35. Walter B. Pitkin, undated memo, c. 1929, in the possession of John Pitkin, Walter B. Pitkin's grandson. Many thanks to John Pitkin for sharing this and other material with me.

36. George W. Stuart to Walter B. Pitkin, October 10, 1929, in the possession of John Pitkin. Quite when the company folded I have been unable to determine. It appears to have still been in business in December 1929, at least according to a press release plainly written by Marston, "Dr. William Marston Becomes Vice President of Equitable," *Exhibitors Daily Review and Motion Pictures Today,* December 18, 1929:

> George W. Stuart, president of the Equitable Pictures Corporation, newly formed production organization which will make pictures for distribution by the Motion Picture Congress of America, Inc., announces the selection of Dr. William M. Marston, eminent expert on emotions and the country's leading authority on "what the public wants," as vice-president of Equitable. . . . Dr. Marston is the best known psychologist in the country. For the past several years, he has applied his analytical prowess to motion pictures and to the reactions, likes and dislikes of motion picture audiences. His production and studio experience include long terms with M-G-M and Universal. During his stay at the Universal studios, he was general consultant on stories, casts and picture values. Among his outstanding achievements while with M-G-M was the celebrated "blonde-brunette" love emotions test held at the Embassy Theatre in New York and which was a newspaper sensation. Dr. Marston gave up the post of lecturer on psychology at Columbia and New York Universities to devote his time to motion pictures. Prior to his lecture work at these two universities, he put in a number of years in government and academic psychoanalysis. He attracted country wide attention as the originator and developer of the now famous "lie detector," a systolic blood pressure deceptive test which he evolved in the Harvard Psychological Laboratory while working together with Dr. Hugo Munsterberg.

18. VENUS WITH US

1. OBR noted the date of her wedding in a Tufts tenth class reunion publication in which she provided an important summary of her career: "OLIVE BYRNE (Mrs. William Richard), Rye, New York (P.O. Box 32, Harrison, N.Y.) In 1927 received an M.A. at Columbia and during the next year worked for a Ph.D. With Universal Studios, Hollywood, during 1929 and then back at Columbia until 1931. From then to 1935 in New York and later in Boston, but back to New York in 1935 and began writing. Staff writer, Family Circle Magazine. Married William Richard November 21, 1928, and has two children, Byrne, born January 12, 1931, and Donn, born September 20, 1932." In "Facts and Fancies of the Class of 1926, Compiled for the Tenth Reunion, June 11, 12, 13, 14, 1936," n.p., Class material, 1922–27, UA039/Classes, 1858–1997, box 7, folder 6, Tufts University Archives. OBR sometimes gave William Richard a middle initial: K. See "OLIVE BYRNE (Mrs. William Richard), 81 Oakland Beach Avenue, Rye, N.Y. Jackson [Tufts's women's college], B.S. English. Columbia University M.A. 1927. Married William K. Richard 1928 now deceased. Has two sons, Byrne Holloway, 20, Harvard '51, and Donn William, 18, Harvard '54. Assistant to Dr. W. M. Marston until his death in 1947, and writes articles for trade papers, etc. Member of Woman's Club of Rye and Coveleigh Club of Rye. Hobby: art." In "Jumbo Looks Back Again at the Great Class of 26, 25th Reunion," Class material, 1922–27, UA039/Classes, 1858–1997, box 7, folder 6, Tufts University Archives.
2. BHRM, "Memories of an Unusual Father," 7.
3. Diary of OBR, entries for November 21 1936, and November 21, 1937, in the possession of BHRM.
4. WMM to Helen M. Voorhees, December 6, 1928 (on Columbia University Department of Psychology letterhead), Mount Holyoke College Archives.
5. WMM, Class Note, *Harvard College Class of 1915: Fifteenth Anniversary Report* (Cambridge, MA: Printed for the Class, 1930), 143–44.
6. United States of America, Bureau of the Census, *Fifteenth Census of the United States, 1930* (Washington, DC: National Archives and Records Administration, 1930), as made available by Ancestry.com, *1930 United States Federal Census* (Provo, UT: Ancestry.com, 2002).
7. In 1939, she was living in Waltham, Massachusetts, at 475 Trapelo Road, and working as a senior library assistant at the Metropolitan State Hospital in Waltham. *U.S. City Directories, 1821–1989* (Provo, UT: Ancestry.com, 2011). In 1941, she was a librarian at the Metropolitan Hospital, New York; that affiliation is given in a newspaper account of a meeting of the American Librarian Association: "Says U.S. History Backs F.D.R.," *New York Times*, June 24, 1941.
8. OBR, Record of Byrne Holloway Richard, notebook, in the possession of BHRM. He was born at the Polyclinic Hospital in Manhattan.
9. Diary of OBR, in the possession of BHRM. In the diaries, OBR referred to EHM as "SM," presumably for "Sadie Marston."
10. Mary Ross, quoted in Chesler, *Woman of Valor*, 314; *New York Herald Tribune*, November 13, 1931, as quoted ibid., 7. MS, *My Fight for Birth Control* (New York: Farrar and Rinehart, 1931); Chesler, *Woman of Valor*, 329.
11. "Hot Babies, Those Co-Eds," *New York Graphic*, November 17, 1931. The article refers to WMM as a visiting professor at Long Island University.

12. WMM, *Harvard College Class of 1915, Twenty-fifth Reunion Report* (Cambridge: Cosmos, 1940), 480–82.

13. WMM, *Venus with Us: A Tale of the Caesar* (New York: Sears, 1932), 4, 20–22, 35, 56, 58, 69, 111–14, 124, 175. On the publication date, see "Books Schedule to Appear During the Summer Months," *New York Times*, June 19, 1932, and display advertisement, *New York Times*, July 24, 1932.

14. The *Boston Globe* called it a curious demonstration of Julius Caesar's contention that while men wage wars, women control the world. A critic for the *Chicago Tribune* praised the book but chastised it for its anachronism: "William M. Marston all but puts his characters in modern dress. They speak in the current slang, they have a sophistication that is indeed familiar to modern ears and eyes and they, for the most part, in action and psychology, bear a definite contemporary stamp." "Critics Acclaim First Novel by Author of 25," *Chicago Daily Tribune*, August 5, 1932. Elisabeth Poe, "The New Books and Their Authors," *Washington Post*, July 31, 1932. "Tense and Thrilling Is This Detective Story," *Daily Boston Globe*, July 30, 1932.

19. FICTION HOUSE

1. James R. McCarthy, "First Full Facts About the Astounding Plague of Organized Kidnappings," *Atlanta Constitution*, June 5, 1932; WMM, *Lie Detector Test*, 81.

2. BHRM, "Memories of an Unusual Father," 7, 15; MM, interview with the author, July 25, 2012. EHM explained her own name this way: "One of the children at age two could not pronounce a pet name Bill used to call me. The little boy said 'Keetsie,' which old and young picked up but shortened it to Keets. Actually, some of the young do not know I have any other names." EHM to Caroline Becker (Alumnae Office), February 26, 1987, EHM Alumnae file, Mount Auburn College Archives.

3. "The Sphinx Speaks of the Class of 1915, Mount Holyoke College: A Biographical History . . . for our Thirty-second Reunion, June 1947" (South Hadley, MA: Mount Holyoke College, 1947), n.p.

4. WMM, *Harvard College Class of 1915, Twenty-fifth Reunion Report*, 480–82.

5. BHRM, "Memories of an Unusual Father," 8.

6. Ibid., 23, 14–15, 13–14.

7. Jack Byrne is listed as editor of *Action Stories*, 271 Madison Avenue, New York, as early as 1927. See the entry for *Action Stories* in William B. McCourties, *Where and How to Sell Manuscripts: A Director for Writers* (5th ed., Springfield, MA: Home Correspondence School, 1927), 8.

8. BHRM, interview with the author, July 14, 2013; adoption record of Byrne Holloway Richard Marston, February 2, 1935, Essex County Probate Court, Commonwealth of Massachusetts, a copy in the possession of BHRM.

9. OBR to MS, August 1935, MS Papers, Library of Congress, microfilm edition, Loo6: 0946. Sanger knew about Olive's affair with Marston. "It didn't bother her," her granddaughter later said. "My Lord, she had so many affairs in her life; Olive's affairs did not trouble her." MSML, interview with the author, July 9, 2013. And Olive and the children visited often; see, e.g., MS to OBR, May 11, 1936, Library of Congress, microfilm edition, Loo6: 0952: "I would love to see you. Why not bring

both children for a week-end soon?" Their correspondence relates many such week-end visits.

10. BHRM, "Memories of an Unusual Father," 8. The house was at 81 Oakland Beach Avenue.

11. BHRM, interview with the author, July 14, 2013.

12. "Every time she came to New York she called up in Rye where I lived." OBR, Van Voris interview, p. 16.

13. WMM to BHRM, undated but the summer of 1942, in the possession of BHRM; OBR to MS, August 1935, MS Papers, Library of Congress, microfilm edition, Loo6: 0946.

14. The phrase "family circle" has an interesting history. In 1931, Inez Haynes Gillmore, the author of *Angel Island*, had published a novel with that name. Inez Haynes Gillmore, *Family Circle* (Indianapolis: Bobbs-Merrill, 1931).

15. Edwin J. Perkins, *Wall Street to Main Street: Charles Merrill and Middle-Class Investors* (New York: Cambridge University Press, 1999), 117–18; Kathleen Endres and Therese L. Lueck, eds., *Women's Periodicals in the United States: Consumer Magazines* (Westport, CT: Greenwood, 1995), 87, xiv.

16. OBR, "Lie Detector," *Family Circle*, November 1, 1935.

17. OBR, "Their Shyness Made Them Famous," *Family Circle*, November 19, 1937.

18. OBR, "How Far Should She Go?" *Family Circle*, November 1, 1935.

19. OBR, "Know Your Man," *Family Circle*, October 23, 1936.

20. Jack Byrne to OBR, February 17, 1958, in the possession of BHRM; OBR.

21. "Live, Love, Laugh, and Be Happy," *Family Circle*, November 27, 1936.

22. OBR, "Ferocious Fiction," *Family Circle*, December 20, 1935.

23. Diary of OBR, entries for January 15, 1936; March 1, 1936; May 28, 1936; November 8, 1936; January 22, 1938; January 31, 1938; and May 27, 1937, in the possession of BHRM.

20. THE DUKE OF DECEPTION

1. "May Use Lie Detector," *Washington Post*, November 22, 1935.

2. Alder, *Lie Detectors*, 148, and chapter 13.

3. "Lindbergh Baby's Murderer to Be Placed Under 'Lie Detector,'" *Times of India*, November 29, 1935. Marston's later account of what happened differs somewhat. He claimed that he had not approached Fisher but that he had been approached, in the fall of 1935, by a detective working for the defense. WMM, *Lie Detector Test*, 82–88. Marston also claimed that Hauptmann, in a letter to Hoffman, had requested a lie detector test.

4. "Gov. Hoffman Urges Lie-Detector Test," *New York Times*, January 24, 1936; "Defense Staff of Hauptmann Adds Attorney," *Washington Post*, January 24, 1936; "Lie Detector Test Backed by Hoffman," *Boston Globe*, January 24, 1936; and "Tells Lie Test He Would Use on Hauptmann," *Chicago Tribune*, January 25, 1936. According to a statement WMM made to the press on January 12, 1936—the day Hoffman granted Hauptmann a thirty-day reprieve—Dr. John F. Condon, who had negotiated the payment of the kidnapper's ransom, had agreed in December to be subjected to a lie detector test, but only after Hauptmann was dead. "Hauptmann Plans to Make New Plea to Highest Court," *New York Times*, January 13, 1936.

5. WMM, *Lie Detector Test,* 87–88.

6. Inscribed copy of *The Lie Detector Test,* in the possession of BHRM.

7. Helen W. Gandy [Hoover's secretary] to Richard R. Smith, March 8, 1938; Richard R. Smith to Helen W. Gandy, March 10, 1938; and Helen W. Gandy to Richard R. Smith, March 16, 1938, William Moulton Marston's FBI File, U.S. Justice Department.

8. My thanks to Hoover's biographer Beverly Gage for this information.

9. WMM, *Lie Detector Test.* And see Verne W. Lyon, "Practical Application of Deception Tests," *Federal Probation* 4 (February 1940): 41–42.

10. E. P. Coffey to Mr. Nathan, memo, May 11, 1938, WMM, FBI File, Department of Justice.

11. WMM, *Lie Detector Test,* 72.

12. The warden at what was then the D.C. Penal Institution in Lorton, Virginia, submitted a letter in support of Frye, citing his work as a switchboard operator and his exemplary behavior: W. L. Peak, Superintendent, to J. A. Finch, Attorney in Charge of Pardons, July 12, 1934, National Archives, RG 204, stack 230, 40:14:2, box 1583, file 56-386. James A. Frye, Application for Executive Clemency, July 12, 1934, National Archives, RG 204, stack 230, 40:14:2, box 1583, file 56-386; James A. Frye to Daniel M. Lyons, Department of Justice, August 2, 1943, National Archives, RG 204, stack 230, 40:14:2, box 1583, file 56-386; Frye's 1945 application for executive clemency, National Archives, RG 204, stack 230, 40:14:2, box 1583, file 56-386, pp. 13–14; James A. Frye to D. M. Lyons, Pardon Attorney, September 7, 1945, and James A. Frye to Harry S. Truman, President of the United States, September 28, 1945, National Archives, RG 204, stack 230, 40:14:2, box 1583, file 56-386.

13. WMM, *Lie Detector Test,* 115.

14. BHRM, "Memories of an Unusual Father," 26.

15. WMM, *Lie Detector Test,* 119.

16. "'Are You in Love?' Check Your Reply with Lie Detector," *Washington Post,* March 9, 1938; Sally McDougall, "Tells Why Women Lie: Dr. W. M. Marston, 'Detector' Inventor, Makes Experiment," *New York World Telegram,* March 9, 1938; and "Scientist Finds Men Prefer Brunettes," *Washington Post,* September 23, 1939.

17. Interview with MM, July 25, 2012.

18. WMM had apparently been saying he was forming a "Truth Bureau." See [redacted] to J. Edgar Hoover, Jacksonville, October 26, 1940: "Having seen in a Jacksonville paper the statement that Dr. William Moulton Marston is to train deception testers preparing them for service in a possible 'Truth Bureau,' I should like to get in touch with Dr. Marston to offer myself for training because I attended Dr. Marston's classes on legal physiology, and the use of the Lie Detector at the American University during 1923." Hoover writes back (Hoover to [redacted], Washington, November 8, 1940): "I must advise that the individual to whom you refer in your letter is not in any way connected with the Federal Bureau of Investigation." WMM, FBI File.

19. OBR, "No Thing Matters," *Family Circle,* April 16, 1937.

20. "The Duke of Deception," *Wonder Woman #2,* Fall 1942. On Upton Sinclair's failed campaign, see Jill Lepore, "The Lie Factory: How Politics Became a Business," *New Yorker,* September 24, 2012.

21. Ad titled "Lie Detector 'Tells All,'" *Life,* November 21, 1938, 65.

22. John S. Bugas to J. Edgar Hoover, July 13, 1939, WMM, FBI File. And see Alder, *Lie Detectors,* 189–90.

21. FEMININE RULE DECLARED FACT

1. "Women Will Rule 1,000 Years Hence!" *Chicago Tribune,* November 11, 1937, and "Feminine Rule Declared Fact," *Los Angeles Times,* November 13, 1937. In 1937, when WMM predicted a matriarchy, he was riding a wave that had to do in part with the prominence of Eleanor Roosevelt and also with a scandal over Mary Woolley, who that year was forced out of the presidency of Mount Holyoke and replaced with a man. "I am one of the many who were greatly disturbed when a man succeeded Miss Woolley as President," Holloway wrote, bitterly. "Women will never develop as leaders unless they are given or seize the chance to lead." EHM to the Mount Holyoke Alumni Office, June 13, 1960, as a handwritten addendum to an alumni questionnaire. Mount Holyoke College Archives.

2. Dave Fleischer, director, *Betty Boop for President* (Paramount Pictures, 1932); "Woman for President Boom Launched," *Milwaukee Journal,* February 26, 1935; "Woman-for-President League 'Nominees,'" *Harvard Crimson,* June 3, 1935; "New League's Aim Is Woman Vice President," *Washington Post,* February 20, 1935; and Mary June Burton, "'We Shall Have a Woman President!'" *Los Angeles Times,* August 11, 1935.

3. Howe's article is quoted in "Among the Magazines," *Washington Post,* May 19, 1935.

4. "Marston Advises 3 L's for Success . . . Predicts U.S. Matriarchy," *New York Times,* November 11, 1937.

5. "Neglected Amazons to Rule Men in 1,000 Yrs., Says Psychologist," *Washington Post,* November 11, 1937.

6. Catt quoted in Cott, *Grounding of Modern Feminism,* 30; also see Cott's discussion of the Janus-faced nature of feminism, chapter 1.

7. Batya Weinbaum, *Islands of Women and Amazons: Representations and Realities* (Austin: University of Texas Press, 1999), 16–27; Laurel Thatcher Ulrich, *Well-Behaved Women Seldom Make History* (New York: Knopf, 2007), chapter 2; and Inez Haynes Irwin, *Angels and Amazons: A Hundred Years of American Women* (Garden City, NY: Doubleday, Doran, 1933).

8. "Dr. Poison," *Sensation Comics #2,* February 1942.

9. MSML, interview by Jacqueline Van Voris, MS Papers, Smith College, 1977, p. 25.

10. WMM, *Try Living.*

11. Diary of OBR, entry for July 10, 1937, in the possession of BHRM.

12. "Bookends," *Washington Post,* October 22, 1937.

13. "Marston Advises 3 L's For Success," *New York Times,* November 11, 1937.

14. H. G. Wells, in a 1935 speech in London, in *Round the World for Birth Control,* Birth Control International Information Centre, 1937, MS Papers, Smith College, microfilm edition, S62: 598; Chesler, *Woman of Valor,* 361–64, 373–76; and Reed, *From Private Vice to Public Virtue,* 121.

15. EHM alumni clipping dated November 1937, Mount Holyoke College Archives.

16. EHM, Mount Holyoke College *One Hundred Year Directory,* 1936, Mount Holyoke College Archives.

17. Diary of OBR, entries for July 8, 1936; July 15, 1936; and July 1, 1937, in the possession of BHRM.

18. MSML to BHRM and Audrey Marston, February 27, 1963, in the possession of BHRM.

19. *1940 United States Federal Census;* place: Rye, Westchester, New York; roll: T627_2813; page: 13A; enumeration district: 60-334.

20. MM, interview with the author, July 25, 2012.

21. Christie Marston, Pete Marston's daughter, said, "Gran [referring to EHM] said that what they did for years is, with friends, Dotsie was mom to Byrne and Donn but with everyone else Gran was mom." Christie Marston, interview with the author, July 25, 2012.

22. Olive Ann Marston Lamott, interview with the author, July 15, 2013.

23. Olive Ann Marston Lamott, interview with Steve Korte, August 25, 1999, DC Comics Archives.

24. Diary of OBR, entry for November 4, 1937.

25. Diary of OBR, entry for February 15, 1938. Relating this story in her diary, OBR added three exclamation points of her own.

26. Diary of OBR, entry for August 3, 1936.

27. Marston's copy of Victor H. Lindlahr's *Eat and Reduce* (1939; repr., New York: Permabooks, 1948) is in the possession of MM.

28. BHRM, "Memories of an Unusual Father," and Olive Ann Marston Lamott, interview with the author, July 15, 2013.

29. WMM, "What Are *Your* Prejudices?" *Your Life* (March 1939).

30. WMM to BHRM, memo, with reply on the back, undated but c. 1940, in the possession of BHRM.

31. WMM, "Dad to Doodle," undated fragment, in the possession of BHRM.

32. "He ruled with an iron hand," MSML, interview with the author, July 9, 2013.

33. Olive Ann Marston Lamott, interview with the author, July 15, 2013.

34. WMM to BHRM, undated, in the possession of BHRM.

35. Diary of WMM, entries for December 24 and 25, 1938, in the possession of BHRM.

36. BHRM, "Memories of an Unusual Father," 9–12.

37. Olive Ann Marston Lamott, interview with the author, July 15, 2013, and OBR to BHRM, undated but c. 1944, in the possession of BHRM.

38. MM told me about this when I interviewed him; BHRM writes about it in his memoir, and OBR writes about it in her diary—e.g., March 1, 1936: "Sunday. Had 'Marston Forum' in evening with all expressing themselves freely. M. recited. B. told story as did Dunn. O.A. on [?] O.A. very tragic."

39. Diary of WMM, entry for June 23, 1935, in the possession of BHRM.

40. BHRM, "Memories of an Unusual Father," 6–9.

41. Olive Ann Marston Lamott, interview with Steve Korte, August 25, 1999, DC Comics Archives.

42. Diary of WMM, entry for September 29, 1940. MM's still got his IQ test: MM, IQ test questionnaire, November 17, 1940, as administered by WMM, in the possession of MM. At age six, Byrne Marston was in the third grade when his brother Donn and his sister, O.A., entered kindergarten. BHRM, "Memories of an Unusual Father," 9–10. And November 1937 clipping in EHM's Mount Holyoke alumni file, Mount Holyoke College Archives.

43. Pete, Byrne, Donn, and O.A. Marston, "The Marston Chronicle," no. 1, July 18, 1939, in the possession of BHRM. And see Diary of OBR, entry for July 6, 1939: "Children getting out a weekly newspaper. Very cute—called The Chronicle."

44. MCG, "Narrative Illustration: The Story of the Comics," *Print: A Quarterly Journal*

of the Graphic Arts 3 (Summer 1942): 12. Gaines quotes LB in this essay, which includes, as an illustration, the cover of *Wonder Woman #1*.

45. The story of the birth of both comic books and Superman is told in many places, but see especially Gerard Jones, *Men of Tomorrow: Geeks, Gangsters, and the Birth of the Comic Book* (New York: Basic Books, 2004); Bradford W. Wright, *Comic Book Nation: The Transformation of Youth Culture in America* (Baltimore: Johns Hopkins University Press, 2001), chapters 1 and 2; Les Daniels, *DC Comics: Sixty Years of the World's Favorite Comic Book Heroes* (Boston: Bulfinch, 1995); and Jean-Paul Gabilliet, *Of Comics and Men: A Cultural History of American Comic Books* (Jackson: University of Mississippi Press, 2005), translated by Bart Beaty and Nick Nguyen, chapter 2.

46. Robbins and Yronwode, *Women and the Comics,* 50–59.

47. Wright, *Comic Book Nation,* 9, 13.

48. Wilson Locke, "Amazona, the Mighty Woman," *Planet Comics #3,* March 1940.

49. OBR, "Don't Laugh at the Comics," *Family Circle,* October 25, 1940, and BHRM, interview with Steve Korte, summer 1999, DC Comics Archives.

50. BHRM, "Memories of an Unusual Father," 27–28.

51. BHRM, interview with the author, July 14, 2013.

22. SUPREMA

1. Gardner Fox with Bill Finger, "Batman Versus the Vampire, Part Two," *Detective Comics #32,* October 1939. Ellsworth is quoted in Daniels, *DC Comics,* 34.

2. Batman's debut: Bill Finger, "The Case of the Chemical Syndicate," *Detective Comics #27,* May 1939; *United States v. Miller,* 307 U.S. 174 (1939). See also Adam Winkler, *Gunfight: The Battle over the Right to Bear Arms in America* (New York: Norton, 2011), 63–65, and Jill Lepore, "Battleground America," *New Yorker,* April 23, 2012.

3. Bill Finger, "Legend: The Batman and How He Came to Be," *Detective Comics #33* (November 1939), and Bill Finger, "The Legend of the Batman—Who He Is and How He Came to Be," *Batman #1,* Spring 1940.

4. Sterling North, "A National Disgrace," *Chicago Daily News,* May 8, 1940, and Bart Beaty, *Fredric Wertham and the Critique of Mass Culture* (Jackson: University Press of Mississippi, 2005), 113.

5. Stanley J. Kunitz, "Libraries, to Arms!" *Wilson Library Bulletin* 15 (1941): 671; Slater Brown, "The Coming of Superman," *New Republic,* September 2, 1940; and "Are Comics Fascist?" *Time,* October 22, 1945. On librarians' responses to comic books, see Carol L. Tilley, "Of Nightingales and Supermen: How Youth Service Librarians Responded to Comics Between the Years 1938 and 1955," PhD diss., School of Library and Information Science, Indiana University, 2007.

6. OBR, "Don't Laugh at the Comics," *Family Circle,* October 25, 1940.

7. Marston describes reading comic-book scripts as a consulting psychologist in WMM, "Why 100,000,000 Americans Read Comics," *American Scholar* 13 (1943–44): 41–42. He does not give a date. Marston does not usually appear on the list of Gaines's advisers. One odd exception is *Wonder Woman #14,* Fall 1945, when he is listed as a member of the board: "Dr. Wm. Moulton Marston, Member of American Psychological Association; Fellow, American Association for Advancement of Science." Notably, in this issue, all of the Wonder Woman stories were written by Joye Hummel, and

the "Wonder Women of History" feature, a profile of Abigail Adams, is only two pages instead of four. Information on the formation of the board, as well as its role, can be found in the papers of several of its members. See, e.g., Josette Frank on how she came to join the board in a letter to Mary Alice Jones, April 15, 1954, a copy of which is in the Lauretta Bender Papers, Brooklyn College, box 16, folder 6.

8. Clara Savage Littledale, "What to Do About the 'Comics,'" *Parents' Magazine*, 1941, 26–27, 93. Hecht's advisory board was aided by a board of "Junior Advisory Editors," whose members included the child stars Shirley Temple and Mickey Rooney. On Littledale and the history of *Parents' Magazine*, see Lepore, *Mansion of Happiness*, chapter 7. Another booster of *True Comics* was the Parents' Institute. See Harold C. Field's reply to Marston's 1944 *American Scholar* essay, letter to the editor, *American Scholar* 13 (Spring 1944): 247–48. *True Comics* is a terrible comic book. Even Stanley Kunitz admitted, "I must confess, despite my sympathetic interest in the experiment, that I am a little skeptical of the ultimate educational value of fighting comics with comics" ("Libraries, to Arms!," 670).

9. MCG to unspecified, memo, undated but c. October 1940, DC Comics Archives.

10. "A Message to our Readers," *More Fun Comics #72*, October 1941. And see Amy Kiste Nyberg, *Seal of Approval: The History of the Comics Code* (Jackson: University Press of Mississippi, 1998), 9–10. David Hajdu suggests that the editorial advisory board was purely for show; see Hajdu, *The Ten-Cent Plague: The Great Comic-Book Scare and How It Changed America* (New York: Farrar, Straus and Giroux, 2008), 45. But this is simply wrong. Gaines called on his advisory board all the time; Frank, Bender, and others who served on the board in the 1940s read scripts and offered commentary. As Frank explained in 1943, "To the best of my recollection, every member, in accepting this assignment, stipulated that he or she would serve only if the service could be real, and signified an aversion to serving on any board that would be merely 'window dressing.'" See also Frank to Mary Bruhnke (Mrs. Charles S. Liebman), January 28, 1947, Child Study Association of America Papers, Social Welfare History Archives, University of Minnesota (hereafter CSAA Papers), box 15, folder 138, in which Frank outlines the duties of the editorial advisory board in great detail.

11. "I had a talk with Mr. Childs yesterday, and as he pointed out to you, Dr. Marston's name will be eliminated as a member of the Editorial Advisory Board on all issues which will come out during the month of January." MCG to Josette Frank, October 15, 1941, CSAA Papers, box 24, folder 239.

12. This remark of EHM's is quoted by MM in "Elizabeth H. Marston, Inspiration for Wonder Woman, 100," *New York Times*, April 3, 1983. See also: "My mother was a prime mover in getting Wonder Woman going. She nagged him for years: 'We need a woman super hero, never mind the guys, we've got enough.'" MM, interview with Steve Korte, July 29, 1999, DC Comics Archives.

13. EHM to JE, January 11, 1973, in the possession of JE; "Marston Advises 3 L's for Success," *New York Times*, November 11, 1937.

14. WMM, "Why 100,000,000 Americans Read Comics," 42–43.

15. Ibid. Marston offers this same explanation in WMM to Coulton Waugh, March 5, 1945, WW Letters, Smithsonian. Waugh was preparing a book about the history of the comic strip: Coulton Waugh's *The Comics* (New York: Macmillan, 1947) is one of the fullest early accounts of the medium, although its treatment of Wonder Woman is quite brief.

16. Anthony Tollin, "Sheldon Mayer: The Origins of the Golden Age," *Amazing World of DC Comics* #5 (March–April 1975), 2–12.
17. Sheldon Mayer, 1975 DC Convention: Wonder Woman Panel, transcript in the DC Comics Archives. Les Daniels, who interviewed Mayer, reports that Mayer first met Marston when Gaines brought Marston onto the editorial advisory board: "In 1941, Mayer met Marston for dinner at the Harvard Club in New York, and an agreement was reached, initially calling for Marston to offer advice on ways to make comic books more psychologically beneficial to young readers." Daniels, *DC Comics*, 58–59.
18. WMM to Sheldon Mayer, February 23, 1941, WW Letters, Smithsonian.

23. AS LOVELY AS APHRODITE

1. WMM to Sheldon Mayer, February 23, 1941, WW Letters, Smithsonian.
2. "Harry G. Peter was the artist. Doctor Marston chose his concept of WONDER WOMAN over the other drawings presented to him." MWH to JE, May 21, 1972, Steinem Papers, Smith College, box 213, folder 5.
3. Mayer, quoted in Daniels, *Wonder Woman*, 24.
4. Sheldon Mayer, 1975 DC Convention: Wonder Woman Panel, transcript in the DC Comics Archives.
5. "Man o' Metal," *Reg'lar Fellers Heroic Comics* #7 (July 1941). Peter's earlier comic credits: "Let's Get into a Huddle," *Famous Funnies* #85 (August 1941). And see Dan Nadel, *Art in Time: Unknown Comic Book Adventures, 1940–1980* (New York: Abrams ComicArts, 2010), 28, with a reproduction of Man o' Metal from nos. 13, 14, and 15 of *Reg'lar Fellers Heroic Comics* (1942), pp. 29–58.
6. MCG to George J. Hecht, November 10, 1941; Hecht to MCG, November 10, 1941; MCG to Hecht, November 14, 1941, in CSAA Papers, box 24, folder 239.
7. Robbins and Yronwode, *Women and the Comics*, 60.
8. On the wealth of women artists working in cartooning and comic strips in the 1920s and 1930s, see ibid., chapters 2 and 3; and on the relative absence of women in the comic-book industry in the 1930s and 1940s, see chapter 4. Most comic-book publishers were averse to hiring women artists. The exception was Fiction House, which, according to Robbins and Yronwode, employed more than twenty women (ibid., 51–52). Judith Schwarz asserts that Rogers was a lesbian (*Radical Feminists of Heterodoxy*, 69–72). But Rogers married the artist Howard Smith in the 1920s, and in 1933 they moved to a farmhouse in Connecticut. In the 1930s, Rogers hosted a popular radio show about animals. Alice Sheppard, "Howard Smith," Archives of AskArt, accessed on January 3, 2014, at http://www.askart.com/askart/artist .aspx?artist=11211519. See Trina Robbins, ed., *Miss Fury by Tarpé Mills: Sensational Sundays, 1944–1949* (San Diego: Library of American Comics, 2011). For more on female comic leads of the 1940s, see Mike Madrid, *The Supergirls: Fashion, Feminism, Fantastic, and the History of Comic Book Heroines* (Exterminating Angel, 2009), 1–29.
9. Daniels, *DC Comics*, 61.
10. Henry George, *An Anthology of Henry George's Thought*, ed. Kenneth Wenzer, 3 vols. (Rochester, NY: University of Rochester Press, 1997), 1:201.
11. HGP's occupation is listed as "Artist, newspaper," in the 1900 federal census, when he was living in a boardinghouse in San Francisco. He gave his birth date as March 8,

1880, and indicated that both of his parents were born in France. *1900 United States Federal Census;* place: San Francisco, CA; roll: 106; page: 7A; enumeration district: 0262; FHL microfilm: 1240106. More details about Peter's life are difficult to find, largely because, after his death in 1958, his estate fell into the hands of dealers, who have been selling off his papers and drawings, one by one, for years, to private collectors. In 2003, for instance, Heritage Auctions sold a number of Peter's drawings, a page of a *Wonder Woman* script, one of Peter's work schedules, along with Peter's address book (Heritage Comics 2003 March Comics Signature Sale #806, Lots 5634, 5635, and 5636). In 2002, Heritage Auctions sold one of Peter's original concept drawings of Wonder Woman (Heritage Auctions October 2002 Comic Auction #804, Lot 7434). I haven't been able to identify the owners of these and similar materials and have therefore not been able to consult them.

12. See, e.g., "Hear Remarks on Equal Suffrage," *San Francisco Chronicle,* October 7, 1906.

13. Edan Milton Hughes, *Artists in California, 1786–1940,* 3rd ed. (Sacramento: Crocker Art Museum, 2002), 1:406; HGP's entry can be found on 2:872. My date for the courtship comes from a Valentine made by HGP and sent to Fulton, dated February 14, 1907. Heritage Comics 2003 March Comics Signature Sale, Lot 5636.

14. "Newspaper Artists Will Make Exhibit," *San Francisco Call,* June 1, 1904, and "Newspaper Artists to Exhibit Their Work," *San Francisco Bulletin,* May 29, 1904. And see the specific mention of Fulton's work at that exhibit in "Newspaper Artists' Exhibition," Camera Craft ([July?] 1904): "Adonica Fulton, of the Bulletin, showed twenty drawings with a wide range of subject and treatment. Her 'French Poster,' was strong and well suited to what it was intended for."

15. An illustrated note from Roth to Fulton is reproduced by Ken Quattro in a blog post chronicling his fantastic investigation into Peter's relationship with Ed Wheelan: Ken Quattro, "The 1905 Comic Fan," *The Comics Detective,* February 13, 2011, http://thecomicsdetective.blogspot.com/2011/02/1905-comic-fan.html. HGP also tended to draw western and animal scenes. For an example from this period, see HGP, "Animals of Prey," pen and ink drawings, in the *Outing Magazine* 56 (1910): 673. A copy of the marriage certificate of HGP and Adonica Fulton was auctioned in 2003: Heritage Comics 2003 March Comics Signature Sale, Lot 5636.

16. Display ad for *Judge* in *Printers' Ink* 90 (1915): 57.

17. "H. G. Peter," *Printers' Ink,* February 26, 1920, p. 161.

18. In 1920, HGP was listed in the federal census as living as a lodger in Staten Island, working as a newspaper artist. In the 1925 NY census and the 1930 and 1940 federal censuses, he and his wife are listed as living at 63 Portland Place, Richmond, New York. In 1925 HGP listed his occupation as "Artist"; in 1940, he said he was a newspaper artist. *1920 United States Federal Census*; place: Richmond Assembly District 1, Richmond, New York; roll: T625_1238; page: 8A; enumeration district: 1586; image: 1257. New York State Archives, Albany, New York; *State Population Census Schedules, 1925;* election district: 12; assembly district: 01; city: New York; county: Richmond; page: 12. *1930 United States Federal Census*; place: Richmond, Richmond, New York; roll: 1613; page: 3A; enumeration district: 0122; image: 431.0; FHL microfilm: 2341347. *1930 United States Federal Census* (Washington, DC: National Archives and Records Administration, 1930), T626, 2,667 rolls. *1940 United States Federal Census*; place: Richmond, New York; roll: T627_2760; page: 8B; enumeration district: 43–54. According to the 1880 census, Adonica Fulton's mother, Mary J. Fulton, was born in Ireland and in 1880 was a widow with five children. Year: 1880;

place: San Francisco, California; roll: 78; family history film: 1254078; page: 581B; enumeration district: 191; image: 0440.

19. *Captain America Comics #1*, March 1941, appeared on newsstands on December 20, 1940.

20. HGP's original 13 × 18.75–inch drawing of the character, with the exchange between HGP and WMM, was sold at auction by Peter's estate, through Heritage Auctions, in 2002. It sold for $33,350 and remains in private hands. It is reproduced in Roy Thomas, "Queen Hepzibah, Genghis Khan, & the 'Nuclear' Wars!" *Alter Ego #23* (April 2003), 5. A drawing of a naked Wonder Woman, signed "H. G. Peter," is reproduced in Craig Yoe, *Clean Cartoonists' Dirty Drawings* (San Francisco: Last Gasp, 2007), 58–59. The attribution is almost certainly spurious.

21. On the episode involving Vargas and the U.S. Post Office, and on the history of pin-ups more generally, see Joanne Meyerowitz, "Women, Cheesecake, and Borderline Material: Responses to Girlie Pictures in the Mid-Twentieth-Century U.S.," *Journal of Women's History* 8 (1996): 9–35.

22. HGP, concept drawing, 1941, in the possession of Stephen Fishler, Metropolis Comics, New York. Fishler bought this drawing from a collector who purchased it "about thirty or forty years ago." Stephen Fishler, interview with the author, January 6, 2014.

23. Alberto Vargas, centerfold, *Esquire*, July 1942, 33–34.

24. WMM, "Wonder Woman Quarterly #1, Episode A," typed script dated April 15, 1942, p. 2; compare to WMM, "The Origin of Wonder Woman," *Wonder Woman #1*, Summer 1942, panel on lower left corner of p. 1A.

25. WMM, "Wonder Woman #2, Episode A," typewritten script, undated, DC Comics Archives, p. 5. Compare to "The God of War," *Wonder Woman #2*, Fall 1942, panel on p. 3A.

26. "Introducing Wonder Woman," *All-Star Comics #8*, December 1941–January 1942. On "Charles Moulton" as the middle names of MCG and WMM, see Steve Ringgenberg, interview with William M. Gaines, May 12, 1998, DC Comics Archives.

27. "The Adventure of the Beauty Club," *Wonder Woman #6*, Fall 1943; WMM to Coulton Waugh, March 5, 1945, WW Letters, Smithsonian; "Dr. Poison," *Sensation Comics #2*, February 1942; "A Spy in the Office," *Sensation Comics #3*, March 1942; and "Introducing Wonder Woman," *All-Star Comics #8*, December 1941–January 1942.

28. WMM to FDR, December 12, 1941, WMM, FBI File.

29. Alder, *Lie Detectors*, preface, 200–210, 250.

30. WW comic strip, June 16, 1944.

31. "Who Is Wonder Woman?" *Sensation Comics #1*, January 1942, and *Sensation Comics #3* (March 1942).

32. Diary of OBR, entry for August 28, 1941, in the possession of BHRM. OBR had also studied shorthand in the summer of 1927, at the Miller School of Business. See OBR, résumé, 1951, in the possession of BHRM.

24. THE JUSTICE SOCIETY OF AMERICA

1. Nyberg, *Seal of Approval*, ix, 25.

2. Anthony Comstock, *Traps for the Young* (New York: Funk and Wagnalls, 1883), introduction.

3. Nyberg, *Seal of Approval,* 2–3, 22–27.

4. MCG to The Most Reverend John F. Noll, D.D., March 10, 1942, Bender Papers, box 16, folder 1.

5. Noll to MCG, March 13, 1942, Bender Papers, box 16, folder 1. In the end, Gaines managed to convince Noll to take *Sensation Comics* off his objectionable list. Noll to MCG, April 30, 1942, CSAA Papers, box 24, folder 239.

6. Gardner Fox, "The Justice Society of America," *All-Star Comics #3,* Winter 1940, and reproduced in *All-Star Comics Archives* (New York: DC Archive Editions, 1991), vol. 1. The best account of the Justice Society is Roy Thomas, ed., *The All-Star Companion: Celebrating the 60th Anniversary of the Justice Society* (Raleigh, NC: Two-Morrows, 2000). The quotation is from Gardner Fox, "The Roll Call of the Justice Society," *All-Star Comics #5,* June–July 1941.

7. "The Justice Society of America Initiates Johnny Thunder!" *All-Star Comics #6,* August–September 1941.

8. *All-Star Comics #8,* December 1941–January 1942.

9. Gardner Fox, "The Justice Society Joins the War on Japan," *All-Star Comics #11* (June–July 1942).

10. Advertisement in *Sensation Comics #5,* May 1942. On the rise of public-opinion polling, market research, and popular quantitative social science, see Sarah Igo, *The Averaged American: Surveys, Citizens, and the Making of a Mass Public* (Cambridge, MA: Harvard University Press, 2007).

11. And there was another interesting result. "For the first time in the past four or five years that I have been getting these polls from readers," Gaines remarked, "we noticed more than the average amount of adults sending in these coupons. For example, in the first thousand or so, over 25 are from men and women—mostly over twenty, whereas in previous polls, we had only one or two out of a thousand, or none at all." MCG to LB, March 20, 1942. The returns are reported in this letter and in another: Dagmar Norgood (from All-American Comics) to LB, March 16, 1942. Both letters are in the Bender Papers, box 16, folder 1. Gaines also sent the results of the survey to Josette Frank: MCG to Frank, March 23, 1943, CSAA Papers, box 24, folder 239.

12. Dagmar Norgood (head of the DC Comics Education Department) to LB, February 12, 1942, Bender Papers, box 16, folder 1.

13. The best source of biographical and autobiographical information about Bender is the biographical material in the Bender Papers, box 18, folder 4. Quotations from Bender's 1916 high school commencement address are taken from her unpublished memoir, "LB, M.D.," Bender Papers, box 18, folder 4. Bender began working in the Psychiatric Division of Bellevue Hospital in October 1934. LB to J. Franklin Robinson, June 13, 1956, Bender Papers, box 1, folder 9. She favored group therapy. In the 1930s, she was especially known for her work in using puppets, art, dance, and music with children. See, e.g., LB to Karl M. Bowman (Bowman was the director of the hospital), November 28, 1939, Bender Papers, box 1, folder 9. She resigned as senior psychiatrist in charge of the children's ward in February 1956; she continued on as an attending psychiatrist. Sol Nichtern and Charlotte Weiss, Annual Report, Ward PQ6, Children's Ward, Bellevue Psychiatric Hospital, November 1, 1956, Bender Papers, box 1, folder 9.

14. LB, Sylvan Keiser, and Paul Schilder, *Studies in Aggressiveness, from Bellevue Hospital, Psychiatric Division, and the Medical College of New York University, Depart-*

ment of Psychiatry (Worcester, MA: Clark University, 1936). Some of Bender's work on childhood schizophrenia later became controversial; in 1944, she conducted an experiment in which she administered electroshock therapy to three hundred children diagnosed with schizophrenia.

15. "Dr. Paul Schilder, Psychiatrist, Dies," *Boston Globe*, December 9, 1940. Bender later published a collection of Schilder's writings, which she dedicated to her three children; she mentions their ages at his death in Paul Schilder, *Contributions to Developmental Neuropsychiatry*, ed. LB (New York: International Universities Press, 1964), x. Bender refers to her own children in her testimony in 1954. U.S. Senate Committee on the Judiciary, *Hearings Before the Subcommittee to Investigate Juvenile Delinquency of the Committee on the Judiciary, U.S. Senate, April 21, 22, and June 4, 1954* (Washington, DC: United States Government Printing Office, 1954). And see the biographical note in the Bender Papers.

16. Bender's testimony, *Hearings Before the Subcommittee to Investigate Juvenile Delinquency*, pp. 154–55.

17. LB and Reginald S. Lourie, "The Effect of Comic Books on the Ideology of Children," *Journal of Orthopsychiatry* 11 (1941): 540–50. A typescript of this article can be found in the Bender Papers, box 16, folder 1. Lourie was a resident for one year; see LB to Marian McBee, September 16, 1942, Bender Papers, box 6, folder 1.

18. H. Carter Dyson, "Are the Comics Bad for Children?" *Family Circle*, April 17, 1942. The accompanying editorial, "Sticking by Superman," had originally appeared in the *Burlington (VT) Daily News*.

19. WMM to Sheldon Mayer, June 3, 1942, WW Letters, Smithsonian, and "The God of War," *Wonder Woman #2*, Fall 1942.

20. Gaines reported early tallies in MCG to LB, April 30, 1942, Bender Papers, box 16, folder 1.

25. THE MILK SWINDLE

1. Gardner Fox, "The Black Dragon Menace," *All-Star Comics #12*, August–September 1942.

2. Gardner Fox, "Food for Starving Patriots!" *All-Star Comics #14*, December 1942–January 1943, and Gardner Fox, "The Man Who Created Images," *All-Star Comics #15*, February–March 1943.

3. Gardner Fox, "The Brain Wave Goes Berserk," *All-Star Comics #17*, June–July 1943.

4. WMM to Sheldon Mayer, April 12, 1942, WW Letters, Smithsonian. See also Roy Thomas, "Two Touches of Venus," *Alter Ego* 3, no. 1 (Summer 1999): 14–18; Thomas, *All-Star Companion*, 67–68; and Karen M. Walowit, "Wonder Woman: Enigmatic Heroine of American Popular Culture," PhD diss., University of California, Berkeley, 1974, pp. 112–18.

5. Ben Proctor, *William Randolph Hearst: Final Edition, 1911–1951* (New York: Oxford University Press, 2007), 135. Proctor cites the *New York American* for October 8–9, 1926, pp. 1–2; October 10, 1926, p. 1L; October 11, 1926, p. 1; October 12, 1926, p. 6; October 13, 1926, pp. 1, 30; then daily to November 1, 1926, p. 1.

6. "The Milk Swindle," *Sensation Comics #7*, July 1942.

7. Chesler, *Woman of Valor*, 75–78.

8. "Department Store Perfidy," *Sensation Comics #8,* August 1942.
9. "The Return of Diana Prince," *Sensation Comics #9,* September 1942.
10. WMM, "Women: Servants for Civilization," *Tomorrow,* February 1942, 42–45.
11. "The Sky Road," *Wonder Woman #10,* Fall 1944.
12. "School for Spies," *Sensation Comics #4,* April 1942.
13. "The Unbound Amazon," *Sensation Comics #19,* July 1943.
14. "The Unbound Amazon," *Sensation Comics #19,* July 1943, and "The Greatest Feat of Daring in Human History," *Wonder Woman #1,* Summer 1942. Wonder Woman's encounters with the king of the Mole Men run in the comic strip from October 28, 1944, to November 18, 1944.
15. "The Secret City of the Incas," *Sensation Comics #18,* June 1943.
16. MS, "The Women's Army Auxiliary Corps," June 17, 1942, in *Selected Papers of MS,* 3:132–33.
17. MS to Robert L. Dickinson, February 20, 1942, in *Selected Papers of MS,* 3:115; Gordon, *Moral Property,* 247; and MS, "Is This the Time to Have a Child?," 1942, in *Selected Papers of MS,* 3:127.
18. [WMM], "Noted Psychologist Revealed as Author of Best-Selling 'Wonder Woman,' Children's Comic," press release, typescript [June 1942], WW Letters, Smithsonian.

26. THE WONDER WOMEN OF HISTORY

1. MCG to LB, June 23, 1942, in Bender Papers, box 16, folder 1.
2. The family was scattered that summer. Byrne was spending a few weeks with family friends in Michigan. "Zaz, M. and I will probably drive up to Boston and some of the beaches up there," Marston wrote to Byrne (that is, he and Huntley and Pete were going to the Cape, to see Ethel Byrne). "Mom is taking Donn and OA up to Aunt Margaret's" (that is, Olive Byrne was taking them to Margaret Sanger's). WMM to BHRM, undated but summer 1942, in the possession of BHRM. Richard Rodgers and Lorenz Hart, "For Jupiter and Greece," *By Jupiter: A Musical Comedy* (New York: DRG Records, 2007).
3. [WMM], "Noted Psychologist Revealed as Author."
4. WMM to Sheldon Mayer, April 16, 1942, WW Letters, Smithsonian.
5. Neither of the two modern reprint editions of Wonder Woman comics, *The Wonder Woman Chronicles* and *The Wonder Woman Archives,* includes the four-page "Wonder Women of History" insert. I read the series as it appeared in the originals, as archived at DC Comics. (In the decades since, the significance of "Wonder Women of History" has been entirely overlooked, partly because it is difficult to find. It has never been included in reprint editions and survives only in the original issues of *Wonder Woman,* which are rare. The artist is unknown.)
6. In the summer of 1942, Marston and Marble were interviewed together on the radio. Alice Marble with Dale Leatherman, *Courting Danger* (New York: St. Martin's, 1991), 177; WMM to BHRM, undated but summer 1942.
7. Alice Marble, Associate Editor of *Wonder Woman,* to LB, July 23, 1942, Bender Papers, box 16, folder 1. The self-addressed, stamped envelope included with the mailing is still with the letter; Bender did not submit any nominations.
8. Bert Dale, "Funny Business," *Forbes,* September 1, 1943, 22, 27. WMM estimated

Wonder Woman's readership in 1945 as two and a half million: WMM to Coulton Waugh, March 5, 1945.

9. On that type of distribution, see MCG to LB, March 14, 1944, Bender Papers, box 16, folder 2. As a promotional campaign, designed as much to defend comics as to promote them, "Wonder Women of History" has much in common with another effort of Gaines's. In 1942, he began printing a comic book called *Picture Stories from the Bible.* As with *Wonder Woman,* he arranged to have the first issue sent to Bender. Gaines donated all the profits from the sale of *Picture Stories from the Bible* to religious organizations. See Edward L. Wertheim, Secretary, Advisory Council, *Picture Stories from the Bible,* press release, November 1, 1945, Bender Papers, box 16, folder 3.

10. The advertisement is reproduced in Daniels, *Wonder Woman,* 92.

11. Marble was a popular lecturer at women's colleges, where she told women students about her tennis career and mentioned, too, her work for Gaines: "I have revealed, to their delight, that I write a comic strip," she later wrote. Alice Marble, *The Road to Wimbledon* (New York: Scribner's, 1946), 161.

12. Although Marble mentioned writing comics in her 1946 autobiography, she did not say anything about it in a later autobiography: Marble with Leatherman, *Courting Danger.* Nor is her affiliation with DC Comics mentioned in Sue Davidson, *Changing the Game: The Stories of Tennis Champions Alice Marble and Althea Gibson* (Seattle: Seal, 1997).

13. WMM to MCG, February 20, 1943, WW Letters, Smithsonian.

14. "The Ordeal of Queen Boadicea," *Sensation Comics #60,* December 1946.

15. Roubicek was very interested in history, according to Jeff Rovin, who was her assistant at DC Comics in 1971 and 1972. He remembers her telling him about how historical stories had been placed in the middle of comic books in the past, saying that it had been a good idea. Rovin, interview with the author, July 25, 2013.

16. Details about the life of Dorothy Roubicek, later Dorothy Woolfolk, are hard to come by. Her papers survive only in fragments, in the collections of other people. Information about her parents and her birth can be found in the U.S. censuses, especially those for 1915, 1935, and 1940. Further details, not all of them reliable, come from Jocelyn R. Coleman, "The Woman Who Tried to Kill Superman," *Florida Today,* August 20, 1993. The only photograph I have come across is from 1955 and appears in Thomas, *All-Star Companion,* 22. Much of my information comes from Roubicek's daughter, Donna Woolfolk Cross. Cross is the daughter of Dorothy Roubicek and William Woolfolk; she was born in 1947. Donna Woolfolk Cross, interview with the author, October 30, 2013, and e-mail to the author, November 7 and 12, 2013. Many thanks to Donna Woolfolk Cross for her candor.

17. [WMM], "Noted Psychologist Revealed as Author."

18. "Wonder Women of History: Susan B. Anthony," *Wonder Woman #5,* June–July 1943.

19. The wave metaphor, while it remains popular, has been subject to serious scholarly criticism. For a representative selection of the range of recent challenges, see the essays in Nancy A. Hewitt, ed., *No Permanent Wave: Recasting Histories of U.S. Feminism* (New Brunswick, NJ: Rutgers University Press, 2010), and in "Is it Time to Jump Ship? Historians Rethink the Waves Metaphor," *Feminist Formations* 22 (2010): 76–135. The introductions by Hewitt (*No Permanent Wave,* 1–12) and Kath-

leen A. Laughlin ("Is it Time to Jump Ship?," 76–81) are valuable summaries of the debate.

20. "Battle for Womanhood," *Wonder Woman #5,* June–July 1943.
21. "The Purloined Pressure Coordinator," *Comic Cavalcade #4,* Fall 1943.
22. "The Adventure of the Life Vitamin," *Wonder Woman #7,* Winter 1943.
23. "America's Wonder Women of Tomorrow," *Wonder Woman #7,* Winter 1943.
24. Gallup's polling on this question over the years is reported and challenged in Streb et al., "Social Desirability Effects and Support for a Female American President," *Public Opinion Quarterly* 72 (2008): 76–89.
25. "A Wife for Superman," *Hartford Courant,* September 28, 1942.
26. "The Amazon Bride," *Comic Cavalcade #8,* Fall 1944.

CHAPTER 27. SUFFERING SAPPHO!

1. OBR, "Our Women Are Our Future," *Family Circle,* August 14, 1942. Marston sent a copy of this article to Gaines and asked him to send it to Bender. The clipping, with a covering note saying, "Dr. Marston thought you might be interested in this," is in Bender's papers, box 16, folder 7.
2. OBR, "Fit to Be Tied?" *Family Circle,* March 21, 1937.
3. "Department Store Perfidy," *Sensation Comics #8,* August 1942.
4. WMM, typewritten script for *Wonder Woman #1,* Episode A, dated April 15, 1942, DC Comics Archives.
5. WMM, typewritten script for *Wonder Woman #2,* Episode A, undated, DC Comics Archives, pp. 7–8, 14, 15. Compare to "The God of War," *Wonder Woman #2,* Fall 1942, pp. 4C, 8A, 19–21, 25.
6. Mayer quoted in Daniels, *DC Comics,* 61.
7. Frank summarizes the report in Josette Frank, "What's in the Comics?" *Journal of Educational Sociology* 18 (December 1944): 214–22. On the background behind this issue, see Harvey Zorbaugh (associate editor of the journal) to LB, July 31, 1944, Bender Papers, box 12, folder 17. Zorbaugh had hoped to include an article by either Sterling North or Clifton Fadiman ("in any case, it will be an article of violent criticism of the comics," Zorbaugh told Bender), but in the end, neither critic contributed.
8. Sidonie Matsner Gruenberg, "The Comics as a Social Force," *Journal of Educational Sociology* 18 (December 1944): 204–13.
9. Josette Frank to MCG, February 17, 1943, WW Letters, Smithsonian. Gaines also forwarded a copy of this letter to Bender; it is in her papers, box 16, folder 1. Frank had been following Wonder Woman from the start. In October 1941, Gaines sent her "an advanced copy of 'All-Star Comics' #8, which contains the introductory episode of 'Wonder Woman.'" MCG to Josette Frank, October 16, 1941, CSAA Papers, box 24, folder 239. She had also long complained about how the magazine "flaunts a partly dressed woman on the cover" and that "the 'ladies' in this strip always seem to appear in chains or irons," as in a letter to Harry Childs, dated February 8, 1943, CSAA Papers, box 24, folder 240.
10. WMM to MCG, February 20, 1943, WW Letters, Smithsonian.
11. BHRM, interview with the author, July 14, 2013.

12. WMM to MCG, February 20, 1943, WW Letters, Smithsonian.
13. Dorothy Roubicek to MCG, February 19, 1943, and Roubicek, pencil sketch of Wonder Woman costume with penciled annotation to WMM from MCG, February 19, 1943, WW Letters, Smithsonian.
14. Francis J. Burke to Alice Marble, February 20, 1943, Bender Papers, box 16, folder 6.
15. MCG to LB, February 26, 1943, Bender Papers, box 16, folder 1.
16. Dorothy Roubicek to MCG, March 12, 1943, Memo, WW Letters, Smithsonian. Bender found the whole controversy truly fascinating, writing to Gaines:

> I must tell you I am really very much interested in the content of the psychological problems of Wonder Woman, and would appreciate it very much if you would keep in touch with me on other material coming in concerning Wonder Woman. . . . I have been discussing some of these problems in various lectures which I am giving and am really interested to go into the psychological implications because these seem to strike at the very heart of masculinity and femininity and of aggression and submission which is very significant in our modern culture.

LB to MCG, April 6, 1943. Gaines replied, assuring her that he would keep her posted. MCG to LB, April 13, 1943. Both letters are in the Bender Papers, box 16, folder 1.
17. LB, "The Psychology of Children's Reading and the Comics," *Journal of Educational Sociology* 18 (December 1944): 223–31; quotations are from pp. 225, 226, and 231. A marked draft of this essay can be found in the Bender Papers, box 13, folder 20.
18. Nyberg, *Seal of Approval,* 14. W.W.D. Sones to MCG, March 15, 1943, WW Letters, Smithsonian. Sones's letter inspired a lengthy, quasi-scholarly reply from WMM: WMM to W.W.D. Sones, March 20, 1943, WW Letters, Smithsonian. It recapitulates the basic arguments of *The Emotions of Normal People.* Gaines sent copies of both letters to Bender; they are in her papers, box 16, folder 1.
19. John D. Jacobs to "Charles Moulton," September 9, 1943, WW Letters, Smithsonian.
20. MCG to WMM, September 14, 1943, WW Letters, Smithsonian.
21. WMM to MCG, September 15, 1943, WW Letters, Smithsonian.
22. Josette Frank to MCG, January 29, 1944, WW Letters, Smithsonian, and Bender Papers, box 16, folder 2. Gaines forwarded a copy of this letter to Bender.
23. WMM to MCG, February 1, 1944, WW Letters, Smithsonian.
24. MCG to Helen Frostenson, Children's Ward, Bellevue Hospital, c/o LB, Psychiatric Division, January 21, 1944, Bender Papers, box 16, folder 2.
25. Bender's 1954 Senate testimony, p. 156.
26. Dorothy Roubicek to MCG, February 8, 1944, Memo, WW Letters, Smithsonian. And see Gaines to LB, February 8, 1944, Bender Papers, box 16, folder 2.
27. See also "Wonder Woman Syndication," *Independent News,* April 1944. This article includes a photograph of John Connolly, the president of King Features, signing a contract with Gaines, Marston and two other guys looking on. A complete set of the Wonder Woman comic strip, edited by Dean Mullaney, will be published in 2014 by the Library of American Comics.
28. On Bender joining the editorial advisory board, see MCG to LB, February 8, 1944; Harry E. Childs (of *Detective Comics*) to LB, February 25, 1944 (this letter is the contract for her services); and LB to Harry E. Childs, March 1944, enclosing correspon-

dence she has had with the American Academy of Medicine, documenting that her serving on this board does not violate the academy's code of ethics. Bender's interest was always chiefly in Wonder Woman. See, e.g., LB to M. C. Gaines, November 16, 1944: "Wonder Woman is still my chief interest because of the problems of femininity and masculinity and passivity and aggression which it deals with." All in Bender Papers, box 16, folder 2. As described by Childs in the February 25, 1944, letter, the duties of the members of the "Editorial Advisory Board of the Superman D-C publications" were to read the comics (all of which would be sent) and to render "any thoughts—favorable or unfavorable—that you may have on their content or any suggestions you might care to make for future issues"; to allow one's name to appear in the magazines; to "consult with us on the subject of children's entertainment in magazines or radio and render us opinions of abstract questions on the subject"; and to "permit us to refer to your position on the Editorial Advisory Board in our direct mail and advertising trade paper for promotion." She was paid $100 per month.

29. WMM's typescripts for the strips for week 1 and week 37 can be found in WW, Selected Continuities, Smithsonian.

28. SUPERPROF

1. On the location of the Marston Art Studio, see EHM to Jerry Bails, sometime in the 1970s, quoted in Roy Thomas, "Two Touches of Venus," *Alter Ego* 3, no. 1 (Summer 1999): 16. The address is given in WMM to JHMK, March 3, 1944, in the possession of JHMK. The office was in room 1403. The business is referred to as the Marston Art Studio in EHM to JHMK, receipt of payment for services, February 3, 1948, in the possession of JHMK.

2. WMM, Psychology Exam, January 25, 1944, typewritten examination, in the possession of JHMK; WMM to JHMK, March 3, 1944. Marston had decided that he needed to hire someone outside the family to help with Wonder Woman. Hummel told me that Olive Byrne, while a beautiful writer, "was not able to write the comic strip," while Holloway "was a lawyer, and not that type of writer at all." JHMK, interview with the author, January 12, 2014.

3. JHMK, e-mail to the author, January 29, 2014.

4. HGP, Draft Registration card, April 1942, *U.S., World War II Draft Registration Cards, 1942* (Provo, UT: Ancestry.com, 2010); EHM quoted in Daniels, *Wonder Woman*, 47; and EHM to JE, January 11, 1973, in the possession of JE.

5. MM, interview conducted by Steve Korte, July 29, 1999, DC Comics Archives.

6. "I got a call from Bellevue Hospital that they had a Harry G. Peter in their charity ward. He was a clean person. But he never worried about how he dressed at all. So when he got a chicken bone in his throat, I had to go rescue him out of the charity hospital." JHMK, interview with the author, January 12, 2014.

7. Olive Ann Marston Lamott, interview conducted by Steve Korte, August 25, 1999, DC Comics Archives; Olive Ann Marston Lamott, interview with the author, July 15, 2013; BHRM, "Memories of an Unusual Father," 28; and BHRM, interview conducted by Steve Korte, summer 1999, DC Comics Archives. "Mr. Peter was a quiet, thoughtful, sensitive man and he liked and approved of Wonder Woman," Huntley said. MWH to JE, June 14, 1972, Steinem Papers, Smith College, box 213, folder 5.

8. JHMK, interview with the author, January 26, 2014; JHMK, interview with the author, January 12, 2014. JHMK also said to me, "Dotsie, although she was related to Margaret Sanger and wrote a beautiful dissertation about Margaret Sanger, she did not, she was not able to write the comic strip." OBR gave oral history interviews about MS, but, as far as I have ever been able to tell, never wrote much about her, beyond testimonials here and there. Walowit corresponded with Hummel in 1974; MS did not come up. "Marston and I would get together at his home in Rye and talk. . . . We definitely had ESP with one another and thought on the same wave lengths. Then the ideas were written into later scripts embodying his psychological beliefs," Hummel wrote on March 8, 1974, in a letter to Walowit, cited in Walowit, "Wonder Woman," 39–40. Walowit was not convinced that Hummel wrote the scripts she claims to have written (see Walowit's discussion of "Wonder Woman and the Winds of Time," *Wonder Woman #17*, on p. 118 of her dissertation).

9. BHRM, "Memories of an Unusual Father," 12; Sue Grupposo, interview with the author, July 15, 2013; and WMM, *March On!*, 214–15.

10. Sheldon Mayer, 1975 DC Convention: Wonder Woman Panel, transcript in the DC Comics Archives.

11. Olive Ann Marston Lamott, interview with the author, July 15, 2013, and BHRM, "Memories of an Unusual Father," 21.

12. Olive Ann Marston Lamott, interview with the author, July 15, 2013.

13. WMM to BHRM, August 16 and 24, 1944, in the possession of BHRM.

14. OBR to MS, May 7, 1936, MS Papers, Library of Congress, microfilm edition, L006: 0948.

15. WMM to BHRM, July 17, 1944, in the possession of BHRM; and WMM, "Queen Hepzibah's Revenge," typewritten script for an extra episode for *Wonder Woman #2*, never printed, DC Comics Archives. The story involves a giant rabbit with wings named Butch.

16. WMM to BHRM, August 4, July 11, and July 21, 1944, in the possession of BHRM.

17. MSML to BHRM and Audrey Marston, February 27, 1963, in the possession of BHRM.

18. WMM, "Sew and Sow," *Family Circle*, March 19, 1943.

19. WMM, "Why 100,000,000 Americans Read Comics," 35–44.

20. Cleanth Brooks and Robert B. Heilman, letter to the editor, *American Scholar* 13 (Spring 1944): 248–52. Brooks was, at the time, defending New Criticism. See Cleanth Brooks, "The New Criticism: A Brief for the Defense," *American Scholar* 13 (Summer 1944): 285–95.

21. Holloway recalls the date and the title of the play in a letter to BHRM, April 5 [no year given but it must be c. 1963], in the possession of BHRM. Her memory was remarkably good. *School for Brides* was staged at the Royale Theatre from August 1, 1944, to September 30, 1944.

22. Diary of WMM, entry for August 25, 1944, in the possession of BHRM; JHMK, interview with the author, January 12, 2014. On MWH and Ethel Byrne: "She had come up from Ethel's at Cape Cod to meet me," Marston wrote in his diary. Diary of WMM, entries for August 26–29, 1944, in the possession of BHRM.

23. Diary of WMM, entry for September 25, 1944, in the possession of BHRM.

24. BHRM, "Memories of an Unusual Father," 17, 21–22. On the leg braces in WW, see "The Case of the Girl in Braces," *Sensation Comics #50*, February 1946.

25. Almost every Wonder Woman comic-book story written in 1945, all of which were

published under the name "Charles Moulton," has since been credited to either JHMK or Kanigher. For a list, see *Wonder Woman Archives*, vol. 7, table of contents. But see also my Comics Index. Kanigher is often thought to have claimed credit for stories he didn't write. The source of the commonly accepted attributions is a set of questionnaires distributed by Jerry Bails in the 1960s, according to an e-mail from Roy Thomas to the author, July 16, 2013.

26. JHMK, interview with the author, January 12, 2014.
27. Ibid.
28. Charles W. Morton (*Atlantic*) to Walter J. Ong, January 19, 1945; Editors of *Harper's Magazine* to Walter J. Ong, undated; H. L. Binsse (*Commonweal*) to Walter J. Ong, March 29, 1945; Editor of the *Yale Review* to Walter J. Ong, received April 15, 1945; Editors of the *Kenyon Review* to Walter J. Ong, received May 18, 1945; Walter J. Ong Papers, St. Louis University, and I have lost track of the box and folder numbers.
29. Walter J. Ong, "Comics and the Super State," *Arizona Quarterly* 1 (1945): 34–48.
30. Harry Behn to Walter J. Ong, August 20, 1945, Walter J. Ong Manuscript Collection, box 7, St. Louis University, and Aldo Notarianni to Walter J. Ong, October 30, 1945, Walter J. Ong Manuscript Collection, box 7.
31. A journal kept by Hummel in 1946 and 1947 records her work, day by day. The work she did that year included typing scripts for Marston, checking art, proofing copy, writing synopses for new stories, writing new stories, and typing them. A record of travel expenses, for taking a train from New York to Rye and a taxi to Cherry Orchard, demonstrates that Hummel went to Rye every two or three days, although there were, at times, gaps of a week or more between visits. JHMK, "Record: Time taken to write Scripts, General work schedule, & Diary," handwritten bound journal, April 24, 1946–January 6, 1947, in the possession of JHMK.
32. BHRM, e-mail to the author, July 25, 2013.
33. "The Battle of Desires," *Comic Cavalcade #16*, August–September 1946.
34. "The Bog Trap," *Sensation #58*, October 1946.
35. BHRM, "Memories of an Unusual Father," 17, 29; JHMK, interview with the author, January 12, 2014; and JHMK, interview with the author, April 26, 2014.
36. "Only a day and a half before his death he was correcting art work on the Wonder Woman strip." C. Daly King, "William Moulton Marston," *Harvard College Class of 1915: Thirty-fifth Anniversary Report* (Cambridge, MA: Printed for the Class, 1950), 212.
37. BHRM, "Memories of an Unusual Father," 17, 29.
38. Olive Ann Marston Lamott, interview with the author, July 15, 2013, and BHRM, "Memories of an Unusual Father," 29–30.
39. "Dr. W. M. Marston, Psychologist, 53," *New York Times*, May 3, 1947. Similar obituaries appeared in Boston: e.g., "Dr. Wm. M. Marston Developed 'Lie Detector,' Taught, Lectured Widely," *Boston Globe*, May 3, 1947. A one-sentence death notice appeared in Los Angeles: "Death Takes Inventor," *Los Angeles Times*, May 3, 1947.

29. THE COMIC-BOOK MENACE

1. EHM to Jack Liebowitz, January 5, 1948, DC Comics Archives.
2. JHMK, interview with the author, January 12, 2014, and JHMK, e-mail to the

author, January 29, 2014. It appears, though, that Hummel's last day of work may have been May 31, 1947. EHM to JHMK, receipt of payment for services, February 3, 1948, in the possession of JHMK, is payment for services rendered between January 1 and May 31, 1947, in the amount of $1,366. This appears to have been a closing of the account. The sum covers twenty-two weeks of work, at about $62 per week. A note written in pencil on the receipt reads, "Hi Joye! Zazzie": greetings from Huntley.

3. Sheldon Mayer, 1975 DC Convention: Wonder Woman Panel, transcript in the DC Comics Archives.

4. EHM believed that the contract WMM had written in 1941 gave his heirs some control over the hiring of writers, and she was determined to exercise it. "The Marston family seemed to have some legal rights to say yea or nay to who took over Wonder Woman," she told Robert Kanigher. Interview, undated, DC Comics Archives.

5. EHM to Jack Liebowitz, January 5, 1948.

6. Donna Woolfolk Cross, interview with the author, October 30, 2013, and e-mail to the author, November 13, 2013.

7. EHM to Jack Liebowitz, January 5, 1948. Donna Woolfolk Cross did not corroborate that her parents created *Moon Girl;* she had never heard of it. But she did corroborate her mother's departure from DC Comics in 1947. My identification of the creator of *Moon Girl* comes from EHM's description of "a very intelligent, well educational professional writer on a share basis, whose wife, for a short time at least, was editor of Wonder Woman." That can't have been anyone else except Woolfolk and Roubicek.

8. *Moon Girl,* initially called *Moon Girl and the Prince,* was published between 1947 and 1949. Issues 1–5 and 7–8 are housed at the Library of Congress (some in print, some on microfiche). "Future Man" appears in *Moon Girl #2,* Winter 1947.

9. EHM to Jack Liebowitz, January 5, 1948. "This summer and fall my work at the Met. has been light so that I have been able to spend whole days on WW," Holloway wrote, but "I will have to decide very soon now whether I am working for Metropolitan Life Ins. Co. or National Comics."

10. Robert Kanigher, interview conducted by Les Daniels, 2004, DC Comics Archives.

11. EHM, "Information for Wonder Woman Scripts," addressed to Robert Kanigher and dated February 4, 1948, DC Comics Archives.

12. Robert Kanigher, "Deception's Daughter," *Comic Cavalcade #26,* April–May 1948.

13. Allan Asherman, interview with the author, August 12, 2013, and Christie Marston, interview with the author, July 25, 2012.

14. The symposium, "The Psychopathology of Comic Books," was held in New York on March 19, 1948, at the Academy of Medicine. LB appears to have attended but not to have presented. A typescript of the proceedings can be found in Bender's papers, box 16, folder 4. The quotations from Gershon Legman are from pp. 20, 36, Bender Papers, box 16, folder 4. And see also Legman quoted in Nyberg, *Seal of Approval,* 39.

15. Fredric Wertham, "The Comics . . . Very Funny!" *Saturday Review of Literature,* May 29, 1948, 6–7, 27. Beaty, *Fredric Wertham and the Critique of Mass Culture,* 118–19. See also John A. Lent, ed., *Pulp Dreams: International Dimensions of the Postwar Anti-Comics Campaign* (Madison, NJ: Fairleigh Dickinson University Press, 1999); William W. Savage Jr., *Comic Books and America, 1945–1954* (Norman: University of Oklahoma Press, 1990), chapter 7; and David Hajdu, *The Ten-Cent Plague: The*

Great Comic-Book Scare and How It Changed America (New York: Farrar, Straus and Giroux, 2008).

16. Baker, *Margaret Sanger*, 199–201.

17. Nyberg, *Seal of Approval*, 88–89; Beaty, *Fredric Wertham and the Critique of Mass Culture*, 16–17; Wertham, "Psychiatry and Sex Crimes," *Journal of Criminal Law and Criminology* 28 (1938): 847–53; and Fredric Wertham, *Seduction of the Innocent* (New York: Rinehart, 1972), 68–69.

18. Wertham, *Seduction of the Innocent*, 76; and Beaty, *Fredric Wertham and the Critique of Mass Culture*, 118.

19. "Psychiatrist Asks Crime Comics Ban," *New York Times*, December 14, 1950; and Beaty, *Fredric Wertham and the Critique of Mass Culture*, 120–25, 156–57.

20. LB to Estes Kefauver, August 17, 1950, Bender Papers, box 16, folder 4, and Kefauver to Bender, August 7, 1950, in the same folder.

21. "Psychiatrist Asks Crime Comics Ban."

22. Beaty, *Fredric Wertham and the Critique of Mass Culture*, 156–57.

23. LB to Whitney Ellsworth, August 22, 1951; Ellsworth, in a letter to Bender on August 27, 1951, agreed. Both letters are in the Bender Papers, box 16, folder 5.

24. Wertham, "Paid Experts of the Comic Book Industry Posing as Independent Scholars," undated scrap. Wertham Papers, box 122, folder 2. Wertham's description of Bender as the nation's top comics flunkie reads, in full: "1. Most important: Dr. Lauretta Bender, whose name appears on the Editorial Board of the National Comics group (National Comics Publications, Inc. 480 Lexington Ave. NYC). She gives as her titles: Assoc. Prof. of Psychiatry, School of Medicine, NYU; Psychiatrist, NY University; Bellevue Medical Center. She has a full-time job in charge of the children's ward in Bellevue Hospital NYC. On crime comics payroll since 1941. Boasted privately of bringing up her 3 children on money from crime comic books." My thanks to Carol L. Tilley for calling this item to my attention.

25. Vernon Pope to LB, October 23, 1953, Bender Papers, box 16, folder 6. Pope had been on the editorial staff of *Look* magazine.

26. Nyberg, *Seal of Approval*, 93.

27. Wertham, *Seduction of the Innocent*, 103, 33, 188–91.

28. Ibid., 192–93.

29. Ibid., 166–67, 192–93, 233–35.

30. The hearings were held in New York to accommodate witnesses from the comic-book industry. Nyberg, *Seal of Approval*, 52–53. *Hearings Before the Subcommittee to Investigate Juvenile Delinquency*.

31. *Hearings Before the Subcommittee on Juvenile Delinquency*, p. 154. Subsequent research on Wertham's papers may bear Bender out. The "case studies" Wertham reported in *Seduction of the Innocent* seem to have been selectively edited composites. Carol L. Tilley, "Seducing the Innocent: Fredric Wertham and the Falsifications That Helped Condemn Comics," *Information & Culture: A Journal of History* 47 (2012): 383–413.

32. LB to Estes Kefauver, August 17, 1950, Bender Papers, box 16, folder 4, and Kefauver to Bender, August 7, 1950, in the same folder.

33. Nyberg, *Seal of Approval*, 76.

34. Ibid., x; Comics Magazine Association of America Comics Code, 1954, as reproduced in Nyberg, *Seal of Approval*, 166–69; and LB to Jack Liebowitz, November 5, 1954,

and Liebowitz to LB, November 10, 1954, Bender Papers, box 16, folder 6. Lauretta Bender's name stopped appearing in DC Comics magazines in November 1954.

35. Robert Kanigher, interview conducted by Les Daniels, 2004, DC Comics Archives.

36. Cover, *Sensation Comics #94*, November–December 1949.

37. Elaine Tyler May, *Homeward Bound: American Families in the Cold War Era* (1988; repr., New York: Perseus, 2000), chapter 3. *Fortune* quoted in Evans, *Born for Liberty*, 221.

38. Daniels, *Wonder Woman*, 93–102. After "Wonder Women of History" stopped appearing in *Wonder Woman*, it ran, irregularly, in *Sensation Comics*. About Kanigher, Walowit wrote, "Shortly after the original author's death, the cohesive concepts which governed the early stories are ignored, and the series focuses almost entirely on Wonder Woman's physical strength. The later comic exhibits neither the imaginative quality for the affirmative image of both human nature and of women which characterize the early stories." Walowit, "Wonder Woman," abstract. Marjorie Wilkes Huntley was distressed as well. In 1955, she was surprised to find that Wonder Woman was still on *Parents' Magazine*'s list of objectionable comics. She wrote to *Parents' Magazine* to complain, noting that Kanigher had taken away from Wonder Woman everything that had been controversial in the 1940s: "I know that the present editor has from his own choice, aside from the pressure of criticism, deleted all those elements which were objectionable in the magazine. So she, Wonder Woman, is now a character which is active in the ways that Superman is active—which you do approve of." MWH to the Cincinnati Committee on Evaluation of Comic Books, c/o Parents Magazine, August 24, 1955, CSAA Papers, box 14, folder 140. Huntley sent copies of her exchange on this subject to Josette Frank.

39. Alder, *Lie Detectors*, 223–28.

30. LOVE FOR ALL

1. BHRM, interview with the author, July 14, 2013.

2. OBR to BHRM, March 16, 1948, in the possession of BHRM.

3. OBR to MS, January 11, 1949, MS Papers, Smith College, microfilm edition, S29: 0495.

4. MS to OBR, January 24, 1952, MS Papers, Collected Document Series, microfilm edition, C09: 314.

5. Audrey Marston, interview with the author, July 14, 2013.

6. MS donated selections of her papers to the Library of Congress in multiple gifts made between 1942 and her death, in 1966. (Jeffrey M. Flannery, Library of Congress, e-mail to the author, March 7, 2014.) MS began handing her papers over to Smith College in 1946 and continued to add to the collection until her death (see the acquisition history in the collection's finding guide). Olive Byrne boxed up many of MS's papers. (Maida Goodwin, Smith College, e-mail to the author, March 7, 2014.)

7. MS to Ethel Byrne, January 22, 1952, *Selected Papers of MS*, 3:292–93.

8. See MS to Juliet Barrett Rublee, February 13, 1955, *Selected Papers of MS*, 3:386.

9. OBR to MS, May 4, 1955, MS Papers, Smith College, microfilm edition, S47: 0273; OBR to MS, January 28, 1955, S45: 1067; MS to OBR, February 1, 1955, S46: 033; and OBR to MS, February 5, 1955, S46: 073.

10. "I gave all my stuff to Margaret so she could give it to Smith or wherever she wanted to give it." OBR, Van Voris interview, 27.

11. OBR to MS, July 14, 1953, MS Papers, Library of Congress, microfilm edition, L007: 0598. MS to OBR, [January? 1954?], *Selected Papers of MS*, 3:353.

12. MS to OBR, November 1, 1954, MS Papers, microfilm edition, Collected Documents Series, CO10: 605. Sanger instructs OBR to call Dr. Abraham Stone or one of his colleagues: "I doubt that the Bureau can afford your high class work, but a part time job is often available." At the time, the Margaret Sanger Research Bureau was having considerable financial difficulties. See, e.g., MS to Abraham Stone, April 2, 1953, and MS to Katharine Dexter McCormick, March 26, 1954, in *Selected Papers of MS*, 3:330, 369.

13. This is told in various places, but see MS, *Selected Papers of MS*, 3:272. On the progesterone tests, see MS to Katharine Dexter McCormick, February 4, 1955, in *Selected Papers of MS*, 3:381.

14. The earliest secretarial correspondence from OBR for MS I can find is OBR to B. D. Danchik, August 26, 1955, MS Papers, Smith College, microfilm edition, S48: 0539, and then running through 0547–0810 there are various letters typed by OBR and signed in this way—that is, through October 17, 1955. At this time, OBR was living in Tucson, in MS's house. See OBR to MS, September 20, 1955, S48: 0710, from 65 Sierra Vista Drive, Tucson, reporting on such matters as mail to the house, as well as OBR to MS, September 30, 1955, S48: 0742.

15. MS to D. Kenneth Rose, August 20, 1956, in *Selected Papers of MS*, 3:402.

16. MS to OBR, October 17, 1955, MS Papers, Collected Document Series, microfilm edition, C10: 965, and MS to OBR, February 2, 1959, MS Papers, Smith College, microfilm edition, S55: 0180.

17. MS to OBR, April 30, 1956, MS Papers, Smith College, microfilm edition, S49: 0945.

18. OBR to MS, May 2, 1956, MS Papers, Smith College, microfilm edition, S49: 0974.

19. OBR to MS, July 19, 1956, MS Papers, Smith College, microfilm edition, S50: 303.

20. OBR to MS, September 30, 1955, MS Papers, Smith College, microfilm edition, S48: 0742, and MS to OBR, April 8, 1957, MS Papers, Smith College, microfilm edition, S51: 0897.

21. MS, Mike Wallace interview, September 21, 1957, transcript, in *Selected Papers of MS*, 3:423–37. See also Chesler, *Woman of Valor*, 440–42.

22. On EHM's retirement: Olive Ann Marston Lamott, interview with the author, July 15, 2013. On the move to Tucson: OBR to MS, February 11, 1959, MS Papers, Collected Document Series, microfilm edition, C11: 539. And see: "Barbara [Stuart Sanger's wife] tells me that you & Betty want to rent a house," from MS to OBR, August 10, 1959, MS Papers, Collected Document Series, microfilm edition, C11: 607. In an alumnae questionnaire dated June 15, 1960, EHM gave her address as 928 North Campbell Avenue, Tucson, Arizona. EHM, Alumnae Association of Mount Holyoke College, Biographical Questionnaire, June 13, 1960, Mount Holyoke College archives. EHM and OBR returned to New York in about 1963. BHRM, e-mail to the author, July 25, 2013.

23. OBR to Justice William O. Douglas, June 9, 1965, in the possession of BHRM.

24. Editorial, *New York Times,* September 11, 1966.

25. "Marston-Sanger Vows Solemnized," *Tucson Daily Citizen,* March 25, 1961.

26. MSML to Byrne and Audrey Marston, February 27, 1963, in the possession of BHRM.

27. MSML to Byrne and Audrey Marston, February 27, 1963.

EPILOGUE: GREAT HERA! I'M BACK!

1. JE, interview with the author, August 5, 2013; JE to EHM, May 8, 1972, Steinem Papers, Smith College, box 213, folder 5; EHM to MWH, June 12, 1972, Steinem Papers, Smith College, box 213, folder 5; and MWH to JE, May 21, 1972, Steinem Papers, Smith College, box 213, folder 5. Huntley told Edgar the story of a letter Marston once got from an eight-year-old girl. "WONDER WOMAN, are you *real*?" the girl asked. "Yes, she was Real!" Huntley answered.

2. Mary Thom, *Inside "Ms.": Twenty-five Years of the Magazine and the Feminist Movement* (New York: Holt, 1997), 1; Amy Erdman Farrell, *Yours in Sisterhood: "Ms." Magazine and the Promise of Popular Feminism* (Chapel Hill: University of North Carolina Press, 1998), 21–22; Evans, *Born for Liberty*, 288; Susan Faludi, "Death of a Revolutionary," *New Yorker*, April 15, 2013; and Flora Davis, *Moving the Mountain: The Women's Movement in America Since 1960* (Urbana: University of Illinois Press, 1999), 110–14.

3. Trina Robbins et al., *It Aint Me Babe* (Berkeley, CA: Last Gasp Ecofunnies Publication, Conceived by the Women's Liberation Basement Press, 1970), July 1970. The cover illustration is by Trina Robbins. "Breaking Out" is credited to the It Ain't Me Babe Basement Collective, with artwork by Carole, whose last name, apparently, has been forgotten by everyone else involved. See Trina Robbins, *A Century of Women Cartoonists* (Northampton, MA: Kitchen Sink Press, 1993), 134. In 1986, Robbins became the first woman to draw Wonder Woman (*A Century of Women Cartoonists*, 165).

4. Kelly Anderson, interview with JE, July 26, 2005, Voices of Feminism Oral History Project, Sophia Smith Collection, Smith College, available at http://www.smith.edu/libraries/libs/ssc/vof/transcripts/Edgar.pdf; and Patricia Carbine, interview with the author, August 9, 2013.

5. "Warner Communications Acquires Interest in New Ms. Magazine," press release, Warner Communications, undated but spring 1972, *Ms.* Magazine Papers, uncataloged but in a box provisionally numbered 90A and in a folder titled Warner Communications, 1972–1977; and Patricia Carbine, interview with the author, August 9, 2013.

6. Patricia Carbine, interview with the author, August 9, 2013; Farrell, *Yours in Sisterhood*, 17–18; and Evans, *Born for Liberty*, 291.

7. EHM to MWH, June 12, 1972, Steinem Papers, Smith College, box 213, folder 5. This letter is in Steinem's papers because after receiving it Huntley forwarded to the offices of *Ms.*, and it seems to have been preserved because it was thought to carry some legal weight. On the envelope in which this letter arrived, postmarked June 14, 1972, someone has written, in pencil, "Good faith—indemnifying us vs. damages." After JE sent EHM a copy of the final book, EHM wrote back with "nothing but praise" for it. EHM to JE, January 11, 1973, in the possession of JE.

8. Thom, *Inside "Ms.,"* 31–33; Daniels, *Wonder Woman*, 131–32; and Farrell, *Yours in Sisterhood*, 28–29, 54–55. Steinem's ties to comics have led to the charge that the arrangement to put Wonder Woman on the cover of *Ms.* was dictated by Warner, not by the editorial staff of the magazine. Warner was formed in 1971 by a former funeral home director named Steve Ross. Daniels claims that Steinem was friends with Ross and entertains the possibility that Steinem made a deal with Ross: Warner would fund *Ms.* if *Ms.* would help promote a Wonder Woman revival. If so, the arrangement was informal and undocumented. No such deal is part of the for-

mal legal arrangement: copies of stock purchase agreements between *Ms.* Magazine Corp. and Warner Communications, Inc., dated April 1972 and May 2, 1972, can be found in the *Ms.* Magazine Papers at Smith College, uncataloged but in a box provisionally numbered 90A and in a folder titled Warner Communications, 1972–1977. That same folder contains *Ms.* magazine's financial reports, submitted to Warner, along with a record of Warner's payments to *Ms.* These documents make no mention of Wonder Woman. (Steinem would not agree to be interviewed by me.)

9. *Wonder Woman: A "Ms." Book* (New York: Holt, Rinehart and Winston, 1972), Gloria Steinem, Introduction. On Roubicek Woolfolk, see Julius Schwartz, foreword to Roy Thomas, *All-Star Companion,* 4, and Robbins and Yronwode, *Women and the Comics,* 104. In the history of comics, Roubicek Woolfolk has been at best neglected and at worst erased. In the mid-1970s, when Joe Brancatelli was writing entries for *The World Encyclopedia of Comics,* his editors threw away his entry on Roubicek Woolfolk: "I wrote a hundred and ninety of the two hundred comic-book entries, which was both character and creator. My job was to submit to Maurice Horn a list of both characters and creators to write about. I would say ninety-five percent of what I submitted was accepted. You know who was knocked out? Dorothy." Brancatelli, interview with the author, November 1, 2013.

10. Patricia Carbine, interview with the author, August 9, 2013; JE, interview with the author, August 5, 2013; Anderson, interview with JE, July 26, 2005; Thom, *Inside "Ms.,"* 41–22; and Anderson, interview with JE, July 26, 2005, p. 23.

11. JE, "'Wonder Woman' Revisited," *Ms.,* July 1972, 52–55. A corrected typescript can be found in Steinem Papers, box 213, folder 5. Edgar received a fair bit of mail about the piece, some from fans of the original Wonder Woman and some from readers very excited to hear about the "New" Wonder Woman. See, e.g., Norma Harrison to JE, July 12, 1972, and Richard J. Kalina to JE, July 4, 1972; Heidi Michalski (chair of NOW) to JE, July 31, 1972, in Steinem Papers, box 151, folder 14.

12. "Dorothy had given me over to Gloria Steinem, who was doing a Wonder Woman book. So I know Dorothy had very specific ideas for what she wanted to do with Wonder Woman. . . . The whole experience was really about Gloria being very, very quickly embracing or dismissive of certain stories that I would present to her. Again, she didn't like the stories, obviously, where Wonder Woman was basically a guy with bracelets and long hair. She wanted me to find the stories that reflected a more contemporary viewpoint. She wasn't around a lot. I would basically show her the bound volumes of what I found and she would say, 'Yes,' 'No.' She was very diligent about reading the stuff, word for word. She was not condescending about comic books; she saw them as a way of communicating with a more visually oriented generation. She was remarkably open-minded," said Jeff Rovin in an interview with the author, July 25, 2013. Steinem's selection amounted to a kind of censorship, though: she carefully steered Rovin clear of scenes of bondage. As Walowit wrote, regarding the *Ms.* anthology, "That the editors could have managed to find twelve stories which avoid the issues of dominance and submission (often depicted in the comics as slavery and bondage) is in itself a *tour de force,* but misrepresents the pervasiveness of these concepts in the original Wonder Woman." Walowit, "Wonder Woman," 8. Walowit adds, "Although Steinem indicates that all twelve stories were written by the original author, two of the reprints are definitively not by Marston. 'The Girl from Yesterday' was written by Lee Goldsmith, and 'The Five Tasks of Thomas Tythe' by Robert Kaniger [*sic*]. 'When Treachery Wore a Green Shirt' is probably also written by Kaniger" (p. 18).

13. "The Return of Wonder Woman," *Ms.,* January 1973, display advertisement. And see the promotional copy from Holt, Rinehart and Winston, undated but mid-1972, *Ms.* Magazine Papers, Smith College, uncataloged but in a folder titled "Wonder Woman: A *Ms.* Book." When Holloway visited the offices of *Ms.* in the spring of 1972, she inspected both the inaugural issue of the magazine and the galleys of the *Ms.*–Wonder Woman anthology. Although Holloway didn't like the cover of the magazine ("done by a man"), she did like the cover of the book ("done by a gal"). EHM to MWH, June 12, 1972, Steinem Papers, box 213, folder 5. Holloway inscribed a copy of the book to Steinem, quoting from Fragment 57A, one of her favorite lines from Wharton's edition of Sappho's poems: "To Gloria, 'Hand Maiden of Aphrodite,' Sappho." EHM, handwritten dedication to *Wonder Woman: A "Ms." Book,* Steinem Papers, box 30, folder 1.

14. Eric Pace, "Lovely and Wise Heroine Summoned to Help the Feminist Cause," *New York Times,* October 19, 1972, and Michael Seiler, "Wonder Woman: The Movement's Fantasy Figure," *Los Angeles Times,* January 17, 1973. The story was picked up all over the country, through wire services. See also, e.g., "Searching for Wonder Woman," *San Francisco Chronicle,* October 27, 1972; "Wonder Woman Lives Again!" in the Long Beach, California, *Press-Telegram,* October 20, 1972; Eric Pace, "Now It's Zap! A She-Wonder for Feminists," *Toledo Times,* October 20, 1972; "Ms. Features the Return of Wonder Woman, *St. Louis Post-Dispatch,* November 5, 1972; "Wonder Woman Will Aid Cause," in the Dover, NH, *Foster S. Democrat,* November 6, 1972; "Wonder Woman Makes Comeback," in the Buffalo *Courier Express,* November 8, 1972; and "Comic-Book Heroine Revived as Symbol of Feminist Revolt," *Dallas Morning News,* November 5, 1972. Clippings can be found in the *Ms.* Magazine Papers, uncataloged but in a box provisionally numbered 52a, Clippings, 1968–1972, and in folders for July–December 1972.

15. "Now, if Ms. owned the rights to Wonder Woman we would be manufacturing a Wonder Woman doll right this moment," Patricia Carbine, *Ms.*'s publisher and editor in chief, wrote to Bill Sarnoff, the head of Warner. Patricia Carbine to William Sarnoff, May 17, 1973, uncataloged but in a box provisionally numbered 90A and in a folder titled Warner Communications, 1972–1977.

16. Cover, *Sister: A Monthly Publication of the Los Angeles Women's Center,* July 1973.

17. Dorothy Woolfolk is listed as editor, and Ethan C. Mordden as assistant editor, in two issues of *Wonder Woman* that are filed with Gloria Steinem's papers: *Wonder Woman #197* (November–December 1971) and *Wonder Woman #198* (January–February 1972). She is not listed as editor in *Wonder Woman #195* (July–August 1971), also filed with Steinem's papers, box 213, folder 5.

18. Steinem quoted in Matsuuchi, "Wonder Woman Wears Pants," 128.

19. Flora Davis to Dorothy Roubicek Woolfolk, June 23, 1972, Steinem Papers, box 33, folder 14. Apparently, Carmine Infantino's idea about Wonder Woman was "OK, we can get publicity as a feminist hero but we don't want her to become really loud about it." Roubicek Woolfolk wanted to be really loud about it. Jeff Rovin, interview with the author, July 25, 2013.

20. Dorothy Roubicek Woolfolk to Gloria Steinem, July 8, 1972, Steinem Papers, box 33, folder 14.

21. Samuel R. Delany, *Wonder Woman #203* (December 1972).

22. Samuel R. Delany, quoted in Ann Matsuuchi, "Wonder Woman Wears Pants: *Wonder Woman,* Feminism and the 1972 'Women's Lib' Issue," *Colloquy* 24 (2012): 118–42;

the quotation is on p. 119. One critic called the special issue "perhaps the worst travesty on feminism ever written." Walowit, "Wonder Woman," 35, 217–21.

23. Robbins and Yronwode, *Women and the Comics,* 106.

24. Allan Asherman (Kanigher's assistant in 1972), interview with the author, August 12, 2013; and Paul Levitz (former head of DC Comics), e-mail to the author, August 11, 2013. Kanigher had been much disconcerted when a reporter from *Ms.* came to interview him, according to Asherman, a story Levitz had also heard.

25. "New Adventures of the Original Wonder Woman," *Wonder Woman #204,* January–February 1973. And see Daniels, *Wonder Woman,* 131–33. Kanigher didn't last, either. In October 1973, he was replaced by Julius Schwartz (Walowit, "Wonder Woman," 36).

26. Susan Faludi, *Backlash: The Undeclared War Against American Women* (New York: Crown, 1991).

27. On the culture of trashing and the fate of Shulamith Firestone, see Susan Faludi, "Death of a Revolutionary," *New Yorker,* April 15, 2013.

28. Anselma Dell'Olio, "Divisiveness and Self-Destruction in the Women's Movement: A Letter of Resignation," 1970, quoted in Faludi, "Death of a Revolutionary." And see Vivian Gornick, "The Woman's Movement in Crisis: Let's Stop the Infighting!" *Village Voice,* November 3, 1975.

29. Dozier's 1967 *Wonder Woman* screen test for Ellie Wood Walker can be seen at http://www.youtube.com/watch?v=VWiiXs2uU1k.

30. "I watched the first part of the T.V. pilot show," EHM wrote to JE, April 19, 1974, in the possession of JE. "The grownups round here were not very responsive. The children—8 to 12—thought it was marvelous and that it should go on forever." See also Walowit, "Wonder Woman: Enigmatic Heroine of American Popular Culture," v–vi.

31. *Wonder Woman,* ABC Television, 1975, based on characters created by WMM, developed for television by Stanley Ralph Ross; the complete first season is available as a DVD distributed by Warner Communications, 2004.

32. "Lib Leader Warns Others Not to Be 'Superwomen,'" *Cleveland Press,* July 19, 1972. This story was picked up by the UP and the AP and reported all over the country; it involves an interview with Friedan after the publication of an essay of hers called "Beyond Women's Liberation," printed in *McCall's* in August 1972.

33. Carole Ann Douglas, "Redstockings Assert Steinem CIA Tie," *Off Our Backs* 5 (May–June 1975), 7. Gabrielle Schang, "Gloria Steinem's CIA Connection: Radical Feminists Won't Be *Ms.*-led," *Berkeley Barb,* May 30, 1975, is a reprint of the Redstockings' statement, illustrated by a picture of Gloria Steinem as Wonder Woman; it can be found in the Steinem Papers, box 203, folder 16.

34. Schang, "Gloria Steinem's CIA Connection," *Berkeley Barb,* May 30, 1975, and "Gloria Steinem's CIA Connection," *Women's Week,* undated feminist newsletter clippings, *Ms.* Magazine Papers, uncataloged. There was much bad blood in the backstory. In 1973, one Redstockings founder, Kathie Sarachild, had sent a résumé to *Ms.,* looking for an editorial position; she was not hired. Kathie Sarachild to *Ms.,* March 23, 1973, Steinem Papers, box 55, folder 10.

35. "Redstockings' Statement," *Off Our Backs* 5 (July 1975): 8–9, 28–33; quotations are from p. 29. A photocopy of the original press release can be found in the *Ms.* Magazine Papers, uncataloged but in a box provisionally numbered 21b and in a folder titled "Redstockings allegations, May–August 1975."

36. Gloria Steinem, "Statement from Steinem," *Off Our Backs* 5 (September–October 1975): 6, 22–23. *Ms.* also distributed the statement by mail, to notable feminists and to feminist publications, including *Lavender Woman, Majority Report,* and *Big Mama Rag.* See, e.g., Mary Daly to JE, September 17, 1975, thanking Edgar for sending Steinem's statement, *Ms.* Magazine Papers, uncataloged but provisionally in Box 21b, in a folder titled "Redstockings allegations, Sept–December 1975"; and Gloria Steinem to Sisters of Hera, August 14, 1975, same box, folder titled "Redstockings Allegations, May–August 1975."

37. JE to William Sarnoff, May 9, 1975, uncataloged but in a box provisionally numbered 90A and in a folder titled "Warner Communications, 1972–1977."

38. The charges continued to resurface, leaving Steinem more than exasperated; she wrote, in 1979, about "the sense of weariness and frustration I feel at having to deal over and over again with hackneyed and un-newsworthy charges" (Steinem to Victor Kovner, April 9, 1979). When Random House published an anthology of Redstockings' writings, it left out the allegations about *Ms.,* fearing legal action. The *Village Voice* planned a story about the allegations in 1979, but after attorneys for Steinem and *Ms.* wrote to the *Voice,* the story was killed.

39. Faludi, "Death of a Revolutionary."

40. Cott, *Grounding of Modern Feminism,* 181.

41. EHM to JE, November 16, 1983, in the possession of JE. "1915 Reviews," unpublished Mount Holyoke College alumni newsletter, May 30, 1975, n.p., entry for EHM.

42. EHM to Karen M. Walowit, May 4, 1974, quoted in Walowit, "Wonder Woman," 84–85.

43. When Ellen Chesler interviewed Olive Byrne in 1985, Byrne made discretion about the Marston family a precondition of the interview. "I promised not to write about Olive's own sensitive personal story as a condition of her agreeing to talk openly to me about Margaret and her mother," Chesler told me. "I am not sure how much of the detail I wrote down, given her concerns." Ellen Chesler, e-mail to the author, February 4, 2014. Byrne might have made a similar stipulation a condition of other interviews, including a lengthy one conducted by Jacqueline Van Voris in 1977.

44. EHM to JE, January 11, 1973, in the possession of JE.

45. Mary Frain, "93 Years Old," *Clinton Item,* October 15, 1982; MWH to BHRM, undated but October 1982. MWH, Funeral and Internment Instructions, November 6, 1974, in the possession of BHRM. The poem Huntley wished to be read is titled, "Only Time Can Die." *All U.S., Social Security Death Index, 1935–Current* (Provo, UT: Ancestry.com, 2011); original data: Social Security Administration, *Social Security Death Index, Master File,* Social Security Administration. Huntley was born on December 29, 1889, and died on December 30, 1986. *Massachusetts Death Index, 1970–2003* (Provo, UT: Ancestry.com, 2005); original data: State of Massachusetts, *Massachusetts Death Index, 1970–2003* (Boston: Commonwealth of Massachusetts Department of Health Services, 2005). These two accounts conflict: the *SSDI* says she died in Clinton (which is where the nursing home was); the *MDI* says she died in Marlborough (which probably means O.A.'s house). Donn Marston died in 1988. His obituary noted that he was survived by his wife and children; by his mother, "Olive Richard"; and by "an aunt, Elizabeth H. Marston." Donn Richard Marston, obituary, *Washington Post,* April 2, 1988.

46. Alder, *Lie Detectors,* chapter 19.

47. BHRM, interview with the author, July 14, 2013.

48. Ibid. OBR died in Tampa, Florida, on May 19, 1990, at the age of eighty-six. *Florida Death Index, 1877–1998* (Provo, UT: Ancestry.com, 2004); original data: State of Florida, *Florida Death Index, 1877–1998* (Jacksonville: Florida Department of Health, Office of Vital Records, 1998).

49. Sue Grupposo, interview with the author, July 15, 2013.

50. EHM died on April 2, 1993, in Bethel, Connecticut. "Elizabeth H. Marston, 100, Inspiration for Wonder Woman." *New York Times,* April 3, 1993. The *Hartford Courant* ran an editorial: "Wonder Woman's Mom," April 5, 1993.

AFTERWORD: THE HYDE DETECTOR

1. "Ah! Sweet Mystery of Life; MGM Tries Out 'Hyde Detector,'" *The Hollywood Reporter,* August 19, 1941. The film, directed by Victor Fleming, was released by MGM on August 12.

2. Several books about Wonder Woman were published either after I completed writing this book: Tim Hanley, *Wonder Woman Unbound: The Curious History of the World's Most Famous Heroine* (Chicago: IL: Chicago Review Press, 2014); Joseph J. Darowski, ed., *The Ages of Wonder Woman: Essays on the Amazon Princess in Changing Times* (Jefferson, NC: McFarland and Company, Inc., 2014); and Noah Berlatsky, *Wonder Woman: Bondage and Feminism in the Marston/Peter Comics, 1941–1948* (New Brunswick, NJ: Rutgers University Press, 2015).

3. EHM to Donn Marston, Sunday, September 22. The year is torn but September 22 fell on a Sunday in 1974, and I believe this letter is from that year. As this afterword went to press, Donn Marston's daughters, Nancy Wycoff and Margaret Van Cleave, had begun arranging to donate his papers to the Houghton Library at Harvard. This letter, and other materials cited in this afterword, will soon be part of the William Moulton Marston Papers, Houghton Library, Harvard University. They are cited here as WMM Papers.

4. "Ah! Sweet Mystery of Life; MGM Tries Out 'Hyde Detector.'"

5. Locks of hair belonging to WMM, cut in 1894 and preserved by ADM, in an envelope in the WMM Papers; and ADM, notebook, 1893–c. 1900, WMM Papers.

6. ADM to WMM, February 19, 1938, WMM Papers.

7. ADM to WMM, May 7, 1941, WMM Papers.

8. EHM, handwritten note bundled with a stack of letters from ADM to WMM, WMM Papers.

9. ADM to WMM, August 13, 1942, WMM Papers.

10. OBR, "Mothers on Trial," unpublished typescript, undated by c. 1937, and apparently an article for *Family Circle,* WMM Papers.

11. Harvard football banner, printed felt, c. 1911, WMM Papers.

12. WMM, *Love in an Apartment Hotel* (Biograph, 1913), dir. D.W. Griffith. My thanks to Joshua Siegel for locating this film, a director's cut, and arranging for me to see it. For more on the film, see Robert M. Henderson, *D.W. Griffith: The Years at Biograph* (New York: Farrar, Straus and Giroux, 1970): "In January 1913, Griffith directed five films, all one-reel pictures, leading off with *Love in an Apartment Hotel,* based on a synopsis purchased from William Marston, who had given his address as Harvard College, Cambridge, Massachusetts" (148). This attribution is from the records of the

Biograph Company, in the Film Department at MoMA. Biograph's studios at the time were at 11 East Fourteenth Street, NY (8), but in December 1912 the studios moved to new quarters in the Bronx, at 175th Street (148), though the company itself moved to California. Griffith left Biograph at the end of 1913. *Birth of a Nation* was produced in 1914 and released in 1915 (159). Robert M. Henderson, *D.W. Griffith: His Life and Work* (New York: Oxford University Press, 1972), 123–124. The story was probably bought by Biograph's story editor, Lee Doughtery (124). And see Library of Congress, *Catalog of Copyright Entries: Works of Part, Part 4* (Washington, DC: Library of Congress, 1913), 142. A discussion of the film is in Roberta E. Pearson, *Eloquent Gestures: The Transformation of Performance Style in the Griffith Biograph Films* (Berkeley, CA: University of California Press, 1992), 106–108.

13. WMM, *The Thief* (Solax, 1913), dir. Alice Guy Blaché. A print is at the Library of Congress, Moving Image Department. Cooper C. Graham et al, *D.W. Griffith and the Biograph Company* (Metuchen, NJ: Scarecrow Press, Inc., 1985) lists *Love in Apartment Hotel,* as "William M. Marston ("The Thief") (au) . . . begun December 1912, finished January 1913 (f); New York/California (l); 27 February 1913 (r)" and "reissued by Biograph 18 June 1915" (171), thereby identifying Marston as the author of a 1913 film called "The Thief." The only film made in 1913 with that title is the one directed by Alice Guy Blaché, at Solax.

14. Marston apparently sent in a letter complaining to the *Boston Evening Record* after it ran a story about his film in which the gambling element was emphasized ("Exposes Harvard Gambling: Movie Scenario a Sizzler," February 26, 1915). The paper later printed a notice, acknowledging his complaint: "Flickerings," *Boston Evening Record,* March 1, 1915. Both clippings can be found in WMM, Scrapbook kept by EHM, WMM Papers.

15. Hugo Münsterberg to WMM, September 9, 1916, Donn Marston Papers.

16. EHM, handwritten note on the envelope containing Hugo Münsterberg to WMM, September 9, 1916, WMM Papers.

17. "Defender of Sex Magazines Stops Reading The World," the [New York] *World,* January 13, 1927, with marginal notation by EHM, in WMM, Scrapbook kept by EHM, WMM Papers.

18. Marston had selected a still for each. *Compliance: The Student Prince in Old Heidelberg* (1927), starring Ramon Navarro; submission: *The Devil Dancer* (1927), starring Gilda Gray; dominance: *Blarney* (1926); and inducement: *Flesh and the Devil* (1926), starring Greta Garbo and John Gilbert. Also fascinating is a clip of a newspaper photograph of Marston giving a lie detector test to two women, one blonde, one brunette, together with them in a cage, with a lion. Unspecified clipping, dated August 11, 1929, in WMM, Scrapbook kept by EHM, WMM Papers.

19. "It gives me much happiness to know that Byrne is so much attached to the old home. The meaning of that year when most of you 'lived with Grandma' is very precious to me." ADM to WMM, April 24, 1941, WMM Papers.

20. WMM, "Why Bruno Hauptmann Dodges the Lie Detector—As Revealed by its Discoverer!" [New York] *Sunday Mirror,* May 5, 1935.

21. ADM to WMM, January 7, 1939, ADM to WMM, February 19, 1938, and ADM to WMM, February 15, 1939, WMM Papers.

22. ADM to WMM, September 14, 1942, WMM Papers. This was in the context of sending them best wishes on their wedding anniversary.

23. Huntley may not have written to ADM as much as the other two women, but it seems she visited her very frequently in Cliftondale. "Glad of a letter from Marjorie—first I have heard from her since Feb.," she wrote to Marston on June 18, 1940, WMM Papers.
24. ADM to WMM, March 2, 1939, WMM Papers.
25. ADM to WMM, October 21, 1940, WMM Papers.
26. ADM to WMM, March 13, 1943, WMM Papers.
27. WMM, diary entry for December 24, 1939, WMM Papers.
28. "A Psychologist Names The Ten Happiest People in America," advertisement, *Look*, March 29, 1938.
29. "Ode to William Moulton Marston, Or, Lines Written While Under the Influence," typescript, undated but c. 1935–1943, WMM Papers.
30. WMM, unpublished, untitled, and undated typescript, WMM Papers. For reference, I will call this manuscript, "A Theory of Personality." It must have been written after 1931 because Marston refers to experiments he conducted at Long Island University in 1931 (see Marguerite Mooers Marshall, "As the Other Sex Sexes Us," *New York Evening Journal*, November 23, 1931) as well as to his book, *Integrative Psychology*, also published in 1931.
31. WMM, "A Theory of Personality," 21.
32. WMM, "A Theory of Personality," 104–105.
33. WMM, "A Theory of Personality," 112–113.
34. WMM, "A Theory of Personality," 156.
35. WMM, "A Theory of Personality," 145.
36. WMM, "A Theory of Personality," 157.
37. WMM, "A Theory of Personality," 161–162.
38. Reid Stewart Austin, *Petty: The Classic Pin-up Art of George Petty* (New York: Gramercy, 1997).
39. WMM, "Miss Elusive," and George Petty, Miss Elusive centerfold, *True*, undated but c. 1938, WMM Papers. I have not been able to figure out how to date the centerfolds. There are no dates on the clippings, except for one, which is dated 1945. The magazine began publishing in 1937. I cannot find extant copies from these years.
40. WMM, "Miss Heartsnatcher," and George Petty, Miss Heartsnatcher centerfold, *True*, undated but some February issue between 1937 and 1945, WMM Papers.
41. WMM, "Miss Bewitching," and George Petty, Miss Bewitching centerfold, *True*, undated but some October issue between 1937 and 1945, WMM Papers.
42. WMM, "Miss Career Girl," and George Petty, Miss Career Girl centerfold, *True*, undated but some issue between 1937 and 1945, WMM Papers.
43. WMM, "Miss Girl of Tomorrow," and George Petty, Miss Girl of Tomorrow centerfold, *True*, undated but some April issue between 1937 and 1945, WMM Papers.
44. WMM, "What Comics Do to Your Children," *Your Life*, October 1939, clipping in the WMM Papers. I hadn't realized before discovering this article that Marston had begun writing about comics as early as 1939. The article, which evaluates many different comic strips and books according to a set of criteria Marston established, likely gained him considerable attention from comic book artists, writers, and especially publishers. One surviving example is a correspondence he subsequently carried out with Al Capp, who'd created *Li'l Abner* in 1934. See Al Capp to WMM, undated but September 1939 (on United Feature Syndicate stationary); WMM to Al

Capp, September 22, 1939; and Al Capp to WMM, undated but late September or early October 1939, WMM Papers.

45. ADM to WMM, August 13, 1942, WMM Papers.

46. ADM to WMM, May 6, 1942, WMM Papers. Then she added, "I meant to say leisurely and placidly," but she didn't cross out the first statement.

47. ADM to WMM, May 6, 1942.

48. ADM to WMM, August 13, 1942.

49. ADM to WMM, October 21, 1942, WMM Papers.

50. ADM to WMM, August 11, 1943, WMM Papers.

51. ADM to WMM, August 11, 1943.

52. E.g., "A thousand thanks for the magnificent flowers." ADM to WMM, November 27, 1942, WMM Papers. These were for Thanksgiving. They usually spent Thanksgiving together, ADM at Cherry Orchard, or the Marstons in Cliftondale, but she seems to have been too ailing to travel.

53. On her last visit, see ADM to WMM and EHM, May 2, 1944, WMM Papers.

54. ADM to WMM, May 8, 1944, WMM Papers.

55. ADM to WMM, May 22, 1944, WMM Papers.

56. I don't know the exact date of her death but it was in 1944, as per the Department of Public Health, Registry of Vital Records and Statistics. *Massachusetts Vital Records Index to Deaths [1916–1970].* Vol. 55, page 553. Facsimile edition. Boston, MA: New England Historic Genealogical Society, Boston, Massachusetts.

57. He wrote doggerel, about the indignities of his illness:
The nurse brought me the bedpan
Slipped it under my backside
While chills ran up and down my spine
As the cold thing touched my hide.
WMM, "Not a Midsummer's Night Dream," undated poem but c. 1944, WMM Papers.

58. MSML to Byrne and Audrey Marston, February 27, 1963, BHRM Papers.

59. EHM, "Family Mementos," typescript, dated February 16, 1975, WMM Papers.

60. Nancy Marston Wykoff and Margaret Marston Van Cleave, interview with the author, February 7, 2015.

61. EHM, "Family Mementos."

ILLUSTRATION CREDITS

Illustrations on the pages listed appear courtesy of the following:

Boston Public Library: 245
Brooklyn College Library Archives: 206
California Digital Newspaper Collection, Center for Bibliographic Studies and Research, University of California, Riverside: 193 (bottom)
Comic Art Collection, Michigan State University Libraries: xiv
Corbis Images: 91, 108 (left)
David Levine Ink: 294
Edward Sorel: 319
Esquire magazine: 197 (top)
Getty Images: 67
Harvard College Library: 9 (bottom), 39, 41, 85 (right), 164, 167, 193 (top)
Harvard University Archives: 27
Heritage Auctions: 178, 179, insert 1
The Library of American Comics: xii, 15, 25 (top and bottom), 62, 69, 76 (top and bottom), 77, 78, 191
The Library of Congress, Manuscripts Division: 266
The Library of Congress, Prints and Photographs Division: 10, 28, 46, 48, 108 (right), 196, 210, 212, 214, 262, 272, 288, 289, insert 3 (bottom), insert 7 (middle, and bottom), insert 8 (middle)
Byrne Marston: 36, 54, 83, 92, 109, 116, 131, 143, 145, 148, 152, 154, 172, 183, 249, 297
The Donn Marston Papers: 299, 303, 304, 305, 306 (bottom), 307, 308, 309
Moulton (Pete) Marston: 4, 5, 6, 21, 42, 43, 44, 61, 118, 133, 137, 138, 146, 151, 153, 246, 254
Metropolis Comics: 197 (bottom)
Mount Holyoke College Archives and Special Collections: 17 (bottom), 19
Museum of Modern Art: 306 (top)
Northwestern University Archives: 68
Rare Book and Manuscript Library, Columbia University: 232 (bottom)
The Rogers Family Collection: 84